ADAM
SMITH

ALSO BY JESSE NORMAN

Edmund Burke: The First Conservative
The Big Society: The Anatomy of the New Politics

ADAM

FATHER OF
ECONOMICS

SMITH

JESSE NORMAN

BASIC BOOKS

New York

Basic Books
Hachette Book Group
1290 Avenue of the Americas, New York, NY 10104
www.basicbooks.com

Printed in the United States of America

First Edition: September 2018

First published in 2018 by Penguin Random House UK

Published by Basic Books, an imprint of Perseus Books, LLC, a subsidiary of Hachette Book Group, Inc. The Basic Books name and logo is a trademark of the Hachette Book Group.

The Hachette Speakers Bureau provides a wide range of authors for speaking events. To find out more, go to www.hachettespeakersbureau.com or call (866) 376-6591.

The publisher is not responsible for websites (or their content) that are not owned by the publisher.

Print book interior design by Amy Quinn

Library of Congress Cataloging-in-Publication Data

Names: Norman, Jesse, author.
Title: Adam Smith : father of economics / Jesse Norman.
Description: First Edition. | New York : Basic Books, 2018. | Includes
bibliographical references and index.
Identifiers: LCCN 2018015933 (print) | LCCN 2018022026 (ebook) | ISBN
9780465093212 (ebook) | ISBN 9780465061976 (hardcover)
Subjects: LCSH: Smith, Adam, 1723-1790. | Economists—Great Britain. |
Economics—Philosophy. | Capitalism—Moral and ethical aspects.
Classification: LCC HB103.S6 (ebook) | LCC HB103.S6 N67 2018 (print) | DDC
330.15/3092 [B] —dc23
LC record available at https://lccn.loc.gov/2018015933

ISBNs: 978-0-465-06197-6 (hardcover), 978-0-465-09321-2 (ebook)

LSC-C

10 9 8 7 6 5 4 3 2 1

In honour of my father and mother,
Torquil and Anne Norman

CONTENTS

LIST OF ILLUSTRATIONS

INTRODUCTION

Adam, Adam, Adam Smith
Listen what I charged you with!
Didn't you say
In the class one day
That selfishness was bound to pay?
Of all your Doctrines, that was the Pith,
Wasn't it, wasn't it, wasn't it, Smith?

Stephen Leacock
(humorist and Professor of Political Economy),
Hellements of Hickonomics, 1936

TODAY, MENTION OF ADAM SMITH OFTEN ELICITS SHARPLY CONTRAST-ing reactions. Especially since the 1980s, he has been at the centre of the ideological battleground for competing views of economics, markets and societies. For many on the right of politics, he is a founding figure of the modern era: the greatest of all economists, an eloquent advocate of the freedom of the individual and the staunch enemy of state intervention, in a world released from the utopian delusions of communism and socialism. For many on the left, he is something very different: the true source and origin of so-called market fundamentalism, author of 'the textbook on contemporary capitalism' according to the activist and writer Naomi Klein, the prime mover of a materialist ideology that is sweeping the world and corrupting real sources of human value, an apologist for wealth and inequality and human selfishness—and a misogynist to boot.

One thing is certain, however: in an era in which economists and economics have become ever more influential, Adam Smith is regarded as by far the most influential economist who has ever lived. In a random survey of 299 academic economists in 2011, Smith came first by a huge margin, with 221 citations vs. 134 for Keynes, the rest all following after. Nor is Smith's academic reputation confined to economists: a detailed study of references on JSTOR, a comprehensive database of largely English-language journals, between 1930 and 2005 showed Smith to be by far the most heavily cited of the economic 'greats'. His latest recorded total was higher than those of Marx, Marshall and Keynes combined, and more than three times as high as that of any modern economist.

Smith's influence has been magnified by the sheer range of his ideas; even outside economics, many of the deepest thinkers of the past 200 years, in a range of fields spanning philosophy, politics and sociology, bear his stamp to some degree, including Burke, Kant, Hegel, Marx, Weber, Hayek, Parsons, Rawls, Habermas and more recently Amartya Sen. Smith's four maxims of good taxation form the basis of tax systems the world over. His famous phrase 'the invisible hand' is ubiquitous in lecture halls and media comment pages alike. He has an institute, a peer-reviewed journal and numerous societies around the world named after him; according to Pushkin, Eugene Onegin studied him; his face stares impassively across the face of the British £20 banknote.

But alongside the admiration and vilification has come a pervasive tendency to recruit Smith to pet causes, and to use his unequalled prestige for ideological purposes. Indeed so powerful has been Smith's thought—and his reputation—that political leaders of every stripe have sought to enlist him as a supporter. In provocative spirit, Margaret Thatcher said at the Scottish Conservative Conference in 1988, 'I'm sometimes told that the Scots don't like Thatcherism. Well, I find that hard to believe—because the Scots invented Thatcherism, long before I was thought of.' Tracing the roots of her political beliefs to the works of Smith, Ferguson and Hume, she laid out a view of a world in which 'wealth would be generated and spread ever more widely' and 'wise Government [stood by to] harness the efforts of individuals to improve the well-being of the whole community.'

On the other side of the political divide, the former British Prime Minister Gordon Brown went one better, often associating himself personally with Smith through the accident of their shared birthplace in Kirkcaldy, Fife. As Chancellor of the Exchequer, he invited Alan Greenspan, then the Chairman of the US Federal Reserve and later one of his economic advisers, to give the Adam Smith lecture in Kirk-caldy in 2005, and was rewarded when Greenspan pondered in his speech 'to what extent the Chancellor's renowned economic and financial skills are the result of exposure to the subliminal intellect-enhancing emanations of this area'. In giving the Hugo Young Memorial Lecture later that year, Brown declared that 'Coming from Kirkcaldy as Adam Smith did, I have come to understand that his *Wealth of Nations* was underpinned by his *Theory of Moral Sentiments*, his invisible hand dependent upon the existence of a helping hand.'

As such examples illustrate, Smith is so intellectually fertile, so multi-faceted and so quotable that he offers constant temptations to over-interpretation or outright misappropriation. Indeed, if context is stretched to breaking point, he can be read as anticipating an astonishing range of contemporary events. One such is the rise of celebrity politics, from the interaction of modern technology with the human disposition to admire the rich and the powerful, and the human capacity for mutual sympathy, both ideas which Smith discusses in *The Theory of Moral Sentiments*. Another is the logic or otherwise of Britain's departure from the European Union. After all, Smith argued in relation to the American colonies that Britain faced a clear choice: either to separate entirely from them, or to form an imperial union, in which case sovereignty, and in due course the seat of government itself, would end up slowly being transferred to America. And so forth and so on.

The result has been to create a caricature known as 'Adam Smith', around whom there is now a vast mythology. These myths tell us little or nothing about Smith himself, but quite a lot about our own changing concerns. And we can see the same patterns in longer-run interpretations. Thus the effect of seeing Smith through nineteenth- and twentieth-century preoccupations with free trade, and through the recent growth of economics itself as a professional and specifically mathematical discipline, has been to highlight the 'economic' Smith, the Smith of *The Wealth of Nations*. This has served to sideline what might be called the 'political' Smith, the Smith who examines how power, property and government co-evolve and the nature and impact of commercial society, both in *The Wealth of Nations* and in his unpublished *Lectures on Jurisprudence*; and the 'moral' Smith, who advances in *The Theory of Moral Sentiments* a startlingly modern account of how moral and social norms are created and sustained by human communities. Part of the point of this book has been to recover these and still other sides to Smith, and integrate them into a fuller picture: that is, to give an introduction not merely to Smith's economics, but to his vastly wider intellectual project.

The fad for selective interpretation has even, perhaps especially, included economists themselves. In the words of the Chicago School economist Jacob Viner on *The Wealth of Nations*, 'Traces of every conceivable sort of doctrine are to be found in that most catholic book, and an economist must have peculiar theories indeed who cannot quote from *The Wealth of Nations* to support his special purposes.' So it has proven.

One example of this tendency will suffice, and from Viner's most famous student no less. In a famous article of 1977 for *Challenge* magazine, Milton Friedman, fresh from winning a Nobel Prize in the previous year, undertook to spell out 'Adam Smith's Relevance for Today'. For Friedman, Smith was 'a radical and revolutionary' in his own time—just as Friedman was in his. Smith was a man who believed his own society was 'overgoverned', and accordingly set himself against state interventions—just as Friedman did in his own time. Smith's 'doctrine of the invisible hand' reflected his view that human sympathy was unreliable, limited and needed to be economized, while free markets generated human well-being—just as Friedman himself held, across a long professional life devoted to expounding these and similar ideas.

Having laid down these basic propositions, however, Friedman found himself in some difficulty. It was true, he explained, that Smith had said various things that conflicted with them: that he had defended a cap on interest rates, and duties on the state to erect and maintain certain public works and public institutions, potentially including roads, bridges and canals, and to establish schools. But these statements were uncharacteristic blemishes, which should not be allowed to detract from the whole.

Now this was a popular article, not a scholarly one. Taken from a paper given to the free-market Mont Pelerin Society, its purpose was to help make the case against what Friedman saw as the economic sclerosis of late 1970s America. But even so, as a case study in adjusting the facts to fit one's own theory, it is a masterclass. For much of Friedman's account is hopelessly wide of the mark. Adam Smith was not a radical, and did not see himself as one; he does not seem to have believed his society was 'overgoverned', whatever that may mean, except perhaps as regards the American colonies; he had no 'doctrine' of the invisible hand, indeed no single theory of how markets work; he did not think free markets always served human well-being; and he did not hold that human sympathy was intrinsically limited or required economizing.

What Smith did in fact think, on these and other issues, and why what he thought still profoundly matters, are the subject of this book. Its further purpose is to puncture myths and establish connections across the whole body of Smith's thought, including its influence on economic thinkers as diverse as Hayek, Keynes and Marx. But even from beyond the grave Smith does not make it easy for the biographer: his life was the very pattern of academic uneventfulness; just before his death he instructed his highly reluctant executors to burn almost all his manuscripts, about whose contents we can only speculate. His *Lectures on Jurisprudence*, an often neglected but vital element in his thought, survive only thanks to some astonishing luck.

Many of the deepest ideas in Smith's thought tie back to those of his closest friend, David Hume. In many ways they were an unusual pair. Hume, the older man by twelve years, was worldly, open, witty, full of small talk, banter and piercing aperçus, a lover of whist, a gourmand and a flirt. Smith by contrast was reserved, private, considered and often rather austere in his public manner, though he could unwind in private. But, far more than any other thinker, Hume is Smith's imagined interlocutor; and, though no real philosophical correspondence between them survives, there are few pages of Smith in which one does not sense the shadow, if not the influence, of Hume. For all the two men's numerous points of difference, it would not be too much to call Smith a disciple of Hume.

By the standards of the time Smith was broadly Whiggish in outlook, a term implying a belief in the virtues of constitutional monarchy, religious toleration and personal freedom. But he remained remarkably close-lipped about his personal political views throughout his life. He never married, and he had no children. As far as we know, there were no secret loves, no hidden vices, no undergraduate pranks, no adult peccadilloes: when it comes to juicy personal detail, Smith's life is a featureless Sahara. In the words of his first biographer, Dugald Stewart, Smith 'seems to have wished that no materials should remain for his biographers, but what were furnished by the lasting monuments of his genius, and the exemplary worth of his private life'.

Despite these unpromising circumstances, Smith has not lacked for biographers. He has been greatly favoured in recent years by works that have painstakingly assembled the details of his life, set it vividly against the intellectual backdrop of Edinburgh and the ideas of the Scottish Enlightenment, presented him anew for a popular audience and explored the span of his intellectual interests, in addition to an ever-expanding academic literature. I have drawn freely and with great gratitude from this body of work.

This book inevitably covers much of the same ground. It is of course not immune to its own preconceptions, and although as balanced and fair-minded as I can make it, it is hardly free from the usual defects of partial knowledge and limited perspective—defects on which I welcome corrections and ideas from readers. But it has three specific points of difference from its predecessors. The first is that it is written not by a professional Smith scholar but by a working politician, albeit one with an academic background in philosophy— that is, by someone both dealing with and trying to understand and explain the nature of political economy in its modern aspects, practical as well as theoretical. The second is that the book makes a deliberate effort to give the reader not merely a taste of Smith's ideas, but a feeling for how those ideas work and fit together, across their whole, very wide-ranging span. Finally, it makes a specific, trenchant and I hope persuasive argument for the importance and continuing relevance of Smith's ideas.

It is an accident of history that Adam Smith and the great Irish philosopher-statesman Edmund Burke—the subject of my last book, *Edmund Burke: Philosopher, Politician, Prophet* (2013)—were good friends. They much admired each other, and there are numerous overlaps in their thinking, as well as points of difference; Smith once reportedly said that Burke was the 'only man, who, without communication, thought on economic subjects exactly as he did'. Together, the two men mark an extraordinary moment in the world's history, a moment at which the political and economic outlines of the present age first become visible, are analysed in depth and given public explanation. Burke is the first great theorist of modern political parties and representative government. Smith is the first thinker to put markets at the centre of political economy, and so of economics, and to place norms at the centre of what we now think of as sociology. As Burke is the hinge of our political modernity, so is Smith the hinge of our economic, and in many ways our social, modernity. These are momentous achievements.

But Adam Smith, like Burke, is not merely a historical figure, and this book is not merely a biography. On the contrary, Smith lives and breathes today through his ideas and his impact. Our present world, developed and developing alike, faces huge challenges, including—but by no means limited to—how to generate and sustain economic growth, how to deal with problems of globalization and escalating inequality, and how to create moral understanding across different communities of history, interest and belief. Smith's ideas still have the capacity to take our breath away, through their ambition and brilliance, their simplicity and scope. They are essential to any attempt to address these challenges, and they need to be widely and fully understood. We need to know not merely what Adam Smith thought, but why it matters; and then to apply his insights again for a new generation.

Part One

LIFE

CHAPTER 1

KIRKCALDY BOY,
1723–1746

I T IS ONE OF THE BETTER WHAT-IFS OF HISTORY. IN AROUND 1726, THE story goes, Margaret Smith took her only son Adam, then aged three, to stay with his uncle at Strathendry, just a few miles from the family home in Kirkcaldy on the east coast of Scotland. There, in the words of his great nineteenth-century biographer John Rae:

> The child was stolen by a passing band of gipsies, and for a time could not be found. But presently a gentleman arrived who had met a gipsy woman a few miles down the road carrying a child that was crying piteously. Scouts were immediately des-patched . . . and they came upon the woman in Leslie wood. As soon as she saw them she threw her burden down and escaped, and the child was brought back to his mother.

The tale has been endlessly told and retold ever since. In first re-counting it, Smith's friend the philosopher Dugald Stewart acclaimed the rescue as 'preserving to the world a genius, which was destined, not only to extend the boundaries of science, but to enlighten and re-form the commercial policy of Europe'. But any resulting benefit was probably a mutual one, since Adam Smith was to amass a formidable reputation later in life for absent-mindedness. As Rae drily remarked, 'He would have made, I fear, a poor gipsy.'

Moments during which the son escaped his mother's watchful eye were rare. The link between them was exceptionally strong, and lasted over six decades. Adam Smith was born on or before 5 June 1723—like Isaac Newton, a posthumous child. His father, also Adam Smith, had died five months earlier at the age of only forty-three, having worked his way up via public service and the law to be Comptroller of Customs in Kirkcaldy. Information is scarce, but this branch of the Smith family seems to have hailed from Seaton, near Aberdeen, from which Adam senior went to Edinburgh to study law. In 1705 he became private secretary to the Earl of Loudon, one of two Secretaries of State for Scotland, in the tumultuous negotiations that preceded the Act of Union two years later between England and Scotland. In that year, 1707, he was made a burgess of the city of Glasgow, strengthening family ties with that city, and received a royal commission as Clerk of the Court Martial, administering military trials. About this time he was also appointed a Writer to the Signet or solicitor, qualified to advise clients on financial matters and estates. It was a post of some professional significance.

Adam Smith senior married twice, both times advantageously for a young man on the rise from the minor gentry. His first wife, Lilias or 'Lillie' Drummond, came from a prominent Edinburgh family, and in 1709 they had a son, Hugh, half-brother to our Adam Smith and older than him by fourteen years or so. However, Lillie died less than a decade later, leaving her husband a widower with a child. The Jacobite rebellion of 1715 had petered out after the inconclusive battle of Sheriffmuir, leaving the Hanoverian party under the 2nd Duke of Argyll in control. Smith senior had plenty of work to do in managing the ensuing courts martial.

By this time he had also taken the post of Comptroller of Customs in Kirkcaldy. He went there from Edinburgh, clearly with misgivings, having hoped for something better from the recent reorganization of the Scottish customs system. By sea, Kirkcaldy was barely more than 10 miles away, across the Firth of Forth; the land route around the bay, in the days before the Forth Bridge, was considerably longer. To locals it was the 'lang toun', the long town, running along a High Street then about a mile in length, close to the shore. It was a place of some substance and history: a free royal burgh since 1450 or so, and thus enabled to trade overseas, to retail foreign commodities and to send representatives to Parliament. In the sixteenth century its port had been a thriving centre for the export of coal, salt and linen to the continent of Europe, but trade had been severely damaged by the civil wars of the 1640s, by the war with France during the reign of William and Mary, and by poor harvests and famine in the 1690s. The balance of Scotland's trading economy was already tilting more to Glasgow and the west with the expansion of the American colonies, fuelled by the tobacco trade in particular, and the Union of 1707 accelerated this process, as Scottish traders joined the much bigger English market under the enforced protection of the Navigation Acts, as we shall see.

By the time Adam Smith senior arrived in Kirkcaldy in 1714 the local economy was in relative decline—by 1755 the town's population of 2,296 was barely more than half what it had been a century earlier—and since the Comptroller's income depended largely on fees from trade, this had a direct impact on his finances. To make matters worse, the new Board of Commissioners of Customs in Edinburgh had ended the practice of farming out tax collection and was seeking to staunch the loss of revenue from smuggling, creating considerable local unpopularity. Smith senior was himself a cultivated and intelligent man, who had travelled to France—and indeed been shipwrecked en route to Bordeaux—in his youth. He kept a liberal-minded household, with a library of some eighty books, some legal, many religious, but also including works of history, literature and self-improvement. Even so, despite Kirkcaldy's geographical proximity to Edinburgh, it was a long way culturally, economically and politically from the coffeehouses and conversations of that great city.

But the town did have one enormous benefit: it introduced Smith to the formidable Margaret Douglas. She was the scion of two large, well-known and influential Fife families: the Douglases on her father's side and the Balfours on her mother's. There were many Douglas army connections, including Margaret's father, Robert Douglas, who had been made a colonel of a militia regiment in 1689, and these appear to have an impression on the young Adam Smith. Many years afterwards, in 1763, James Boswell noted that 'Mr Smith at Glasgow once told me that his friends had cut his throat in not allowing him to be a soldier,' a possibility Boswell—who had been Smith's student—found 'completely ridiculous'. Others who knew the fêted philosopher and political economist in later life would not have demurred.

Margaret married Adam Smith senior in 1720, but less than three years later he was dead, the cause unknown to us. His death must have been a shattering blow for the expectant mother and her young stepson Hugh, now twice orphaned. Little wonder, perhaps, that Margaret named Adam after his father. Little wonder that she and the boy were so close for the rest of their lives. And little wonder that, as is often the way with dead or absent fathers, the older Smith's life had overtones for the younger's. Adam Smith grew up as a serious young man. He would spend much of his life reflecting on issues of law and trade and economic self-improvement; and he would become, not the Comptroller of Customs in little Kirkcaldy, but one of the Commissioners of Customs for all Scotland.

Tradition has it that Adam Smith was born on the High Street in Kirkcaldy; alas, the house has long since been demolished. His father may have feared for his own death, for he made a new will in November 1722, just two months before he passed away. It appointed 'tutors and curators', all male, to support Margaret in bringing up the child. These included two uncles, but also a range of other men of some distinction, bearing testimony to the personal and social regard in which the couple were held. Among them was Captain James Oswald of Dunnikier, fairly recently arrived but already the largest local landowner, who paid for the funeral; a nephew and cousin, both called William Smith, who became secretary to the powerful 2nd Duke of Argyll and Regent at Marischal College in Aberdeen respectively; Henry Miller, a relative of the highly reputed David Miller, schoolmaster of the burgh school in Kirkcaldy; and two members of a remarkable family, the Clerks of Penicuik. Sir John Clerk, 2nd Baronet, had studied law in Leiden and history, architecture and music—under Corelli, no less—in Rome, sat in parliaments before and after Union, and held the lucrative position of Baron of the Court of Exchequer, from which he energetically promoted the cause of advanced Enlightenment thinking in a range of scientific, artistic and cultural fields. The other, Dr John Clerk of Listonshiels, was an innovator on issues of sanitation and public health, and a co-founder of Edinburgh's Infirmary in 1729. Thus, although Adam Smith grew up without a father, he did so within a mixed and extended network of family and friends who were well connected, supportive, independent-minded and oriented towards the future.

Even so, life was hard for the young mother. Adam was a sickly boy and Hugh not a strong one, in a period when one child in every four died at birth or in infancy. And at times there was very little money. In 1730 Margaret had to write to Lord Loudon, who had been financially destroyed by the collapse of the South Sea Bubble, seeking six years' interest on a bond owed to the young Adam; she described herself then as 'very much straiten'd'. Nor were her Douglas relatives of much financial help: she did not receive the cash from her dowry or her father's inheritance until December 1750, twenty-seven years after Adam's birth.

Money may have been tight, but Margaret evidently lavished love and attention on Adam, and he reciprocated in kind. Writing a short life of Smith in 1793, shortly after his subject's death and with memories still relatively fresh, Dugald Stewart remarked that 'She was blamed for treating him with an unlimited indulgence; but it produced no unfavourable effects on his temper or his dispositions; and he enjoyed the rare satisfaction of being able to repay her affection, by every attention that filial gratitude could dictate, during the long period of sixty years.'

Hugh was sent to a boarding school in Perth and, like his father and other Smith relatives, ended up working locally at the Customs House until his death in 1750. Adam, however, went to the burgh school in Kirkcaldy. This in itself was an unusual institution. In 1496 the Scottish Parliament had passed an Education Act requiring 'all barons and freeholders who are wealthy' to send their eldest sons to grammar schools at the age of eight or nine to learn Latin, and for three years afterwards to study law. The purpose of the Act, which created the first compulsory education in Scotland, was to strengthen local government and improve the administration of justice 'that the poor people should have no need to seek our sovereign lord's principal auditors for each small injury'. One of its effects was to strengthen the burgh or parish schools which offered their pupils a grammar school education. Kirkcaldy's was such a school. Founded in 1582, it had been recently taken in hand by David Miller, who had been lured from his position as schoolmaster in nearby Cupar. Perhaps at the prompting of the energetic and ambitious 'Lady Dunnikier', as Mrs Oswald was known, herself now prematurely widowed and with a son to educate, the Town Council agreed in 1724 not merely to increase Miller's salary, but to raise the fees, build a new schoolhouse and adopt his curriculum.

It was a wise investment. Miller set himself to give his pupils not merely the basics of reading, writing and arithmetic but a classical education, including some ancient history and a grounding in standard Latin texts (and it seems at least a start in Greek); and a religious education, including questions in the Catechism. But he also brought to the school a focus on effective self-expression and rhetoric. This was not unknown in similar schools, which performed such improving plays as Joseph Addison's *Cato*, much admired in the eighteenth century for its strong Stoic message of discipline and self-reliance. Miller, however, went one step further; we know that he composed a drama of his own at this time in which Adam Smith took part. Grandly entitled 'A Royal Council for Advice, or the Regular Education of Boys the Foundation of all other Improvements', it cast the boys as a council petitioned by and responding to the members of a range of different trades and professions. It thus introduced Miller's pupils to public oratory and, indeed, to public life—with, perhaps, a not so subtle accompanying message to their parents that if they wished to enjoy their fruits they should keep sending their sons to school even at the higher fees. The drama was well received.

In *The Wealth of Nations* Smith praises Scotland's system of parish schools, contrasting them favourably with the less than universal charity schools in England; and he must have had his own burgh schooling partly in mind. He expresses regret that Latin was preferred to elementary geometry and mechanics, but he was sufficiently well schooled in the classics himself to be later excused the remedial first year of the Glasgow University curriculum. And he was lucky in his friends and contemporaries. Foremost among these was the younger James Oswald: eight years older than Smith, later a distinguished local MP, a lifelong friend and credited by some as encouraging Smith's interest in political economy. Another was John Drysdale, an important member of the Moderate grouping within the Church of Scotland. And then there was the brilliant Adam family of architects, the father William and his three sons, including Robert Adam, later Architect of the King's Works, designer of the Curzons' magnificent country seat Kedleston Hall and of the Edinburgh Royal Exchange, and a pioneer of his own named style of neoclassicism.

For the young Smith, Kirkcaldy was undoubtedly something of an education in itself: small enough for him to know intimately, yet oddly worldly and diverse in other ways. Its market, like all such markets then still a mass of guild regulation and restrictive practices, lay virtually on the family doorstep. The same was true of the local Presbyterian church or kirk, which played a central role in the life of the community. But Kirkcaldy was also an active international port, which in the previous century had had a Latvian consulate. As such, it offered a wealth of information and potential insights into trade, its types, conditions and patterns, and especially so to one familiar with the Customs House. The prevalence of smuggling in particular would have been obvious to young Adam, and perhaps encouraged youthful speculation into its causes and effects. So too the effects of growth, for by the mid-1730s the economy in Fife was starting to improve, with the development of the linen trade in particular spurred on by entrepreneurial local landowners. But perhaps most suggestive of all, given Smith's later emphasis on the division of labour, is the fact that the Oswalds owned a nailery in Pathhead, just outside town. Smith would have had many opportunities to observe the process of nail-manufacturing on his walks up to the big house at Dunnikier. If so, they served him well, for this simple example of industrial specialization would have a central place in *The Wealth of Nations*.

Young Adam was not physically robust, and his handwriting never evolved beyond a 'round, schoolboy hand'—the large, looping and laborious script still to be found in one of his school textbooks. But he was evidently a very good student, and he earned a reputation among his fellows as a genial figure. Stewart records that 'Mr Smith soon attracted notice, by his passion for books, and by the extraordinary powers of his memory. The weakness of his bodily constitution prevented him from partaking in their more active amusements; but he was much beloved by them on account of his temper, which, though warm, was to an uncommon degree friendly and generous.'

In October 1737 Adam Smith went up to the University of Glasgow. The choice was not foreordained—St Andrews was close at hand, Edinburgh not so far by a sea crossing, and the Smiths had links with Marischal College in Aberdeen as well—but it was a fateful one. For Scotland, Glasgow and the University of Glasgow were all at that time in the process of rapid change, change to which Smith would make no small contribution.

THE ACT OF UNION IN 1707 BETWEEN ENGLAND AND SCOTLAND WAS highly contentious at the time, and it has been much contested in recent years, as old disputes over Scottish independence have been fought and refought. Was Union the result of Scottish economic and political weakness, or of English oppression and manipulation? Was it the means by which Scotland was protected as a nation and set on a path to long-term greatness, or a basic act of treachery which took from it the independence that was its birthright? So the arguments have flowed to and fro.

The idea that the interests of the Scots and the English are and have always been opposed, let alone that unionism itself is intrinsically anti-Scottish, is a modern invention. But whatever one's views on these questions, on certain key matters the facts are relatively clear. The first is that Scotland was struggling economically and financially at the turn of the eighteenth century. The country had little manufacturing industry and its economy was small, overwhelmingly rural and limited in exports to food and raw materials. Harvests failed repeatedly in the 1690s, causing many deaths from famine. There was huge emigration, with as many as 100,000 Scots leaving to settle in Ulster between 1650 and 1700. In an age not of free trade but of the struggle by states to control it, the country lacked the economic or military power to hold its own, especially in the face of the high tariffs imposed by England and of the Navigation Acts, which required trade with the English colonies to use English ships, and important 'enumerated commodities' such as tobacco, cotton and sugar to be landed in England and taxed there before being shipped on.

The Navigation Acts and English mercantile policy were significant constraints on Scotland, its foreign policy and its potential for economic growth before 1707. But Scottish trade had also been undermined by the effects of war with the Dutch in the 1660–70s and with France after the coronation of William and Mary in 1689. And the first and only Scottish attempt to found a colony, at Darien on the coast of Spanish-controlled Panama in 1698–1700, had been a calamitous failure. Seen as a provocation by the English, who were desperate to keep Spain away from any alliance with France, it was brought low by poor leadership and planning, a robust Spanish response, rampant disease—and, it was soon bitterly alleged, by withdrawal of secondary financing from London merchants. With the colony's collapse went perhaps a quarter of the capital circulating in lowland Scotland.

In part as a result of its economic weakness, Scotland in 1700 was also weak politically. The highlands and islands and the lowlands were very different places, not merely geographically but linguistically— most highlanders then spoke Gaelic—socially and economically, with cross-cutting religious allegiances. And while it was a source of pride that the English had been forced to look north for their sovereign in 1603 with the so-called Union of Crowns, when James VI of Scotland had also been made James I of England after the death of Queen Elizabeth, the bitter fact remained that foreign policy had moved to London with the new King as well. England and Scotland remained formally separate kingdoms, each with its own institutions of government, but as the much larger country England had been favoured. For its part, with only a few exceptions, the Scottish Parliament had shown neither the power nor the will for independent action.

The idea of a deeper political union was not itself a new phenomenon. Oliver Cromwell's Second Protectorate Parliament of 1657 had been a union parliament, with thirty Scottish members (and thirty Irish), who had petitioned to remain there after it was dissolved on the restoration of Charles II in 1660. The two nations had taken a further step towards each other in 1689, when William and Mary were specifically invited by the Scottish Convention of Estates to accept the crown of Scotland. Their acceptance was no usurpation, nor did it come about through the pretended exercise of any divine or hereditary right; and it showed how, quite apart from the monarchy itself, there could be a wider community of interest between Scotland and England. But in thereby rejecting the claims of the Catholic James II/VII to the throne, the Scots were also deliberately opting for a Protestant and specifically Presbyterian settlement, and this in turn was highly contested. The Jacobite rising of 1689–91 was crushed by William, but the flame of Jacobitism in Scotland would smoulder and periodically flare up into rebellion over the following fifty years and more.

English sentiment had long been opposed, or at best indifferent, to the idea of a closer union with Scotland, and various attempts to achieve it during the seventeenth century had failed. But by 1705 all this had changed. The main reason was the accession of Queen Anne to the throne three years earlier. Whereas the Act of Settlement 1701 had ensured a future Protestant succession for England and Ireland after Anne's death, no such agreement had been reached in Scotland. The effect of Anne's installation was thus to rekindle dispute in Scotland, fuelled by the recent electoral success of the Jacobites. This in turn fed longstanding resentments within the Scottish Parliament, which now refused financial supply—the revenue required to administer the government—and passed a series of measures designed to tie the succession and so the rights to make peace and war to liberalization of trade. These actions were regarded as aggressive by the English, and doubly so because of the extreme delicacy of the international situation. England had gone to war with France again in 1701 over the Spanish Succession, Louis XIV continued to give encouragement to the Jacobites, and there were even rumours of a possible French invasion of Scotland.

By late 1704 these tensions had somewhat abated, following the Duke of Marlborough's decisive victory over the French at Blenheim. But that victory only emphasized the basic point, since the Queen's armies, then as now, relied heavily on Scotland for many of their best troops. Accordingly the Westminster government, led by Anne's First Minister Lord Godolphin and Marlborough, her Captain-General, pushed hard for an 'incorporating union', by which the governments of the two nations would be combined into one, thus resolving, it was hoped, the economic, political and security issues at a stroke. But there was strong popular opposition in Scotland, led by the Kirk, which feared that Union would mean the imposition of an episcopacy, and this inflamed popular sentiment into violent protests and rioting.

The Act of Union creating the United Kingdom of Great Britain was finally passed by the Scottish Parliament on 16 January 1707 by 110 votes to 67, a substantial majority. The circumstances of its passage are still the subject of scholarly dispute, but it cannot be doubted that financial and other inducements were deployed on a large scale, especially to lure over to the winning side the previously uncommitted twenty-five votes of the small and aptly named Squadrone Volante party, all of whom eventually voted for the Bill. There were also threats of retaliation from England if it did not go through.

But the Bill's passage was greatly eased by two other crucial factors. First, the opposition was divided: between the Country party, who were Presbyterians utterly hostile to the return of James II, and the so-called Cavaliers, who were Jacobites and in favour of it. Conceivably this disagreement could have been temporarily overcome with effective leadership tied to the strong anti-Union feeling among the wider populace, but this too was sorely lacking.

Still more important, perhaps, were the nature and scale of the concessions made by Westminster to secure support for the Act of Union. An Act of Security in 1706 guaranteed the historic rights and Presbyterian governance of the Kirk. While Scottish public law was incorporated into the Union, the status of Scottish private law, and of its legal practice, courts and tribunals, was protected. So too were the privileges of the royal burghs, and the Scots' system of local government. The Scottish education system, in many ways superior to the English, was not affected, and the electoral system was untouched. Many of the country's most important institutions, including the banks, remained intact. The Scots were enabled to compete for the great tide of patronage—domestic and imperial, civil and military—that emanated from Westminster. And the substantial sum of £398,000 was set aside to defray Scotland's share of England's national debt, and to reimburse losses from the Darien disaster—losses which, cynics might and did note, had particularly affected members of the Squadrone party. These were not trivial matters, nor did they mark merely political concessions. They reflected a recognition of the importance and distinctiveness of Scottish institutions, and they suggested that Union would not be marked by a desire for insolent domination by the English. So it largely proved.

For the Scots the greatest long-term prize was that Scotland and England now formed a single economic entity. Scottish merchants were at last enabled to benefit from the common market—protected from foreign competition by the tariffs and enforced by the Navigation Acts they had long despised—which England's fast-developing colonial trade had created. Scotland was badly under-represented in the new Union Parliament, which was based on imputed wealth, not on population. But the economic advantages of Union were overwhelming.

Writing in 1760 and with the benefit of hindsight, Adam Smith was unequivocal: 'The Union was a measure from which infinite good has been derived to this country.' This view was widely shared by the leading Scottish thinkers of the day. The benefits were not simply economic: as Smith wrote in *The Wealth of Nations*, 'By the union with England the middling and inferior ranks of people in Scotland gained a complete deliverance from the power of an aristocracy which had always before oppressed them.' In effect, the way had started to open for the equalizing benefits of commercial society to be felt north of the border. Yet as Smith also pointed out, 'The immediate effect of it was to hurt the interest of every single order of men in the country.' The new Union did indeed start badly. There were very serious Jacobite rebellions in 1708 and, especially, 1715; Scottish anti-Union sentiment was swiftly reignited by new laws from London which appeared to undermine the Kirk; there was great popular anger at increased customs dues and excise payments, matched by anger in England at rampant Scottish smuggling; while the unexpected abolition of Scotland's Privy Council reduced the effectiveness of its government in managing these periodic crises. It would be at least three decades before the

Union started to show its value, and even then it would be threatened by the last great Jacobite rebellion in 1745–1746.

Adam Smith's early life was thus spent during a period of painful economic dislocation, adjustment and uncertainty in Scotland. The problem was not that the country was being bled white by high taxes, as was alleged; the vast preponderance of tax revenues stayed within its borders. It was more basic than that: Scotland lacked the agricultural techniques, the commercial skills and the capital needed to take early advantage of the newly opened markets, in which English merchants were already well entrenched. At the same time, competition from England hit Scottish trades hard, from wool to brewing to paper manufacture, and the economic tilt from an eastern orientation facing the North Sea to a western one facing the Atlantic, already under way for at least a century, rapidly accelerated.

The Scots were ingenious both in finding new markets and in financing trade with them. But their extraordinary expertise in smuggling also played its part. It has been estimated that Scottish merchants did not pay customs duty on as much as half the goods imported from the colonies, enabling them to undercut the English. Even as early as the 1720s Glasgow, favoured by the prevailing trade winds, by its northerly latitude and by its position on the Clyde, was becoming a centre for the tobacco trade, controlling some 15 per cent of legal American imports. By the 1740s that trade was expanding rapidly; and by the following decade Glasgow alone was importing more tobacco than all the English ports combined, including London.

This was the era of the city oligarchs known as the Tobacco Lords, the greatest of them John Glassford, who was said by the novelist Tobias Smollett to own a fleet of twenty-five ships and to have traded more than half a million pounds of goods a year. Their profits were recycled into other trades, into agriculture, into industry and into spectacular houses and the western expansion of the city. Glasgow had been ravaged by fire in 1652, when a third of the buildings had been destroyed, and again in 1677. But fifty years later Daniel Defoe was able to acclaim it as 'a very fine city . . . the houses are all of stone . . . in a word, 'tis the cleanest and beautifullest, and best built city in Britain, London excepted.'

FOR A MOTHER LIKE MARGARET SMITH, AMBITIOUS FOR HER CLEVER younger son, Glasgow was a glimpse of the future. In administration the city had been dominated by the Crown, by local magnates and, increasingly, by the tobacco merchants. In religion, it drew from the heavily Presbyterian south-west of Scotland, and this gave it a pious and straitlaced character. Commerce and religion did not always sit happily alongside each other, but together they engendered a strict adherence to the so-called Glorious Revolution settlement of 1688, the Union and the Hanoverian succession. This would not have deterred Margaret, or Adam's sober-minded 'tutors and curators'. The boy was destined for Glasgow University.

Founded by William Turnbull, Bishop of Glasgow, under a Papal letter or Bull of 1451, the university had originally been located within the precincts of Glasgow Cathedral. But by the early eighteenth century it had expanded to include some 200 to 300 students, and it was located in a very imposing building with a tall tower, constructed in the style of Oxford and Cambridge colleges around two quads, or courts, on the High Street. It was a small academic community: less worldly, more collegiate and more intellectually austere than its Edinburgh counterpart, but considerably more moderate than the stoutly and suspiciously Presbyterian city that surrounded it. It suited Adam Smith perfectly. But when he arrived in 1737 at the age of fourteen— not then an unusual age to matriculate—Glasgow University was itself emerging from a period of significant change.

The cause was a clash between Church and Crown. The Presbytery of Glasgow was responsible for religious affairs in the city. It kept a jealous watch for signs of possible unorthodoxy at the university, and in the 1720s its particular attention had focused on the teaching of

John Simson, the Professor of Divinity. Simson's offence was to seek a basis for the Protestant Confession of Faith—the Kirk's core statement of Calvinist orthodoxy—in human reason rather than in revelation or in God's grace. His professorship was suspended, and after a furore and two ecclesiastical trials before the general assembly of the Church of Scotland, he was eventually forced to stop teaching divinity altogether. For its part, the Crown—in the person of the Earl of Ilay (later the 3rd Duke of Argyll), an adroit politician who was becoming the *de facto* 'King of Scotland' with the support of the Prime Minister, Sir Robert Walpole—controlled the city government alongside the local magnates. It had long been concerned at the growth of radical Presbyterianism, and it responded by supporting moderate Presbyterian professors at the university and by seeking to sideline those of more extreme views.

More widely, there was growing pressure for academic reform from civic fathers, merchants and the increasingly prosperous and ambitious 'middling sort', who reacted against pettifogging interpretation of the scriptures, blind obedience to authority and dictated lectures in Latin, and who wanted to open up university education while retaining its broader moral and religious basis. In 1726, at the insistence of Ilay, the university began a rapid process of modernization. Its constitution, curriculum and teaching were all reformed. The regenting system, under which each class was taken by a single 'regent' through four years of study, was abolished and specialist professorships were established for the first time, in logic and metaphysics, moral philosophy and natural philosophy. It would be in character for Smith to note and appreciate the benefits to students of this new division of labour, and in due course he would hold the first two of these chairs himself.

Like his fellow students, Smith studied these subjects as well as the ancient languages and authors, and of course divinity. But his greatest early interest lay in natural philosophy—we should say the sciences today—and specifically in physics and mathematics. These subjects had been revolutionized after 1687 by Isaac Newton's

Principia Mathematica, which had set out from first principles a new and extraordinarily powerful theory of the movements of the planets and other heavenly bodies, and of gravity. The Professor of Mathematics at Glasgow, Robert Simson, nephew of the banned theologian John, was a follower of Newton and an expert on the ancient Greek geometer Euclid, whose *Elements* was still seen as the gold standard for demonstrative reasoning in the exact sciences. It was this combination—the quality of Simson's teaching, the power of Newton's dynamics and the clarity of reasoning to be found in Euclid—that Adam Smith seems to have found intoxicating.

Still more important in shaping the young Smith was the influence of Francis Hutcheson, Professor of Moral Philosophy since 1730, whose lectures Smith attended in his second year. Hutcheson was a Scots-Irishman, born in Ulster but trained for the Church in Glasgow. Distancing himself from radical Protestantism, he had then moved to Dublin and become a leading figure among the moderate or 'new light' Presbyterian ministers there, before returning to Glasgow as the acknowledged leader of the moderates on the faculty. Like his teacher John Simson, Hutcheson had been the subject of a prosecution attempt by the Presbytery for his religious views, this time unsuccessful.

Hutcheson had published widely while in Dublin, including treatises on aesthetics and ethics, and to these he later added a further book on ethics, and works on logic, mind and knowledge. His writings had earned him a considerable reputation across Europe, as they did later in the American colonies. But he was also known as a superb teacher, an innovator who lectured in English rather than Latin, striding around informally before his students and seeking to convey not merely knowledge but understanding, and to kindle a spirit of inquiry. And he was a highly engaging man, whose warmth, gentleness and courtesy made him widely loved and admired.

Hutcheson's influence on Smith was thus both personal and intellectual. Many years afterwards, in 1787, Smith referred to his teacher as the 'never-to-be-forgotten Hutcheson'. The only other person to whom he is known to have applied that unusual and loving epithet is David Hume, now regarded as one of the greatest philosophers ever to have written in English. What, then, did Smith find so stimulating in Hutcheson's thought?

For one thing, its starting point. Much seventeenth-century philosophy had been based on the bleakest of assumptions about human nature. For the great English philosopher Thomas Hobbes, humans in the state of nature were perpetually engaged in 'a war of all against all', in which life was, famously, 'solitary, poor, nasty, brutish and short'—a war from which only a social contract could deliver them, by creating a legitimate basis for government. The great German jurist Samuel von Pufendorf—seeking to give a legal basis to the fragile peace and the idea of the nation-state which emerged from the Treaty of Westphalia in 1648—had extended a broadly Hobbesian analysis of human nature into the international sphere. For Hutcheson, however, Hobbes and Pufendorf defended an individualistic ethics in which only authority backed by power could bring peace and order. Hutcheson particularly reacted against what he saw as their pessimism and narrow conception of human motivation. For him the crucial fact about human beings was their sociability, and this was not derived from sovereign power or the fear of God; it was intrinsic and basic to human nature itself. The effect of this founding assumption was to make Hutcheson's thought both more optimistic and more realistic at a time when the demands of commercial society were beginning to supersede the historic necessities of war.

The idea of sociability runs through all of Hutcheson's work and binds it together. At its core is what he calls a 'moral sense', a divinely inspired but instinctive capacity for moral feeling which operates naturally and immediately, and thus prior to human reason or calculation and independently of human will. Humans are not amoral animals governed merely by the pursuit of advantage, but human reason is weak: the effect of the moral sense is to indicate the path of virtuous conduct and to explain how humans can come to instant moral views—sometimes mistakenly—about others' conduct, without the need for reflection. In particular, Hutcheson claims that the moral sense leads to the judgement that 'that action is best, which procures the greatest happiness for the greatest numbers', a formula that was later adapted by Jeremy Bentham and his nineteenth-century utilitarian followers. But Hutcheson's focus is quite different, not on how to procure and maximize happiness, but on happiness as the result of moral conduct. For him there is no necessary opposition between selfish and virtuous behaviour, for taken as a whole 'self-love' and the moral sense both work towards human self-preservation and well-being. They are 'as necessary to the state of the whole as gravitation'.

From this basic line of thought Hutcheson attempted to derive a general account not merely of moral conduct but of politics and society as a whole, including what would now be called economic behaviour. For in his view the moral sense is what allows people to conceive not merely of moral but of political rights and obligations. It grounds within individuals the development of a society committed to shared moral norms in the light and the love of God; and it encourages a limited constitutional monarchy based on a social contract, respect for property rights, religious toleration and a right to resist authoritarian government.

In effect, Hutcheson sought to knit three things together: his own distinctive moral psychology, a natural-law theory of government, and many of the classic Whig political demands of the time. It was not an entirely easy combination. Nevertheless, this was a liberal, moderate and in many ways strikingly egalitarian vision. Its tone, its specific ideas and its ambition were to have a deep impact on Adam Smith, as we shall see. Indeed, according to Dugald Stewart, Hutcheson's lectures guided Smith to the 'study of human nature in all its branches, more particularly of the political history of mankind'.

But equally striking are the ways in which he would disagree with Hutcheson. Smith's thought differs sharply in its treatment of the idea of natural law; it is not utilitarian in the classical Benthamite sense;

it disputes the claim that civil society rests on a social contract; and above all, it rejects the core idea of a 'moral sense'. The basic question addressed by Hutcheson, of how humans know right from wrong, was fundamental to the very possibility of moral reflection. But it would receive a very different solution—and a far deeper, more elegant and intellectually fertile one—from his pupil.

In his final year at Glasgow Smith continued his studies, including further immersion in Newtonian physics. The quality of his work had not escaped notice, for he was described by the Professor of Greek as 'a very fine boy as any we have', and in 1739 he was awarded one of two prestigious Snell Exhibitions to study at Balliol College, Oxford. The Exhibitions had been originally established to support Glasgow graduates who were preparing for ordination in the Church of England, but the rules had recently been relaxed and the awards were worth the decent sum of £40 a year for up to eleven years. By June 1740 Smith had made the week-long journey, travelling on horseback through the border country via Carlisle, Lichfield and Warwick to Oxford.

As far as we know, this was Adam Smith's first journey outside Scotland, and he must have been struck by England's more developed agriculture and expanding industry. But he was very far from impressed by Oxford itself. The university had contrived to lose its medieval reputation for scholarship, while maintaining a strong commitment to the Crown and specifically to Jacobitism, much to the distaste of moderate Whigs. Eighteenth-century thinkers from Bishop Butler to Jeremy Bentham united in despair at their inability to learn while at Oxford. The great historian Edward Gibbon, who attempted to study there twelve years after Smith, was unsparing but not untypical in his denunciation:

> To the university of Oxford I acknowledge no obligation . . . I spent fourteen months at Magdalen College; they proved the fourteen

months the most idle and unprofitable of my whole life . . . The schools of Oxford and Cambridge were founded in a dark age of false and barbarous science; and they are still tainted with the vices of their origin . . . The legal incorporation of these societies by the charters of popes and kings had given them a monopoly of the public instruction; and the spirit of monopolists is narrow, lazy, and oppressive; their work is more costly and less productive than that of independent artists; and the new improvements so eagerly grasped by the competition of freedom are admitted with slow and sullen reluctance in those proud corporations, above the fear of a rival, and below the confession of an error.

Gibbon's analysis of the vicious effects of monopoly is that of Smith himself in *The Wealth of Nations*. And he goes on to quote Smith's own words: 'In the university of Oxford, the greater part of the public professors have, for these many years, given up altogether even the pretence of teaching.' What they did teach was far from the new science of Newton and Locke; Oxford must have been among 'the learned societies' which, he said in *The Wealth of Nations*, 'have chosen to remain, for a very long time, the sanctuaries in which exploded systems and obsolete prejudices found shelter and protection, after they had been hunted out of every other corner of the world'.

Nor, alas, was Balliol an exception to this rule. By the end of the nineteenth century the college would become an academic power-house under Benjamin Jowett, and a nursery of statesmen famed for instilling what its alumnus the Prime Minister H. H. Asquith once supposedly described as 'the tranquil consciousness of an effortless superiority'. But when Smith arrived there in 1740 the college had become mired in internal rivalries, dullness and debt under the Mastership of Theophilus Leigh. As John Rae said, 'A claim is set up in behalf of some of the other Oxford colleges that they kept the lamp of learning lit even in the darkest days of [that] century, but Balliol is not one of them.' Even by Oxford's standards, moreover, the college was known for its strong Jacobite sympathies, and it had crossed swords repeatedly with the authorities at Glasgow University over the terms of the Snell bequest. Exhibitions went unfilled while the college retained the income; the Scotsmen who did come got the worst rooms and the surliest treatment; and they regularly objected. The Little Library open to undergraduates was not well stocked and, to make matters still worse, college life was expensive, especially compared to the Scottish universities. In short, Balliol at that time was Jacobite, Tory, factional, costly and Scotophobic; and Adam Smith was Presbyterian, Whiggish, sociable, impecunious and a Scot. It is perhaps surprising that he lasted there as long as he did.

The particular combination of slackness and expense did not endear Balliol to Smith, though it seems to have inspired his later view that, whatever the personal inclinations or moral character of those involved, the superiority of Scottish universities lay in the fact that their professors relied not on college stipends but on income from fees paid by students, which made the professors harder-working and more attentive to student needs. Even as they were, however, the college's own fees evidently hurt. In his first known letter, to his guardian William Smith, he complained about the 'extraordinary and most extravagant fees we are obliged to pay . . . it will be his own fault if anyone should endanger his health at Oxford by excessive study, our only business here being to go to prayers twice a day, and to lecture twice a week.' Gentlemen commoners at Oxford at that time rarely spent less than £60 a year; Smith's income of £40 was supplemented by a Warner Exhibition worth £8 5s a year, but still fell well short of that total. Even with frugal living, he must have required periodic top-ups from home. In almost every way, then, the contrast with Glasgow could hardly have been greater.

Oxford's lecture schedule may not have endangered Smith's health, but there were moments when he was far from well. We know very little about the six years he spent at the university; not where he lived, nor what he studied nor which lectures he attended, nor even the names of his lecturers or tutors. But we do know from his college bills that he spent the vast majority of his time in residence; he could probably have ill afforded to travel. And from his very few surviving letters of the time we also know that in 1743–4 he was afflicted with some kind of nervous disorder. He wrote to his mother in November 1743 that 'I am just recovered of a violent fit of laziness, which has confined me to my elbow chair these three months.' And in another letter to her, of the following July: 'I am quite inexcusable for not writing to you oftener. I think of you every day, but always defer writing till the post is just going, and then sometimes business or company, but oftener laziness, hinders me.'

Smith's condition is more likely to have been exhaustion or a mild form of depression than laziness. To combat it he took 'tar water', a mixture of water and pine tar which had just become fashionable through the endorsement of no less an authority than the great idealist philosopher and scourge of Newtonianism, Bishop Berkeley himself. So enthusiastic was Berkeley on the topic of tar water that he opened his last major work, *Siris* (1744), with a breathless panegyric to the remedy, recommending it 'for the cure or relief of most if not all diseases, in ulcers, eruption, and foul cases; scurvies of all kinds, disorders of the lung, stomach, and bowels; in nervous cases, in all inflammatory distempers and in decays, and other maladies'. This was an imposing list, and tar water was clearly effective as a marketing ploy if for no other purpose, for *Siris* sold better than any of the Bishop's other books during his lifetime. Smith was sufficiently persuaded of the potion's merits to recommend it in a letter to his mother: 'It has perfectly cured me of an inveterate scurvy and shaking in the head. I wish you'd try it. I fancy it might be of service to you.'

Last but not least, with the exception of some of the other Snell fellows, Smith does not seem to have found his undergraduate colleagues particularly congenial—just one became a friend thereafter. Rae says of them, 'I have gone over the names of those who might be Smith's contemporaries at Balliol . . . and they were a singularly undistinguished body of people.' Writing to Smith from Balliol in 1754, ten years later, his friend Alexander Wedderburn drily contrasted London with Oxford, 'where the acquaintances I have found are so totally different from those I have left that my studies run no risk of being much interrupted'.

Yet if Oxford had its drawbacks it also offered things to be grateful for. Many ambitious Scotsmen of the time were self-conscious about their accents, and a certain English poise and polish were much sought after. One effect of Smith's time at Oxford was to knock the edges off his accent so that, in Rae's words, 'Englishmen . . . were struck with the pure and correct English he spoke in private conversation.' A more tangible benefit was Adderbury Manor. Smith's custodian and kinsman William Smith was steward to the dukes of Argyll, and lived at the family's fifty-six-room country seat at Adderbury, some 20 miles north of Oxford. Visits to the house must have provided a blessed refuge for the young Scotsman, and an invaluable introduction to a wider and grander social world.

But above all Oxford gave Smith what the great twentieth-century philosopher Michael Oakeshott once called 'the gift of an interval . . . an opportunity to put aside the hot allegiances of youth . . . a period in which to look round upon the world . . . a moment in which to taste the mystery without the necessity of at once seeking a solution'. And Smith, ever the autodidact, used this interval to good effect. In later life he was renowned for the breadth and depth of his learning, and his habit of work was formidably intense. Looking back from the perspective of Smith's later achievements, Dugald Stewart suggests that he devoted his six years at Oxford to English literature; to extending his knowledge of ancient authors; to learning some French and Italian, with an emphasis on practising translations, which always fascinated him; and to reading history and acquiring 'a familiar acquaintance with everything that could illustrate the institutions, the manners, and the ideas of different ages and nations'. This is surely right. The great continental masters such as Machiavelli, Pascal,

Descartes, Bayle, Voltaire and Montesquieu, to say nothing of Racine and La Rochefoucauld, now fell to his hand. It was during this time that Smith laid the intellectual foundations for his mature thought, including *The Theory of Moral Sentiments* and *The Wealth of Nations*.

There is one other fascinating possibility, reflected in a plausible story from John Leslie, a mathematician whom Smith recruited forty years later to teach his heir, David Douglas. Leslie wrote in a 1797 letter about Smith that 'We have heard that the heads of college thought proper to visit his chamber, and finding him reading Hume's *Treatise* . . . then recently published, the reverend inquisitors seized that heretical book and severely reprimanded the young philosopher.'

Why does this matter? David Hume's *Treatise of Human Nature* had been published in 1739–40, just before Smith arrived at Oxford. The book is a philosophical masterpiece, which has proven to be foundational to modern reflection on human knowledge, personal identity, the emotions, causation and many other areas. It was far from a critical failure on publication, despite Hume's mournful words that it 'fell dead-born from the press'. But, seeking to build a wider audience, two years later Hume recast some of his ideas in the more accessible form of a set of elegant and discursive *Essays, Moral and Political*, with great success. So even if Leslie's plausible story is wrong, it is highly likely that Smith knew something, perhaps a good deal, of Hume's work while he was at Balliol.

All the more so because in religious terms the *Treatise* was dynamite from the moment the printer's ink was dry. Hume had removed some of its most controversial passages at the last minute, but even so the book soon earned its author a notorious reputation for religious scepticism, indeed atheism. Francis Hutcheson was among those appalled by the supposed heresies of the *Treatise*; and he went out of his way in 1745 to prevent Hume from obtaining the chair in moral philosophy at Edinburgh.

But, though they disagreed over religion, Hutcheson and the early Hume shared a philosophical ambition, to discharge one of the great projects of the Enlightenment by producing a 'science of man': a unified and general account of human life in all its major aspects, based on facts and human experience, which could sit without embarrassment alongside, indeed potentially embrace, Newton's towering *Principia*. Hutcheson's attempt, as we have seen, had been grounded on a divinely inspired 'moral sense' and on the theory of natural law rooted in the belief in God. But Hume turned in a very different direction, away from God and towards nature itself. In the Introduction to the *Treatise*, he had written: 'There is no question of importance whose decision is not comprised in the science of man.' It followed from this that 'Even mathematics, natural philosophy and natural religion are in some measure dependent on the science of man.' In his essay 'That Politics may be Reduced to a Science' Hume went on to explain: 'So great is the force of laws, and of particular forms of government, and so little dependence have they on the humours and tempers of men, that consequences almost as general and certain may sometimes be deduced from them, as any which the mathematical sciences afford them.' But, he emphasized, such a science could be based only on observation and experience; and not, by implication, on divine inspiration or religious dogma. Natural law would not be reliant on the concurrence or continuing support of the deity; it would, in effect, be returned to nature. This stricture cut both ways. Yes, it clipped the wings of religion. But it did the same thing to mathematics and the exact sciences, by insisting that for all their claims of universality and objectivity they too were in some sense dependent parts of a wider science of man. The implication was not lost on Smith.

A science of man, then, would combine core areas of human experience, however apparently subjective, into a single unified theory founded on a few simple propositions about man and the world, without any reliance on supernatural powers or divine intervention. It was, and remains, a dazzling idea, with potentially revolutionary implications. The phrase 'science of man' itself appears nowhere in the writings of Adam Smith, but the idea of it underlies and motivates all of his works—including, it appears, those that have not survived. Smith's particular interest would focus on the possibility that such a general explanation could be given of human behaviour, public and private, from the home to the law court and the legislature to the marketplace. What would this be? How could it possibly work? It would not be until 1750 or so that Smith and Hume would finally meet. But their intellectual engagement would inspire, sustain and provoke Smith for the rest of his life.

CHAPTER 2

'THE MOST USEFUL, HAPPIEST AND MOST HONOURABLE PERIOD OF MY LIFE', 1746–1759

IN THE LATE SUMMER OF 1746 ADAM SMITH LEFT OXFORD AND RE-turned to his mother in Kirkcaldy. He found the country of his birth in a state of shock, reeling from the convulsive effects of the Jacobite rebellion of '45, which had culminated that April in the slaughter of the rebels by the forces of the Crown at the battle of Culloden. In such a context, the High Church and Jacobite Toryism of Balliol must have felt less hospitable than ever to the young Presbyterian from Fife. But, after six years at Oxford, he had got what he needed.

In retrospect, the '45 feels like the last birthing pains of a commercial Scotland. But there was nothing foreordained about it at the time. It arose as a piece of astonishing adventurism by the twenty-four-year-old Charles Edward Louis John Casimir Sylvester Severino Maria Stuart, known as Bonnie Prince Charlie or the Young Pretender. In exile in France, his grandfather King James II of England and VII of Scotland had been forced by pressure from the 'Sun King' Louis XIV in 1692 to accept most of the settlement that had followed the Glorious Revolution, including its emphasis on constitutional and not absolute monarchy. But the flame of Jacobitism had never been entirely extinguished in any part of Britain. In Scotland, it was kept alive by an uneasy alliance of three groups. The most committed of these were the Catholics, who retained their personal allegiance to James. They were not large in number—perhaps 1 per cent of the total Scottish population—but they were well organized. Two centuries of religious persecution had created highly effective secret networks of information and mutual support, and the Catholics contributed disproportionately to the maintenance of different Jacobite armies and to the support of the exiled court in France. Alongside the Catholics were the Non-Jurors—the relatively small number of Anglican clergy who had refused to swear the oath of allegiance to William and Mary as co-regents after 1689. These men were devout believers in the Stuart succession, and as staunch Anglicans they and their followers were more visible and better publicly placed than the Catholics to press for the Jacobite cause.

But by some way the largest group were the Scottish Episcopalians. The Episcopalian Church had formed in the decades immediately after the Scottish Reformation of 1560, when the Church of Scotland had broken with Rome and adopted the Confession of Faith. Believing strongly in the importance of the Church hierarchy, Episcopalian clergy pledged their allegiance to the Crown, and so to the Stuart line. Many had been radicalized by the religious settlement of 1688–9, which they saw as intolerant, discriminatory and triumphalist. They and their adherents were largely located in parts of the highlands, and in the north-eastern lowlands, and these areas remained long resistant to the spread of Presbyterianism.

The three groups had clearly different histories, different beliefs and different goals, and on some points—Catholicism, hierarchy—they were in outright opposition to each other. The Jacobites were thus badly conflicted from the outset, and those internal conflicts grew worse as their leaders sought to build popular support by committing to other political and social causes. As a result, the clear and focused discontent created by the eviction of James II from the throne in 1688 gradually blurred into a more general spirit of protest. Against this, however, the different groupings were brought together periodically by recurrent hopes of an armed intervention from France. France was Catholic, it was in a protracted geopolitical struggle with England, it had long supported the Stuarts financially, and it was home to the exiled court. Above all, it was the great continental superpower of Europe, with an immense army located just a few miles away across the Channel. Surely it could simply wave its wand and send troops in support of a Scottish Jacobite insurrection?

In 1708, it did. The scheme had two aims: to place the 'Old Pretender' James Francis Edward, son of King James II, on the throne of Scotland, and to create a diversion that would draw English troops away from the Duke of Marlborough's highly successful campaign against the French in the War of the Spanish Succession. A small flotilla was mustered at Dunkirk with troops assembled, while a welcome party of Scottish rebels awaited their landing at the Firth of Forth. But the whole scheme proved abortive. James Francis went down with measles at the last moment, and when the flotilla finally sailed with him two weeks later it was harried by an English squadron which prevented it from landing, despite his entreaties to the captain to do so.

Seven years later the Jacobites tried again, and this attempt was much more serious. As the 1708 rebellion had been partly triggered by the Scottish reaction to the Act of Union, so was that of 1715 by reaction to the death of Queen Anne in the previous year. Taking up the succession in the Hanoverian line, George I had made plain his preference for an overwhelmingly Whig administration, and the Whigs went on to win a huge victory in the general election in the spring of 1715. In this they capitalized highly effectively on anti-French feeling, claiming that the recently signed Treaty of Utrecht—negotiated by the previous Tory government to settle the war—had been too lenient to Louis XIV. Election victory was swiftly followed by impeachment proceedings against the main Tory leaders, provoking widespread indignation.

The 1715 rebellion thus arose not merely from Jacobite longing for a Stuart restoration after the death of Anne, but from a Tory political reaction in England as well. In southern England and the midlands, where Jacobitism was weak, the agitation was populist and noisy but ineffective. The north did somewhat better. A small Jacobite force assembled, advanced on the city of Newcastle and was repelled. It then moved on to take Preston and was successfully resisting a siege by government troops when it suddenly capitulated, to the amazement and rage of its Scottish allies.

But Scotland itself was a very different matter. For one thing, even among the unaffiliated Scots, many had some sympathy for the Jacobite cause. For another, the highlands—harsh, isolated, sparsely populated, Gaelic speaking and poor—were home to the highland clans, who were very well organized for war. Each clan had its own hereditary ruling dynasty, and an intricate feudal structure of kin relationships, which spread authority and mutual support throughout its subordinate branches. The main obligation owed was for the 'man-rent'—the number of men a junior officer undertook to provide and lead in battle. As a result, the clans could mobilize large numbers of experienced and very tough soldiers at short notice. There were thus plenty of men in Scotland who were willing to take up arms for the Jacobite cause. Perhaps as many as 20,000 came and went in 1715–16.

In late summer the clan chieftains and leading north-east sympathizers gathered troops at the behest of the Earl of Mar. Advancing after some successful raids, they encamped at Perth. However, they allowed themselves to become entranced by the possibility of reinforcements from France, and again they were disappointed. The resulting delay allowed the Duke of Argyll to muster forces of his own for the government, and on 13 November the two sides met at Sheriffmuir, near Dunblane. The Jacobites were vastly greater in number—some 10,000 men against 3,000 on Argyll's side—and had the better of the fighting. But they failed to strike the decisive blow and the final result was inconclusive. By spring the rebellion had melted away.

Apart from a few plots, the spirit of rebellion would not return for the next thirty years. Louis XIV had died in 1715, the new French King was just a baby, and an Anglo-French alliance the following year kept the Jacobites' hopes of an intervention by France at bay. But by 1745 they were ready to try again, this time under the wild but charismatic leadership of the young Charles Edward Stuart. This time, too, the French looked to be more committed. They had carefully planned an invasion in 1743, with 10,000 troops assembled on the coast, only to be thwarted by an appalling storm which drove back the fleet and scattered their supply vessels. This was followed by a long period of indecision at the court. Eventually Charles Edward could stand the delay no longer. He arrived in Scotland in July 1745 with virtually no military support, but through a mixture of persuasion and financial promises quickly induced clan chiefs to rise, despite their initial scepticism. Within weeks the combined army had taken Perth.

Charles Edward now moved on Edinburgh, which fell (apart from the castle) on 17 September without a shot fired, to its considerable later embarrassment. Three days later the rebel army of 2,500 men destroyed a similarly sized government force in very short order at the battle of Prestonpans. At this point, however, the Jacobites made a fateful decision. Lord George Murray, who had led a brilliant flanking manoeuvre at Prestonpans and who was distinguishing himself as the Jacobites' most effective field commander, now argued that they should pause, consolidate what had been achieved and await news of the French. Carried away by visions of glory, however, Charles Edward persuaded himself and the clan chiefs that English Jacobite leaders had promised him their support in numbers in the event of an invasion. After a month's delay, they marched into England, ultimately reaching Derby, just 129 miles from London.

To Charles Edward, the way to the throne now lay open. But to the clan chiefs the situation looked very different. They were operating far from home, in hostile territory and in winter. Far from rising up in support as promised, moreover, the English Jacobites had so far signally failed to move. Nor was there any sign of a supportive invasion from France, while fresh intelligence suggested a new Hanoverian army at Northampton near by. At a stormy council of war on 5 December Charles Edward was confronted by the clan chiefs, and despite his protestations they determined to retreat. Scholars still disagree on this vital question, but some have argued that if the Scots had now marched on London, they might have succeeded. For, as we now know, the crucial new intelligence was false, and had been provided by a spy for the English named Dudley Bradstreet. The oncoming army did not in fact exist. Not only that: the English Jacobites had finally decided to come out in support; the French were poised to invade; and London was lightly defended. If Charles Edward had pressed on, he might conceivably have had the capital by Christmas.

But the Scots turned back. The winter weather was bad, and they were beset by sickness and fatigue. Their prince Charles Edward was now angry, obstructive and withdrawn. Meanwhile King George II's son, the young Duke of Cumberland, was in pursuit. Nevertheless, led by Murray, the Jacobite army executed a superb fighting retreat back to the Scottish borders. There they reprovisioned before withdrawing further, to Stirling and finally into the highlands. Cumberland paused, reinforced his troops with a substantial body of paid Hessian auxiliaries and continued his pursuit. On the moor at Culloden near Inverness on 16 April 1746, Charles Edward overruled his officers to insist that they stand their ground and fight a setpiece battle—as it proved, the last on British soil. The Jacobite army was under-equipped and tired from an abortive overnight raid. It found itself exposed on open and marshy terrain unsuited to its famous charges, and was routed and murderously put to flight. Charles Edward fled to the Hebrides, was famously smuggled to Skye dressed as a lady's maid by Flora Macdonald and then escaped to France. The last Jacobite campaign was over.

There followed a period of violent suppression of the Jacobites, led by Cumberland. Several of their leaders were summarily executed, a further 116 rebels were hung, drawn and quartered, and over 3,000 more died in prison, disappeared or were subject to transportation. The highlands had always been a source of political instability, and the British government now moved to incorporate them fully within the wider nation. Episcopalian clergy were required to swear oaths of allegiance to the Crown. Scottish landowners were stripped of hereditary judicial rights in return for compensation, while clan chiefs who had supported the rebellion saw their lands forfeited and sold. Additional roads were built to facilitate the rapid transfer of troops around the highlands. The formation of Scottish militias was prohibited. Tartan was forbidden except when worn by the British army. New emphasis was given to the use of English over Gaelic.

Thus when Adam Smith arrived back in Kirkcaldy in August 1746, barely four months after Culloden, Scotland was in a state of total upheaval. And nowhere more so than Edinburgh, just a few miles across the Firth of Forth. Unlike Glasgow, the capital was not renowned for trade. But it was already developing the distinctively polite culture for which it would later be famed, as different streams of civic, academic, professional, political and commercial society came together with a religious sensibility that was moderate in both doctrine and commitment. Far from being an academic redoubt, the university was unusual in that it had originated in a petition of the Town Council, and the Council exercised authority over it for nearly 300 years after its foundation in 1567. This helped to make the university an integral part of the city, and created a highly productive relationship from which sprang Scotland's first hospital, the Royal Infirmary in 1729. In physical terms, the atmosphere was often rank; to the locals it had long been 'Auld Reekie' due to the smoke that filled the Old Town, and the stench of sewage abated only with the draining of the fetid North Loch in the 1760s. Intellectually, however, Edinburgh was highly civilized, a city of coffeehouses, conversation and debate; and its people had fully shared the eighteenth century's obsession with clubs, most notable among them the Philosophical Society, founded in 1737 and still flourishing today as the Royal Society of Edinburgh.

But the city was not famed for its fighting spirit, and when the Jacobite army marched on Edinburgh in 1745 its civic, cultural and professional life had very quickly shut down. The Bank of Scotland closed its doors, as did the university, the courts and the administration of government. Most of the leading citizens decamped at speed. Only a rag-tag collection of volunteers went to its defence, and these quickly surrendered to spare further bloodshed. It took Edinburgh many years to recover from this catastrophe, and still the '45 cast a long shadow. To many, especially among 'the middling sort', it was a brutal and demoralizing reminder of the fragility of polite society. The suppression of the rebellion raised the lingering and highly unpleasant possibility of direct rule from Westminster. And in the contrast between Edinburgh's coffeehouse gentility and the brutal clan blood feuds of the highlands, there lay the more fundamental issue of whether Scotland, with its deep divisions of language, religion and geography, was really one nation at all.

FOR ADAM SMITH, IT MUST HAVE RAISED A STILL DEEPER QUESTION, about the very basis of human sociability. If, as Hutcheson had taught, man was in essence a social being, how was this so? If Hutcheson's own idea of a 'moral sense' was unsatisfactory, then what, if anything, could replace it? Indeed, how and under what conditions was it possible for people to live or flourish together at all? To these questions Smith would soon start to develop his own magnificent and comprehensive answer.

For the next two years Smith lived at home with his mother, and about this time we know virtually nothing. Doubtless he continued to read voraciously, and to think. But the way forward was not clear. Having turned away from the possibility of a clerical career, he had hopes at one point of a life as a tutor in one of the great families, a not uncommon first step for a university graduate. But this did not come to pass, and academic posts were few and far between. His 'never to be forgotten' teacher Francis Hutcheson had died in 1746; but Hutcheson's professorship at Glasgow had passed to Thomas Craigie of St Andrews, and Smith cannot have expected to succeed his mentor, given his own youth and lack of public reputation at the time.

But in 1748 Smith was invited to give a series of lectures in Edinburgh, and this offered an unmissable opportunity to gather his ideas together and make a public mark. The invitation came from one of the less famous but more important figures of the Scottish Enlightenment, the jurist Henry Home, later Lord Kames. Kames was close to Smith's dear friend James Oswald, and a cousin of David Hume; it was Kames who had persuaded Hume to drop some of the more incendiary language of the *Treatise*. A Jacobite in his youth, he was a prolific author and an energetic but controlling man; according to Boswell, Hume said, 'When one says of another man, he is the most arrogant man in the world, it is meant only to say that he is very arrogant. But when one says it of Lord Kames it is an absolute truth.' For all this, though, Kames was also a great patron of younger talents, an inveterate networker and institution-builder and in many ways a quintessential Enlightenment figure, who sought to establish Scotland as both a literary and commercial force in the world.

Impressed by Smith, Kames had earlier pushed him into print for the first time by commissioning him to write a preface to—and, it seems, to edit—a collection of poems by a Jacobite poet in exile, William Hamilton. Now Kames followed this up by commissioning the younger man to give a series of lectures on rhetoric and belles lettres in the autumn of 1748. These were repeated the following year and again in 1750–51. The central topic—how to communicate effectively in writing and speech—was well chosen to appeal to an Edinburgh audience, to flatter Smith's interests and ability and to prepare the way for a professorship, and a second series was added, on jurisprudence. Both sets of lectures were well received, and they helped to make Smith's name.

We do not know exactly where in Edinburgh Smith gave what

were later published as his *Lectures on Rhetoric and Belles Lettres*. It was not at the university—he never in fact taught at the University of Edinburgh—but may conceivably have been under the auspices of the Philosophical Club, perhaps to help keep the club alive in the difficult years after the rebellion. The lectures were received by 'a respectable auditory, chiefly composed of students of law and theology', which included friends such as Oswald and luminaries-to-be including Alexander Wedderburn, a future Lord Chancellor; and they earned Smith the professorial sum of £100 a year for three years. The text of the lectures has come down to us only indirectly, primarily in the form of two sets of students' notes from 1762–3, when Smith delivered them as a set of thirty lectures in Glasgow. Those notes are more of a digest than a literal transcription, however, and the lectures themselves were significantly reorganized by Smith at this time. This makes it impossible to trace the exact progression of his thought, especially in relation to his first published book, *The Theory of Moral Sentiments* of 1759. But he was a great creature of habit, there are relatively few references to works published after 1748, and the lectures' overall thrust is clear enough. So they may well have had much of the same content from the outset.

Rhetoric—the art of persuasion—had ancient roots in the writings of Aristotle in Greece, and later of Cicero and Quintilian in Rome. But in the seventeenth century it had come under severe criticism from those in and around the new Royal Society, who followed Francis Bacon in seeking to purge science of the false and 'idolatrous' influences of human subjectivity, culture and religion, even of language itself. The brilliant mathematician Colin Maclaurin, a student of Isaac Newton and vigorous defender of Newtonianism against religious attack, kept the flame of scientific expression alive in Scotland—as it was remarked, his 'pure, correct and simple style inducing a taste for chasteness of expression [and] . . . a disrelish of affected ornaments'. But, if rhetoric was an intellectually contested topic, it was also one of considerable practical importance in lowland

Scotland after the disaster of the '45, and especially so in Edinburgh, whose professional young men needed to be able to communicate well—both in speech and on paper—if they were to make their way in the courts, in politics, in the Church or as soldiers. This pointed the other way, away from scientific dryness and towards a cultivated elegance and ease of style. And that importance was accentuated by the rising levels of hostility to the Scots in England, where jealousy of Scotland's rapid rise would spill into rampant 'Scotophobia' in the 1760s, lashed on by John Wilkes's scandalous journal the *North Briton* and by public hostility to George III's favourite, the Earl of Bute. As Hume wrote in 1764, 'I do not believe there is one Englishman in fifty, who, if he heard that I had broke my neck to-night, would not be rejoiced with it. Some hate me because I am not a Tory, some because I am not a Whig, some because I am not a Christian, and all because I am a Scotsman.' In this context, Scottish dialect, a pronounced brogue or lack of idiomatic English self-expression could be a serious impediment to future success.

Smith's lectures were thus of both considerable theoretical and practical interest. They are full of useful tips and advice, and Smith was himself an excellent model for, as one of his obituaries noted, 'His pronunciation and his style were much superior to what could, at that time, be acquired in Scotland only.' The inclusion of belles lettres—covering works of modern and ancient literature—made the lectures less formal and more rounded than a strictly rhetorical approach, and hinted at their value both in communication and in literary criticism. In structure, the lectures fall into two parts. The first concerns language and style, the origins of language and its effective use. The second, longer part focuses on different types of communication: descriptive, narrative, poetic, demonstrative, didactic and judicial. The emphasis is on rhetoric and not grammar; indeed, Smith is positively disdainful of 'grammatical parts we must altogether pass over as tedious and unentertaining'. And he peppers the lectures with quotations and criticism, drawing on a formidable array of authors, ranging from Demosthenes, Thucydides and Tacitus to Shakespeare, Milton, Swift and Pope.

In an essay of 1742, 'Of Eloquence', David Hume had seemed to celebrate the grand style of the classical masters Cicero and Demosthenes, which sought to inflame an audience's passions and to lament its usurpation by modern politeness and 'manners'. Smith, however, was in no doubt in siding with the more modern trend—to seek to create for Scotland an effective common language which would permit professional work, commercial exchange and scientific inquiry to progress. Most importantly, for Smith language was a crucial entry point to the development and explication of a projected science of man. As his pupil John Millar put it, 'The best method of explaining and illustrating the various powers of the human mind, the most useful part of metaphysics, arises from an examination of the several ways of communicating our thoughts by speech, and from an attention to the principles of those literary compositions which contribute to persuasion or entertainment.'

Both here and in an important later essay, 'Considerations Concerning the First Formation of Languages' (1761), Smith sees effective communication as requiring what he calls perspicuity and propriety. Perspicuity is to be achieved through a plain and unadorned style, in contrast to—a favourite target—the artificial and pompous labourings of Lord Shaftesbury in his 'dungeon of metaphorical obscurity'. A perspicuous language is one that clearly projects, but also thereby reveals, the thoughts of its speakers. Propriety, or correctness in the use of language, fits language both to the speaker's natural character and communicative intent on one side and to the expectations of the audience on the other. Effective communication requires the speaker to anticipate what effect their words will have on the hearer. Propriety thus carries with it a host of tacit assumptions about norms of grammar and presentation, about the speaker's persona, the occasion, social context and audience; and it is through propriety that sympathy, that communicative bond between speaker and audience, is conveyed.

41

As Smith put it, 'when the sentiment of the speaker is expressed in a neat, clear, plain and clever manner, and the passion or affection he is possessed of and intends, by sympathy, to communicate to his hearer, is plainly and cleverly hit off, then and then only the expression has all the force and beauty that language can give it.' *'By sympathy'*: the phrase looks forward to a key idea of Smith's *Theory of Moral Sentiments*, and illustrates the interconnectedness of his thought from the very start of his intellectual journey.

Gone, therefore, are the tropes, the figures of speech, the topics, the minutious divisions and subdivisions of ancient rhetoric. For Smith they are like the epicycles of Ptolemaic astronomy: expedient features added in no systematic way to save a dying theory, when what is required is a reorientation of the whole subject itself. And more striking still is his view of language: not merely as a human artefact or convenience, but as autonomous and self-creating. Smith is anthropomorphic about words. They are unruly, energetic, not to be contained; their meanings jostle and compete with each other for our attention: 'New words are continually pushing out our own original ones; so that the stock of our own is now become but very small and is still diminishing.' Not only that: whole languages are in a dynamic state of flux. On the one hand, increasing sophistication breeds complexity; on the other, the need for mutual intelligibility with other languages is a force for simplification. For a science of rhetoric to be even possible it must be, not formal, individual and static, but dynamic, social and relational. This is a view of human interaction that runs throughout his thought, including in *The Theory of Moral Sentiments* and *The Wealth of Nations*.

How is such a teeming, shape-shifting hubbub to be properly understood and explained, let alone tamed? In lecture 24 Smith recommends the use of the 'didactical method' for the presentation of a scientific system, and describes the alternative approaches:

> we may either like Aristotle go over the different branches in the
> order they happen to cast up to us, giving a principle commonly

a new one for every phenomenon; or in the manner of Sir Isaac Newton we may lay down certain principles known or proved in the beginning, from whence we account for the same phenomena, connecting all together by the same chain. This latter, which we may call the Newtonian method, is undoubtedly the most philosophical, and in every sense, whether of Morals or Natural Philosophy, etc., is vastly more ingenious, and for that reason more engaging, than the other.

Here we see for the first time in print Smith's deep preference for the simplicity, coherence and economy of the 'Newtonian method' of scientific presentation, and for the approach to science that it exemplified. His positive theory is embryonic at best—at best a sketch of how rhetoric might be reconceived in more coherent terms. Even so the thought is telling on several counts: for the novelty of extending Newtonianism even to language itself; insofar as it anticipates the same themes across Smith's later thought; and for the way it seeks to temper and balance his theory with specific observations. Smith discards the elaborate rules and structures in the works of the ancient rhetoricians—'They are generally a very silly set of books and not at all instructive'—in favour of an approach based on a few fundamental principles, but at the same time the whole has an empirical and naturalistic feel. There is no dismissal here of inconvenient data, and no suggestion that language is a divine bequest to man, above human understanding, or subject to rules independent of human society.

Smith's *Lectures on Rhetoric and Belles Lettres* are, then, not merely about the tradecraft of effective communication, but about language as a medium of social and intellectual exchange, and as an illustration of the powers and working of the human mind. They are little known today and little studied, and Smith's own tastes in literature— for Livy among historians, for Swift among prose stylists, with a rather qualified admiration for Shakespeare—have struck some people ever since as distinctly idiosyncratic. But they were not without influence or adherents. One such was Kames himself, who published his own (in places rather Smithian) *Elements of Criticism* in 1762. Another was the young Hugh Blair, who was among Smith's initial audience and who would be appointed to the first ever chair in rhetoric and belles lettres, at Edinburgh in the same year. If, as has been suggested, the Scots of the late eighteenth century invented the academic study of English literature, then Smith deserves mention as one of its inventors.

Above all, however, the *Lectures* can be viewed as a way into Smith's wider thought. Several of Smith's leading later ideas can already be found here in embryo: we can see the auditors and readers of the *Lectures* as precursors of the 'impartial spectator' of *The Theory of Moral Sentiments*, the early emphasis on perspicuity of communication anticipating his later stress on sympathy and mutual recognition, while the rhetoric and suasion here anticipate the disposition to 'truck, barter and exchange' of *The Wealth of Nations*.

However, the central philosophical question, of what form a science of man could properly take, still remained. Smith's answer comes in an essay on the *History of Astronomy* which he wrote at about this time. This was the product of great study, intended to be part of a larger inquiry; and a work of which he remained proud to the end of his life. Its full title reveals its purpose: *The Principles which Lead and Direct Philosophical Enquiries; Illustrated by the History of Astronomy*. This is an essay about philosophical, and specifically natural-philosophical or scientific, method. The work has a distinctly Humean stamp. In particular, Hume had launched a subversively sceptical attack on the deepest foundations of the natural sciences in his *Treatise*, by arguing that human experience of causation only really amounts to one of a 'constant conjunction' between specific causes and effects. But if all we can know of is a constant conjunction, then it seems we can have no access to or knowledge of underlying causal laws, and our understanding of what they amount to can never outrun human experience. Causation becomes limited and contingent: not a deep natural phenomenon, but an accident of human psychology.

Smith's essay carefully respects this point. Nature's laws are 'invisible chains' whose effects cause us wonder, surprise and admiration, and seduce us into believing we can know them directly. As with his theory of rhetoric, the task of philosophy is 'to introduce order into this chaos of jarring and discordant appearances, to allay this tumult of the imagination, and to restore it, when it surveys the great revolutions of the universe, to that tone of tranquillity and composure, which is both most agreeable in itself, and most suitable to its nature'. Scientific discovery is reliant on the imagination, according to Smith, and the history of astronomy illustrates this through a succession of imaginative attempts to find such order in chaos: first among the ancients, then in the Ptolemaic system, more recently in the work of thinkers such as Copernicus, Brahe, Kepler, Galileo, Descartes and Newton.

Each system succeeds the other not so much by giving us knowledge of nature's laws—for Humean reasons this is impossible—but by resolving our doubts insofar as evidence allows, bringing intellectual coherence to our understanding and delight to our sense of beauty and order. In Smith's words, 'Systems in many respects resemble machines. A machine is a little system, created to perform, as well as to connect together, in reality, those different movements and effects which the artist has occasion for. A system is an imaginary machine invented to connect together in the fancy those different movements and effects which are already in reality performed.' With time comes clarity, simplicity and order: 'The machines that are first invented to perform any particular movement are always the most complex, and succeeding artists generally discover that, with fewer wheels, with fewer principles of motion, than had originally been employed, the same effects may be more easily produced.'

In specifying and emphasizing the machine-like aspects of systematic natural science, and starting to form them into a sophisticated account of scientific method, Smith went some way beyond Hume, and embarked on a line of thought that has had many imitators. Indeed, in the modern era the view has arisen that Newton's scientific worldview was entirely mechanistic and deterministic, an account of the cosmos as working by clockwork which he regarded as closed, completed and the final truth. This suggestion has proven useful as a basis from which to argue against the existence of God; or, more recently, to draw comparisons with general equilibrium theories in economics, as we shall see. But the truth is very different: Newton regarded his own scientific advances as part of a wider process aimed at discovering the real underlying nature of things. As he said in Rule 4, added to the third edition of his *Principia*, 'In experimental philosophy, propositions gathered from phenomena by induction should be considered *either exactly or very nearly true* notwithstanding any contrary hypothesis, *until yet other phenomena make such propositions either more exact or liable to exceptions*' (emphasis added). Newton's thought is not closed but open-ended. In other words, scientific thinking moves iteratively and reflectively between phenomena and potential explanations for them; any scientific theory is approximate, conditional and future-oriented, awaiting new evidence for or against.

This crucial aspect of Newton's thought was something Smith thoroughly understood. It means for him that a theory can emerge as a coherent explanation of a set of phenomena, without the need to make grand assumptions about unknowable natural laws. The result is that there is much less of a gap within a Humean or Smithian science of man between what would now be termed the exact and the social sciences: both in effect simply present a set of phenomena to be examined, explained and understood. If we take the essay on the *History of Astronomy* together with Smith's lectures on rhetoric, what is so striking is not merely Smith's depth of engagement with physical theories of the cosmos, but his unwillingness to confine systematic thinking to what would today be called the 'hard' sciences, let alone in any closed or static way. By the mid-1750s, perhaps earlier, he was starting to develop a clear—and remarkably modern—idea of what a science of man could be.

SMITH'S LECTURES ON RHETORIC—WITH THEIR EMPHASIS ON RIGOUR and practicality, on Newtonian method and effective performance—are not merely a way into his own thought. They also exemplify a blend of assumptions and concerns utterly characteristic of what has come to be called the Scottish Enlightenment.

The idea of 'the Enlightenment'—what, where, how and who it was, and what it meant—remains a contested one among scholars. But by the turn of the eighteenth century it was becoming clear across Europe that a rapid evolution in thought was under way. In part this was the result of scientific advance: the dethroning of the Ptolemaic view of the universe described by Smith, in favour of the heliocentric view of Copernicus and his followers; the astonishing discoveries of Newton; major mathematical developments by Descartes in geometry, and Leibniz and Newton with the calculus; the invention of the telescope and microscope, and the new natural philosophy of Galileo, Boyle and Hooke. But these achievements in turn betokened a much wider intellectual, social and cultural realignment, away from religion, deference to institutions and received wisdom and towards individual reason, scepticism and the exchange of ideas. In due course they led to calls for religious toleration, legal rights and moral equality that many princes and governments across Europe found profoundly threatening.

Scotland at the turn of the eighteenth century was fertile territory for these ideas. The Presbyterian Church was still an institution of huge influence, as its contest for power with the Crown in Glasgow demonstrated. But the covenanting character of much Scottish Protestantism, which had led the country first to protest and then to war with Charles I in 1638–40, once again evinced its independence of spirit, alongside its specific rejection of episcopacy and hierarchy. Moreover, Scotland's intellectual culture was well developed. It had five universities—St Andrews, King's and Marischal colleges in Aberdeen, as well as Glasgow and Edinburgh—versus England's two at Oxford and Cambridge; and there was a large network of parish schools across the lowlands. Finally, national pride had been stung with the failure at Darien, and stung again for many people with the Act of Union. The effect of these different elements was to give the Scottish Enlightenment a strong orientation towards practice in relation to theory, and towards individual self-improvement and social advance. The result, increasingly nurtured by societies, clubs and coffeehouses, was a remarkable outpouring of ideas and thinkers whose interests ranged from geology to law, medicine to chemistry, anthropology to the arts. And at its intellectual core, reflecting on the deepest workings of human nature and the social world, were Adam Smith and David Hume.

It was probably around 1750 that Smith finally met David Hume, and formed the most intellectually important friendship of his life. Hume had recovered from his disappointment at the public reception of the *Treatise* to compose his *Essays, Moral and Political*, and he was about to write his *History of England*, published in six volumes over 1754–62 to tremendous critical and popular success—so much so that when his publisher then entreated him for another volume Hume memorably replied, 'I have four reasons for not writing: I am too old, too fat, too lazy and too rich.' Hume was celebrated in later life almost as much for his affable and ironic temper as for his intellect, which was fortunate given the various setbacks which dogged his early career. In 1745 he had been denied the chair in moral philosophy at Edinburgh, due to his reputed atheism. Events were soon to repeat themselves.

In the winter of 1750–51, at the age of twenty-seven, Smith was elected Professor of Logic and Metaphysics at Glasgow, with the support of Kames and the Duke of Argyll. As was customary, in January 1751 he read an inaugural dissertation ('On the Origin of Ideas', now lost), signed the Confession of Faith before the Presbytery of Glasgow and swore an oath of faithful service. He arrived in Glasgow the following October, and was joined in due course by his mother and his cousin Janet Douglas, who kept house for him. He had agreed to take on some of the teaching duties of Thomas Craigie, the Professor of

Moral Philosophy, who was ailing. Craigie died soon afterwards, however, and Smith—preferring both its subject matter and its income—was elected to the chair in moral philosophy in April 1752. This left the logic and metaphysics professorship vacant. Again Hume applied for it, and whatever his reputation for irreligiosity it seems he would willingly have signed the Confession and taken the oath. But again he was turned down on religious grounds, with both Argyll and the Presbytery set against him. Thus Glasgow joined Edinburgh in the notable distinction of rejecting one of the greatest thinkers of that or any age for an academic job.

Smith had evidently seen the flow of opinion against Hume, and was not minded to contest it. As he wrote to his friend William Cullen, the Professor of Medicine, 'I should prefer David Hume to any man for a colleague; but I am afraid the public would not be of my opinion; and the interest of the society [that is, the university] will oblige us to have some regard to the opinion of the public.' It was a pragmatic judgement, not a heroic one, for this was a world of patronage and Hume's nomination lacked both religious and political support. Smith generally sought to avoid personal bother wherever possible, and there is no reason to think his backing would have changed the final outcome. Hume was, however, found a position as librarian at the Faculty of Advocates in Edinburgh, 'an office from which', he said, 'I received little or no emolument, but which gave me the command of a large library'.

Hume was twelve years older than Smith, and the two men were rarely in the same place together over their future lives. Nevertheless the relationship was both close and intellectually respectful from early on, and it steadily deepened. By the time of Hume's death in 1776 they were addressing each other as 'My dearest friend'. In 1752, in the first letter we have between them, Hume promises to send a copy of the *Essays*, saying, 'If anything occur to you to be inserted or retrenched, I shall be obliged to you for the hint.' And as so often he adds a droll aside: he had resolved to exclude the sixth and seventh essays, he said,

'But Millar, my bookseller, made such protestations against it; and told me how much he had heard them praised by the best judges; that the bowels of a parent melted, and I preserved them alive.'

A further letter of Hume's expresses his concern at Smith's ill-health; and given the latter's commitments at this time it is little wonder if he was exhausted. The university session ran from mid-October to mid-June. At 7.30 a.m. every weekday Smith gave a one-hour moral philosophy class for public students; at 11 a.m. there was a one-hour period of discussion and examination of the morning's lecture; and he taught a further private class of one hour at noon three times a week for part of the term. Rae suggests that eighty or ninety students attended the public class, and twenty the private, out of a total enrolment of some 300 or 400 at the time. There were also discussions with students during the afternoons. Smith seems to have earned between £150 and £300 a year in salary and fees, a distinctly respectable amount, and this was further supplemented by rent-free housing, and by income from periodic boarders.

By the end of his life Smith would come to be regarded as the very image of the absent-minded professor. One anecdote has him expounding so vigorously to Charles Townshend on the division of labour that he fell into a tanner's pit. Lady Mary Coke recounted to her diary in February 1767 that 'going to breakfast, and falling into discourse, Mr Smith took a piece of bread and butter which, after he had rolled round and round, he put into the teapot and poured the water upon it; sometime after he poured it into a cup, and when he had tasted it, he said it was the worst tea he had ever met with.' There are many other such tales.

Yet the tag of absent-mindedness sits oddly alongside the fact that Smith was clearly an excellent teacher, both well organized and compelling in class. In Dugald Stewart's words, 'There was no situation in which the abilities of Mr Smith appeared to greater advantage than as Professor. In delivering his lectures, he trusted almost entirely to extempore elocution. His manner, though not graceful, was plain and unaffected; and, as he seemed to be always interested in his subject, he never failed to interest his hearers.' One of those hearers was the young James Boswell, who went to Glasgow in 1759 largely on the strength of Smith's reputation, and was not disappointed. 'My greatest reason for coming hither was to hear Mr Smith's lectures (which are truly excellent),' he wrote to a friend. No less impressive was Smith's own character: 'He has none of that formal stiffness and pedantry which is too often found in Professors. So far from that, he is a most polite well-bred man, is extremely fond of having his students with him, and treats them with all the easiness and affability imaginable.'

Smith was also an effective administrator, first at the University of Glasgow and then later in life as a Commissioner of Customs in Edinburgh. At Glasgow he sat on several college committees, helped manage a complex web of property negotiations, was involved in a range of building projects including restoration of the Principal's house and moved the library successfully into a new, albeit initially damp-afflicted building designed by William Adam. He was Quaestor or treasurer, was twice unanimously elected Dean of Faculty, and served as Vice-Rector. These are not the marks of someone out of touch or inept in the art of administration. And such extra duties did not diminish his affection for the university. An attempt by Hume in 1758 to woo him to take up the professorship of the law of nature and nations in Edinburgh came to nothing.

Amid all these commitments Smith also somehow found time to support the launch of the short-lived *Edinburgh Review* in 1755–1756, and used its first issue to write an assessment of Samuel Johnson's *Dictionary of the English Language*, which had just appeared. The review is warm but critical. The author was to be commended for his labours, according to Smith, but there was a deep flaw in his whole approach: the work was 'not . . . sufficiently grammatical'. Johnson had gathered together key instances of words, but he had not analysed what general principles or concepts underlay them, with the result that 'sufficient care is not taken to distinguish the words apparently synonymous.' The word *but*, for example, could be rationally reduced from seventeen senses in the *Dictionary* to seven, Smith argued.

The *Dictionary* had been the result of herculean labours by Johnson and a group of devoted clerks over nearly a decade, marked a decisive advance on previous efforts and had been widely acclaimed on publication. As Boswell later wrote, 'The world contemplated with wonder so stupendous a work achieved by one man, while other countries had thought such undertakings fit only for whole academies.' In contrast to Smith's own preference for minutious grammaticality, the book is far from being a dry compendium, and deliberately so. Indeed it is lit up by Johnson's own personality, and his choice of citations and ironic turn of phrase: he famously defines *lexicographer* as 'a harmless drudge', for example, and *patron* as 'commonly a wretch who supports with insolence, and is paid with flattery'. Johnson himself, moreover, was acutely sensitive to criticism, and—especially when teasing Boswell—often was or pretended to be more than a little Scotophobic. His definition of *oats* is 'a grain which in England is generally given to horses, but in Scotland supports the people'.

To be thus reviewed by a little-known and scantly published Scottish academic must have chafed the great man indeed, and it set the terms for a very cool relationship between the two in the future. They appear to have first met around 1762, and 'did not take to each other', in Johnson's words. Smith can have had little taste for Johnson's Tory politics, while for his part Johnson distrusted philosophy and despised Hume's religious scepticism, which he suspected Smith shared. And relations did not improve when Smith moved to London in 1773.

As the sheer range of his interests—from rhetoric to moral psychology to jurisprudence to political economy—testifies, the 1750s were a time of extraordinary intellectual productivity for Smith. Always prickly about protecting the priority of his own ideas, he expressed alarm at the possibility of plagiarism by others, on one occasion by Hugh Blair and, later, by the historian William Robertson and all-round Scottish *philosophe* Adam Ferguson. According to Dugald

Stewart, Smith's response in 1755 was to present a paper to a local society: 'a pretty long enumeration . . . of certain leading principles, both political and literary, to which he was anxious to establish his exclusive right'. Among them were words that would carry through the ages:

> Little else is requisite to carry a state to the highest degree of opulence from the lowest barbarism, but peace, easy taxes, and a tolerable administration of justice; all the rest being brought about by the natural course of things. All governments which thwart this natural course, which force things into another channel, or which endeavour to arrest the progress of society at a particular point, are unnatural, and to support themselves are obliged to be oppressive and tyrannical.

This is the first statement of what would become Smith's 'system of natural liberty', and it comes four years before his first book, *The Theory of Moral Sentiments*, was published, and twenty-one years before the publication of *The Wealth of Nations*. It reminds us that Smith had conceived some of the leading ideas of his great published works almost from the very outset of his working life.

Smith appears at this time to have been something of a protégé of the great Andrew Cochrane, Lord Provost of Glasgow, and it was likely Cochrane who convened the audience for this important early paper. He had made a fortune in the tobacco trade before immersing himself in public administration. A staunch Hanoverian, as Lord Provost he had fought to reduce Jacobite demands for ransom from the city in August 1745, then journeyed to London to negotiate compensation for its losses, and thereby saved Glasgow from bankruptcy. Noting the younger man's ability, he appears to have recruited him early on to his 'commercial club' and this brought Smith into contact with the city's merchant class, including the tobacco magnates John Glassford, Alexander Speirs and James Ritchie. It must have been a superb intro-duction for the young man to the commercial ways of the world, and in particular to the power of the trading interests and their often close relationship with government.

Smith later remembered his thirteen years at Glasgow 'as by far the most useful, and therefore as by far the happiest and most honourable period of my life'. It is a typically Smithian move to construe happiness in terms of usefulness, and typically self-effacing, for it has the effect of drawing attention away from love and friendship and the other intrinsically valuable but highly personal things that make people's lives happy. We know virtually nothing about any romantic attachments, for in such matters Smith was an all but closed book throughout his life. He was later described as having loved a lady in Fife, and—they may be the same person—as having been 'seriously in love with a Miss Campbell of—— . . . a woman of as different dispositions and habits from his as possible'. But on these topics, as a recent biographer has aptly observed, 'We can do little more . . . than contribute a footnote to the history of sublimation.' Intimacy apart, however, Smith had a wide and increasing circle of friends, correspondents and admirers; and, as his fame grew over time, busts of him could reportedly be bought in local bookshops. He was also elected to numerous clubs: as well as Cochrane's Club in Glasgow, these included the Literary Society, the Philosophical Society, the intellectual Select Society and the pro-militia Poker Club, all in Edinburgh. Apart from the 1755 essay and a few other references, there is very little to suggest that he made any great impact on these institutions. But they allowed him to see friends and enjoy the benefits of social intercourse without compromising the routine of his life, or his unbending desire to work.

And work he did. For during this period, despite all his other commitments, Smith somehow found time to write his first acknowledged masterpiece, *The Theory of Moral Sentiments*.

THE THEORY OF MORAL SENTIMENTS HAS LABOURED IN RECENT TIMES IN the shadow of *The Wealth of Nations*. It is Smith's 'other work', far less well known than its younger sibling, less widely read and frequently treated as something of a problem child: an unsuccessful youthful foray into moral philosophy soon to be overshadowed by the great works of Immanuel Kant.

By the time of its final edition *The Theory of Moral Sentiments* included a long analysis 'Of the character of virtue', and a review of different systems of moral philosophy against which Smith argued that his theory should be read. But the book is not first and foremost a work of moral philosophy, let alone a hymn to altruism. Rather, it is a work of moral psychology and sociology. In particular, Smith is not engaged in an early Kantian-style project of providing a justification or basic grounding for moral principles. Instead, he is addressing the psychological question of how our moral feelings arise in the first place. By what individual and social processes do humans become morally aware? Can there be universal moral principles? Is there such a thing as human nature, or does it change from time to time and place to place? *The Theory of Moral Sentiments* is thus intended to be not merely the title of a book, but the demarcation of a whole field of actual and possible inquiry. It is about how humans become human.

The target of the book is clear; indeed Smith had framed it in a letter published in the second and final issue of the *Edinburgh Review* in 1756, in a discussion of Jean-Jacques Rousseau's *Discourse on Inequality*. As we have noted, seventeenth-century thinkers such as Hobbes and Pufendorf had built great theories on highly pessimistic assumptions about human nature. But Rousseau went much further: his *Discourse* launched a blistering critique of civilization itself, arguing that mankind had been seduced and corrupted by its illusory benefits. Justice had become a vehicle for oppression of the weak by the strong; private property, instead of giving scope to human possibility, had deformed it. In Smith's translation, 'But from the instant in which one man had occasion for the assistance of another, from the moment that he perceived that it could be advantageous to a single person to have provisions for two, equality disappeared, property was introduced, labour became necessary, and the vast forests of nature were changed into agreeable plains, which must be watered with the sweat of mankind, and in which the world beheld slavery and wretchedness begin to grow up and blossom with the harvest.' Far from being a morally estimable source of well-being, civilization was in fact a gross deception, creating not freedom but dependency amounting to enslavement.

As Smith pointed out, this critique itself built on *The Fable of the Bees*, a wonderfully funny and ironic satirical poem by Bernard Mandeville of 1705, which the author added to and defended in a series of further essays over the next twenty years. Mandeville's is an extraordinary work, which sets the agenda for Smith in *The Wealth of Nations* in several ways: it considers the 'division of labour' and touches on the benefits of specialization; as its subtitle *Private Vices, Public Benefits* hints, it argues that self-interested individual behaviour can have unexpected positive consequences; and against orthodox religious opinion it urges that luxury is economically beneficial and frugality vain. Above all, though, *The Fable of the Bees* is a full-throated denunciation of cant and hypocrisy. For Mandeville, Shaftesbury's (and later Hutcheson's) belief in human benevolence, indeed all talk of nice moral distinctions, principles and standards, virtues and vices, is really just hot air. There are only two human motivations that matter, 'self-liking' and 'shame': civility, culture and the rest are at root merely camouflage for the human hunger for approbation and hatred of embarrassment. 'Virtue' and 'vice' are names used by skilful 'politicians' to control the masses by channelling human passions against each other.

Mandeville's parable of the bee colony makes the point perfectly. Originally, the bees are prey to every vice, happy and prosperous: 'Vast numbers thronged the fruitful hive / yet those vast numbers made 'em thrive; / millions endeavouring to supply / each other's lust and vanity.' Then suddenly, however, the colony suffers an onset of moral virtue. The effect is catastrophic: competition, ambition and consumption are replaced by thrift and kindness, prices fall, trade dries up, the choice and quality of goods decline, the economy stagnates. Thus, Mandeville argued, inverting the very logic of the Fall of Man, benevolence and altruism were disastrous for society while selfishness and greed led to triumphant success. Even justice itself had been corrupted: in Smith's words, 'According to both [Rousseau and Mandeville], those laws of justice, which maintain the present inequality among mankind, were originally the inventions of the cunning and powerful, in order to maintain or to acquire an unjust superiority over the rest of their fellow-creatures.'

There are moments when Smith can sound rather like Rousseau, for example in denouncing man's preoccupation with material objects and with status in the eyes of others. Rousseau's important distinction between *amour propre*, or a love of how one appears in other people's eyes, and *amour de soi,* or self-love, evidently made an impression on the Scotsman. The two men both offer 'stadial' or staged theories of human development; both reflect at length on the origins and impact of commercial society and human nature in relation to society and, in different ways and to differing degrees, on inequality and oppression. But temperamentally they are poles apart: Smith level-headed and pragmatic, Rousseau swinging with astonishing rhetorical force between violent pessimistic denunciation and utopian optimism. And overall Smith's work is a comprehensive rebuttal of the Genevan *philosophe*: a defence of civility, of the liberating effects of commerce, of private property and personal freedom under law, and of the capacity of uncoordinated individual actions to yield not evil but social good in unexpected and unintended ways. A core purpose of *The Theory of Moral Sentiments* is, by explaining how moral feelings arise from human sociability, to vindicate the claims of civilization itself as a force for moral improvement. Smith rejects Mandeville's rather Manichean worldview, but he respects his injunction that 'One of the greatest reasons why so few people understand themselves, is that most writers are always teaching men what they should be, and hardly ever trouble their heads with telling them what they really are.'

Smith's *Theory of Moral Sentiments* is very much focused on 'telling them what they really are'. Nevertheless, this is a work of constructive theorizing, not of mere scepticism. But it is also careful to steer clear of familiar traps, such as an appeal to divine grace, or to a Hutchesonian 'moral sense' which assumes what in fact needs to be proven. The style is varied, but often straightforward. There is little logic-chopping or disputatious debating, and the book abounds in homely examples carefully chosen to illustrate its general themes. The deceptively simple opening words show the way: 'How selfish soever man may be supposed, there are evidently some principles in his nature, which interest him in the fortune of others, and render their happiness necessary to him, though he derives nothing from it except the pleasure of seeing it. Of this kind is pity or compassion . . . '

Compassion is thus a basic principle of human nature for Adam Smith. Yet it quickly becomes clear that the key idea here is not so much compassion in the sense of pity, but rather compassion as empathy or fellow feeling. In the *Treatise* Hume had argued that 'sympathy' with those affected by an action could give rise to feelings of moral approval and disapproval. Smith uses the same word in several ways, but in its key sense he goes rather further than Hume, by expanding the idea of sympathy to include not merely pity and compassion, but 'our fellow-feeling with any passion whatever'. In this sense, sympathy is the capacity to detect and reflect the emotions of others. This then in turn enables the operation of what would now be called empathy: the imaginative capacity to place ourselves mentally, to greater or lesser extent, in the position of those who may be far removed and wildly different from us. We may, then, in Smith's sense sympathize with or imaginatively grasp emotions we find unpleasant or offensive, or with emotions of joy or self-satisfaction in others that would not elicit sympathy in its more usual sense.

It is this capacity for sympathy that first interests us in the lives and fates of others. As such, it allows us to compare our feelings of approval or disapproval with theirs. What is the source of our capacity for moral self-awareness and judgement? In Smith's words:

> To judge of ourselves as we judge of others . . . is the greatest exertion of candour and impartiality. In order to do this, we must look at ourselves with the same eyes with which we look at others: we must imagine ourselves not the actors, but the spectators of our own character and conduct . . . We must enter, in short, either into what are, or what ought to be, or into what, if the whole circumstances of our conduct were known, we imagine would be the sentiments of others, before we can either applaud or condemn it.

Smith underlines the social dimension of individual self-consciousness by considering someone cut off from society altogether: 'Were it possible that a human creature could grow up to manhood in some solitary place, without any communication with his own species, he could no more think of his own character, of the propriety or demerit of his own sentiments and conduct, of the beauty or deformity of his own mind, than of the beauty or deformity of his own face.' To have a self, to be self-conscious or self-aware, to draw on social and moral values or exercise judgement in relation to ourselves, thus always involves what Smith calls 'an immediate reference to the sentiments of others'.

But to 'look at ourselves with the same eyes with which we look at others' is also to allow the possibility that we can be seen by them, and that we can see them looking at us, and that they can see us looking at them, and so on. And, moreover, that they can see our actions, and see us acting as agents, and vice versa. It is a way in which humans can form the collective self-consciousness that amounts to common knowledge. Sight is immediate and often mutual in its operation; as with linguistic exchange, for Smith it is a fundamental way in which human beings lift themselves by their boot straps from a raw awareness of others into sociability, into moral self-consciousness and so into an understanding of obligations owed to and owing from others. Moreover, Smith's analysis goes beyond a simple two-way relationship between a moral actor and an action. It adds a third element: how the action would, if all the facts were known, be viewed in its context by others. This triadic relation brings an element of futurity, and so the possibility of evolution, to his moral theory.

But by saying 'if the whole circumstances of our conduct were known' Smith also hints at the need for a further, corrective element. He calls this, adapting a phrase of Hume's, the 'impartial spectator'. This is the idea of a 'cool' and 'indifferent' bystander who can see matters objectively, without passion or bias and with understanding of the different sides of an issue. Seeing ourselves through the eyes of others frees us from the idea that we are somehow special, and allows the possibility of impersonal judgement, Smith seems to say; but it is the device of the impartial spectator that corrects for human weakness and allows us to set up norms or standards of behaviour that are superior to mere conventional wisdom.

Robert Burns was a great admirer of Smith, and he picks up this theme in his poem 'To a Louse' of 1786. The work is a little gem in Burns's favourite Habbie stanza form, driven on by the querulous tone of the poet as he upbraids a louse for its impertinence in crawling on a young lady's bonnet:

> *Ye ugly, creepin, blastit wonner,*
> *Detested, shunn'd by saunt an sinner,*
> *How daur ye set your fit upon her—*
> *Sae fine a lady!*
> *Gae somewhere else and seek your dinner*
> *On some poor body*

. . . then turns to warn the lady herself, both of the impending attack and of the spectacle of herself she is creating:

> O Jeany, dinna toss your head.
> An set your beauties a' abread!
> Ye little ken what cursed speed
>   The blastie's makin!
> Thae winks an finger-ends, I dread,
>   Are notice takin!

But the *volta*—the turn which gives the poem its further punch and meaning—comes in the last stanza, complete with a final anti-clerical flourish:

> O wad some Power the giftie gie us
> To see oursels as ithers see us!
> It wad frae mony a blunder free us,
>   An' foolish notion
> What airs in dress an gait wad lea'e us,
>   An ev'n devotion!

The words directly echo *The Theory of Moral Sentiments*. For Burns, seeing ourselves as others see us can be a deflating and chastening experience. For Smith, its collective implications fall little short of revolution: 'If we saw ourselves in the light in which others see us, or in which they would see us if they knew all, a reformation would generally be unavoidable. We could not otherwise endure the sight.'

The idea of an impartial spectator is a fascinating one, but it faces an obvious objection: isn't this just another name for a 'moral sense', or for God? The answer is no. In effect, Smith is seeking to capture the idea of conscience, but his account is both analytic and based in human experience. In effect, his theory goes not from the inside out, but from the outside in. Instead of arguing that our individual moral judgements are primary, the result of divine inspiration or primeval instinct, he argues that they are secondary and derived from looking at others: we draw such judgements from the comparison between our actual and possible conduct and that of others, and our moral principles evolve in reaction to and through norms set in society at large. We may give the resultant moral understanding different names. But it derives from human nature and human sociability. The result is a theory of moral sensibility which is naturalistic and empirical in approach, which does not rely on a Hutchesonian moral sense, and which implicitly debunks any claims of morality to be a distinct or higher sphere of human appraisal.

However, Smith's enlarged conception of mutual sympathy also has some fascinating and counter-intuitive implications, from which he does not shrink. In particular, he uses it to explain what he sees as man's automatic and demeaning admiration for those in positions of power and wealth, and hard-heartedness towards the poor. This theme runs through Smith's thought from beginning to end. He had touched on it in his earlier lectures on rhetoric, saying, 'There is in humane nature a servility which inclines us to adore our superiors and an inhumanity which disposes us to contempt and trample under foot our inferiors.' But *The Theory of Moral Sentiments* gives a deeper explanation in terms of sympathy:

> It is because mankind are disposed to sympathise more entirely with our joy than with our sorrow, that we make parade of our riches and conceal our poverty . . . When we consider the condition of the great, in the delusive colours in which the imagination is apt to paint it, it seems to be almost the abstract idea of a perfect and happy state . . . We feel therefore a peculiar sympathy with the satisfaction of those who are in it. We favour all their inclinations, and forward all their wishes . . . Great King, live forever! is the compliment which, after the manner of eastern

adulation, we should readily make them, if experience did not teach us its absurdity.

In principle, then, his theory can explain the spread of norms that are convenient but corrupting, as well as those that are socially beneficial.

So much, so apparently Mandevillian—mankind is dominated here by base instincts which conventional morality is supposed to correct. As Katharine Hepburn says to Humphrey Bogart in *The African Queen*, after pouring all his gin into the Ulanga River: 'Nature, Mr Allnut, is what we are put in this world to rise above.' Yet it is clear that Smith's overall notion of human nature is vastly more positive than that of Mandeville. In particular, he takes pains to distinguish between 'the desire of acquiring honour and esteem by really deserving those sentiments' and 'the frivolous desire of praise': 'There is an affinity between vanity and the love of true glory, as both these passions aim at acquiring esteem and approbation. But they are different in this, that the one is a just, reasonable, and equitable passion, while the other is unjust, absurd, and ridiculous.' More positive, too, is his belief in the power of morality. Thanks to sympathy and the impartial spectator, human beings have the capacity for self-conscious moral introspection; they know the difference between honest ambition and a yearning for undeserved approbation, and that shows itself in their moral judgements of themselves and others. Mandeville's attack on virtue, by contrast, uses the one to criticize the other, and thus rests on an equivocation.

Smith also contradicts Rousseau's idea of an original state of nature, which had been corrupted by human society and dependency on others. Smith in effect denies that any such state of nature exists, or ever could exist, for the very reason that human nature arises within and is shaped by human society: 'All the members of human society stand in need of each other's assistance, and are likewise exposed to mutual injuries. Where the necessary assistance is reciprocally afforded from love, from gratitude, from friendship, and esteem, the society flourishes and is happy. All the different members of it are bound together by the agreeable bonds of love and affection, and are, as it were, drawn to one common centre of mutual good offices.' There is no single rationalistic point from which man can survey, or like Archimedes with his lever can move, society as a whole. Societies hang together pluralistically, through bonds of interest, mutual obligation and affection mediated by social and moral norms.

As with language, this is a dynamic picture. Our moral life is constantly and continuously changing, developing, feeding off that of others; it has no first foundation or final resting point. Sympathy feeds reciprocity, the trading of assistance and obligation, reciprocity feeds commerce and mutual security, and these in turn shape the social virtues, in a spreading and self-reinforcing pattern. Moral judgements are constantly being made to fit action to emerging norms within specific contexts, selecting and penalizing behaviour as appropriate. In modern terms, Smith's theory is thus a genuinely evolutionary one, but it operates via processes of social rather than natural selection. And it carries within it a crucial Smithian insight, that innumerable human interactions can yield vast but entirely unintended collective consequences— social benefits, yes, but also social evils, as we shall see in Chapters 9 and 10—and do so, moreover, in a way that is self-organizing and that yields what we would now call a spontaneous social order. The theory remains factual and descriptive, as befits the attempt to outline a genuine science of morals. It offers both a general framework for thinking about how morality comes into being and specific ways to analyse its emergence in different circumstances. Yet by describing how recognized and recognizably moral standards emerge, it carries clear moral implications as well. It moves from facts to values via norms.

Even for individuals who are or appear to be entirely unselfconscious, feelings of remorse or guilt show how far sympathy—and so an awareness of moral norms—is embedded in human action. Contrariwise, a society without sympathy cannot engender reciprocity, and this in turn will shape the morality of its members. Smith respects the nobility of the noble savage, but he denies him any moral purchase. Quite the opposite: 'Every savage . . . is in continual danger: he is often exposed to the greatest extremities of hunger, and frequently dies of pure want . . . He can expect from his countrymen no sympathy or indulgence . . . A savage, therefore, whatever be the nature of his distress, expects no sympathy from those about him.' And in contradiction to Rousseau, with civility—even partial—comes moral improvement: 'A polished people, being accustomed to give way, in some measure, to the movements of nature, become frank, open and sincere. Barbarians, on the contrary, being obliged to smother and conceal the appearance of every passion, necessarily acquire the habits of falsehood and dissimulation.'

We are now close to the philosophical heart of the matter, for the 'harmony' among or interdependence of humans is the hinge of Smith's entire system, which is admirably summarized by Knud Haakonssen: 'It is basically this continuous exchange that underlies all human culture. It probably underlies language; through vanity it is the foundation for all distinctions of rank; in the form of bartering it is behind any economy; and through the mechanism of sympathy it gives rise to human morality.' This is a fundamental assumption that underlies Smith's whole system of thought. But, in his words, 'this . . . harmony cannot be obtained unless there is a free communication of sentiments and opinions.' The benefits of spontaneous order thus depend on the freedom of the individual.

GIVEN THE NATURE OF THE TIMES, IT IS PERHAPS NO SURPRISE THAT such an ingenious paean to politeness, civility and self-improvement was warmly received. *The Theory of Moral Sentiments* was published in the spring of 1759 and sold well in both London and Edinburgh. Indeed, Smith's London publisher Andrew Millar was able to boast that two-thirds of his first printing had been sold before publication. The book was also, with a few exceptions, a widespread *succès d'estime*. Notably, one reviewer was the young Irishman Edmund Burke, then just twenty-nine, the little-known editor of the *Annual Register*, and still six years away from launching a glorious public career with his election to Parliament. David Hume had been charged with distributing copies of the book to influential figures in London, and he did his job well: the list of recipients reads like a *Who's Who* of courtiers, politicians and grandees. Even so, Hume had wit enough to include one to Burke, ingeniously spying the latter's potential value to Smith, for 'he wrote lately a very pretty treatise on the sublime.' In his review for the *Register*, Burke said that 'making approbation and disapprobation the tests of virtue and vice, and showing that those are founded on sympathy, he raises from this simple truth one of the most beautiful fabrics of moral theory that has perhaps ever appeared.' In a letter of thanks to Smith for the book, Burke did not shrink from friendly criticism, but he also noted appreciatively 'those easy and happy illustrations from common life and manners in which your work abounds', and begged Smith for the chance to introduce himself when he next came to London. It was the beginning of a long and mutually admiring friendship.

Given Smith's closeness to Hume, it must have been the latter's good opinion that he most sought for the new book. Hume did not pass judgement immediately. But he was not the man to let an opportunity like this slip, and sent Smith a lovingly teasing letter from London on 12 April 1759 which must have driven the younger man mad. 'Tho' it has been published only a few weeks,' Hume begins, 'I think there already appear such strong symptoms, that I can almost venture to foretell its fate. It is in short this——But I have been interrupted in my letter by a foolish impertinent visit . . . ' This proves to be from a fellow Scot with extensive news, which Hume lingeringly reports. Then: 'But to return to your book, and its success in this town, I must tell you—a plague of interruptions!' Hume has another visit and retails more gossip, this time from the continent about new books by Helvétius and Voltaire.

He continues: 'But what is all this to my book? say you. My dear Mr Smith, have patience: compose yourself to tranquillity: show yourself a philosopher in practice as well as profession. Think on the emptiness, and rashness, and futility of the common judgements of men.' There follows a homily on the Stoic virtue of temperance, complete with a quotation in Latin from Persius, before Hume mock-reluctantly concludes: 'Supposing, therefore, that you have duly prepared yourself for the worst by all these reflections, I proceed to tell you the melancholy news, that your book has been very unfortunate; for the public seem disposed to applaud it extremely.' Even now he cannot resist a dig at established religion: 'Three Bishops called yesterday at Millar's shop to buy copies . . . The Bishop of Peterborough said he had . . . heard it extolled above all books in the world. You may conclude what opinion true philosophers will entertain of it, when these retainers to superstition praise it so highly.' By the end one can only pity the emotions of the wretched Smith, for the letter is a masterpiece of tantric epistolation.

The Theory of Moral Sentiments was a great success in its own right. But Smith made quite clear that it was also intended to be part of a much bigger project. At the very end of the book he wrote, 'I shall in another discourse endeavour to give an account of the general principles of law and government, and of the different revolutions they have undergone in the different ages and periods of society, not only in what concerns justice, but in what concerns police [that is, public administration], revenue and arms, and whatever else is the object of law.' As we shall see, he spent the next thirty years seeking to discharge this promise. He failed in the attempt; but in failing he composed the greatest work of social science ever written.

CHAPTER 3

ENLIGHTENED INTERLUDE, 1760–1773

I N EARLY 1760 ADAM SMITH WAS THIRTY-SIX YEARS OF AGE, UNMAR-
ried and still living in Glasgow with his mother and his cousin (and
housekeeper) Janet Douglas. He was a respected university professor
and administrator, and the author of a highly successful first book.
True, he was then temporarily in the grip of one of his regular ill-
nesses, of cause unknown, for which his doctor's prescription was the
admirably sensible demand that he ride 500 miles by summer's end.
But otherwise his life was a model of domestic serenity.

Yet if Smith's life was serene, the same was very far from true
of the world around him. Britain had been at war with France since
1756, and while war with France was nothing new, for the first time
it had escalated into a global conflict. The so-called Seven Years War
was a true world war, which stretched from the North American colonies to Guadeloupe in the Caribbean, to the Atlantic coast of Europe,
down to Senegal in West Africa and around to India up to and including Bengal. It pitted France's waning colonial ambitions and enormous
armed strength on land against insurgent British economic power and
the domination at sea of the Royal Navy.

The situation on the European mainland was complex and
multi-faceted. Britain's European policy was then what it has broadly
remained for more than 400 years: to try to manage the balance of
power in Europe as far as possible so as to prevent the emergence

of an unchallenged continental superpower. To that end, Britain had effectively concluded a decade earlier that its ally Austria was no longer an adequate check on the ambitions of France. In the Peace of Aix-la-Chapelle, which concluded the War of the Austrian Succession in 1748, Britain had obliged Austria, much to its anger, to cede the valuable province of Silesia to Frederick the Great of Prussia. Now the two sides changed partners altogether: in 1756 Austria joined with France, its historic enemy, while Britain allied itself with Prussia, a move which also assuaged the fears of King George II about the safety of his homeland, Hanover.

As the fighting between Britain and France escalated across four continents, the year 1759 was to prove pivotal. A planned French invasion of 50,000 troops via Portsmouth—combined, inevitably, with a further Jacobite uprising—was averted, despite renewed entreaties to Louis XV by Charles Edward Stuart and his dwindling court in exile. The French were fought to a standstill along the western frontier of the thirteen colonies in North America, and the year closed with a series of remarkable victories for the British. In August the brilliant Admiral Edward Boscawen destroyed the bulk of the French Mediterranean fleet off Lagos in Portugal. In September, General James Wolfe achieved the seemingly impossible in the Canadian territories with a daring night ascent of the cliffs around the Plains of Abraham, defeating the French General Montcalm and taking French-controlled Quebec. In November Admiral Hawke broke the French Atlantic fleet in an action of astonishing bravery at Quiberon Bay off the coast of Brittany.

The events of 1756–63 were to prove highly consequential. If the French had won in North America, there might have been no American revolutionary war, and perhaps no emergence of the continental United States at all. If the French had held the British in India, there would have been no Raj, and the English language might never have achieved its present global reach. If the French had achieved mastery of the seas, British trading ambitions and the later growth of the British Empire might have been stifled altogether.

Much of the significance of the Seven Years War was appreciated at the time. Horace Walpole—Prime Minister's son, a diarist of insight and wit, and a colossal snob—wrote to Sir Horace Mann in 1761, 'You would not know your country again. You left it a private little island, living upon its means. You would find it the capital of the world; and, to talk with the arrogance of a Roman, St James's Street crowded with nabobs and American chiefs, and Mr Pitt attended on his Sabine farm by Eastern monarchs and Borealian electors, waiting till the gout has gone out of his foot for an audience.'

But 1760 also marked a crucial change in British domestic politics. In October George II died and—his son Frederick having predeceased him in 1751—his grandson George III succeeded to the throne. The new King was a very different kind of monarch from his grandfather and great-grandfather. The first two Georges had been born in Hanover and spoke English with a strong German accent. They cared more for hunting than for public administration, and had been quite willing to hand over the domestic business of government to Sir Robert Walpole and his successors, provided of course that they were Whigs. But George III, born in England and speaking English as a native, was emphatically not German—a point he rammed home by adding to his accession speech the words 'Born and educated in this country, I glory in the name of Briton.' Owing to his father's premature death, he came to the throne at the very young and opinionated age of just twenty-two. He was highly critical of the politicians—the hitherto dominant Whigs in particular—and was determined to insert himself into the political arena, thereby to reassert what he saw as the constitutionally proper powers and duties of the monarch.

The crucial question which both the politicians and the new King had to address was a simple one: how to pay down the war debt. As Prime Minister, the elder William Pitt had not scrupled to spend money freely to support the navy and reinforce and reimburse the colonies, using the British government's unrivalled access to domestic and international credit at low interest rates. In 1757, Britain's national debt stood at around £75,000,000, or roughly the same as its gross domestic product. But just seven years later this had risen by nearly 75 per cent to £130,000,000, to say nothing of the £250,000 a year required to keep British troops in North America. The bills were coming due, and by the standards of the time the amounts were prodigious.

In due course Adam Smith would have much to say about the effects of war on public debt, and the taxation needed to pay for it. But the combined effect of the change of monarch, George III's own ambitions and the overwhelming need to balance the books was to unsettle British politics over a decade of rotating governments and political tumult. The irony was that when stability finally arrived, with the administration of Lord North in 1770, the results would be disastrous.

Smith had himself been thinking hard about the nature of government and law since before 1750, when they had been the subject of a set of lectures on jurisprudence commissioned from him in Edinburgh by Lord Kames—a second set, alongside the lectures he gave on rhetoric. Once he had taken over the moral philosophy chair at Glasgow, he reshaped and expanded those lectures, perhaps with an eye to a future publication. This, and not *The Wealth of Nations*, is the 'other discourse' referred to in Smith's teasing final remarks in *The Theory of Moral Sentiments*—'an account of the general principles of law and government, and of the different revolutions they have undergone in the different ages and periods of society'—remarks which remained in the *Theory* through six editions, until his death in 1790.

As so often with Smith, the primary evidence here is scarce. Indeed, it is a miracle that we know anything much at all about the lectures. Near the end of his life Smith wrote, poignantly, about his earlier hopes:

My very advanced age leaves me, I acknowledge, very little expectation of ever being able to execute this great work to my own satisfaction; yet, as I have not altogether abandoned the design, and as I wish still to continue under the obligation of doing what

I can, I have allowed the paragraph to remain as it was published more than thirty years ago, when I entertained no doubt of being able to execute everything which it announced.

Yet he evidently could not bear publication of the uncompleted work, for on his deathbed he was insistent to his executors that the lectures and other unfinished materials be destroyed. And so they were.

We cannot measure the loss. But through sheer luck—as with the *Lectures on Rhetoric and Belles Lettres*—student notes on Smith's lectures on jurisprudence have survived, in this case in three sets. One, transcribed by Smith's contemporary John Anderson from some student notes, is short and probably dates from 1753–5; it confirms the order in which the materials were originally presented, shows the extent of some of Smith's early intellectual debts and underlines the early provenance of the key ideas of his theory of government.

The other notes, from a decade later, are still more interesting. One dates from 1762–3, the other most likely from the following year. They appear to be fair copies of notes taken during the lectures themselves, the first a partial but detailed set for private use, the second set more polished and complete, of the kind then occasionally sold by students. In content, they are inconsistent, patchy and (the first in particular) obviously incomplete in places. But even so they are of immense importance, for they act as a vital intellectual bridge between Smith's two great published works. On the one hand, they recapitulate key aspects of *The Theory of Moral Sentiments* in 1759. On the other, they give a clear sense of Smith's developing thought, as he began to frame what would become *The Wealth of Nations*.

IT IS CLEAR THAT SMITH REGARDED HIS WORK ON JURISPRUDENCE AS an important part of a much larger whole. His student John Millar, who audited both sets of his lectures in logic and moral philosophy at Glasgow, described his thought in four parts immediately after his death to Dugald Stewart. Millar's words are highly significant:

> The first [part] contained Natural Theology, in which he considered the proofs of the being and the attributes of God, and those principles of the human mind upon which religion is founded. The second comprehended ethics strictly so called, and consisted chiefly of the doctrines which he afterwards published in his *Theory of Moral Sentiments*.
>
> In the third part he treated at more length of that branch of morality which relates to justice, and which, being susceptible of precise and accurate rules, is for that reason capable of a full and particular explanation. Upon this subject he followed the plan that seems to be suggested by Montesquieu; endeavouring to trace the gradual progress of jurisprudence, both public and private, from the rudest to the most refined ages, and to point out the effects of those arts which contribute to subsistence and to the accumulation of property, in producing corresponding improvements or alterations in law and government. This important branch of his labours he also intended to give to the public; but this intention, which is mentioned in the conclusion of *The Theory of Moral Sentiments*, he did not live to fulfil.

And finally,

> In the last part of his lectures, he examined those political regulations which are founded not upon the principle of justice, but that of expediency, and which are calculated to increase the riches, the power and the prosperity of a state. Under this view, he considered the political institutions relating to commerce, to finances, to ecclesiastical and military establishments. What he

delivered on these subjects contained the substance of the work
he afterwards published under the title of *An Inquiry into the
Nature and Causes of the Wealth of Nations.*

We have next to nothing now from Smith on 'Natural Theology . . . and
the proofs of the being and attributes of God', and little about his
views on religion. But in relation to the other parts, given Millar's and
Stewart's closeness to Smith, and the prominence of these words in
Stewart's posthumous biographical note, there is every reason to treat
them as authoritative. Millar's description suggests that Smith's projected work on jurisprudence was designed to play a key linking role:
both to explain the origins and leading principles of law and government and, in so doing, to show that such an account could take its
place within a coherent and well-grounded theory joining individual
moral psychology and sociology to politics and law and ultimately to
economics and commerce. It is, overall, a staggeringly ambitious intellectual undertaking.

'Jurisprudence' is defined by Smith as 'the theory of the general
principles of law and government', and as 'that science which inquires
into the general principles which ought to be the foundation of the
laws of all nations'. The subject had become a staple of eighteenth-
century moral philosophy classes, especially at Glasgow under the
influence of Gershom Carmichael, and it became more prominent
after the curriculum reforms of 1727. Among the great works of the
field, Hobbes's *Leviathan* (1651) was known but not widely read for
religious reasons. Montesquieu's *The Spirit of Laws* fared rather better. But no less influential were the broad and systematic natural law
traditions of jurisprudence focused on rights and 'offices' or duties,
given new life by Hugo Grotius' foundational work *De Jure Belli ac
Pacis* (On the Rights of War and Peace) in 1625, and by Samuel von
Pufendorf's textbook *On the Duty of Man and Citizen* of 1673. These
works were brought to Glasgow and studied by Pufendorf's follower

Carmichael, and were well known in turn to Carmichael's successor, Francis Hutcheson.

As with *The Theory of Moral Sentiments*, Smith's unpublished *Lectures on Jurisprudence* are generally naturalistic in approach; they seek to offer explanations of laws and government not through any deduction from first principles or divine edict but via the analysis of social norms and practices, both in contemporary societies and through examples from history. For him every system of law has four goals: the maintenance of justice; the orderly administration of government, in particular to promote 'opulence' or wealth-creation; the raising of public revenue; and the management of arms to defend the state. But of these the idea of justice, analogous to the idea of sympathy in the *Theory*, is the most fundamental, for without justice there can be no social order. As Smith says, no society 'could subsist among those who are at all times ready to hurt and injure one another'. Without justice 'the immense fabric of human society . . . must in a moment crumble into atoms.'

Once again, Smith's approach is distinctive. For Hutcheson, justice had its origins in benevolence and the 'moral sense'. For the sceptical Hume, in sharp contrast, it was an 'artificial virtue', not rooted in any specific human instinct or faculty but in conventions spontaneously developed within society largely over property rights, and for reasons not of morality but of utility. For Smith the first view was insufficient, as we have seen; it hardly explained justice to say that it derived from a moral sense, let alone to say so as part of a science of man.

But also insufficient, albeit more subtly, was the second. Hume's theory had one remarkable virtue, that it was an evolutionary account of justice: perhaps the first, coming as it did some twenty years before the publication of *The Theory of Moral Sentiments*. Indeed, the *Theory* may have arisen precisely in part from Smith's attempts to generalize and improve upon Hume's view of justice. And through its use of conventions Hume's theory also illustrated the Mandevillean lesson that individual actions could have unexpectedly beneficial social effects, indeed took that lesson from Mandeville's world of commerce into that of morality and politics. But Hume's utility-based conventions seemed unable to account for some obvious features of the idea of justice: its rather compelling authority, the deep obligations and duties it imposes on human behaviour, and the feelings of resentment induced when it is violated, all features which had been highlighted as part of a well-known earlier theory of conscience by Bishop Butler in his *Fifteen Sermons Preached at the Rolls Chapel* (1726).

Smith highlights these weaknesses in *The Theory of Moral Sentiments*. In his view the very nature of justice, and its centrality to wider moral and political deliberation, made it easier to theorize than other virtues. 'The general rules which determine what are the offices of prudence, of charity, of generosity . . . admit of many exceptions and require so many modifications' as to make them impossible to analyse in any general way. Justice, by contrast, could be specified in a series of general rules, at least when it was seen as 'a negative virtue, [which] only hinders us from hurting our neighbour'.

The *Lectures* enlarge on this basic thought, deploying and extending the spectatorial framework of the *Theory*. 'Justice is violated', Smith says, 'whenever one is deprived of what he has a right to and could justly demand from others, or rather, when we do him any injury or hurt without a cause.' Resentment was justified when 'an impartial spectator would be of opinion he was injured, would join with him in his concern and go along with him when he defended the subject in his possession against any violent attack, or used force to recover what had thus been wrongfully wrested out of his hands'. Here, as in the *Theory*, the key idea of the impartial spectator functions as a kind of moral conscience, offering an explanation of the duties imposed by justice and the feelings of resentment that accompany injustice, and lifting the treatment of these ideas above the purely conventional.

The effect of tackling justice even in this relatively modest way is to allow Smith more scope to address fundamental issues of the scope and limits of human liberty. He does so using traditional juris-prudential categories, through a very detailed analysis of the different kinds of injury to rights exercised 'as a man'—injury to person, repu-tation and estate—rights 'as a member of a family'—including injury to wife, offspring and servants—and rights 'as a citizen or member of a state'. Much of its analysis is technical and legalistic, but there are also numerous telling examples from history and from other cultures designed to illustrate key points of argument. And the overall thrust is clear: not merely to outline and explain his conception of justice, relatively limited and 'negative' though it is, but also to show how it is recognizably rooted in human life, albeit in different forms across different societies. Smith's goal is, in other words, to reconnect the ideas of property and propriety: to produce both a legal understanding of the rules that define the ownership, use and transmission of private property and a moral understanding of the sense of justice proper to a commercial society.

By contrast with his own realistic approach to justice, Smith has nothing but distaste for utopian ideas, and specifically for the idealized notion of a state of nature which somehow predated human civiliza-tion. Whether it was Hobbes's 'war of all against all', Rousseau's primal state or Pufendorf's more benign vision made no difference: 'It in real-ity serves no purpose to treat of the laws which would take place in a state of nature . . . as there is no such state existing.' It makes no sense to speak of humans in a state of nature prior to society, because hu-mans are social by nature. But, crucially, Smith's historical approach also dissolves the Humean distinction between the artificial and the natural virtues. For Smith artifice—what humans create—is itself a natural phenomenon. It is governed by human expectations, conven-tions and norms, because all human activities are so governed.

But there is another kind of theorizing on display in the *Lectures*, of which Smith is arguably one of the originators. This is akin to what Dugald Stewart described as 'conjectural history': the attempt to imagine how a particular institution or practice might originally have arisen, and to deploy that imagined history as part of a wider theory. In this case, Smith's target is nothing less than the origins of the political-legal realm. Based on his analysis of property rights, he introduces the idea of 'four distinct states which mankind pass through'. The first stage, the 'age of hunters', rests merely on what the members of a group can catch for themselves. But 'as their numbers multiplied, they would find the chase too precarious for their support,' encouraging the domestication and fattening of animals, and so 'the age of shepherds'. Yet while nomadic shepherding tribes could be much larger still, as they too became more numerous 'they would find a difficulty in supporting themselves by herds and flocks. Then they would naturally turn themselves to the cultivation of land . . . [and] gradually advance into the age of agriculture.' But the effect of specialization and growing technical skills would be to generate surpluses, and so the exchange of commodities under the law of contract 'not only betwixt the individuals of the same society but betwixt those of different nations . . . Thus at last the age of commerce arises.'

Smith is quickly able to show the value of this stadial theory by applying it to property rights, and then to government itself. In the age of hunters, he argues, property rights would largely be those of immediate possession ('occupation') of what had been killed; in that of shepherds, they would cover herds and land, and rights of use ('accession') as well as occupation. But in the age of agriculture, and still more in that of commerce, property rights would cover land and so 'multiply to a number almost infinite'. And, he suggests, the forms of government would change to suit the demands of the society so created. It is only with the age of shepherds that individuals can hold stock, allowing inequality and dependency to arise between them and so requiring government to maintain order. But these fledgling institutions of law and adjudication are quite inadequate to the needs of agricultural societies, which first display the outlines of modern jurisprudence in their different parts of government, and that early jurisprudence itself must develop in order to meet the needs of commercial society as it evolves.

Finally, Smith relates the whole theory to what he takes to be the actual historical development of government in Britain. Before the time of William the Conqueror, Britain appears to have sat in Smith's estimation somewhere between the age of shepherds and that of agriculture. Property was held, he says, 'allodially'—that is, without being subject to superior authority—and the 'great lords were continually making war upon one another'. William changed all the allodial lordships in England to feudal tenures, subject to Crown authority, establishing himself at the head of the aristocracy. But it was only with the Crown's escalating need for revenue and thus taxation in the seventeenth century that Parliament was enabled to exercise powers that secured the liberty of the individual and restrained that of the monarch. These measures, supported by the growth of the courts, helped to usher in an age of commerce.

There are classical antecedents, and a brilliant unfinished paper discussing the subject from the early 1750s by the scholar-statesman Anne Robert Jacques Turgot in France; but, these apart, Smith's appears to be the first fairly full stadial theory of human development, and the first giving due measure to the importance of the fourth stage, that of commercial society. We cannot be sure of the theory's precise roots, but they may even go back to Smith's earliest lectures on jurisprudence in Edinburgh in 1750–51. The theory itself was to prove extremely influential; in due course it became an important part of *The Wealth of Nations*, and excited much comment and imitation. But the *Lectures* anticipate the later work in other crucial respects as well, for having developed his core theory of justice Smith could now proceed to the subjects of wealth-creation, public revenue and arms, all more familiar to his modern readers. We have seen how Smith was laying claim to core ideas from *The Wealth of Nations* as early as his 1755 talk at Cochrane's Club, and the *Lectures on Jurisprudence* reinforce this picture. By 1764 Smith was already thinking deeply about such fundamental issues as the division of labour, the effects of market size and specialization, consumer culture and preferences, man's

ADAM SMITH

'disposition to barter and exchange', 'natural' and market prices, the nature of money and bullion, banks and bankruptcy, international trade, interest rates, competition, markets, trust, standing armies vs. militias, and the law of nations. All of these issues would be revisited in *The Wealth of Nations*.

The *Lectures on Jurisprudence* thus serve as a crucial missing link in Smith's work. Unpublished in his own time and little known even today, they tie together leading themes from *The Theory of Moral Sentiments* and *The Wealth of Nations*, themes which must be restored to their proper place if we are to have any deep understanding of the whole structure. They are hardly unproblematic: in particular, there is an interesting tension between the traditional jurisprudential categories of property rights and the way in which they are reconstrued historically in the conjectures of Smith's stadial theory, while the *Lectures'* relatively tight focus on negative justice bypasses many issues, notably of distributive justice, that would be considered central to the idea of justice today. But the lectures deserve far more attention than they have received. Their function is broadly descriptive, but despite the appearance of paradox this does not prevent Smith from reaching firm judgements of his own. His subject is the study of good government and law, and he is quite clear that certain institutions fail any such test. Some, such as slavery, are morally outrageous. Others, such as primogeniture, which required that property be inherited through the first-born, and entails, which constrained how land could be passed through the generations, he thinks evidently unjust and unwise.

But what perhaps cast the longest shadow forward are his trenchant remarks about government measures or interventions that hurt 'the progress of opulence'. These include such familiar items as war, taxation, monopolies, the privileges of chartered corporations and subsidies, but also more intangible matters such as weak government, bad contract law and enforcement and poor public infrastructure. They point to Smith's belief not merely in the centrality of markets to the process of wealth-creation and economic and social development, but

80

also in the importance of an effective state. As he remarked, 'Property and civil government very much depend on one another.' The achievement of his jurisprudence is to show how and why they do.

In 1762, the University of Glasgow showed its appreciation of Smith by awarding him an honorary doctorate of laws. He was already the object of a highly tempting offer which would take him away from the university, and from academic life. By this time his reputation had attracted various scions of the aristocracy as pupils, most notably Thomas Petty Fitzmaurice, second son of the Irish peer the Earl of Shelburne, and brother of the future Prime Minister of that name. That engagement had been an evident success. Shelburne clearly valued Smith's moral guidance as well as his scholarship, and for good reason. Removed from the temptations of English worldliness, the boy had prospered under Smith's careful supervision, as the latter's detailed and solicitous progress reports to his father testify. Pupil and tutor had formed a close and affectionate relationship. The same was true of Smith and François Louis Tronchin, whose father Théodore, a leading doctor in Geneva and contributor to the *Encyclopédie*, had entrusted the boy to his care in 1761.

David Hume had ended his teasing letter of April 1759 by mentioning a still more interesting potential engagement: 'Charles Townshend, who passes for the cleverest fellow in England, is so taken with the performance [that is, *The Theory of Moral Sentiments*] that he said to Oswald he would put the Duke of Buccleuch under the author's care, and would endeavour to make it worth his while to accept of that charge.' This was something rather different, for the dukes of Buccleuch were some of the greatest landowners in Scotland. Townshend, later to achieve considerable notoriety as Chancellor of the Exchequer for his 'Townshend duties' imposed on trade with the American colonies, had married into the family and become the stepfather of Henry Campbell Scott, the young Duke, then aged twelve and studying at Eton.

Hume had also gently pointed out that 'Mr Townshend passes for being a little uncertain in his resolutions,' and nothing immediate came of the latter's sally. Perhaps this was not surprising, given Horace Walpole's acid appraisal of him: 'The greatest man of this age . . . if he had had but common truth, common sincerity, common honesty, common modesty, common steadiness, common courage and common sense'. However, Townshend had high political ambitions for the young Duke, who he thought required a bracing intellectual and moral education. Four years later, in October 1763, he approached Smith directly. The offer was a very handsome one—£500 a year, with an annual pension thereafter of £300 for life, to accompany and instruct his charge during a European tour. Travel costs were included, but even so this was much more than Smith could expect to earn in a good year at Glasgow. In addition the duties would be lighter and more varied than at the university, the tour would take him overseas for the first time, there would be scope to continue with his intellectual work, and on his return he would be set up with a life pension sufficient to bring that work to conclusion, with the advantageous Buccleuch connection also in hand.

As if to drum the opportunity in, Smith had a highly enticing letter just a few days later from Hume himself, who had recently moved to France as secretary to the Earl of Hertford, the British Ambassador. 'I . . . have everywhere met with the most extraordinary honours which the most exorbitant vanity could wish or desire,' Hume wrote. 'The compliments of Dukes and Marischals and foreign ambassadors go for nothing with me at present: I retain a relish for no kind of flattery but that which comes from the ladies.' It was an alluring prospect.

Smith swiftly accepted Townshend's offer, resigned his professorship and assigned his remaining teaching elsewhere. He also very honourably insisted on repaying his students the fees they had paid for the remaining lectures, but they baulked at this, leading to his only recorded example of (rather modest) physical violence. 'But Mr Smith was not to be bent from his purpose,' it was reported. He said, '"You must not refuse me this satisfaction. Nay, by heavens, gentlemen, you shall not," and seizing by the coat the young man who stood next to him, he thrust the money into his pocket, and then pushed him from him. The rest saw it was in vain to contest the matter, and were obliged to let him take his own way.'

Smith and Buccleuch arrived in Paris in February 1764, and proceeded south to Toulouse, then the second city of France. In many ways it was a shrewd choice. The young Duke was a gentle and inexperienced soul, as yet unsuited to the social rigours of Paris; and Toulouse should have been familiar territory, as a university city, with a large professional and clerical population. However, when they arrived the city was convulsed by popular resistance to the *vingtième*, a tax of 5 per cent on income imposed in a vain attempt to tackle France's own immense war debts. This can only have drawn Smith's mind deeper into vital issues of public finance. In case further stimulus were needed, there was a stream of letters from Townshend to the Duke, encouraging him to examine and reflect on the many inadequacies of the French economy and financial system under the *ancien régime*.

Toulouse was also filled with a more sinister source of unrest, however. In 1762 a local merchant, a Huguenot named Jean Calas, had been convicted of the murder of his own son, supposedly for converting to Catholicism. Calas had been tortured, beaten and executed—still bravely maintaining his innocence—after a kangaroo trial dominated by anti-Protestant religious prejudice. By 1764 the case had been taken up by the great Voltaire himself, who turned it into a *cause célèbre* and succeeded in getting the verdict overturned, the Chief Magistrate ejected and the family paid compensation. It was a triumph, but as with the anti-Catholic Gordon Riots of 1780 in London—in which a drunken mob had raided distilleries, released prisoners from Newgate Prison and made a sustained attempt to capture the Bank of England—the episode vividly illustrated how quickly it was possible for supposedly civilized societies to disintegrate into violence.

In their own ways, France's financial difficulties and Toulouse's conflicting religious undercurrents were both grist to Smith's theorizing. More immediately problematic was the failure of Townshend's chosen contact, the Duc de Choiseul, to provide any useful introductions once Smith and Buccleuch had arrived, a particular necessity given Smith's poor spoken French. In July Smith reported despairingly to Hume that 'The progress we have made is not very great. The Duke is not acquainted with any Frenchman whatever . . . The life which I led in Glasgow was a pleasurable, dissipated life in comparison of that which I lead here at present. I have begun to write a book in order to pass away the time.' We cannot know for sure, but it is fascinating to speculate that *The Wealth of Nations* may have been spawned by Smith's boredom in Toulouse.

The city became more hospitable over time, however, and there were visitors from Britain and trips to Bordeaux and Montpellier to vary Buccleuch's educational diet. In April 1765 Townshend agreed that they were ready to move to Paris. But before that they took a summer tour to the south of France, and then to Geneva in the autumn. Geneva was very different to Toulouse: a republic, a city-state of strongly Protestant stamp, and the birthplace of the notorious Jean-Jacques Rousseau. Aided by Théodore Tronchin, the father of one of his earlier pupils and an admirer of his, Smith moved immediately with Buccleuch into the highest Genevan social and intellectual circles. Rousseau had departed, and the two men never met. But during his stay Smith was able to meet Voltaire, who lived across the border in France and whom he had long admired. It was a good preparation for Paris.

The tutor and his increasingly accomplished pupil finally arrived in the French capital at Christmas 1765, and spent nine months there. Hertford was, alas, recalled to London, taking Hume with him. But even without his friend Smith now found himself the toast of polite society. To be fêted by the salons of Paris was joy enough, especially after the barrenness of his early months in Toulouse. But it also introduced him to some of the greatest French minds of the time, among them Turgot, the financier Necker, the social philosopher and notorious atheist Helvétius, the mathematician d'Alembert and most significantly, as it proved, the royal physician and political economist François Quesnay and his followers, later known as the Physiocrats. In 1758–9 Quesnay had published his *tableau économique*, a pioneering attempt to capture in a highly simplified form the flows of goods and money circulating around the French economy—indeed to see 'an economy' itself as a self-standing entity or system, whose key elements could in principle be theorized and depicted—and he and those around him published a series of further works expounding their ideas at the end of the 1760s. They were forming what was, in effect, the first coherent school of thought in the burgeoning new field of political economy, at a time when elite opinion in France was struggling to understand and come to terms both with domestic challenges of indebtedness and economic stagnation, and with the broader and still more unwelcome idea of growing British economic and military superiority.

Intellectually, this was an extraordinarily pregnant moment, and by implication at least the Physiocrats offered a formidable challenge to Smith to test and develop his own ideas. He liked and greatly respected Quesnay, and described the Physiocrats' theorizing as 'with all its imperfections perhaps the nearest approximation to the truth that has yet been published upon the subject of political economy, and [it] is upon that account well worth the consideration of every man who wishes to examine with attention the principles of that very important science'. There was much in it that Smith thought of importance, including the idea of an economy as a circulating system; the status of private property; the emphasis on individuals pursuing their own interests through free exchange; and the focus on labour as a source of economic value.

In the modern era these areas of agreement have led some commentators to regard Smith as intellectually derivative of the Physiocrats. This is a mistake, for though he learned from them, he was also pitiless in analysing their errors, notably in Book IV of *The Wealth of*

Nations. The Physiocrats were agrarians: the central plank of their approach was the belief that only the agricultural sector generated surplus economic value, that merchants, traders and artisans were therefore unproductive and merely 'sterile'—a view that Smith had already opposed in his *Lectures on Jurisprudence*—and that cities were artificial impositions on the natural order. These were all claims which Smith vigorously rejected.

And as for policy, how was this agricultural transformation to be achieved? The Physiocrats' proposals—a radical simplification of taxation and the removal of the thicket of barriers to internal trade in France—struck Smith as utopian and potentially revolutionary. Dr Quesnay imagined, Smith wrote in *The Wealth of Nations*, that an economy would 'thrive and prosper only under a certain precise regimen, the exact regimen of perfect liberty and perfect justice. He seems not to have considered that, in the political body, the natural effort which every man is continually making to better his own condition is a principle of preservation capable of preventing and correcting, in many respects, the bad effects of a political economy, in some degree, both partial and oppressive.' The inspiration here is, surely, Mandeville's *Fable of the Bees*, with its subtitle *Private Vices, Public Benefits*. In Smith's hands the idea that individual enterprise—'the natural effort which every man is continually making to better his own condition'—could be of value to all was to prove a remarkably powerful one.

The last months of the tour fell under something of a cloud. Over the summer of 1766 Smith and Buccleuch learned to their great sorrow that Sir James Macdonald, a friend of the Duke's who had stayed with them in Toulouse, had died in Rome. In August the Duke himself fell ill, apparently of food poisoning, while hunting with Louis XV in the forest of Compiègne. He recovered fairly quickly, after 'three moderate tea-cupfuls of blood' had been taken from him, but not before Smith had written detailed and anguished letters to Townshend recounting the course of the illness.

But still worse was to follow. The Duke's younger brother Hugh Campbell Scott had joined them earlier in Bordeaux. In mid-October he suddenly sickened and despite the best efforts of Quesnay and of Tronchin, whom Smith had called in from Geneva, he died on 19 October. A distraught Smith wrote to Scott's sister, Lady Frances: 'It is my misfortune to be under the necessity of acquainting you of the most terrible calamity that has befallen us. Mr Scott died this evening at seven o'clock . . . He expired about five minutes before I could get back [from warning the Duke] and I had not the satisfaction of closing his eyes with my own hands. I have no force to continue this letter; the Duke, though in very great affliction, is otherwise in perfect health.'

Smith and Buccleuch instantly cancelled their remaining plans and returned to Britain with the body. By 1 November they were back in London. Smith never went abroad thereafter. As he had written to his London publisher Andrew Millar, 'I long passionately to rejoin my old friends, and if I had once got fairly to your side of the water, I think I should never cross it again.' So it proved.

HAVING MADE IT BACK OVER THE CHANNEL, HOWEVER, SMITH DID NOT immediately travel home. Instead he stayed in London for six months. He put through corrections to the third edition of *The Theory of Moral Sentiments*, instructing his publisher Strahan in Scotland to 'call me simply Adam Smith without any addition either before or behind' on the frontispiece; in the event the letters LLD were added to his name. But Smith may well also have stayed to help prepare the Duke for the management of the vast estates which would fall to him when he attained his majority the following September, and perhaps to see him through preparations for his marriage, which took place on 3 May. Smith was then released from service, and almost immediately began to collect his pension. He rejoined his mother and Janet Douglas in Kirkcaldy, and wrote to Hume from there in June 1767: 'My business here is study in which I have been very deeply engaged for about a month past. My amusements are long solitary walks by the seaside. You may judge how I spend my time. I feel myself, however, extremely happy, comfortable and contented. I never was, perhaps, more so in all my life.'

The next nine years were largely devoted to the reflection and research that would culminate in *The Wealth of Nations*. During this period Smith took considerable pains to keep his work on an even keel and minimize interruptions. The one exception was for Buccleuch himself. Townshend had died unexpectedly in September at the age of only forty-two, and with him went the heavy burden of his political expectations for the young man, much to the latter's relief. Perhaps as a result, the relationship between Smith and his former pupil continued to deepen.

In the years to come Smith would make regular visits to see Buccleuch at Dalkeith House, his palatial residence outside Edinburgh, which had been recently modernized by the Adam brothers. On his return to Scotland the Duke had been faced with the onerous task of taking over and managing the family estates, now heavily encumbered with debt. The urgent priority was to reissue hundreds of leases to tenant farmers, and doubtless on Smith's advice the Duke adopted a very enlightened approach, investing heavily in roads and other infrastructure, extending lease lengths to encourage investment and balancing existing obligations with an appeal to good new potential tenants.

The whole scheme was a great success, and the Duke was increasingly recognized as an innovative landowner at a time when agricultural improvement was both fashionable and good business. But his fortunes were gravely damaged once more just five years later in 1772 by the collapse of Douglas, Heron & Co., better known as the Ayr Bank, in which he and many other leading Scottish landowners had invested. This was little short of a financial disaster. The bank had been launched amid high hopes in 1769, to feed the growing local demand for agricultural credit. But if the expectation had been one of financing long-term investment, the reality was radically different. The Scottish banking system was structurally undercapitalized at that time, short on deposits and thus reliant for financing on the costly flow of bills of exchange and other paper circulating locally and with the London banks.

The lack of capital had been a spur to innovation, notably with the invention of the 'cash account', the world's first overdraft, by the Royal Bank of Scotland. But it meant that the easy-lending Ayr Bank had quickly been swamped by demand, including from speculators, and it over-expanded. There was a sharp recession in Scotland in 1771, causing many of its loans to turn sour; and lacking access to liquidity and capital, the whole structure came crashing down in the classic pattern of banking failures ever since. This then resulted in a secondary banking crisis which only four private banks in Edinburgh survived, and which inflicted enormous losses on the Ayr Bank's original partners, who, unlike the investors in today's incorporated limited-liability banks, were exposed to the full extent of their wealth. Their creditors were ultimately paid in full, but at the horrendous total cost to the partners of £663,397. It was said that as much as £750,000 in landed property was sold to fund the losses.

But if the Ayr Bank was a local calamity, it was also indirectly a sign of something far more positive: the rapid growth of the Scottish economy. As we have seen, Glasgow had been the first to profit from the economic benefits of Union, ramping up trade in the 1730s and 1740s, and making itself the world's pre-eminent tobacco port in the process. The failure of the last great Jacobite rebellion in 1746 marked the start of a period of social and political stability that assisted the growth of private enterprise. But even before that there were more general signs of growth, and that growth accelerated after the '45, aided by the construction of new roads, harbours and bridges. Ambitious plans for the development of Edinburgh, including the magnificent Georgian New Town, were laid after 1753. Civic-minded bodies such as the Convention of Royal Burghs promoted public investment in lowland Scotland, while special corporations were set up to fund particular projects such as the Forth and Clyde Canal linking the two great firths, work on which began in 1768. Commercial Scotland was—indeed still is—a relatively small place; there was much less distance, either of geography or class, between landowners, industrialists and merchants than in England, and more of a common framework of values. These factors, and the perennial shortage of capital, encouraged the great landowners to invest in new ventures alongside an emerging generation of traders and entrepreneurs.

The overall effects were dramatic. The tonnage of vessels cleared at Scottish ports more than doubled between 1759 and 1775. The production of linen was the country's largest industry, employing many tens of thousands of weavers and spinners, supported by government export subsidies; and it was booming, so that by the early 1770s there were 120 sailings a year to Russia alone to import flax to feed it. While the British tobacco trade had massively expanded in mid-century, Scotland's share had expanded still faster, from 10 per cent in 1738 to 40 per cent in 1765. The great Carron ironworks was founded near Falkirk in 1759, and despite a difficult start became both an icon of Scottish industrial transformation and famous for its lethal light, short-barrelled naval cannon, known as the carronade.

Despite the gradual growth of industry and trade, in 1750 Scotland remained very much a rural society. On average less than one in ten people lived in a large town, half the rate of occupation in England, and the structures of rural society, cultivation and ownership remained broadly traditional, notwithstanding the fashion for agricultural improvement. By the 1760s, however, the country was entering a long period of explosive growth—indeed, it has been argued that town and city growth in Scotland was faster than anywhere else in Britain or the continent of Europe between 1750 and 1850. In his essay 'Of the Protestant Succession' (1754) Hume had praised the social, political and economic improvements of the previous sixty years, attributing them to 'our constitution' and the effects of the Hanoverian parliamentary establishment: 'Public liberty, with internal peace and order, has flourished almost without interruption: Trade and manufactures, and agriculture, have increased: The arts, and sciences, and philosophy, have been cultivated. Even religious parties have been necessitated to lay aside their mutual rancour; and the glory of the nation has spread itself all over Europe.' When Adam Smith wrote to his friend and future publisher William Strahan in April 1760 that the Union of 1707 was 'a measure from which infinite good has been derived to this country', he was observing the early stages of what would become an extraordinary process of sustained economic development from poverty to riches, of a kind arguably not seen again until the emergence of the so-called Asian Tigers such as Singapore and South Korea in the twentieth century.

This remarkable expansion was not inevitable; by comparison, growth in Ireland also rose at this time, only to peter out twenty years later. Scottish urbanization was powered by industrialization, especially in textiles, and later by growth in coal-mining, paper manufacture, brewing and distilling, among other industries. As the economy grew, so it further benefited from a happy combination of natural and human factors—copious coal reserves, the proximity of major ports, a land frontier with England, expanding export trade, a vibrant (sometimes too vibrant) banking system, low labour costs and a dynamic spirit of entrepreneurship among them.

Such growth required capital, and Scotland's shortage of capital meant that the country was ill equipped to ride out periodic recessions resulting from over-expansion, shifts in demand or bad harvests, all of which played a role in the Ayr Bank crisis of 1772. It seems very likely that Smith worked to assist his patron Buccleuch in dealing with the consequences of that crisis; but even if he did not he had a ring-side seat in Dalkeith from which to watch the ramp-up in the bank's loans, its rapid collapse and the aftermath. Part of Smith's genius is to take his personal experience and to draw out both telling anecdotes and general lessons from it in his writings. Book II of *The Wealth of Nations* is dedicated to money and capital, and in it he puts the 1772 crisis to good use, with a careful and incisive analysis of its causes and consequences. It is a superb cautionary tale of the abuse of paper money and the banking system. The Scottish banking market had long been characterized by speculative lending, as Smith explains, and speculators and promoters were fearful of a crackdown by the Bank of England on the overheated market in bills of exchange, which could potentially ruin them as signatories. The result was severe social and political pressure: 'Their own distress . . . they called the distress of the country; and this distress . . . they said, was altogether owing to the ignorance, pusillanimity and bad conduct of the banks . . . It was the duty of the banks, they seemed to think, to lend for as long a time, and to as great an extent, as they might wish to borrow.'

The bank's origins lay in a response to this pressure. 'In the midst of this clamour and distress, a new bank was established in Scotland . . . more liberal than any other had ever been, both in granting cash-accounts, and in discounting bills of exchange.' Its basic purpose was highly ambitious, but also fatally compromised by competitive rivalry: not merely to support business activity, but also 'by drawing the whole banking business to themselves, to supplant all the other Scotch banks, particularly those established in Edinburgh'. It is, in effect, a perfect illustration of the economic logic of a financial bubble, of the way on which social and political factors can quickly turn a smaller problem into a larger one, and, when the money ran out, of its ultimately disastrous consequences.

In a striking image, Smith emphasized the value that banking, if properly conducted, could offer an economy: 'The judicious operations of banking, by providing, if I may be allowed so violent a metaphor, a sort of waggon—way through the air, enable the country to convert, as it were, a great part of its highways into good pastures and corn fields, and thereby to increase very considerably the annual produce of its land and labour.' This carried risks of its own, however: 'The commerce and industry of the country . . . it must be acknowledged, though they may be somewhat augmented, cannot be altogether so secure, when they are thus, as it were, suspended upon the Daedalian wings of paper money, as when they travel about upon the solid ground of gold and silver.' The Ayr Bank debacle perfectly illustrated the potential for catastrophe.

But Smith also coolly noted that the failure of the Ayr Bank in fact assisted its competitors, by breaking the circulation of expensive bills of exchange: 'Those other banks, therefore, were enabled to get very easily out of that fatal circle, from which they could not otherwise have disengaged themselves without incurring a considerable loss, and perhaps too even some degree of discredit.'

All in all, then 'In the long run . . . the operations of this bank increased the real distress of the country, which it was intended to relieve; and effectually relieved, from a very great distress, those rivals whom it meant to supplant.' The whole affair was an object lesson, not merely in the need for care, thought and prudence in banking, but in the law of unexpected consequences.

THE COLLAPSE OF THE AYR BANK, AND THE PARAMOUNT NEED TO SAVE Buccleuch from disaster, dragged Smith away from his work. There were other factors in play as well. As he guardedly wrote to his friend the MP William Pulteney in September 1772:

> Though I had no concern myself in the public calamities, some of the friends for whom I interest myself the most have been deeply concerned in them; and my attention has been a good deal occupied about the most proper method for extracting them . . . My book would have been ready for the press by the beginning of this winter; but the interruptions occasioned partly by bad health arising from want of amusement and from thinking too much upon one thing, and partly from the avocations above mentioned will oblige me to retard its publication for a few months longer.

Smith's struggle to complete the book was a matter of some comment among his friends. In a letter of 1773 to Daniel Fellenberg, a Swiss lawyer, Kames remarked that 'Dr Smith's friends are like you solicitous for a publication. For some time past he has been employed in building and demolishing; and I am afraid that the delicacy of his taste exceeds his powers of execution, so that the delivery of this child may yet be at a distance, though the time of reckoning is long past.' One particular obstacle for him was the physical difficulty of writing itself. Smith's handwriting remained a large and cumbrous script throughout his life, not given to long or rapid self-expression. We know he used others to transcribe *The Wealth of Nations*; one story has him dictating passages to a clerk in his study at the family home in Kirkcaldy while periodically rubbing his head against the wall, to the point where the pomade in his wig left a mark.

Progress on the book was also slowed by a potential offer to join a commission into the activities of the East India Company, which fell through, and a suggestion that he should become tutor to the Duke of Hamilton on a visit abroad, which he refused. Whether from overwork, stress or loneliness—or a combination of all three—his health remained fragile. A letter from Hume in November 1772 implores him to finish the book, see it into print in London and then settle in Edinburgh. Five months later Smith wrote to Hume, whom he had appointed as his literary executor, in frankly despairing terms, and with detailed instructions:

> My dear friend, as I have left the care of all my literary papers to you, I must tell you that except those which I carry along with me, there are none worth the publishing but a fragment of a great work which contains a history of the astronomical systems that were successively in fashion down to the time of Descartes . . . This little work you will find in a thin folio paper book in my writing desk in my book-room. All the other loose paper which you will find either in that desk or within the glass

folding-doors of a bureau which stands in my bedroom, together with about eighteen thin paper folio books, which you will likewise find within the same glass folding-doors, I desire may be destroyed without any examination. Unless I die very suddenly, I shall take care that the papers I carry with me shall be carefully sent to you.

Shortly afterwards, he headed with 'the papers I carry along with me' to London. He would not return till 1776, and then it would be, with *The Wealth of Nations* in his hand.

CHAPTER 4

'YOU ARE SURELY TO REIGN ALONE ON THESE SUBJECTS', 1773–1776

ADAM SMITH ARRIVED IN LONDON IN MAY 1773, MOVING INTO rooms in Suffolk Street, near the present National Gallery and Trafalgar Square. He must have known the capital city quite well by now from previous visits, and the location was wisely chosen: just a short walk from Parliament, the river and St James's Park, and very close to the British Coffeehouse, which was much frequented by the Scots in London. The change of scene appears to have worked, for although we can only catch glimpses of Smith during the three years he spent in London, he seems to have thrived amid its bustle.

Smith's main purpose was to get *The Wealth of Nations* finished and through the press. But his first business, and the original reason for his journey, lay with the proposal that he should act as travelling tutor to the Duke of Hamilton, presumably on a European tour. In the event, however, he was persuaded by Buccleuch to reject the offer in the expectation of something better after the new book was completed, and in due course Buccleuch did indeed procure for him the post of Commissioner of Customs in Edinburgh.

But all this lay in the future. For the present, London offered much to entertain him, and Smith was quickly admitted as a Fellow of the Royal Society. Founded in 1660 at the instigation of Sir Christopher Wren to promulgate the 'new science', the Society had experienced something of a decline since the days of Newton, Hooke and Herschel, but it remained highly prestigious even so. Smith periodically attended lectures at the Society's premises off Fleet Street, and carefully collected copies of its *Transactions*. No less distinguished in its membership was Dr Johnson's Club, to which Smith was elected soon afterwards. The Club, as it is still known today, was founded by the inveterately clubbable painter Joshua Reynolds in 1764 at the Turk's Head tavern in Soho, to entertain his friend Samuel Johnson. Its original nine members ranged across the arts, and included Edmund Burke and the brilliant playwright Oliver Goldsmith; these were soon joined by David Garrick, James Boswell, Charles James Fox and Edward Gibbon, among others.

It was a dazzling array of talents. But, even so, towards the end of his life Johnson came to deplore what he saw as the change in character and loss of exclusivity of the Club, and he may have had Smith particularly in mind. According to Boswell, Johnson thought Smith 'as dull a dog as he had ever met with' and 'a most disagreeable fellow after he had drunk some wine, which . . . "bubbled in his mouth"'. When Smith was rash enough to commend the architecture of Glasgow, which had been much adorned and enhanced in the previous two decades, Johnson replied caustically, 'Pray, sir, have you ever seen Brentford?' And Smith's view of Johnson was no better: 'I have seen that creature . . . bolt up in the midst of a mixed company and, without any previous notice, fall upon his knees behind a chair, repeat the Lord's Prayer, and then resume his seat at table. He has played this freak over and over perhaps five or six times in the course of an evening. It is not hypocrisy, but madness.'

On Johnson's side at least, the personal animus may have had long-standing roots. Johnson was a man of profound but tortured Christian beliefs; as we have seen, he abhorred Hume's religious scepticism, and suspected Smith on the same grounds. More specifically, he is unlikely to have forgotten the notice Smith had given to his *Dictionary* in the short-lived *Edinburgh Review* almost twenty years earlier, including Smith's argument that the book's lexicography was insufficiently grammatical and nuanced in its definitions. Though the criticism had little public impact at the time, it was still a potentially lethal blow to the intellectual core of Johnson's endeavour, and 'the Great Cham of Literature' knew how to bear a grudge. Yet there were also flashes of mutual respect amid the darkness. Smith is said to have admired Johnson's political pamphlets, while Johnson dismissed the suggestion that Smith's lack of experience made him unqualified to write upon trade: 'There is nothing which requires more to be illustrated by philosophy than trade does . . . To write a good book upon it a man must have extensive views. It is not necessary to have practised, to write well upon a subject.'

No great number of Smith's letters survive today, and they were evidently infrequent at the time, to judge by his repeated apologies to his correspondents. But there is one letter from this period that bears the distinctive stamp of his economic ideas. In 1774 the College of Physicians in Edinburgh petitioned Parliament to require that medical degrees should be awarded by examination only to those able to show two years of certified medical study. To modern ears this may seem like an entirely common-sense proposition; it was less so in the late eighteenth century, when scientific medicine was still in its infancy. At any rate, Smith—whose close friend William Cullen, the Professor of Medicine at Edinburgh University, had sought his views—was vehemently hostile to the proposal. Here he smelled the rank odours of monopoly and restraint of trade.

Replying to Cullen, Smith opens by dismissing the universities of Oxford and Cambridge without even a mention: 'In the present state of the Scotch universities, I do most sincerely look upon them as . . . without exception the best seminaries of learning . . . anywhere in Europe.' The reason was simple: in contrast to their English counterparts, as he had discovered at Oxford, the professors in Scotland relied heavily on students' fees for their income, forcing them to attend to students' needs; there were few if any bursaries or scholarships which, Smith thought, burdened and diverted students from their calling; and there was open competition for degrees. But this great achievement would, he thought, be prejudiced by the new proposals, which would limit competition and provide medical credentials without guaranteeing medical quality. Drawing on recent research of his own into the leading universities of Europe, Smith averred that 'Monopolists very seldom make good work, and a lecture which . . . students must attend, whether they profit by it or no, is certainly not very likely to be a good one.' Talk of high standards was merely camouflage for what was actually at stake: 'The strictest universities confer degrees only upon students of a certain standing. Their real motive for requiring this standing is that the student may spend more money among them and that they may make more profit by him.' This is the true and chastening voice of *The Wealth of Nations*.

Smith's letter to Cullen begins in typical fashion by acknowledging the distraction created by 'some occurrences, which interested me a good deal'. One of these was a protracted dispute over an annuity involving the brilliant but volatile Adam Ferguson, the Professor of Moral Philosophy at Edinburgh, whom he had recommended to the Earl of Stanhope as a travelling tutor for his ward—a matter in which Smith himself behaved with conspicuous propriety. But there was one vastly larger public issue that was clearly absorbing Smith at this time, indeed transfixing much popular and political opinion across Britain. That was the possibility of war with the thirteen American colonies.

IN 1772 HUME HAD WRITTEN TO SMITH WITH NEWS OF THE DISAStrous fall-out from the Ayr Bank collapse. But he also put the theoretical question to the toiling scholar as well: 'Do these events anywise affect your theory? Or will it occasion the revisal of any chapters? . . . What say you? Here is food for your speculation.' Smith was adept at turning recent events to intellectual advantage, and using them to make political economy more immediately interesting and relevant. The Ayr Bank debacle did feature prominently in *The Wealth of Nations*. But so too, and far more so, did the causes, course and implications of the dispute with the colonies, in which he buried himself while in London.

The thirteen colonies were not the only British possessions on the American continent; these also included Nova Scotia, acquired in 1713, and French Canada and East and West Florida, acquired in 1763. But the colonies had their own distinct history, dating back to the original settlement in Jamestown, Virginia in 1607. By the early 1770s American grievances against the mother country had ramified and escalated almost to the point of no return. Fundamentally they originated from the clash between the colonies' growing commercial power and political self-consciousness on the one hand and the constrictions of British policy on the other. Bolstered both by a high birth rate and by immigration, the colonial population in America had risen by a factor of ten over the previous century, and now stood at some 2 million people. Many of the new immigrants were not of British extraction, felt no great sense of deference to British laws and customs, and brought along their own traditions of Protestant dissent. Yet paradoxically they seemed to mix quite easily alongside colonial elites who were well schooled in English law and administrative practice. It was said that Blackstone's *Commentaries on the Laws of England* was second only to the Bible on colonial bookshelves.

Wisely enough, Sir Robert Walpole had largely left the American colonies to their own devices, and after he fell from power in 1742 this habit persisted in British government for another two decades. But the same latitude did not extend to trade. Ever since the time of Henry VII, piecemeal regulations had coalesced into a view of trade that would later be known as mercantilism: the function of the colonies was to produce inexpensive raw materials and purchase expensive finished goods; that of the mother country to turn the one into the other, thereby adding the greatest possible economic value at the least cost; that of merchants to manage the trade between the two sides, all to be carried in British vessels according to the dictates of the Navigation Acts. Mercantilism was lucrative to the mother country, and it had the collateral benefit from a British perspective of keeping American merchants and farmers perennially short of cash, and so dependent for finance on the City of London. The system had emerged from circumstance as well as from design, and it reflected the desire to project power and collect revenue rather than any deep underlying philosophy. To British politicians it seemed—when they considered it at all—like simple common sense, and it persisted. The colonies themselves continued to grow, local grievances of law and administration were regularly addressed, and smuggling flourished. It was simply too expensive for Westminster to impose a more rigorous policy in America, and too risky given the presence of the French to the colonists' north and west.

All this changed with the Seven Years War. The loss of New France—the French Canadian territories along the St Lawrence River—to the British removed the French threat to the thirteen colonies and emboldened those in London who had feared driving the colonists into their embrace. At the same time, the war had come at huge cost, nearly doubling the national debt to £130 million. To British eyes, the response of George Grenville as Prime Minister in 1763 was entirely understandable: reduced public expenditure, stricter enforcement of the Navigation Acts and the imposition of a new stamp duty on legal transactions in the colonies, the proceeds to go on colonial defence. The colonies had been secured and protected by force of arms at British expense; they imposed continuing administrative costs; they should pay their share of these costs themselves through local taxation; and they would benefit as a result. It all seemed quite straightforward.

Yet, as Burke and some others saw quite clearly, the new policy was in fact catastrophic. The colonies had never been directly taxed, and they were outraged by the imposition of the stamp duty. The duty had to be quickly repealed by the new government, led by the Marquis of Rockingham, but Rockingham's administration simultaneously compounded colonial discontents by bowing to domestic pressure and promoting the passage of a Declaratory Act which insisted on Britain's right to levy taxes in principle. The continuing pressure for revenue then pushed Buccleuch's stepfather Charles Townshend, the Chancellor of the Exchequer, into a series of additional duties in his budget of April 1767, notoriously on tea, which further inflamed colonial sentiment.

Townshend's budget was 'received with universal satisfaction and applause' in the House of Commons, but it has been much criticized ever afterwards. He appears to have consulted Smith about taxation in late 1766, while the latter was in France, and Smith corrected some calculations of his relating to a new proposed Sinking Fund, into which a portion of tax revenue would be set aside. But it was clear to Townshend that the new fund, even with other tax expedients, was not growing fast enough by itself to pay off the debt, and in a letter to Smith of the time he scouted other 'methods of quickening and invigorating the measure', adding at the end the fateful line 'I will add to these a *real* American Revenue' (emphasis in the original).

Smith was acting as an adviser to Townshend on taxation. Was he indirectly responsible for the loss of the American colonies, as has been suggested? Or more precisely, did his advice play a part in the crisis over the Townshend duties? The possibility is a tantalizing and ironic one. But the answer is probably not. Smith had no objection in principle to taxing the colonies, and we know from a later memorandum of 1778 that he thought it wrong for the colonists to enjoy the benefit of British defensive power without contributing to it. But the taxes actually levied contradicted a host of Smithian principles: they were inefficient, they helped protect the East India Company's monopoly on re-exporting tea, and they were imposed by Britain and not passed by colonial legislatures, contributing to their lack of political authority. So it is unlikely that Smith gave any such advice. Not for the first time—or the last—a British Chancellor of the Exchequer was besieged by political opponents, short of funds and in a tearing hurry. He raised money from many sources, where he could and at what he thought was the lowest political cost. In this, to say the least, he badly miscalculated.

Over the next few years organizations and networks of resistance— and talk of rebellion—became increasingly prominent in America, and colonial grievances about 'taxation without representation' were joined by radical arguments that Britain had no right to legislate for its colonies at all. In 1770 the governmental merry-go-round at Westminster finally ended with the arrival of an administration led by Lord North, which withdrew all the Townshend duties except for that on tea, left as a symbol of Britain's presumed right to tax. However, relations were now so bad that, far from assuaging the colonists, the withdrawals of duty only fed claims that the British were trying to destroy the colonial economies by flooding them with cheap imports.

During Smith's time in London, British relations with America accelerated towards war. On the night of 16 December 1773 rebels, some disguised as Mohawk warriors, boarded three ships in Boston harbour and dumped 342 cases of tea from them into the water. When news of the Boston Tea Party, as it became known, got to London in January 1774, it sharply intensified and unified opinion in Parliament, and led to draconian measures to reassert British control in Massachusetts and punish the colonists, reinforcing their sense of oppression. The protests and petitions to the King of the Continental Congress, the proto-national representative assembly which met in Philadelphia in September and October, were officially ignored. With Parliament despised, the King unavailing and the colonies in uproar as a result, it was only a matter of time before war broke out, and the revolution duly sputtered into life in April 1775 with firefights in Lexington and Concord, just outside Boston. Colonial governments were overthrown and new state constitutions drafted. On 4 July 1776 the Declaration of Independence was signed.

BY THEN, HOWEVER, THE GREATEST EARLY ANALYSIS OF THE DEEP causes of the American war had already been out for four months. *The Wealth of Nations* was published in London on 9 March 1776, in two rather expensive volumes and a print run of 500–750 copies.

The sheer range, length and brilliance of Smith's work render any summary inadequate. But the full title of the book gives a flavour of its contents: *An Inquiry into the Nature and Causes of the Wealth of Nations*. This is not an economic textbook, though it is full of analysis, lessons and information. Rather, it is a book about economic processes and economic development. Nations, it argues from a vast array of evidence, can be wealthy and prosperous, or poor and struggling. But national wealth is not merely circumstantial or divinely bequeathed, it is created by human hand. It is not a stock of currency or bullion, or indeed a stock of anything, but 'the annual produce of the land and labour of any nation'.

Moreover, what wealth really amounts to, and the causes of it, can be studied: political economy can be used to evaluate policy choices, and such choices can create or destroy wealth. An important goal of *The Wealth of Nations* is not merely to understand but to shape human actions; and to shape both how policy choices are made, individually and collectively, and the very idea of political economy itself. It is a contribution to 'the science of a legislator, whose deliberations ought to be governed by general principles which are always the same'. The book's panoramic sweep extends in space from the subsistence economy of the Scottish highlands to the developed nations of Europe and colonial trade with the Indies, and in time from ancient civilizations to contemporary events. But nowhere, it would transpire, are the effects of bad policy-making better illustrated than in the discussion of America.

As Smith explained in his introduction, the work itself has a clear structure, moving in Book I from the sources of wealth or 'opulence' to the nature and uses of capital within an economy (Book II), to the causes of economic progress and development (Book III), to trade policy and its failure in Britain (Book IV), and finally to government revenues, taxation and other domestic policy issues (Book V). In effect, the first two books set out Smith's basic economic theory, while the last three apply the theory in different contexts, adumbrating en route his 'natural theory of liberty' and its sometimes revolutionary implications.

He starts, famously, with an arresting example which drew his own experience of the Oswalds' nailery outside Kirkcaldy together with evidence from the French *Encyclopédie*: the case of a pin factory. By himself 'A workman . . . could scarce, perhaps, with the utmost industry, make one pin in a day, and could certainly not make twenty.' In a pin factory, however, the process is broken down into eighteen different specialized operations. The result of this division of labour is a dramatic increase in productivity: 'Each person . . . might be considered as making four thousand eight hundred pins in a day.' Specialization raises productivity in three ways, according to Smith: by improving skills, by reducing disruptions and by creating scope for the use of dedicated machinery. This in turn generates surpluses that can be used to pay for new investment, further boosting specialization and so productivity, in a virtuous cycle.

If human labour creates value, the division of labour supercharges that process. It is the principal source of wealth-creation for Smith, and its full implications are momentous. But Smith sees it, like so much else in our economic lives, as the result of something more fundamental still. For him there are two great dynamic principles of human behaviour. The first is what he memorably describes as a 'propensity . . . which has in view no such extensive utility; the propensity to truck, barter and exchange one thing for another'. This is distinctive of humans as a species, and it draws on Smithian 'sympathy' and the human capacity to empathize with another's desires and values: 'Nobody ever saw a dog make a fair and deliberate exchange of one bone for another with another dog. Nobody ever saw one animal by its gestures and natural cries signify to another, this is mine, that yours;

I am willing to give this for that.' Smith's second dynamic principle is a 'desire of bettering our condition' which is 'universal, continual and uninterrupted'. The man who has more pins or apples or cloth than he needs will seek to better his condition by exchanging some of them with someone who has what he lacks, and the result is trade.

Trade is mutually beneficial when, and because, it is freely and voluntarily undertaken; both the buyer and the seller gain from the transaction. This in turn encourages further specialization and division of labour, since the man who can trade his surplus pins or apples or cloth successfully has a direct interest in their further production. But it also has the result that even in the poorest areas of a civilized country people are dependent on each other for all but their most basic economic needs. Even to produce an item as familiar as an ordinary woollen coat, Smith points out, requires the cooperation of a vast number of skilled workers, from shepherds to spinners and weavers, from shears-makers to sailors.

As Smith says, 'It is but a very small part of a man's wants which the produce of his own labour can supply. He supplies the far greater part of them by exchanging that surplus part of his own labour . . . Every man thus lives by exchanging, or becomes, in some measure, a merchant, and the society itself grows to be what is properly a commercial society.' What sustains people in this mutual economic dependence? Simply, the insistent press of the desires for exchange and self-betterment: 'It is not from the benevolence of the butcher, the brewer or the baker that we expect our dinner, but from their regard to their own interest. We address ourselves, not to their humanity, but to their self-love, and never talk to them of our own necessities, but of their advantages.' Self-love is just one among a wide range of human emotions, but it is a key to explaining the economic and social value created by commercial society.

Goods are traded in markets, and Smith tends to think of markets as places of business rather than in more general terms. Over time, it makes no sense to produce goods or services that cannot be sold, and this simple thought leads to another crucial Smithian insight, that in his words 'The division of labour is limited by the extent of the market.' Small markets are not able to attract the customers or generate the surpluses that reward specialization and investment. In effect, the virtuous cycle of the division of labour struggles to get going, or runs slowly. In big markets, by contrast, with a multiplicity of wealthy customers, the cycle runs fast. As so often, Smith piles up evidence for his argument via everyday or historical examples which stand for wider human experience. You never see porters except in great towns, he says, while in remote rural areas people have no choice but to be more self-sufficient, because exchange is more difficult. Cities are centres of economic growth bringing together dozens of different trades, while ports generally do better than inland towns in virtue of their wider market access. European civilization begins with trade in the Mediterranean. And so on.

Any trade involves some estimation of value, but what is value? The ultimate answer, Smith insists, lies in labour: 'the real measure of the exchangeable value of all commodities' is the amount of labour in it, or 'the toil and trouble in acquiring it'. But estimating amounts of labour is impractical, and in the meantime markets need some common medium of exchange. If what you really desire is oranges it may make no sense at all to trade your grain for my pans; and even if you do, it would be hopelessly time-consuming and expensive to have to trade them directly. This, Smith speculates, is the source of the early trade in precious metals and so ultimately the use of money, which is 'in all civilised nations, the universal instrument of commerce, by the intervention of which goods of all kinds are bought and sold for each other'.

Money need not be metal: in Homer's Greece, cattle were used as money. In Abyssinia salt was money, in India shells, in Newfoundland dried cod, in other places and times tobacco, sugar, hides or nails. But for reasons of convenience and mutual recognition money gradually settled as standardized gold and silver coinage, and this association helped to foster a central illusion which Smith makes great efforts to dispel later in the book: the idea that money and wealth are the same thing. In particular, money is not capital, and the function of banks is not to increase capital as such, but to make it available for productive use: 'It is not by augmenting the capital of the country, but by rendering a greater part of that capital active and productive . . . that the most judicious operations of banking can increase the industry of the country.'

How do markets for goods actually work? In a society of hunters all a man has is his labour. In agricultural societies capital can be created from trade, and used to employ people for wages. Where land is privately owned the landlords will demand rent for use of the land. This enables Smith to analyse what he calls the real price of a given commodity in terms of rent, wages and profit, or of the returns—including profit—demanded by land, labour and capital respectively. When a market is operating competitively, if the market price of grain, say, falls below the real price, then the drop in expected returns will cause landowners to withdraw the use of land, labourers their work and employers their capital. When market prices exceed real prices, however, the same process works in reverse, generating profits and stimulating new supply.

Thus the market dynamically adjusts by means of competition to bring supply and demand into balance; producers have an incentive to supply no more and no less than customers demand. Moreover, the market is self-regulating; its balancing adjustments occur automatically as a result of trading, without any external intervention. As Smith puts it, 'The natural price, therefore, is, as it were, the central price, to which the prices of all commodities are continually gravitating.' In normal markets with freely working supply and demand, the natural price will thus equal the real price. Smith's idea is of a possible equilibrium between supply and demand, though he generally uses the very similar language of 'balance'. But his whole picture is dynamic. In normal markets prices tend towards equilibrium, but they may not achieve it for any length of time; and the equilibrium or balancing point constantly changes as markets shift and evolve.

The effect of competition in free markets is thus to keep profits at a minimum. High profits over any sustained period are a sign for Smith of poorly functioning markets, shortage of capital or labour, or the operation of some special (sometimes necessary) privilege. They are associated with poorer, not richer, societies; and with failure not success: 'The rate of profit does not, like rent and wages, rise with the prosperity, and fall with the declension of the society. On the contrary, it is naturally low in rich, and high in poor countries, and it is always highest in the countries which are going fastest to ruin.'

Of course markets are often not free, calm and competitive, as regards either prices or wages. Smith is unsparing in his criticism of the 'exclusive corporation spirit' by which producers seek to exercise control over their disaggregated and unorganized customers: 'People of the same trade seldom meet together, even for merriment and diversion, but the conversation ends in a conspiracy against the public, or in some contrivance to raise prices.' The same is true in relation to labour, since there is an asymmetry in economic power between the relatively small number of employers and the vastly larger number of workers: 'We rarely hear, it has been said, of the combinations of masters, though frequently of those of workmen. But whoever imagines, upon this account, that masters rarely combine, is as ignorant of the world as of the subject. Masters are always and everywhere in a sort of tacit, but constant and uniform combination, not to raise the wages of labour above their actual rate.' Even the law of the time was not symmetrical, he complains, since it punished workers but not masters for any attempt to act in combination.

The goal of public policy, therefore, is clear. As Smith later put it, 'Consumption is the sole end and purpose of all production; and the interest of the producer ought to be attended to, only so far as it may be necessary for promoting that of the consumer.' Far from promoting the interests of the consumer, however, British public policy had often done the opposite, restricting competition and encouraging producers to come together through trade privileges, guilds, public registers, welfare funds and the like. The apprenticeship laws, such as the Elizabethan Statute of Artificers 1563 which prevented men from practising any trade or craft without a compulsory seven-year apprenticeship, are thus a restraint of trade for Smith; and even the poor laws are singled out for their counter-productive effects in discouraging people from moving house and being able to look for work.

If the division of labour is the mainspring of wealth-creation, its counterpart is capital accumulation, for increased specialization both generates and demands capital, and this is the subject of Book II. A manufacturer needs capital to invest, while a trader must be able to pay for new inventories of goods to sell; and more specialized economies demand more capital in creating greater prosperity. 'Circulating capital' flows around an economy and is lent and re-lent, often to pay for raw materials and other short-term items, while 'fixed capital' is used to fund longer-term investments in land, plant and machinery.

Much of this is now—thanks to Smith—familiar to us. But it seemed little short of miraculous to many at the time, and even now his core ideas still have the capacity to surprise us in their astonishing simplicity and fertility. But, Smith points out, capital can be used not merely for investment but also for consumption, and here his views—and his tone—diverge quite sharply from those of modern economics. His strong conviction is that the use of capital should be to aid further capital accumulation, and he criticizes those who spend their capital, especially on 'trinkets' and other frivolous or extravagant items: 'Capitals are increased by parsimony and diminished by prodigality and misconduct . . . By not confining his expenses within his income, [the prodigal] encroaches upon his capital . . . he pays the wages of idleness with those funds which the frugality of his forefathers had, as it were, consecrated to the maintenance of industry.' The tone is almost Rousseauesque, with an echo of their shared Calvinist background.

Similarly, Smith is highly censorious about 'unproductive labour'. He sees that services can help to build capital in principle but, in keeping with his dislike of extravagance, he is scathing about the unproductive work which menial servants must do, whose 'services generally perish in the instant of their performance, and seldom leave any trace of value behind them'. Even the monarch does not escape his censure, on the same grounds: 'The sovereign, for example, with all the officers both of justice and war who serve under him, the whole army and navy, are unproductive labourers.' This does not rule out the possibility that public servants may be 'honourable', 'useful' or 'necessary' for other reasons, of course.

At this point Smith may seem perilously near to the moralistic and close-handed Presbyterian Scotsman of myth. But he is saved from caricature by the implications of his remarks for public policy. First of all, for societies as much as for individuals, 'Parsimony, and not industry, is the immediate cause of the increase of capital,' since without it no proceeds of industry would be saved. Secondly, while 'every prodigal appears to be a public enemy', in reality 'Great nations are never impoverished by private, though they sometimes are by public, prodigality and misconduct. The whole or almost the whole public revenue is, in most countries, employed in maintaining unproductive hands.' It follows that import bans or sumptuary laws to control personal spending on luxury items are not merely bad policy, but 'the highest impertinence and presumption . . . in kings and ministers . . . They are themselves always, and without any exception, the greatest spendthrifts in the society. Let them look well after their own expense, and they may safely trust private people with theirs.'

But decrying import bans is just one small aspect of a much greater enterprise in which Smith is engaged, and *The Wealth of Nations* is not merely a work of analysis, but a polemic against bad policy-making. Writing in 1780 to a Danish friend, he described the book as 'the very violent attack I had made upon the whole commercial system of Great Britain', and so it is. The thrust of the attack is

111

both intellectual and practical. In his words, 'The great object of the political economy of every country is to increase the riches and power of that country.' How to achieve this? Political economy seemed to offer just two options. The older one was a system of thought based on agriculture, pioneered—though Smith rarely names any of them—in France by Quesnay and the Physiocrats. On this view agriculture is 'the mother of all goods' and land alone is the source of national wealth and income. Proprietors create wealth by improving their land, and farmers by cultivating and working it, but artificers, manufacturers and merchants are seen as useful but economically unproductive middlemen. Their labour 'adds nothing to the value of . . . the rude produce of the land', but competition between them serves all those involved by lowering prices and generating markets for produce.

This 'agricultural system' had its virtues, as Smith acknowledged: they included a recognition of 'the wealth of nations as consisting, not in the unconsumable riches of money, but in the consumable goods annually produced by the labour of the society', and an understanding of the importance of freedom and competition. However, in the Physiocrats' hands it resulted in over-precise and exacting, indeed utopian, policy prescriptions, and the whole was brought down by its evident drawbacks. Its preoccupation with agriculture caused investment to be diverted into unprofitable channels, and failed to grasp the importance of manufacturers and merchants in improving product quality and routes to market. And its focus was too narrow, on France and national policy rather than on the demands of an emerging global trading order.

The other great system of thought was mercantilism, and this is Smith's main target. Book III of *The Wealth of Nations* explores the dynamics of economic progress, charting the progress of nations from great baronies to the feudal system and the emergence of cities, and feudalism's supersession in turn by commercial society. The 'mercantile system' emerges as a pathology of contemporary commercial society. It had grown up as gospel among the great nations over the previous century with the development of international trade: 'It is the modern system, and is best understood in our own country and in our own times.' Great Britain had done more than any nation to spread trade around the world, but in so doing it had helped to spawn a body of mercantilist practices that, far from enriching the country, were actively undermining it.

FOR SMITH, THE MERCANTILE SYSTEM IS MARKED BY ITS OBSESSION with money. It sees wealth as money, and in particular gold and silver. Just as a merchant seeks to acquire wealth by storing up money, so a mercantilist nation seeks to acquire wealth by storing up bullion. How is this bullion to be obtained? By foreign conquest and the acquisition of mines, traditionally, but also and more insidiously by attempts to manage the balance of trade. Complex networks of regulation and inducement had thus been developed to inhibit the export of gold and silver themselves, while promoting other exports and limiting imports, and so the loss of gold and silver in exchange. These included duties, prohibitions, bounties, subsidies, reliefs, advantageous commercial treaties and colonies, with their attendant privileges and monopolies.

Yet, Smith argued, the domestic effects of mercantilism were highly damaging as well, for every export bounty or restraint on imports was, in effect, a subsidy to producers at home. Mercantilism thus tended to distort trade and investment, boost profits, discourage competition and indirectly raise prices. Worse, it fed the 'monopolising spirit' of manufacturers and merchants, whom it taught to recognize that government action could increase their profits at little or no direct cost. The result was a further boost to the growth of what would now be called business lobbies and special interests, and further detriment to customers and workers. Smith's verdict on such actions is careful but damning: 'The proposal of any new law or regulation of commerce which comes from this order ought always to be listened to with great precaution . . . It comes from an order of men . . . who have generally an interest to deceive and even to oppress the public.' For Smith this insight had important implications: 'Whenever the legislature attempts to regulate the differences between masters and their workmen, its counsellors are always the masters. When the regulation, therefore, is in favour of the workmen, it is always just and equitable; but it is sometimes otherwise when in favour of the masters.'

Furthermore, Smith sees colonialism itself as intimately tied to the growth of the mercantile system. The idea of colonization began as a route to the acquisition of mines and so bullion, but it broadened over time into a quest for sources of raw materials for, and captive demand for finished goods from, the mother country, and into control of trade. It had even extended to include trade in slaves, which Smith roundly condemns, as we have noted. Chartered companies such as the East India Company had extracted exclusive privileges and trading monopolies, and had assumed sovereignty over entire countries by force of war. Parts of India, for example, had been rich, civilized and prosperous before the arrival of the East India Company. Yet the Company's restrictions on the rice trade had helped turn a shortage into a famine.

The mercantile system and its flawed assumptions about trade and prosperity had thus lain at the root of Britain's imperial ambitions—so much so as to be a principal cause of the American war then under way. In the American and West Indian colonies, in Smith's later words, 'A great empire has been established for the sole purpose of raising up a nation of customers, who should be obliged to buy, from the shops of our different producers, all the goods with which these could supply them.' The roots of the Seven Years War, similarly, lay in colonial expansion, which had created 'the whole expense of the late war', the overall result of which had been a catastrophic increase in debt, far above anything hitherto known in Britain; indeed escalating public debt is itself a by-product of the 'commercial system'. And the ultimate cause? 'It cannot be very difficult to determine who have been the contrivers of this whole mercantile system; not the consumers, we may believe, whose interest has been entirely neglected; but the producers, whose interest has been so carefully attended to; and among this latter class, our merchants and manufacturers have been by far the principal architects.'

Thus, whatever its apparent allure, the entire mercantile system was in fact utterly misguided and counter-productive. In reality 'Nothing . . . can be more absurd than this whole doctrine of the balance of trade.' Trade was not a zero-sum game in which each nation could gain only by beggaring its neighbour, as the mercantilists imagined. On the contrary, such a view was not merely individually unwise but collectively incoherent. There could never be a trading system of any kind in which every country ran a positive balance of trade. Indeed, it seemed that some societies—notably, the American colonies—could run a negative balance for decades while flourishing for other reasons. Rather than fixating on the balance of trade, there was far more to be gained from placing trade with other major nations and even France, Britain's historic enemy, on a rational economic basis.

What was that basis? Smith never sets out his own alternative to the agricultural and mercantile systems in any detail, not least because as a 'system of liberty' it has and can have no final settled form. Yet it is fairly clear what he has in mind. 'All systems, either of preference or of restraint, therefore, being thus completely taken away, the obvious and simple system of natural liberty establishes itself of its own accord.' This encompasses principles of freedom in four great areas of human life: freedom of occupation or employment, of ownership of land, of internal commerce and of foreign trade. In such a system, individuals should be left free to pursue their own commercial interests in competition with others. Commercial privileges and legal monopolies, duties, prohibitions and bounties should be curtailed or abolished. Britain's self-enforced monopoly of trade with its colonies should be relaxed, and the colonies given political representation in proportion to their contribution to the public finances, balancing taxation with representation. The restrictive laws of primogeniture and entail should be repealed, and restraints on the place and type of a man's occupation done away with. And the sovereign power or state should be entirely relieved of 'the duty of superintending the industry of private people, and of directing it towards the employments most suitable to the interests of the society', a duty for whose proper discharge 'no human wisdom or knowledge could ever be sufficient.'

Nevertheless, there are and must be enabling constraints on individual enterprise. In particular, for such a system of natural liberty to flourish the sovereign must retain just three plain and simple duties, 'of great importance': protection of society itself from foreign foes; protection of its members from each other, via 'an exact administration of justice'; and 'the duty of erecting and maintaining certain public works, and certain public institutions, which it can never be for the interest of any individual, or small number of individuals, to erect and maintain.' These include certain kinds of building projects, a system of local schools, and instruction for those of all ages, especially in positions of public or professional responsibility, in the 'study of science and philosophy' in order to reduce their dependency on religion for guidance in moral matters.

In each of these areas, Smith points out, the impact of commercial society, and the limitations of the mercantile system, could be felt. In the first place, they raised the complexity and expense of war. Wars over trade were international: in the case of the Seven Years War 'more than two-thirds of [its cost] were laid out in distant countries; in Germany, Portugal, America, in the ports of the Mediterranean, in the East and West Indies.' Secondly, the emergence of capital and so private wealth resulted in economic inequality, which in turn demanded strong institutions capable of maintaining and administering justice. Indeed, Smith coolly observes, 'Civil government, so far as it is instituted for the security of property, is in reality instituted for the defence of the rich against the poor, or of those who have some property against those who have none at all.' And, thirdly, commerce itself might demand a measure of public expenditure. Specific commercial initiatives should be funded by specific taxes, or even by 'temporary monopolies' granting the exclusive right to trade a commodity for a limited period. More generally, investment on infrastructure such as roads, canals and bridges should where possible be paid for by charges on those who use them, to inhibit frivolous or economically irrelevant schemes from being built.

But, Smith suggests, unlike the societies of hunters or shepherds, commercial society also places particular strain on the working poor. 'No society can surely be flourishing and happy, of which the greater part of the members are poor and miserable. It is but equity, besides, that they who feed, clothe and lodge the whole body of the people, should have such a share of the produce of their own labour as to be themselves tolerably well fed, clothed, and lodged.' Their well-being is to be judged not by income alone, but also in relative terms, by the capacity to lead a life that is decent and respectable in the eyes of others: 'Under necessaries therefore, I comprehend, not only those things which nature, but those things which the established rules of decency have rendered necessary to the lowest rank of people.' But the poor 'have little time to spare for education', and the very division of labour that creates so much wealth also has the unintended consequence of damaging and dehumanizing them. They often work in highly repetitive manual trades which create 'torpor', 'corruption and degeneracy', and which sap their 'intellectual, social, and martial virtues'. The remedy Smith advances is for government to establish a widespread system of local schools able to provide a basic education to all, paid for partly at public expense and partly through very moderate fees.

Finally, *The Wealth of Nations* addresses issues of public finance, and in particular the nature of the three duties of the sovereign—of defence, the administration of justice and public works—their associated costs, and how those costs are to be funded. Here Smith was unafraid to engage with several of the most contentious issues of the day: on militias, on church funding and on taxation. In each case, what he has to say is important.

Debate had long raged in Scotland over the merits of armed citizen bands or militias as against a standing army, particularly one composed of mercenaries. It fed off a strand of civic republican thought that had long opposed standing armies as instruments of absolute rule, and that contrasted martial virtue with the supposed softness, luxury and corruption of commercial society. In 1698 the ardent republican Andrew Fletcher of Saltoun had published *A Discourse on Government with Relation to Militias,* in which he denounced the precariousness of Scottish liberties, criticized mercenary armies as 'calculated to enslave a nation' and argued that a militia was essential to free government. The argument for militias as a vital expression of nationhood grew after the Act of Union. But it was confronted with a new and brutal reality during the '45 Rebellion, when the Edinburgh militia instantly dispersed rather than fight the Jacobites and highlanders, only for the latter to be destroyed themselves by Cumberland's professional and mercenary army at Culloden.

The prohibition on militias by the English after 1746 was widely read as an affront to Scottish national pride, and the wider argument was taken up again by Adam Ferguson in a pamphlet ten years later entitled *Reflections Previous to the Establishment of a Militia.* Ferguson too was a supporter of the Union, and far from naive about the extraordinary changes taking place in Scotland, or the wider value of commercial society. But he insisted on the importance of militias nonetheless as a means of maintaining martial virtue, fearing that without them the people's attachment to 'a constitution of liberty' would be eroded, and 'a Caesar will arise'.

Adam Smith had a keen ear to both sides of this debate, and to the classical republican and humanist traditions that inspired support for militias. In 1762 he had joined Ferguson as one of the original members of the Militia Club, quickly renamed the Poker Club on the grounds that its purpose was to poke or stir up the flames of support for militias. In his other writings, notably in the *Lectures on Jurisprudence,* Smith often comes across as a supporter of militias. But he is pragmatic, here as elsewhere, about the merits and demerits of the two forms of defence.

In *The Wealth of Nations*, Smith's realism comes through, in an analysis that reflects considerations both of history and of political economy. Yes, important historical precedents spoke against standing armies: 'The standing army of Caesar destroyed the Roman republic. The standing army of Cromwell turned the long parliament out of doors.' But defence was no less subject than other parts of human life to changes in technology and the division of labour. In primitive societies, seasonal wars meant people could leave their fields to fight, and then return without the loss of their livelihoods. However, 'In a more advanced state of society, two different causes contribute to render it altogether impossible that they, who take the field, should maintain themselves at their own expense. Those two causes are, the progress of manufactures, and the improvement in the art of war.'

War demanded specialization:

When the art of war too has gradually grown up to be a very intricate and complicated science, when the event of war ceases to be determined, as in the first ages of society, by a single irregular skirmish or battle, but when the contest is generally spun out through several different campaigns, each of which lasts during the greater part of the year; it becomes universally necessary that the public should maintain those who serve the public in war, at least while they are employed in that service.

Indeed a standing army was the sole way in which modern, commercial societies could defend themselves: 'Such an army, as it can best be maintained by an opulent and civilized nation, so it can alone defend such a nation against the invasion of a poor and barbarous neighbour. It is only by means of a standing army, therefore, that the civilization of any country can be perpetuated, or even preserved for any considerable time.'

Smith remained aware of and supportive of militias; indeed he predicted accurately that 'Should the war in America drag out through another campaign, the American militia may become in every respect a match for [the British] standing army.' Overall, however, 'A militia . . . in whatever manner it may be either disciplined or exercised, must always be much inferior to a well disciplined and well exercised standing army.' But he placed one important caveat on this ambiguous and provocative statement: such a standing army must be not merely well disciplined but 'necessarily connected with the support of the constitution of the state'. Only thus could the insurrection of a Caesar be avoided.

No less controversial was the question of church funding. In his *History of England* David Hume had made a highly provocative argument for established churches. At first, he says, it might seem wise for government to encourage the funding of churches through private donations rather than state subsidy: 'But if we consider the matter more closely, we shall find, that this interested diligence of the clergy is what every wise legislator will study to prevent; because in every religion, except the true, it is highly pernicious . . . in the end, the civil magistrate will find, that he has dearly paid for his pretended frugality.' Much better, Hume says, for the legislator to offer public funding: 'In reality the most decent and advantageous composition, which he can make with the spiritual guides, is to bribe their indolence, by assigning stated salaries to their profession, and rendering it superfluous for them to be farther active, than merely to prevent their flock from straying in quest of new pastures. And in this manner ecclesiastical establishments, though commonly they arose at first from religious views, prove in the end advantageous to the political interests of society.' The effect of church establishments is thus, in effect, to nationalize a major part of religious instruction and practice; and Hume suggests, thereby reduce their vigour and growth.

Smith quotes Hume verbatim, but his position is the direct inverse of Hume's: it highlights the advantages of separating Church and state entirely. His argument ties together a series of familiar Smithian points. Faction is to be avoided wherever possible, but factionalism is often stoked by religion: 'Times of violent religious controversy have generally been times of equally violent political faction.' Successful religious factions seek to enfranchise themselves through corrupting demands for public subsidy. Moderate religious instruction and education can be of genuine benefit to society. Yet in religion, as in education and in commerce, people are affected by the incentives they face. And so: 'If politics had never called in the aid of religion, had the conquering party never adopted the tenets of one sect more than those of another, when it had gained the victory, it would probably have dealt equally and impartially with all the different sects, and have allowed every man to choose his own priest and his own religion as he thought proper.'

Avoiding established churches thus opens the field for competition between churches: 'There would in this case, no doubt, have been a great multitude of religious sects.' But the effect of this, Smith says, would be not to inflame enthusiasm but to tamp it down, because 'Each teacher would no doubt have felt himself under the necessity of making the utmost exertion, and of using every art both to preserve and to increase the number of his disciples. But as every other teacher would have felt himself under the same necessity, the success of no one teacher, or sect of teachers, could have been very great.' Some, perhaps most, churches might remain immoderate in their views, 'yet provided those sects were sufficiently numerous, and each of them consequently too small to disturb the public tranquillity, the excessive zeal of each for its particular tenets could not well be productive of any very hurtful effects.' It is impossible not to read this exchange between Hume and Smith without considering it in relation to established religions and religious extremism in the world today.

Thirdly, Smith turns to issues of taxation. In contrast to the complexity and ramification of many modern tax systems, in eighteenth-century Britain there were only four sources of tax revenue: taxes on land, stamp duties on legal documents and other papers, 'assessed taxes' such as the window tax, and customs and excise duties. Income tax was first introduced by William Pitt in 1799 to help pay for the Napoleonic Wars, abolished after them, and reintroduced by Sir Robert Peel in 1842. Smith's goals are simply to set out what makes for good tax policy, and how the tax system shapes economic incentives more widely.

Particularly worth noting are his four maxims of good taxation. First, 'The subjects of every state ought to contribute towards the support of the government, as nearly as possible, in proportion to their respective abilities; that is, in proportion to the revenue which they respectively enjoy under the protection of the state.' This thought is then unpacked as follows: 'The expense of government to the individuals of a great nation is like the expense of management to the joint tenants of a great estate, who are all obliged to contribute in proportion to their respective interests in the estate. In the observation or neglect of this maxim consists what is called the equality or inequality of taxation.' And there is evidence that at least in certain contexts Smith supported not merely proportional but progressive taxation, in which the tax rate increases with the taxable amount. Certainly he says, in relation to land taxes, 'A tax upon house-rents, therefore, would in general fall heaviest upon the rich; and in this sort of inequality there would not, perhaps, be anything very unreasonable. It is not very unreasonable that the rich should contribute to the public expense, not only in proportion to their revenue, but something more than in that proportion.' This fits with his wider egalitarianism, evident in his views on the poor, on 'savages' and on slavery, as we shall see.

Secondly, Smith says that 'The tax which each individual is bound to pay ought to be certain, and not arbitrary. The time of payment, the manner of payment, the quantity to be paid, ought all to be clear and plain to the contributor, and to every other person.' This prevents unfair targeting of taxation and reduces uncertainty and corruption. Thirdly, 'Every tax ought to be levied at the time, or in the manner, in which it is most likely to be convenient for the contributor to pay it.'

This happens on the spot today with consumable goods, preventing people from being caught out; with bigger amounts, it prudently allows the tax to be levied when the individual has the funds required. Lastly, 'Every tax ought to be so contrived as both to take out and to keep out of the pockets of the people as little as possible over and above what it brings into the public treasury of the state.' For inefficient taxes increase bureaucracy, undermine the incentive to be productive, encourage smuggling and create vexation.

These maxims—of fairness, certainty, convenience and efficiency—have been consulted by tax policy-makers ever since Adam Smith, and they retain their value today.

FROM A STRICTLY COMMERCIAL PERSPECTIVE, SMITH FOUND HIMSELF eclipsed by his friend Edward Gibbon, whose *The Decline and Fall of the Roman Empire*, published the previous month, sold out almost immediately. Nevertheless, *The Wealth of Nations* did well. William Strahan, who published both books, remarked that 'the former is the more popular . . . but the sale of the latter, though not near so rapid, has been much more than I could have expected from a work, that requires much thought and reflection (qualities that do not abound among modern readers).'

Smith must have known that *The Wealth of Nations* was by far the most comprehensive and acute analysis of its kind yet published. But even so he was grateful for the serious reviews of his book when they emerged, remarking drily that 'I have . . . upon the whole been much less abused than I had reason to expect.' But, as with *The Theory of Moral Sentiments*, the earlier and more important reactions came from his friends. On 1 April, scarcely three weeks after publication, Hume wrote to him about the new book, in exuberant style: 'Euge! Belle! Dear Mr Smith, I am much pleased with your performance, and the perusal of it has taken me from a state of great anxiety. It was a work of so much expectation, by yourself, by your friends, and by your public, that I trembled for its appearance; but am now much relieved . . . it has depth and solidity and acuteness, and is so much illustrated by curious facts, that it must at last take the public attention.' Yet Hume was far too fastidious not to mention several areas of friendly disagreement in passing as well, in relation to the prices of produce, seigniorage—the profits made by a government on the issuance of currency—'and a hundred other points . . . fit only to be discussed in conversation'.

Hugh Blair wrote at greater length two days later: 'I expected much, yet I confess you have exceeded my expectations. One writer after another on these subjects did nothing but puzzle me. I despaired at ever arriving at clear ideas. You have given me full and complete satisfaction and my faith is fixed.' Blair was especially complimentary about the style, structure and arrangement of the work, but recommended the addition of an index and 'syllabus' setting out the main heads of the argument; Smith subsequently added the first but not the second. But Blair also cautioned his friend: 'By your two chapters on universities and the church, you have raised up very formidable adversaries who will do all they can to decry you.'

Other friends quickly added their own judgements. The historian William Robertson wrote of the book that 'I had raised my expectations of it very high, but it has gone far beyond what I expected. You have formed into a regular and consistent system one of the most intricate and important parts of political science . . . your book must necessarily become a political or commercial code to all Europe.' Adam Ferguson echoed these sentiments: 'On further acquaintance with your work my esteem is not a little increased. You are surely to reign alone on these subjects, to form the opinions, and I hope to govern at least the coming generations.' But in typically forthright fashion he continued, 'You have provoked, it is true, the church, the universities, and the merchants, against all of whom I am willing to take your part; but you have likewise provoked the militia, and there I must be against you.' Since Ferguson was a former Chaplain to the Black Watch and had been a leading promoter of a Scottish militia, this was perhaps not so surprising. But it underlined the extent to which Smith's views cut against both the Scottish and English establishments.

As he had *The Theory of Moral Sentiments*, it seems to have been Edmund Burke who reviewed the new book anonymously in the *Annual Register*, again in warm and highly perceptive terms: 'The French economical writers undoubtedly have their merits. Within this century they have opened the ways to a rational theory, on the subjects of agriculture, manufactures, and commerce. But no one work has appeared amongst them, nor perhaps could there be collected from the whole together, anything to be compared to the present performance, for sagacity and penetration of mind, extensive use, accurate distinction, just and natural connection, independence of parts. It is a complete analysis of society.' Burke instantly saw that Smith's book was nothing less than a fundamental attempt to draw out the full implications of market exchange and humans' desire 'to better their condition', and so to reorient entirely the public understanding of government and society.

Yet if Smith rejoiced in this acclaim, a much sadder note was sounded by his Scottish friends as well. While he had been working on *The Wealth of Nations* in London, David Hume, his inspiration, friend and intellectual companion of a quarter-century, had gone into a sharp physical decline.

CHAPTER 5

WORKING TO THE END, 1776–1790

I N RETROSPECT, THE SIGNS OF HUME'S LAST ILLNESS MAY HAVE AP-
peared as early as September 1773. But they were well disguised.
Adam Ferguson wrote to Smith then that '[Hume] is in perfect good
health . . . he had a cough, and lost flesh, soon after you went from
home . . . he has still some less flesh than usual, which nobody re-
grets, but in point of health and spirits I never saw him better.' Widely
celebrated, and prosperous in later life thanks to sales of his *History of
England*, Hume had moved the previous year to St Andrew Square in
the New Town in Edinburgh, advertising to his friend Gilbert Elliot
the excellence of his 'old mutton and old claret' and 'sheep-head broth',
and explaining that his previous rooms were 'too small to display my
great talent for cookery, the science to which I intend to addict the
remaining years of my life'.

By early 1776, however, the disease—it may have been cancer of
the bowel—had clearly taken hold. In February Hume wrote, in wry
but mournful reproach, 'By all accounts you intend to settle with us
this spring; yet we hear no more of it . . . I weighed myself t'other day,
and find I have fallen five complete stones [70 pounds, or just under
32 kilos]. If you delay much longer, I shall probably disappear altogether.' A mutual friend, the chemist and physician Dr Joseph Black,
wrote in April to urge Smith to come north, and included a full diagnosis for Smith to pass on to another of Hume's friends, the eminent

doctor and President of the Royal Society, Sir John Pringle: 'He has been declining several years and this in a slow and gradual manner until about a twelve month ago, since which the progress of his disorder has been more rapid.'

Hume travelled to London for a physical examination, and on 23 April he had dinner en route with Smith, who was then heading north to Kirkcaldy and his very elderly mother, at Morpeth in Northumberland. They discussed what had evidently become a rather ticklish issue for Smith. Hume had appointed him as his literary executor in January, and given him a legacy of £200 in his will. Yet it was Hume's earnest desire that his *Dialogues Concerning Natural Religion* should be published after his death. Framed in the style of Plato's Socratic dialogues, the *Dialogues* explored—and in some cases exploded—a wide range of contemporary religious arguments, in particular as to whether belief in God was reliant on revelation or could be grounded in evidence from nature and the temporal world. They were brilliant, amusing and, Smith acknowledged, 'finely written'. But they were also highly provocative, and at the urging of his friends Hume had held them back from publication ever since 1751, merely allowing them to be circulated in manuscript form.

The friends' concern was not a vain one: they knew that Hume had been blocked from professorships at both Glasgow and Edinburgh, and that in 1755–7 serious efforts had been made to have him and Kames formally excommunicated from the Church of Scotland. It is not clear that Hume was in fact an atheist in the strict sense. Although deeply sceptical of much church practice and religious belief, he never formally denied the existence of God and, as we have seen, he seems to have been willing to take the religious oath required for a university appointment. Such dogmatism was not his style, for his abiding goal as a philosopher was to get others to see matters, including religious matters, in a detached, analytic and inevitably conditional way. However, such nice distinctions made little difference in the minds of churchmen of every creed; for them he was an infidel, 'the great infidel' in Boswell's words, whose philosophy undermined morality and true religion.

Smith seems to have had mixed reasons for declining to publish the *Dialogues* posthumously, over and above his own retiring nature and dislike of bother: that they were sure to inflame religious opinion, that he as executor would be held responsible, and that—given the £200 legacy—he might even be thought to have published them for profit. The ailing Hume vainly tried to persuade him that his fears were groundless; but Smith was reluctant, as Hume perceived. In the end nothing came of the matter. Hume gave the task to his nephew instead, and the *Dialogues* were finally published in 1779, arousing relatively little controversy. But the matter hung unhappily over Hume's last weeks, and it may have left a later mark on Smith's last adieu.

Hume took the waters in Bath and Buxton, initially with some success, but he returned to Edinburgh in a still more weakened state, deriving some amusement from the conflicting diagnoses and evident confusion of his many doctors. Smith stayed with him in July, before returning to his mother. No believer in an afterlife, Hume needed no such belief to remain cheerful in the face of death, and his composure was widely noted among those who saw him. Nor had his famously urbane sense of humour left him. On 4 July 1776, while Jefferson, Adams, Franklin and their fellow revolutionaries were meeting in Philadelphia to publish the Declaration of Independence and launch a new nation, Hume gathered Smith and a few other friends around him for one last dinner in company. When Smith complained of the cruelty of the world in taking him from them, Hume replied, 'No, no. Here am I, who have written on all sorts of subjects calculated to excite hostility, moral, political, and religious, and yet I have no enemies; except, indeed, all the Whigs, all the Tories, and all the Christians.'

Evidently in some distress at his friend's decline, Smith put the point pungently in a letter from Kirkcaldy on 14 August to his friend and former student Alexander Wedderburn, 'Poor David Hume is dying very fast, but with great cheerfulness and good humour and with more real resignation to the necessary course of things, than any whining Christian ever died with pretended resignation to the will of God.' His final exchange of letters with Hume, on 22 and 23 August, touched on the vexed question of the *Dialogues*. But Smith was also careful to secure his friend's agreement to publish 'a few lines' of his own alongside a short autobiography which Hume had composed in April. And knowing Hume's end was near, both men opened and closed each letter in terms of the most touching love and friendship, terms which echoed each other, surely deliberately. Smith: 'My dearest friend . . . I ever am, my dearest friend, most affectionately yours'; Hume, in what appears to be his last letter: 'My dearest friend . . . Adieu, my dearest friend'.

DAVID HUME DIED ON 25 AUGUST 1776—AS HIS DOCTOR PUT IT, 'IN such a happy composure of mind that nothing could have made it better'. As Boswell noted, his coffin was conveyed in pouring rain amid a large crowd to the burial ground on Calton Hill, where—much to Smith's displeasure—a grandiose mausoleum was later erected to a design by Robert Adam.

The rest of Smith's year was partly taken up by negotiations with his publisher Strahan, who duly agreed to publish his 'few lines' alongside Hume's *My Own Life* as a pamphlet, without the addition of either the *Dialogues* or any of Hume's letters. *My Own Life* is a brief and highly engaging autobiographical note by Hume, designed as a preface to his writings, which casts his life as a journey from relatively obscure and impecunious origins to wealth and celebrity. As such, it is as much literary performance as history: a 'funeral oration' which underplays his early success—including the famous line that his *Treatise* 'fell dead-born from the press'—and emphasizes his warm and sociable character, and his detached composure in the face of death. 'In spring, 1775, I was struck with a disorder in my bowels, which at first gave me no alarm, but has since, as I apprehend it, become mortal and incurable. I now reckon upon a speedy dissolution. I have suffered very little pain from my disorder; and . . . never suffered a moment's abatement of my spirits . . . I consider, besides, that a man of sixty-five, by dying, cuts off only a few years of infirmities . . . It is difficult to be more detached from life than I am at present.'

Smith was careful to clear his contribution with the family and friends of the dead man, and it took the form of an open *Letter to Strahan* from Kirkcaldy, dated 9 November. The *Letter to Strahan* was a perfectly crafted counterpart to Hume's *Life*. Any bad conscience Smith may have felt over the *Dialogues* is more than assuaged by the pathos and elegance of his tribute to his dead friend. Picking up where Hume leaves off, it recounts his last weeks and days, repeatedly emphasizing his good spirits, while the inclusion of letters from Dr Black helps to chart the final stages of the disease. When its symptoms set in again in late spring, 'He submitted with the utmost cheerfulness, and the most perfect complacency and resignation . . . though he found himself much weaker, yet his cheerfulness never abated.' Hume had been reading the *Dialogues of the Dead* by Lucian, Smith says, and in similar spirit he thought of excuses he might offer to Charon, the boatman who ferries souls over to the underworld of Greek myth: '"Have a little patience, good Charon, I have been endeavouring to open the eyes of the public. If I live a few years longer I may have the satisfaction of seeing the downfall of some of the prevailing systems of superstition." But Charon would then lose all temper and decency. "You loitering rogue, that will not happen these many hundred years. Do you fancy I will grant you a lease for so long a term? Get into the boat this instant . . . "'

The *Letter* closes with a beautiful final encomium:

Thus died our most excellent and never to be forgotten friend; concerning whose philosophical opinions men will, no doubt, judge variously . . . but concerning whose character and conduct there can scarce be a difference of opinion . . . Even in the lowest state of his fortune, his great and necessary frugality never hindered him from exercising, upon proper occasions, acts both of charity and generosity . . . And that gaiety of temper, so agreeable in society, but which is so often accompanied with frivolous and superficial qualities, was in him certainly attended with the most severe application, the most extensive learning, the greatest depth of thought, and a capacity in every respect the most comprehensive. Upon the whole, I have always considered him, both in his lifetime and since his death, as approaching as nearly to the idea of a perfectly wise and virtuous man, as perhaps the nature of human frailty will permit.

There is a striking parallel here with Plato's famous description in the *Phaedo* of the last days of Socrates, who had been condemned to death on charges of impiety and corrupting public morals in ancient Athens. Both show the philosopher on his deathbed, his friends saying goodbye, the progressive final onset of death, their obvious grief contrasting with his own imperturbability, cheerfulness and acceptance. And Smith's letter specifically echoes Plato's final line: 'Such was the end, Echecrates, of our friend; concerning whom I may truly say, that of all the men of his time whom I have known, he was the wisest and justest and best.'

A funeral oration, Lucian's *Dialogues of the Dead*, Charon, the death of Socrates—all of these elements spoke of ancient Greece, not contemporary Scotland; of paganism, not Presbyterianism. Make Hume into a moral paragon, throw in a reference to him as an exemplar of the specifically Christian virtues of frugality, humility and charity, emphasize the absence of any last search for solace, add a joke apparently calling for the overthrow of established religion . . . it is not hard to see how offensive the *Letter to Strahan* would prove to be. And there can be little doubt that Smith deliberately drew on the *Phaedo* for this final tribute, knowing that some readers would note the parallel.

Yet what is astonishing is how little inkling he seems to have had of the likely public reaction when the letter was published in March 1777. No less a figure than George Horne, Vice-Chancellor of Oxford University, rushed out a *Letter* which denounced Hume as seeking to 'banish out of the world every idea of truth and comfort, salvation and immortality, a future state, and the providence and even existence of God', and reprimanded Smith for eulogizing an avowed atheist. Horne's pamphlet was much reprinted, and Smith was vigorously attacked in the press. James Boswell used it as an excuse to end relations altogether with his old friend and formerly much admired teacher. 'Is this not an age of daring effrontery?' he wrote toadyingly to Johnson; 'you might knock Hume's and Smith's heads together, and make vain and ostentatious infidelity exceedingly ridiculous. Would it not be worth your while to crush such noxious weeds in the moral garden?' The ironies of the situation were exquisite: as Smith wrote in 1780 to Andreas Holt, Commissioner of the Danish Board of Trade, 'A single, and, as I thought, a very harmless sheet of paper, which I happened to write concerning the death of our late friend, Mr Hume, brought upon me ten times more abuse than the very violent attack I had made upon the whole commercial system of Great Britain.' Smith can hardly have failed to notice that, despite his qualms, the publication two years later of Hume's *Dialogues* passed without any great controversy. But perhaps his *Letter to Strahan* had already drawn the sting.

The sequence of events says much about both Smith and Hume, but it did not affect Smith's livelihood. In January 1778, at the prompting of the Duke of Buccleuch, he was appointed a Commissioner on the Customs Board in Edinburgh. Given the closeness of the two men, and the Duke's significant powers of patronage, it is not hard to see why Smith accepted the position. Yet it proved to be a fateful choice. For as he later admitted, although the Commissionership was well paid, 'I am occupied four days in every week at the Custom House; during which it is impossible to sit down seriously to any other business: during the other three days too, I am liable to be frequently interrupted by the extraordinary duties of my office.' These were hardly the right conditions for productive intellectual work, let alone for a man with several further books planned or in progress.

But there was much to be said for the new position: it echoed and surpassed his father's appointment as Comptroller of Customs in Kirkcaldy, it provided occupation and company to someone prone to loneliness, and at £600 per annum it paid very well. In his characteristic way, Smith then attempted to give up his pension from Buccleuch, and was politely rebuffed: 'his Grace sent me word by his cashier, to whom I had offered to deliver up his bond, that though I had considered what was fit for my own honour, I had not considered what was fit for his; and that he never would suffer it to be suspected that he had procured an office for his friend, in order to deliver himself from the burden of such an annuity.'

On the strength of his new income Smith moved into Panmure House, a large house just off the Canongate in a well-to-do part of the Old Town. Edinburgh at that time was still in the midst of a wave of new building, which included the draining of the polluted and malodorous North Loch and the construction of a major new bridge connecting the medieval city with the decorous Georgian squares and boulevards of the New Town. But Smith had chosen well. The neighbourhood was central without being too busy, and Canongate Church stood right by the house and so very conveniently as a place of worship for his devout mother. Moreover, it had views across to Calton Hill, was well placed for long walks to the top of Arthur's Seat and yet was situated a very short distance from the Customs House and other official buildings. Margaret Smith and Janet Douglas moved down from Kirkcaldy, and the three of them were soon joined by David Douglas, the nine-year-old son of Smith's cousin Robert Douglas, and later his adopted heir.

Intellectual work was not impossible, but it was unquestionably becoming more difficult as age—Smith was fifty-five in 1778—and the world's business encroached yet further upon him. He had been trying to make progress with a book on the imitative arts at the time of Hume's death. On its face, the question of why and how human tastes differ posed a threat to a science of man: for if tastes differed fundamentally and irreconcilably, then how could there be any kind of rigorous account of the arts? How could there be an objective standard for assessing or criticizing works of art, or an objective explanation of the pleasures afforded by them? This work resulted in two papers that Smith finally gave to the Glasgow Literary Society in 1788, which address these questions in 'the imitative arts', curiously including not merely painting but music and dancing. But interesting though these papers are—and Smith evidently thought they were, since they were spared the bonfire of his unpublished papers at his death—they constitute no more than a fragment of a wider theory. It is notable that the unifying treatment of his other work, the emphasis on sympathy, on exchange, on the impartial spectator, is absent from these essays. This may be one reason why the book never emerged.

Smith also made continuing efforts to spread the gospel of *The Wealth of Nations*. The book had arrived too late to have any impact on policy over the American crisis, and its key political recommendation—to have American representation in the British Parliament—struck many people as impractical. It did not make an appearance itself in parliamentary proceedings until November 1783, and even that was in a speech by Charles James Fox, who described it as 'an excellent book' although, as John Rae noted, he 'was neither an admirer of the book, nor a believer in its principles, nor a lover of its subject'. Such misdirection was quite in character for Fox. Still more characteristically—and setting the pattern for future generations—he later admitted that he had never read the book at all.

But in other quarters *The Wealth of Nations* was increasingly recognized as a treasure-trove of economic insight. Smith seems to have given advice himself to Lord North on tax policy in 1777, as he was thanked in the Prime Minister's budget speech. In February 1778, four months after the decisive American victory at Saratoga, he submitted to Wedderburn a memorandum now known as 'Thoughts on the State of the Contest with America'. The memorandum analysed in fairly pitiless terms four different possible outcomes to the conflict: renewed British control and military government of the colonies; total emancipation; restoration of the old colonial system; and British control of some of the colonies, the others being free. Smith extended his earlier arguments with a call for a consolidating union by treaty, local taxation being matched by American representation at Westminster. He conceded without irony that this was 'not very probable at present', and few would have disagreed. But, as the memorandum hinted, there were no good options left for the British. And Smith's views on the evils of war and their ruinous effect on trade were only reinforced in September 1779 when a French squadron led by the American John Paul Jones nearly landed troops at Leith, the port of Edinburgh, and then destroyed the frigate *Serapis*, escorting a convoy of merchantmen, off Flamborough Head.

Smith's acquaintance Henry Dundas had been Lord Advocate of Scotland since 1775, and was in the process of establishing a vice-like grip over Scottish politics which eclipsed even that of Argyll. Dundas had become a convert to many of the doctrines of *The Wealth of Nations*—though not, alas, to the abolition of slavery, which as a secretary of state he obstructed in the 1790s—and he may have influenced his close friend the younger William Pitt in regard to them. In 1779 he solicited Smith's advice directly on the topic of free trade for Ireland. Irish trade had long laboured under the imposition of the Navigation Acts, despite the efforts of Burke and a few others to highlight their punitive effect. But Irish demands for relief had assumed new potency after the American revolution, with calls for political independence and a pending threat of invasion by France. The big question was whether Britain and Ireland should form a union, as England and Scotland had in 1707. There was significant opposition from commercial interests, but Dundas, ever the politician, was calculating the odds and sanguine about the prospect: 'There is trade enough in the world for the industry of Britain and Ireland . . . an union would be best if it can be accomplished, if not the Irish Parliament must be managed by the proper distribution of the loaves and the fishes.'

For his part, Smith was categorical in support of a union with Ireland, on economic and moral grounds: 'To crush the industry of so great and so fine a province . . . in order to favour the monopoly of some particular towns in Scotland or England, is equally unjust and impolitic.' Reviewing the options, he made clear his preference for Irish trade to be as free as possible, including with the colonies: 'Nothing, in my opinion, would be more highly advantageous to both countries than this mutual freedom of trade.' He elaborated on these views a few days later to Lord Carlisle, the President of the Board of Trade, saying, 'A very slender interest of our own manufacturers is the foundation of all these unjust and oppressive restraints . . . I never believed that the monopoly of our plantation trade was really advantageous to Great Britain . . . [and] the competition of Irish goods in the British market might . . . break down that monopoly which we have most absurdly granted to the greater part of our workmen against ourselves.' Quite consistently and properly, Smith argued strongly in private at the highest levels for the abolition of unreasonable duties and prohibitions, even as he found himself having to impose some of the same by law through the Customs Board. And to cap it off, all these laws were, he thought, an invitation to personal dishonesty and hypocrisy, as well as smuggling: 'About a week after I was made a Commissioner . . . I found, to my great astonishment, that I had scarcely a stock, a cravat, a pair of ruffles, or a pocket handkerchief which was not prohibited to be worn or used in Great Britain. I wished to set an example and burnt them all.' Nothing, it seems, could better illustrate the foolishness and futility of the mercantile system, or Smith's own sense of duty.

Smith spent the last twelve years of his life largely in Edinburgh. Though not an especially gregarious man, he clearly enjoyed life in the city. Among other things, he co-founded yet another society, the

Oyster Club—named, it appears, after the mollusc, a popular dish then as now—with his friends Joseph Black, Hume's physician at the end, and James Hutton, the man who first established geology as a science. The club met on Friday nights in the Grassmarket. It was no seminary of debauch, since all three men were bachelors of austere personal habit, but it quickly attracted a clutch of Enlightenment literati. As Hutton's biographer, the mathematician John Playfair, recounted, 'round them was soon formed a knot of those who knew how to value the familiar and social converse of these illustrious men.' The same was true of the Royal Society of Edinburgh, which in 1783 became the chartered successor to the Philosophical Society which Smith had originally joined in 1752. And it was doubtless true too of Smith's private Sunday-night suppers at Panmure House, which became something of an Edinburgh institution. Dugald Stewart remarked that 'in the society of his friends, he had no disposition to form those qualified conclusions that we admire in his writings; and he generally contented himself with a bold and masterly sketch of the object, from the first point of view in which his temper, or his fancy, presented it.' The picture is of a man quite at ease with his friends.

NEVERTHELESS, THERE REMAINED CONSIDERABLE WORK TO BE DONE, in particular in preparing a heavily revised new, third edition of *The Wealth of Nations*. There had been a second edition in 1778, with numerous small changes, but the third was to prove a much more ambitious undertaking. The most powerful and detailed early criticisms of the book had come in an open letter from Thomas Pownall MP. Pownall was a man of wide experience, who had served in America for six years, latterly as Governor of Massachusetts Bay. He was, therefore, quite familiar with the realities of colonial trade. He described the book glowingly in Newtonian terms as 'A system, which might fix some first principles in the most important of sciences, the knowledge of the human community and its operations. That might become *principia* to the knowledge of politic operations; as mathematics are to mechanics, astronomy and the other sciences.' Even so, he faulted Smith's attack on colonial monopolies; questioned his command of detail, such as on rates of return from the colonies; and highlighted a supposed tendency to treat merely probable and derived claims as though they were certain and based on fact. Among other things, the new edition was intended to address these and other criticisms. As Smith said to Strahan, 'This edition will probably see me out and I should therefore choose to leave it behind me as perfect as I can make it.'

In early 1782 Smith took a four-month leave of absence in London, mainly to work on the new edition, though he also did some customs business. It was a politically pregnant moment for him to be in the capital. The American war had ended the previous October in an ignominious surrender by Cornwallis at Yorktown, and in March 1782 Lord North was finally forced to resign on a motion of No Confidence. After sixteen years out of office the Marquis of Rockingham's group of Whigs, arguably the first modern political party and with Burke at its intellectual and organizational centre, finally returned to power. But they had a desperately fragile base of political support. The government had to be reconstructed under Lord Shelburne following Rockingham's sudden death in July, and Shelburne was in turn evicted by Charles James Fox and Lord North, erstwhile enemies acting in coalition, in April 1783. It seemed the political merry-go-round had returned.

In the intimate world of eighteenth-century politics, Smith stood as a friend of both North and Shelburne—Shelburne said that he owed to a coach journey with Smith in 1761 'the difference between light and darkness through the best part of my life'—as well as Dundas. As a member of Dr Johnson's Club he dined alongside Fox and Burke. So he was well connected across the political spectrum. His relationship with Burke, now of almost twenty-five years, had become a close one. Smith must have suspected that Burke lay behind the admiring reviews his books had received in the *Annual Register*, and he had sent letters of sympathy and admiration when Burke resigned as Paymaster-General rather than serve under Shelburne. Smith's reported line about Burke being the only man who thought on economic subjects as he did may be apocryphal, and there were clear points of disagreement, but it correctly hints at the intellectual sympathy between the two men.

With the arrival of the Fox–North Coalition, Burke was again back in post and, as the Commons' leading expert on India, he was determined to restrain, through committee reports and indeed by Act of Parliament, what he saw as the undue influence of the East India Company overseas. Smith thus had much clearer insight into the history of the Company in India and its effects on colonial trade. This gave further inspiration to his revisions to *The Wealth of Nations*, in which he planned to include 'a short history and, I presume, a full exposition of the absurdity and hurtfulness of almost all our chartered trading companies'.

The revisions dragged on through 1783. Back in Edinburgh, Smith bewailed his many book purchases in London, for 'the amusement I found in reading and diverting myself with them debauched me from my proper business.' He resumed work at the Customs House and awaited information on the financial effects of bounties from the Treasury. He planned another trip to London, but this was aborted when he decided to give the £200 required for it to a needy Welsh nephew instead. And he watched from afar as Fox's India Bill, which Burke had drafted to curb and reconstruct the East India Company, passed triumphantly through the Commons, only for it to be destroyed by the King's unconstitutional machinations in the Lords, bringing down the coalition government with it. On 20 December 1783 William Pitt kissed hands as the new Prime Minister, at the tender age of twenty-four. He would remain in office for the next eighteen years.

The inevitable general election opened on 30 March 1784, and after just a few days' polling it was clear that Pitt would be returned to office in a landslide. The previous November Burke had been appointed to a two-year term as Lord Rector of Glasgow University. Although politically despondent, he used the election period to visit Smith for ten days or so in early April, over Easter. After meeting some of Smith's notable Edinburgh friends, the two men travelled over to Glasgow for Burke's installation as Rector, and then to see Loch Lomond. It must have been a welcome interlude.

But then on 23 May Smith's mother died. Her death was hardly unexpected, for Margaret Smith had lived to a great age, but it was nevertheless a terrible blow. She had raised him as a widowed mother, had cared for him over long periods of adulthood and kept house for him, latterly with Janet Douglas. On and off, mother and son had shared a house over nearly sixty-one years. Little wonder, then, that he was distraught. As he wrote to Strahan in June:

> Though the death of a person in the ninetieth year of her age was no doubt an event most agreeable to the course of nature; and, therefore, to be foreseen and prepared for; yet I must say to you, what I have said to other people, that the final separation from a person who certainly loved me more than any other person ever did or ever will love me; and whom I certainly loved and respected more than I shall ever love or respect any other person, I cannot help feeling, even at this hour, as a very heavy stroke upon me.

It evidently took Smith some time to recover from the shock. But in November 1784, having been further delayed by Strahan in hope of a bigger sale once Parliament had reconvened, the third edition of *The Wealth of Nations*, and a separate volume of *Additions and Corrections* to the first and second editions, were finally published. The earlier editions had built Smith's reputation considerably, and the loss of the American colonies, scandals at the East India Company, escalating unrest in Ireland and political upheaval at Westminster undoubtedly boosted public interest in what was increasingly being seen as a landmark in political economy. Commercially, the new edition was squarely aimed at this growing market, and it was printed in the smaller octavo size and priced more affordably.

There were two more editions during Smith's lifetime, but neither made more than small changes. Those for the third edition, however, ran to some 24,000 words, including the index. They contained new pages on the malign effects of bounties and inveighing against restrictions on trade with France. But the centrepiece was Smith's last and most vigorous attack on the mercantile system, much filled out by the evidence of statutes showing just how far Parliament itself had been co-opted by the merchants' interests. He hammered home his case with a long inventory and discussion of prohibitions, bounties and duties on linen, wool and a host of other items. This was supplemented with a history and analysis of the chartered companies, culminating in a direct assault on the East India Company. He said, 'By a perpetual monopoly, all the other subjects of the state are taxed very absurdly in two different ways: first, by the high price of goods, which, in the case of a free trade, they could buy much cheaper; and, secondly, by their total exclusion from a branch of business which it might be both convenient and profitable for many of them to carry on.' The solution was to remove that monopoly, 'But in this situation, the superior vigilance and attention of private adventurers would, in all probability, soon make [the Company] weary of the trade.'

Smith was now at the height of his fame. It was reported that the Prime Minister as well as Dundas had become converts to 'the system of natural liberty', and there was a distinct positive shift in parliamentary opinion. Pitt had read *The Wealth of Nations* and discussed its ideas with Smith, and while others deserve credit for the wider change of mood as well—notably Josiah Tucker, who was the Dean of Gloucester and a vociferous advocate of free trade—the new administration's emphasis on liberalization was evident.

Among other things, Pitt pushed for a single free-trade area with Ireland in 1785, only for this to be rejected by the Irish on political grounds; he secured a treaty with France in 1786 which lifted duties and opened up new markets on both sides; and his great domestic reforms of February 1787 swept away a complex mass of duties, then payable into 103 different government accounts, and created a single Consolidated Fund. In March 1787, when Smith was struggling with illness, Dundas wrote to him with what must have been a very pleasing invitation: 'I am glad you have got vacation. Mr Pitt, Mr Grenville and your humble servant are clearly of opinion you cannot spend it so well as here. The weather is fine, my villa at Wimbledon a most comfortable healthy place. You shall have a comfortable room and as the business is much relaxed we shall have time to discuss all your books with you every evening.'

This may have been the occasion of a famous anecdote told by John Rae:

> No-one in London therefore was more interested to meet Smith than the young minister who was carrying the economist's principles out so extensively in practical legislation. They met repeatedly, but they met on one occasion, of which recollection has been preserved, at Dundas's house on Wimbledon Green—Addington, Wilberforce, and Grenville being also of the company; and it is said that when Smith, who was one of the last guests to arrive, entered the room, the whole company rose from their seats to receive him and remained standing. 'Be seated, gentlemen,' said Smith. 'No,' replied Pitt, 'we will stand till you are first seated, for we are all your scholars.'

SMITH'S CLOSE FRIEND AND PUBLISHER WILLIAM STRAHAN DIED IN July 1785. Despite his advancing age, Smith had not given up hope of completing the other great works that were forming themselves in his mind, but his priority was to issue a new and revised edition of *The Theory of Moral Sentiments*, as he had done with *The Wealth of Nations*. The Duc de La Rochefoucauld had written to object to the coupling in the *Theory* of the despised name of Mandeville with that of his ancestor, the author of the celebrated maxims. Writing to reassure the Duc in November 1785, Smith said:

> I have not forgot what I promised to your Grace in an edition of the 'Theory of Moral Sentiments', which I hope to execute before the end of the ensuing winter. I have likewise two other great works upon the anvil; the one is a sort of philosophical history of all the different branches of literature, of philosophy, poetry and eloquence; the other is a sort of theory and history of law and government. The materials of both are in a great measure collected, and some part of both is put into tolerable good order. But the indolence of old age, though I struggle violently against it, I feel coming fast upon me, and whether I shall ever be able to finish either is extremely uncertain.

Presumably, as we have seen, the projected work on government was to derive from his *Lectures on Jurisprudence*. But of the 'philosophical history' we know nothing, though it is not hard to see Smith's surviving lectures on rhetoric and essays on the imitative arts and the history of different sciences as offshoots.

Smith's own health was now clearly deteriorating. He had been extremely diligent in his attendance at the Customs House. But after suffering through the winter with what was described as a 'chronic obstruction in his bowels', by early 1787 he had recovered enough to take a six-month leave of absence in which he travelled to London, in part for medical advice and treatment. In March he wrote to his friend and fellow Snell Exhibitioner John Douglas, Bishop of Carlisle, referring only half humorously to ancient astrological theories of health, in which sixty-three was deemed a critical year: 'This year I am in my grand climacteric; and the state of my health has been a good deal worse than usual. I am getting better and better, however, every day; and I begin to flatter myself that, with good pilotage, I shall be able to weather this dangerous promontory of human life; after which, I hope to sail in smooth water for the remainder of my days.'

In London he was treated by John Hunter, surgeon to the King, and made a partial recovery. In June a friend of Gibbon's reported seeing him 'very weak and not far from the end of his career . . . [I] fear that the machine is nearly worn out.' But it was at about this time that James Tassie, a Scottish jeweller in London, modelled two variants of a medallion showing Smith in profile, one in contemporary dress and wig, the other bare-headed and bare-shouldered like a Roman. Dugald Stewart, who knew Smith personally, said the medallion 'conveys an exact idea of his profile, and of the general expression of his countenance'. Dated 1787, it appears to be the only portrait for which Smith ever sat. In each version, despite his wavering health, he appears quite full of face.

Having returned to Edinburgh, by November Smith was well enough to accept the Rectorship of Glasgow University, much to his delight. He wrote to the Principal, Dr Archibald Davidson, 'No preferment could have given me so much real satisfaction. No man can owe greater obligations to a Society than I do to the University of Glasgow . . . and now, after three and twenty years absence, to be remembered in so very agreeable manner by my old friends and protectors gives me a heartfelt joy which I cannot easily express to you.'

Meanwhile, his work with the new edition of *The Theory of Moral Sentiments* ground on. First published in 1759, the *Theory* had been materially revised for its second edition in 1761, and had then run through three further editions without major changes. This sixth edition, however, was a different matter altogether. In writing to La Rochefoucauld, Smith had expressed his hope of completing the revisions in early 1786, before turning his attention to 'the two other great works upon the anvil'. By 1788, however, he was forced to admit partial defeat. In a letter of 15 March to Thomas Cadell, who was to publish the work in London, he wrote, 'As I consider my tenure of this life as extremely precarious, and am very uncertain whether I shall live to finish several other works which I have projected and in which I have made some progress, the best thing, I think, I can do is to leave those I have already published in the best and most perfect state behind me.' He had taken a third leave of absence from the Customs House, this time for four months, to make the necessary additions and corrections, but 'I am a slow a very slow workman, who do and undo everything I write at least half a dozen of times before I can be tolerably pleased with it.'

Even apart from all the other recent demands on his time, the new materials themselves were proving more arduous than anticipated. The changes to *The Wealth of Nations* had been time-consuming but fairly straightforward, for on the whole they were extensions to the book's core of leading ideas based on new research. Those to the *Theory*, however, were not just longer still—amounting to almost a third of the work—but much more intellectually demanding. As befitted nearly three decades of reading and reflection, they made important changes to the theory itself, and so required Smith to try to think through the whole thing once again. One of the editors of the authoritative Glasgow edition has described what resulted as 'almost a new book'.

In the event the revisions were not complete till November 1789. They disconnected La Rochefoucauld from Mandeville, as Smith had promised, and included new paragraphs on 'the corruption of moral sentiments' and on the idea of praiseworthiness and the limits of conscience; and they enlarged Smith's closing remarks about different systems of moral philosophy. But the greatest single change was the insertion of an entirely new Part VI, 'Of the Character of Virtue', which explored how social interaction and law helped to shape moral character, and the nature of the duties owed to family, nation and the world as a whole. Smith's moral philosophy is highly eclectic—he is happy to take ideas from diverse traditions—but the new materials

have a strongly Stoic feel about them, in their emphasis on the benevolence of the created order, and on the virtues of prudence, self-
command and duty. Their style is also rather different: less rhetorical,
less addicted to homely examples and with less of the air of the
lecture-hall, more free flowing and readable, and thus closer to that
of *The Wealth of Nations*. And, as one might expect, there is a distinct
sense of the philosopher nearing the end of his life, who wishes to
share his wisdom.

In the *Theory*, Smith had argued that moral values and standards
derive not from divine revelation or an innate 'inner sense'. Rather,
they are created by human interaction itself. Humans naturally identify with each other imaginatively; they see each other's actions, and
by means of what Smith calls sympathy they come to see themselves
as judgeable, and so to judge their own conduct. But, he made clear,
something else is needed to make these norms more than merely reflections of public opinion or conventional wisdom, and that is the
idea of an 'impartial spectator', the 'cool' and 'indifferent' bystander
who can see matters objectively, without bias and the distortions of
perspective.

Even so, however, by the time of the sixth edition Smith seems
to have felt that there was more to be said about why and how any
such norms could be genuinely moral ones, as opposed to mere reflections of public opinion. His solution is twofold. First, he acknowledges
that public opinion can be morally mistaken, and indeed damaging.
In such cases sympathy can lead people astray: 'This disposition to
admire, and almost to worship, the rich and the powerful, and to
despise, or, at least, to neglect persons of poor and mean condition,
though necessary both to establish and to maintain the distinction of
ranks and the order of society, is, at the same time, the great and most
universal cause of the corruption of our moral sentiments.' The social
norms generated through sympathy and the judgements of the impartial spectator can have both positive and negative effects, he argues;
as a source of recognition and consent they can support the ordered

structure on which society relies, but the encouragement they can offer for people to exalt the powerful and despise the weak is morally corrupting.

But Smith offers one important further vindication of his account of moral norms. This is his claim that humans do not merely seek praise and shun blame, they seek to be worthy of praise, and not of blame: 'Man naturally desires, not only to be loved, but to be lovely; or to be that thing which is the natural and proper object of love. He naturally dreads, not only to be hated, but to be hateful; or to be that thing which is the natural and proper object of hatred. He desires, not only praise, but praiseworthiness; or to be that thing which, though it should be praised by nobody, is, however, the natural and proper object of praise.'

At first glance this argument may seem circular: what can 'lovely' here mean if not 'morally worthy of love'? And if it means that, then hasn't Smith smuggled a moral judgement into his supposedly naturalistic and scientific account? No: the best evidence for what is lovely is that people find it so. Smith's view appears to be that we grasp what it is to be praiseworthy by comparing our introspective understanding of our own actions with the praise or no of others for them. Once we have grasped it, we do not require praise in order to retain that understanding, or the desire to be worthy of praise. And we can use our knowledge of what is praiseworthy to assess our own motivations 'from the inside' as moral agents, and to see what is wrong about exalting the powerful and despising the weak. His account thus arguably remains a naturalistic one.

A particularly striking feature of the new Part VI is how Smith extends his reflections on moral character and duties into a commentary on different societies and styles of political leadership. He is careful to distinguish love of country from love of mankind.

We do not love our country merely as a part of the great society of mankind: we love it for its own sake, and independently of any such consideration. That wisdom which contrived the system of human affections, as well as that of every other part of nature, seems to have judged that the interest of the great society of mankind would be best promoted by directing the principal attention of each individual to that particular portion of it, which was most within the sphere both of his abilities and of his understanding.

Burke expressed a very similar thought in his almost exactly contemporary *Reflections on the Revolution in France* (1790): 'To be attached to the subdivision, to love the little platoon we belong to in society, is the first principle (the germ as it were) of public affections. It is the first link in the series by which we proceed towards a love to our country, and to mankind.' One may see in both these reflections an empirical assault on the kind of abstract universalism that after Kant has been taken as the hallmark of moral theory.

For his part, Smith acknowledges the moral supremacy of 'the interest of that great society of all sensible and intelligent beings, of which God himself is the immediate administrator and director'. But this does not mean that humans should ignore their more mundane duties from a preoccupation with universal ideas or ideals: 'To man is allotted a much humbler department, but one much more suitable to the weakness of his powers, and to the narrowness of his comprehension; the care of his own happiness, of that of his family, his friends, his country: that he is occupied in contemplating the more sublime, can never be an excuse for his neglecting the more humble department.' There can be no escape from the duties of the moment into the timeless abstractions of philosophy.

Sometimes a country can come under threat from what Smith calls 'public discontent, faction and disorder', and here both his language and thought are very Burkean. The wisdom of the great political leader lies in balancing the claims of existing authority and 'the more daring, but often dangerous spirit of innovation'. But there is special danger, he argues, in giving power to the 'man of system'—the autocrat who insists on imposing some idealized plan on society—for 'amidst the turbulence and disorder of faction, a certain spirit of system is apt to mix itself with that public spirit which is founded upon the love of humanity.' This 'spirit of system' can infect and inflame moderate public opinion. 'The leaders of the discontented party seldom fail to hold out some plausible plan of reformation . . . They often propose, upon this account, to new-model the constitution, and to alter, in some of its most essential parts, that system of government under which the subjects of a great empire have enjoyed, perhaps, peace, security, and even glory, during the course of several centuries together.' As with 'prodigals and projectors' in business, so with the 'man of system' in politics.

But this spirit of innovation, Smith insists, is mistaken: not merely because it sacrifices those benefits of peace and security, but because the new model constitution often fails to achieve what was first desired. 'The violence of the party, refusing all palliatives, all temperaments, all reasonable accommodations, by requiring too much frequently obtains nothing; and those inconveniencies and distresses which, with a little moderation, might in a great measure have been removed and relieved, are left altogether without the hope of a remedy.' As in political economy, human action can have unanticipated consequences, while revolutionary zeal can swamp genuine reform.

Smith reserves his harshest words for those 'sovereign princes' who are 'of all political speculators . . . by far the most dangerous'. This is because they unite absolute power to the 'spirit of system'. But political leaders can fall far short of absolutism and still be disastrous, if such a spirit takes hold: 'The man of system . . . is apt to be very wise in his own conceit; and is often so enamoured with the supposed beauty of his own ideal plan of government, that he cannot suffer the smallest deviation from any part of it . . . He seems to imagine that he can arrange the different members of a great society with as much ease as the hand arranges the different pieces upon a chess-board.' But this geometrical dogma—the use of system as a means of direct control—mistakes both the nature of society and the nature of governing. 'He does not consider that the pieces upon the chess-board have no other principle of motion besides that which the hand impresses upon them; but that, in the great chess-board of human society, every single piece has a principle of motion of its own, altogether different from that which the legislature might choose to impress upon it.' This 'idea of the perfection of policy and law' fails to grasp the nature and necessity of human freedom, and under its influence 'the society must be at all times in the highest degree of disorder.' Again, there are close parallels here with the language of Burke, notably in the *Reflections*.

In attacking the mercantile system, *The Wealth of Nations* had not shrunk from engaging with current events in the form of the war in America, and it is hard not to read these revisions to *The Theory of Moral Sentiments* against the backdrop of the French Revolution. On 18 November 1789 Smith wrote to Cadell to say that the 'book is now at last perfectly finished to the very last sentence'. By that time France was in uproar. Financially, the country was indebted to the point of bankruptcy. Its tax system was regressive, narrow and unjust, yet incapable of reform. Politically, it was in crisis, following the abolition of the Estates-General in June and the storming of the Bastille in July. The revolutionaries had quickly moved to destroy the power of the Church and the nobility. Local militias were being formed amid widespread unrest. In October an attempt had been made on the life of Marie Antoinette, when the royal family was forcibly moved from Versailles to Paris.

All this would have been well known to Smith. He understood the inadequacies of the French tax system well from personal experience, he was in touch by letter with opinion in France, and news from that country was quickly relayed to Edinburgh. Smith's words about the 'man of system' might properly be applied to the 'enlightened despots' of the time, Frederick the Great of Prussia and Catherine the Great of Russia; and as a philosopher Smith offered, and doubtless meant to offer, a general analysis. Did he intend these remarks to have special relevance to France? The matter is much contested, though he must have had at least the Physiocrats in mind. What we can say with certainty is that the words bear this interpretation; that they convey his fully considered thoughts; that between November 1789 and publication of the sixth edition in the following May, despite failing health, Smith had the opportunity to reflect and make final changes; and that he did not do so. We can also be certain that he would have despised the revolution's successive plunges into mob rule, organized terror and war. As he wrote at the time, 'Of all the corrupters of moral sentiments . . . faction and fanaticism have always been by far the greatest.'

SMITH WAS NOW AT THAT STAGE OF LIFE WHERE DEATH SEEMS EVERY-where. His cousin and housekeeper Janet Douglas had passed away in the autumn of 1788. As with Hume, he admired her fortitude at the end: '[She] seems to die with satisfaction and contentment, happy in the life that she has spent, and very well pleased with the lot that has fallen to her, and without the slightest fear or anxiety about the change she expects so soon to undergo.' But the mask slipped slightly as he testified to another friend of her importance to him: 'Her humour and raillery are the same as usual. She will leave me one of the most destitute and helpless men in Scotland.'

February 1790 saw the death of Smith's lifelong friend William Cullen, Professor of Medicine in Glasgow, and later Edinburgh. Writing to his son, Smith apologized in abject terms for his inability to attend the funeral: 'A stomach complaint has weakened me so much that I can bear no fatigue, not even that of walking from my own house to the Custom House.' As late as May he entertained hopes of a visit to London, 'But my progress to recovery is so very slow, and so often interrupted by violent relapses that the probability of my being able to execute that journey becomes every day more doubtful.' Neverthless he was, a friend noted, 'perfectly patient and resigned'.

But, as the *Letter to Strahan* made clear, a philosopher's death was not merely a matter of personal equanimity, and in his declining years Smith took care to leave life as far as possible on the right terms. In an age when nepotism was both common and expected, he regularly sought to advance the interests of younger friends and family with supportive letters and money—though not, it seems, beyond their merits. He also appears to have given away substantial sums privately—according to Dugald Stewart, 'on a scale much beyond what might have been expected from his fortune'—abiding by the maxim that anonymous donation is the most virtuous form of charity. Perhaps as a result, his final estate was small.

His books were in as fit a state as he could place them, but there remained his personal papers. Smith had named his distinguished friends and fellow Oyster-clubbers Joseph Black and James Hutton as his literary executors, and it was a judicious pairing: in Playfair's words, 'Dr Black hated nothing so much as error, and Dr Hutton nothing so much as ignorance. The one was always afraid of going beyond the truth, and the other of not reaching it.' How they must have agonized over Smith's repeated instructions to destroy all but a few of his manuscripts! The two men had promised they would, but they temporized. As the end approached, however, Smith made clear he was not to be fobbed off. At his direct insistence on 11 July all barring 'some detached papers' were burned, including, it seems, the 'eighteen thin paper folio books' which Smith had previously mentioned to Hume. Several essays and Smith's beloved *History of Astronomy* were excepted, but it appears his lectures on rhetoric and natural religion, his work on jurisprudence and the drafts of the 'philosophical history' which he mentioned to La Rochefoucauld were lost to the flames. To Dugald Stewart, who knew him well, 'He seems to have wished, that no materials should remain for his biographers, but what were furnished by the lasting monuments of his genius, and the exemplary worth of his private life.' To modern readers accustomed to a more confessional style of dying, Smith's actions may seem perverse, and the loss nothing other than an intellectual calamity.

Adam Smith died on Saturday, 17 July 1790, aged sixty-seven. His last recorded words, uttered to friends as he retired to bed before dinner a few days earlier, were 'I believe we must adjourn this meeting to some other place.' He was buried five days later in the Canongate churchyard, a few dozen yards from Panmure House, under a plain stone listing his two great published works. Almost all his property and possessions, including his books, were left to his nephew and heir, David Douglas.

What, all in all, can we say about Smith's character and personality? Among his many biographers the first, and the only one to know Smith personally, was Dugald Stewart. He gives us the picture of a professor and a philosopher 'eminently distinguished . . . [by] the originality and comprehensiveness of his views; the extent, the variety, and the correctness of his information; the inexhaustible fertility of his invention; and the ornaments which his rich and beautiful imagination had borrowed from classical culture'. There were many testimonials to his absent-mindedness, to 'peculiarities, both in his manners, and in his intellectual habits', which made him 'certainly not fitted for the general commerce of the world, or for the business of active life'. Yet this underplays Smith's record as an academic administrator at Glasgow, as we have noted, and his effectiveness as a Commissioner of Customs in the distinctly worldly areas of the collection of duties and the prevention and prosecution of smuggling.

From other sources we can fill out the picture of Smith a little further. According to his friend the printer and antiquarian William Smellie, 'In stature he somewhat exceeded the ordinary size; and his countenance was manly and agreeable.' In character, he was a man with an unwavering sense of the paramount importance of the public good, and an unwavering desire to think matters out for himself. Intellectually fastidious to a degree, and eclectic in his philosophical views, he combined a Stoic sense of virtue, personal duty and the particular importance of self-command with a Presbyterian commitment to education and an informed public realm. He was a Scot, and fully persuaded of the superiority of Scottish educational institutions, yet an habitué of London and well aware of the social and economic value to Scotland of the Union of 1707. Remarkably egalitarian both in thought and practice, he appears to have disliked hierarchy in any form.

Smith was generous to those in need and generally careful in discharging his debts, including to thinkers he admired such as Hume, Hutcheson and Quesnay and the Physiocrats. But, as his jurisprudence shows, he believed in a *jus sincerae aestimationis*, or right to an unspoiled reputation, and on occasion he could be prickly in defence of his own achievements and dismissive of those, such as the political economist Sir James Steuart, whom he deemed second-rate. His personal reticence makes his religious views impossible to determine exactly, though they seem to have combined belief in a providential deity with distaste for Church hierarchy and organization. He was a shy man—he once remarked, 'I am a beau in nothing but my books'—publicly rather formal, short of small talk and with a tendency to lecture, but relaxed among friends and loved by those who knew him well. His tastes in literature were idiosyncratic. In politics, he was a Whig, but drawn to Pitt for his reforming belief in the 'system of natural liberty'. Of any sexual or romantic interests, of a personal life that ventured at any point beyond the morally upright, let alone into indiscretion, we know virtually nothing. Can he have entertained a hope of fatherhood, even later in life? In writing to Lord Stanhope in 1777, at the age of fifty-three, he asked to keep Stanhope's latest letter (now lost) 'to leave it a legacy to my family and Posterity, if it should ever please God to grant me any, as an example of inflexible probity, which they ought to follow upon all occasions'. But of course this may simply be Smith's usual courtesy at work.

Smith was evidently much admired by his pupils, such as John Millar; the same was true of James Boswell, until he turned away

from Smith under the influence of Dr Johnson and for religious reasons. Smith's closest and most extended relationship with a pupil was
with the Duke of Buccleuch. After his death the Duke said of their
European tour and its aftermath, 'In October 1766, we returned to
London, after having spent near three years together, without the
slightest disagreement or coolness on my part, with every advantage
that could be expected from the society of such a man. We continued to live in friendship to the hour of his death; and I shall always
remain with the impression of having lost a friend whom I loved and
respected, not only for his great talents, but for every private virtue.' It
was a handsome tribute.

Smith's relationship with David Hume deserves special comment.
Intellectually, these are two of the most remarkable men that ever
lived. Chronologically, the flow of ideas is heavily in one direction,
from Hume to Smith. But Smith is his own man, there are innumerable points of overlap—and some of disagreement—in thought between them, and the intensity of this implied exchange, together with
their close personal friendship, made them the great engine of ideas at
the centre of the Scottish Enlightenment. It is striking that despite a
gap in age of twelve years—a gap if anything made greater by Hume's
early-breaking genius—they seem always to have conversed on equal
terms; indeed there are moments when the desire of the sociable
Hume for them to meet can almost seem precatory on his cooler and
more self-contained friend. Yet it is from Hume that Smith derives
his great project; and while Hume turned outwards over time from
philosophy to essays and history to spread his ideas, Smith did the opposite, working and reworking his central body of thought in an effort
to perfect it.

In his final additions to *The Theory of Moral Sentiments*, Smith
wrote 'Happiness consists in tranquillity and enjoyment. Without
tranquillity there can be no enjoyment; and where there is perfect
tranquillity there is scarce any thing which is not capable of amusing.'
He had the closest possible relationship of son to mother, he clearly

adored Janet Douglas, and he was reliant on these two women for many decades. To a man who believed that 'the very suspicion of a fatherless world, must be the most melancholy of all reflections', they were his source of tranquillity, and a precious and loving support.

It was with that domestic support over four decades, with Hume's friendship and in the milieu of the Scottish Enlightenment, that Smith was able to complete two of the most intellectually significant and far-reaching books ever written, and to frame a body of ideas whose power, even today, is still to be fully appreciated. To the development and impact of those ideas we now turn.

Part Two

THOUGHT

CHAPTER 6

REPUTATION, FACT AND MYTH

I F YOU WALK UP THE ROYAL MILE IN EDINBURGH'S OLD TOWN TODAY, from Adam Smith's house off the Canongate and up towards the Customs House, you pass two great statues. The first, raised by recent public subscription outside St Giles's Cathedral, is of Smith himself, standing tall and noble. Behind him is an old plough and by his side a beehive, symbolizing the transition from agricultural to commercial society and the market economy. His left hand holds a gown before him, hinting at his largely academic life. His right—less prominent, and occasionally described as the 'invisible hand'—rests on a globe, a gentle reminder of his intellectual ambition and worldwide renown.

The second statue, a few hundred yards further up, is of David Hume; and it is very different. It depicts Hume as a Roman senator, togaed, sprawling back and balancing a book on a right leg extended towards the viewer. His foot, poking off the podium, invites students and tourists alike to rub it, as many do, for luck. The attitude is languorous, yet the face unsmiling. If the Smith statue appears straightforward, this by contrast is a work of ironies. The partly bare-chested Hume shows little sign of his actual corpulence; there is no trace of humour in this most humorous of men; and the big toe is an invitation to superstition from a man who in fact despised it.

Yet one further irony is rarely noted. Thanks mainly to the great eighteenth-century Scottish portraitist Allan Ramsay, Hume's face is familiar to us: fleshy, amused, intelligent, with a touch of the voluptuous—and, it may be said, not much like his statue. By contrast, we may admire Smith's statue, but in fact we have relatively little idea of what Smith looked like. There is just one contemporary image which shows his face in any detail—the medallion from life by Tassie—and even that only in profile. Numerous portraits exist of the great Scottish figures of the day, including thinkers such as Adam Ferguson, Francis Hutcheson, Lord Kames, John Millar, Thomas Reid and Dugald Stewart as well as Hume, of writers such as Robert Burns, James Boswell and Tobias Smollett, and there is even an astonishing painting by Ramsay of Jean-Jacques Rousseau in Armenian costume during his visit to Britain. Yet no portrait of Smith survives; and, Dugald Stewart suggests, none was ever painted. Smith's dislike of personal exposure could hardly be plainer.

Today, the contrast between Smith's personal elusiveness and the apparent familiarity of his ideas is a stark one. But what is still more striking is how little, even now, both the man and his thought are really understood in the world at large. The problem is made worse by three complicating factors. In the first place, although a man of modest and retiring habits, Smith was aware of what he had achieved, and he was punctilious about his reputation—indeed he saw reputation itself as akin to personal property. In his own case, as we have seen, he took elaborate measures to preserve a particular presentation of his life and work for future generations. Secondly, while the later success of *The Wealth of Nations* has given Smith extraordinary fame, it has also had the effect of overshadowing his *Theory of Moral Sentiments* and other writings—some only relatively recently published—and of distorting the public understanding of his thought in a way that Smith himself might never have expected; and he wrote no brief digest or overview to clarify errors and assist subsequent interpretation. The result is that people know little enough about the real Smith today—and what they think they know is mainly about his economics.

Thirdly, the sheer capaciousness of Smith's writings, their multiplicity and the manner in which they lend themselves to quotation, create vast scope for ambiguity. Virtually every great economist of the past two centuries has claimed Smith's influence; virtually every major modern branch of economics, from the so-called neoclassical mainstream to the Austrian and Marxist schools—of which more anon—and the more recent offshoots of institutional, developmental and behavioural economics, traces its lineage back to Smith. Politicians, academics and pub bores around the world have found the authority of *The Wealth of Nations* and the simplicity of its core ideas an irresistible combination, and routinely draw on them to dignify and adorn their own beliefs or arguments. The result has been to obscure Smith, to mistake the range and power of his ideas and to breed myths without number.

Smith's reputation advanced by stages throughout the nineteenth century. By the 1820s he was being acclaimed by no less an authority than the great population theorist Thomas Malthus, who echoed Pownall's early review by remarking that *The Wealth of Nations* had 'done for political economy what the *Principia* of Newton had done for physics'. But Smith's death itself excited very little immediate comment at the time; and so it remained for several decades. There were few obituaries, and they were desultory and brief: twelve lines in the *Annual Register*, nine in the *Scots Magazine*. *The Times* condescended to a note focusing on Smith's 'laboured eulogium on the stoical end of David Hume', and then a longer piece of grudging hackwork, which described *The Theory of Moral Sentiments* as 'ingenious but fanciful', disclaimed any originality in *The Wealth of Nations* and suggested that Smith 'had early become a disciple of Voltaire's in matters of religion'.

The early reaction was warmer in the American colonies, where *The Wealth of Nations* was widely bought, cited in the debates on the Constitution in 1787–8 and referred to in several of the Federalist Papers urging its ratification. And it was warmer still in revolutionary France, where the *Moniteur Universel* commented that 'Europe has just been deprived of this famous philosopher.' But the early 1790s were hardly a suitable time for balanced evaluation. There had been great excitement among British radicals, Whigs and intellectuals after the fall of the Bastille on 14 July 1789, which many saw as the dawn of a new age of enlightened government in France. But this had long been superseded by events. By early 1793 Britain was in the grip of a moral panic about possible sedition and 'the French treason': not merely the replacement of one ruler by another—the good old 'English treason'—but the overthrow of monarchy itself. These fears were only magnified by the execution of Louis XVI at the guillotine on 21 January of that year.

In this context it was easy to misunderstand Smith, or to co-opt him to a specific cause, in a way all too familiar today. Apologists for events in France in particular associated him with a Humean religious scepticism amounting to atheism, while celebrating him as a revolutionary advocate of free trade. But a more subtle effect of the heightened feeling was to start to detach political economy from politics as such. Dugald Stewart read his long biographical note—the first and still the most important life of Smith—to the Royal Society of Edinburgh in January 1793, at the same time as notorious trials for sedition were getting under way there. He was careful to separate out 'speculative doctrines of political economy' from 'the first principles of government'. He emphasized that Smith's indignation with established arrangements had extended to commercial matters rather than to politics, so that any debts he owed to the French lay in economic theory rather than in politics and government.

Over time, the subject of political economy would become further detached from politics. Indeed, in the nineteenth century a thoroughgoing attempt was begun to recast political economy as the new subject of economics, and to separate out not merely economics and politics, but economics and ethics, in the name of science. As economics became more scientific, so it became more mathematical; and as it became more mathematical so it became more removed from everyday life, from human institutions and human values, and indeed from the idea of value itself.

The chapters that follow step back from Smith himself to look at his ideas and their later impact in closer detail. In particular, they focus on four areas—economics, markets, crony capitalism and moral norms and values—in which Smith's thought is both profound and of huge contemporary relevance. But first we look at that thought as a whole, and try to scrape away some of the barnacles and limpets that have encrusted it over more than two centuries.

A SCIENCE OF MAN

To assess Smith's thought it is helpful to start not with Smith himself, but almost two centuries earlier, with Francis Bacon (1561–1626). Bacon is one of the most complex and ambiguous figures of an ambiguous and complex age. He once remarked that 'All rising to great place is by a winding stair,' a dictum perfectly illustrated by the labyrinthine twists of his own political career. Driven on by an unceasing desire for preferment, he fought and insinuated his way through the shifting politics and bitter personal rivalries of the courts of Queen Elizabeth I and King James I, to the Lord Chancellorship—and ultimately to public disgrace on charges of bribery. Yet at the same time he helped to lay the foundations of a scientific revolution.

Medieval philosophy ranged far more widely than is often understood today, and it had a strongly rationalistic cast. It focused on logic, metaphysics and rhetoric rather than on nature; on reason rather than on experience, or experience's cousin, experiment; on the elaboration and defence of religious dogma rather than on the acquisition of knowledge of the world. Over time the mainstream tradition came to be that of the so-called scholastics who followed Thomas Aquinas, for whom the articles of faith of the Catholic religion and—insofar as they did not conflict—the works of Aristotle were paramount. What mattered, both in the schoolroom and more widely, was acknowledgement of the divine order of this world and the next, and knowledge of the scriptures; and it was impious to inquire too deeply into God's creation. At the beginning of the sixteenth century even humanists such as Erasmus and Thomas More did not take much if any interest in natural philosophy.

Born a generation after Henry VIII broke with Rome and launched the English Reformation, however, Francis Bacon had a very different view. For him, the scope of knowledge was constantly growing, and the age of exploration that had taken Magellan round Cape Horn and Columbus to the New World required as its counterpart an exploration of nature itself. And this exploration in turn demanded iconoclasm: a smashing of false idols and a desire to rid oneself of faulty presuppositions which, Bacon believed, inhibited or prevented the advance of knowledge.

Bacon's targets included metaphysical theorizing, and the narrow verbal disputatiousness of the scholastics. But he also rejected the occult arts of the alchemists of the day. For him, scientific investigation was a shared, public endeavour, ideally to be conducted by specialists in a college—in *The New Atlantis* (1627) he calls it Salomon's House—dedicated to that purpose. 'Knowledge and human power are synonymous,' he said; man should understand nature in order to control her, and thereby bring about material improvement. The justification was not the joy, elegance or intrinsic value of learning as such, but what would today be called its technological, and ultimately economic, utility.

In a series of works, Bacon laid out an astonishingly broad intellectual programme for the natural sciences, according to a division of knowledge into different branches. While remaining carefully respectful of religious dogmas, his conception of natural philosophy is independent of religion. Rather, it is a cumulative, gradual and public activity, and its method emphasizes very careful processes of tabulation and recording of data; these are taken to disqualify or support inductive reasoning from facts to generalizations, which can then form the basis for inference to scientific laws.

Bacon's cheerful contempt for metaphysics and his emphasis on discovery, induction, technology and the growth of useful knowledge stood in stark contrast to the rational theorizing of his near contemporary René Descartes, with its relentless search for certainty; and it is tempting to see here in embryo the often overwrought contrast between British empiricism and the Pascalian *esprit géometrique* of the French. But Bacon tries to steer a middle path: the natural philosopher, he says, must resemble not the ant, which merely heaps up its own store, or the spider, which only spins out its own webs, but the bee, which 'extracts matter . . . [and] works and fashions it by its own efforts'.

Bacon made no discoveries himself, and his thought has its weaknesses: he failed to recognize the centrality of mathematics to scientific advance, and his specific account of scientific method has few adherents today. Indeed, Newton's *Principia Mathematica*—by any measure one of the very greatest scientific advances in history, and a work which unites mathematical precision with imaginative theorizing—stands not as an exemplar of Bacon's ideas, but as a partial demonstration of their insufficiency in relation to pure science. But in what are now called the applied sciences Bacon's ideas exercised enormous influence at the time; indeed they, and the explosion of cataloguing, classifying and measuring that they helped to spawn over the next two centuries, laid some of the groundwork for the industrial revolution.

In developing his own science of man over some forty years, Adam Smith accepts many of Bacon's governing assumptions. Like Bacon, Smith is seeking a naturalistic, empirical theory; indeed his ambition appears for it to have been a unified and general account of human life in its major aspects—moral, social, artistic, political and commercial—grounded in facts of nature and human experience. Like Bacon, Smith recognizes the importance of human specialization and cooperation. And like Bacon he offers a body of ideas that is designed to be public, intellectually accessible and broadly independent of religion.

But the contrasts run deeper. Smith, in so many ways an intellectual disciple of Hume, follows Hume's view of causation by insisting that we can never know the 'invisible chains' that are nature's laws. Moreover, his essay on the *History of Astronomy* evinces a far more sophisticated view of the logic of scientific discovery than Bacon's: a view which places human imagination and hypothesis at the centre of a progressive series of attempts 'to introduce order into this chaos of jarring and discordant appearances' and so restore 'tranquillity and composure' to the tumult of our imagination.

Above all, however, Smith's theory is dynamic, where Bacon's is static. Despite his claims to have left Aristotle behind, Bacon still thinks of science in terms of essences, rather than of change; he asks what something *is*, not what it *does*. Smith, by contrast, is acutely aware of change. And he has a much more supple sense of his intellectual inheritance. Aristotle used the so-called *Organon* of his metaphysical and logical writings to give a grounding to his *Ethics*, and that in turn to his *Politics*. In similar fashion Smith's *History of Astronomy* essay functions as the grounding to his *Theory of Moral Sentiments*, and that in turn to *The Wealth of Nations*, and also, it would appear, to the unfinished works, his 'philosophical history of all the different branches of literature, of philosophy, poetry and eloquence', and his 'theory and history of law and government'.

At the core of the whole enterprise is a Newtonian conception of scientific procedure. Smith had made clear in his early *Lectures on Rhetoric and Belles Lettres* his admiration for the way in which Newton presented his findings, 'lay[ing] down certain principles known or proved in the beginning, from whence we account for the same phenomena, connecting all together by the same chain'. And in the same work he underscored his view that this procedure can be extended beyond physics and astronomy and into the realms of human thought and action: 'This latter, which we may call the Newtonian method, is undoubtedly the most philosophical, and in every sense, whether of Morals or Natural Philosophy, etc., is vastly more ingenious, and for that reason more engaging, than the other.' It is notable that Smith follows this approach at the outset of both *The Theory of Moral Sentiments* and *The Wealth of Nations*.

But that was the method of presentation of results, not the method of their discovery, which in the *Principia* is notably open-ended. In the words of his student Colin Maclaurin, Newton proposed that 'we should begin with phenomena, or effects, and from them investigate the powers or causes that operate in nature; that, from particular causes, we should proceed to the more general ones, till the argument end in the most general.' Inductive generalizations should be regarded as true pending further data, and the scientist thus open to future exceptions or confirming evidence. This is not the closed world of geometrical proof, but the provisional, hypothetical world of modern scientific inquiry.

Newton was quoted as saying in relation to the South Sea Bubble of 1720–1721, a stock-market panic in which he lost a fortune, that 'I can calculate the movement of the stars, but not the madness of men.' Similarly, Smith's Newtonianism is not naive: he does not suppose that human beings behave like inanimate atoms, planets or billiard balls, and that their movements are exactly predictable by scientific law. Indeed, we have seen how he specifically rejects as utopian dogma the idea that people's actions are controllable as on a chessboard. As he notes, 'Every single piece has a principle of motion of its own,' creating what would now be called feedback loops as they adjust to changing circumstances in a dynamic and not exactly ascertainable way. His science of man is thus not a science or technology in the schoolbook physics sense. Rather, in a standard eighteenth-century usage, it is science as an organized body of thought, whose purpose is to render into an intelligible whole a set of phenomena that may be widely and wildly disparate. The explanations and understanding it creates may perhaps be the basis for future expectations, perhaps even the possibility of predictions as in the physical sciences, but that is another matter. It is notable that Smith himself ventures very few predictions in any of his works. This can hardly be by accident. It suggests that he was well aware of the complexity and uncertainty of his subject in the face of the sheer unpredictability of human behaviour.

A Theory of Evolution

We can go further. Smith's science of man is not merely aware of change, it presupposes it. It is in part an examination of the causes of human progress. Indeed, it is a theory of evolution—a proto-theory, to be sure, but a theory of evolution nonetheless. The *Astronomy* essay is not merely a study of the logic of scientific discovery, but an account of the evolution of mind. The *Lectures on Rhetoric* argue for a dynamic, complex understanding of language, which recognizes the potentially conflicting demands of changing use and changing standards of mutual intelligibility. *The Theory of Moral Sentiments* offers an evolutionary account of social and moral norms, mediated as with language by the operation of sympathy or fellow feeling. *The Wealth of Nations* focuses in part on one specific aspect of human interaction, market exchange, locates it within a historical transition from feudalism to commercial society and shows how that idea can be used to explain economic development and the evolution of a global trading order. It has been plausibly argued that one effect of Smith's jurisprudence, especially as developed by his pupil and protégé John Millar, the Regius Professor of Civil Law in Glasgow, was to stimulate the growth of a case-based common-law—and so evolutionary—tradition in Scottish jurisprudence. It may be that the deep reason why Smith was ultimately determined to destroy his unfinished works was that, however fertile in ideas they might be, he had not yet succeeded in bringing them under the same unifying set of evolutionary concepts as he had with his two great published works.

But Smith's science of man is not merely a theory of evolution: it is almost certainly a core part of *the* theory of evolution. There is specific reason to think that Smith's writings exercised a strong indirect influence on Charles Darwin himself. Darwin spent two rather unhappy years in 1825–7 at medical school in Edinburgh, an institution at which Smith's friend and executor Joseph Black had taught for thirty years, in a city which celebrated Smith, at a time when the issue of protectionism vs. free trade was becoming ever more a subject of public debate. At Cambridge in 1829 Darwin reported in a letter that 'My studies consist in Adam Smith and Locke,' while through a family connection he often met the philosopher and historian Sir James Mackintosh, who had grown up in Enlightenment Scotland a generation after Smith. On HMS *Beagle*, Darwin saw how the French naturalist Henri Milne-Edwards had applied Smith's idea of the division of labour to the organs of the human body, and promptly adapted it himself to the diversification and specialization of species within an ecosystem. In his formative decade of the 1830s, Darwin was close to the brilliant Harriet Martineau, whose best-selling *Illustrations of Political Economy* (1832) had a potent effect in bringing the ideas of Adam Smith to a wider public. It is highly likely that Smith left a considerable mark on the great natural scientist.

How exactly is Smith's thought evolutionary? In the modern, Darwinian sense, evolution is described as descent with modification: the heritability of traits in different forms from one generation of a species to the next, with natural selection weeding out the less successful forms through the so-called survival of the fittest. In Smith's theory there appear to be two main mechanisms. The first is cultural. In the *Lectures on Rhetoric* Smith notes how new linguistic practices and usages continually emerge 'without any intention or foresight in those who first set the example, and who never meant to establish any general rule'. In *The Theory of Moral Sentiments* he goes further, outlining a process by which people learn to view their own behaviour in part through that of others, and form judgements as to its actual or possible effects. At the same time, through the moderating influence of the impartial spectator, they come to see their behaviour impersonally, without undue passion or bias. The result, Smith argues, is not merely a prudential grasp of the impact of their actions but, once internalized, a moral one. That is, in evolutionary terms, patterns of actual and possible behaviour emerge, spontaneously and through imitation, and some of them are then passed over or selected for; the latter in turn become norms and are passed on to others through further rounds of behaviour and selection. And so it continues. This process of copying and selection is generally socially beneficial, but it need not always be so. Sometimes, as with our disposition to admire the rich and famous, it can be morally dubious but economically valuable. Sometimes it can select for norms that are beneficial to an in-group, but not to wider society. Over time, however, the tendency is to spread norms beneficial to society as a whole.

There is an important contrast here with Darwinian natural selection. In natural selection, the attribute selected for—faster speed, greater strength, better disguise etc.—typically benefits the individual involved as well as the population as a whole. Faster cheetahs do better than slower ones, they are favoured by natural selection, and genes for speed are passed down to their offspring. And so forth. But here the focus is in both directions. Smith recognizes that human lives offer huge potential for individually advantageous behaviour to have not positive but negative social effects. The question then is not just why individual behaviour benefits the group, as in much evolutionary theory, but how moral norms that can effectively constrain and penalize bad individual behaviour arise at all. His answer, as with biological evolution, is through descent with modification. Its effect is dynamic: to create emergent moral and social order, spontaneously if not necessarily immediately, from the bottom up. And the norms and values thereby formed evolve into human institutions. As Smith's friend Adam Ferguson said in 1767, 'Every step and every movement of the multitude, even in what are termed enlightened ages, are made with equal blindness to the future; and nations stumble upon establishments, which are indeed the result of human action, but not the execution of any human design.' David Hume gave an influential refutation of the argument that the world must be the product of divine intention in his *Dialogues Concerning Natural Religion*, composed in 1779. But twenty years earlier, in 1759, partly under Hume's influence, Smith had outlined a cultural mechanism by which moral and social norms could arise by themselves purely from human interaction.

THE INVISIBLE HAND

Yet there is of course a second, far more famous evolutionary mechanism in Smith's thought: the 'invisible hand'. As he says in Book IV of *The Wealth of Nations*:

> As every individual, therefore, endeavours as much as he can both to employ his capital in the support of domestic industry, and so to direct that industry that its produce may be of the greatest value; every individual necessarily labours to render the annual revenue of the society as great as he can. He generally, indeed, neither intends to promote the public interest, nor knows how much he is promoting it. By preferring the support of domestic to that of foreign industry, he intends only his own security; and by directing that industry in such a manner as its produce may be of the greatest value, he intends only his own gain, and he is in this, as in many other cases, led by an invisible hand to promote an end which was no part of his intention. Nor is it always the worse for the society that it was no part of it. By pursuing his own interest he frequently promotes that of the society more effectually than when he really intends to promote it.

The idea of the invisible hand has been celebrated or denounced for many decades. For some, it is nothing less than the fundamental idea that the market is an equilibrating mechanism that transforms individual greed via competition into general welfare. For others, the invisible hand is the symbol of a winner-takes-all economic system that uses an appeal to impersonal market forces to legitimize coercion of those without economic power. For the former, government is at best an impediment to efficient markets and general welfare; for the latter, it is an essential safeguard against unfairness and inequality. And there have been many other interpretations of the invisible hand, from the ironic to the providential.

It is, therefore, vital to be clear about what the invisible hand is and is not for Smith, and whether and why it matters. First of all, it is important to note that there are only three mentions of the phrase in the entire corpus of his writings. Far from being the centrepiece of *The Wealth of Nations*, the metaphor of the invisible hand appears exactly once there, and receives no specific elaboration or development. Nor, even there, is it the paean to unfettered markets and the beneficent effects of self-interest claimed by some. Rather, it occurs in the context of the investor's desire for security: Smith is arguing for the narrow and common-sense proposition that domestic capital is a valuable resource for a nation's defence, and that capital regulations are not required because the extra cost and risk of foreign trade give people natural economic incentives to invest in domestic markets anyway.

There are two more mentions of the phrase elsewhere in Smith's work. The first is in the *History of Astronomy* essay, in a quite different context, and need not concern us. The second, however, occurs in *The Theory of Moral Sentiments*, and is more relevant. Smith argues that the desire for wealth and status acts as the spur to extraordinary efforts at self-improvement. Once the rich have achieved their wealth they consume relatively little more than the poor, and may come to see their riches as delusive. But 'It is this deception which rouses and keeps in continual motion the industry of mankind. It is this which first prompted them to cultivate the ground, to build houses, to found cities and commonwealths, and to invent and improve all the sciences and arts, which ennoble and embellish human life; which have entirely changed the whole face of the globe.' The effects of their collective effort are thus colossal improvements, which benefit humankind as a whole. 'In spite of their natural self-ishness and rapacity, though they mean only their own conveniency', he argues, the rich benefit the poor through their investment and employment. Thus 'they are led by an invisible hand to make nearly the same distribution of the necessaries of life, which would have been made, had the earth been divided into equal portions among all its inhabitants, and thus without intending it, without knowing it, advance the interest of the society, and afford means to the multiplication of the species.' Whatever one thinks of this rather ambiguous argument, it clearly points once again to what would now be called beneficial spillover effects, and 'establishments, which are . . . the result of human action, but not the execution of any human design'.

With just three references in total, there is no theory of the invisible hand as such in Smith's work; and though he discusses many different markets, and looks in detail at market functioning in his extended 'Digression Concerning the Corn Trade and Corn Laws' in Book IV of *The Wealth of Nations*, the phrase does not recur. But as Smith notes in the quotation above, the invisible hand operates 'in many other cases', and in a wider sense the idea which it expresses is indeed a key part of his thought, and has been fundamental to the social sciences ever since. For in many circumstances markets mediated by open competition and voluntary exchange can play a role analogous to natural selection. In general, the theory goes, individuals and companies able to make sustainable profits will survive over time, while those that cannot will fail. This is, in Darwinian terms, a form of descent with modification. Its result is the emergence of spontaneous order—but in this case political-economic, not specifically moral, order—not in any form imposed from above, but from the bottom up. And as Smith makes quite clear, this can be the unintended consequence of individual decisions. Those involved need know or want nothing of the kind, and they might fail to have a similarly beneficent effect if they acted deliberately. The phenomenon is ubiquitous, and it is a kind of miracle.

This allows us to get clearer on Smith's putative science of man. This is not merely very wide in scope, potentially tying language, individual and social psychology, ethics and political economy—and, arguably, aspects of law and government—together in a coherent and broadly unified way. It is also dynamic and evolutionary in character. It is, in effect, a theory of collective mind, premised on free human interaction and open communication. Understood in this way, it has— even now, more than two centuries after Smith's death, and despite vast differences of context and circumstance—an astonishingly contemporary feel about it.

But this also brings out the magnitude of Smith's achievement in political economy. However familiar it may sometimes appear, the world of the late eighteenth century was very different from that of today. Most people worked in agriculture; those who owned factories were generally individuals, families or small partnerships, and personally involved; and the owners often knew each other. Child labour was common. Most banks issued their own notes. There were not many commercial organizations; and they generally had unlimited liability, so that if they failed—as with the Ayr Bank—the owners had to pay off the debts involved or go to prison. The modern worlds of technology, finance and business, of international corporations raising capital at will and employing tens or even hundreds of thousands of people on multiple sites across different continents, were unimaginable. To discern among this thronging mêlée abiding principles of private ownership, commercial interest, market exchange, the division of labour, capital, profit-seeking and wage employment is no small thing. To tie these principles not into a theory of enlightened princely behaviour, but into a wider theory of evolving economic order and unintended collective benefit is stupendous.

To be clear: there are things that Smith fairly evidently got wrong, and key areas of modern economics which he failed to anticipate. He did not foresee the rapid industrialization of the nineteenth century, though he had the (lone) example of the massive Carron Iron

Works in nearby Falkirk before him. He did not grasp the full importance of technological change, though he was a friend of James Watt and sponsored him to set up a workshop at Glasgow University. He would likely have been surprised, and perhaps dismayed, by the rapid subsequent growth of joint-stock companies. His speculations about the origins of money are interesting but mistaken. His remarks on value are confusing, and his cost-of-production theory and its cousin, the labour theory of value, proved to be a blind alley to most nineteenth-century theorists, and command little support today except among some Marxist economists. And there are central areas of modern economic theory—concerning demand, marginal utility, monetary policy, mass unemployment, the business cycle, to name a few—on which *The Wealth of Nations* has little if anything direct to say. Much of this is to be expected, since Smith wrote at the last moment of the pre-industrial age.

Moreover, though Smith often has moments of startling originality in his moral, historical and jurisprudential writings—the impartial spectator, his stadial theory of development, much of his detailed analysis of commercial society—he was not especially original in his political economy. The great economist Joseph Schumpeter wrote in his *History of Economic Analysis* that 'The fact is that *The Wealth of Nations* does not contain a single analytic idea, principle, or method that was entirely new in 1776.' The accuracy of this bald and bold assertion is open to debate, and Schumpeter remained an admirer of Smith, if a rather qualified one. But his remark captures a wider truth: that Smith's instinct in that book was towards the collation, development and synthesis of ideas, whatever their source. His originality shows itself in his willingness to press economic thinking into unexpected areas, such as his analysis of slavery, and indeed parts of politics itself, as we shall see. In this, again, he anticipates much modern economics.

What is perhaps more surprising, especially in someone so historically minded, is that Smith often appears to be unaware of, or to ignore, much of what is of value in earlier work on political economy. In particular, his use of 'mercantile system' as a catch-all portmanteau term, while rhetorically convenient, has had the effect of blurring distinctions between previous thinkers and consigning them all to a box marked 'political economy before Smith'. The 1750s, however, had seen an explosion of important writing and ideas in this area, including the publication of works by Ferdinando Galiani, Josiah Tucker and Richard Cantillon, as well as by Quesnay and Hume. In his *Essays* Hume had anticipated many of Smith's key themes, including the idea that 'men and commodities [not silver and gold] are the real strength of any community,' the adverse impact of many government attempts at intervention, the mutual benefits of free trade, and the economic foolishness of the attempt to beggar one's international neighbours. But Smith's claim in *The Wealth of Nations* that 'Mr Hume is the only writer who, so far as I know, has hitherto taken notice of' the link between commerce and manufactures and 'the liberty and security of individuals' can at best have been regarded with bemusement by his informed contemporaries.

A particular victim of Smith's selective approach to his predecessors is Sir James Steuart, the Jacobite author of *An Inquiry into the Principles of Political Economy* (1767). Smith dismissed Steuart's book in a letter of 1772 to William Pulteney, saying, 'Without once mentioning it, I flatter myself, that every false principle in it will meet with a clear and distinct confutation in mine.' This goes too far. Yes, Steuart is often prolix, plodding and dull to read. But he usefully emphasized aspects of political economy—in relation to employment, uncertainty and ignorance, for instance—that are wholly or partly missing in Smith, but that have since assumed importance. One effect of the success of *The Wealth of Nations*, however, has been to eclipse Steuart's work almost entirely.

These shortcomings are important, though they pale beside the breathtaking sweep and richness of *The Wealth of Nations*. And there is one thing that Smith gets triumphantly, monumentally right, that guarantees his place among the immortals: he sets himself to address the foundational question of how far the pursuit of individual self-interest through cultural and market exchange can yield economic growth and socially beneficial outcomes. That marks the moment at which economics starts to come of age.

In posing this question, Smith highlighted the division of labour: one of the most extraordinary and important phenomena in all of human existence. More prosaically, he was also the first thinker to place markets, competition and market exchange squarely at the centre of economics. Others before him had noticed the effects of excess supply or demand on price, the tendency towards equilibrium under certain conditions and the effects of market exchange in promoting capital accumulation and lifting prosperity. But only Smith formed these ideas into a general theory, his 'system of natural liberty', explored its implications both for individual markets and for commercial society as a whole, and then applied his ideas to some of the key economic issues of the day. And, more than two centuries after his death, his analysis remains absolutely fundamental to mainstream economics. Microeconomists still operate in the shadow of Smith's analysis of market dynamics, and macroeconomists in that of his theories of interest, saving and investment. Not for nothing, then, is Smith acclaimed today as the father of economics.

FIVE MYTHS

But this is only part, albeit the larger part, of the story. Getting clearer on what Smith thought and what he achieved also requires us to get clear on what he was not. This is much harder than it seems, because a formidable mythology has arisen over the past two centuries around Adam Smith. That mythology remains staunchly defended by those—academics, economists, politicians, ideologues, enthusiasts—who have sought to recruit the wisdom of Smith's ideas, and more frequently the prestige of his name, to projects of their own. In five key areas, it demands to be tackled head-on.

Myth 1: There is an 'Adam Smith Problem'

The first myth is, in a way, a numerical one. In the nineteenth century a debate originated among German scholars over what came to be called *Das Adam Smith Problem*. Was there just one Adam Smith, with one overarching theory, or were there two: the Adam Smith of *The Theory of Moral Sentiments* and the very different Adam Smith of *The Wealth of Nations*? Isn't the former work really about altruism and human goodness, and the second about selfishness and human greed? And if that is so, surely there is a fundamental contradiction between them? But then, some have reasoned, Smith must have had a dramatic change of heart, perhaps in the 1760s when he visited France and met Quesnay and the Physiocrats: the soft-hearted young moral philosopher must have yielded at that time to the flinty older economist. Yet this in turn only compounds the difficulty, for how could Smith have failed to notice such a glaring disagreement between the two books, especially while putting through his late revisions to the *Theory*? And why did he apparently do nothing to soften or reduce the contradiction? Smith may have been a great economist, on this view, but he was a philosophical fool—or worse, a knave.

These questions have been much debated, and the idea that there are two Smiths continues in different ways to fascinate some of his interpreters. In the absence at that time of conventions over citation, there is a small puzzle about why Smith did not decide to cross-reference the two books so as to bring out the linkages between them, as well as any evolution in his thought. This applies, for example, to his late additions to *The Theory of Moral Sentiments*, where he deploys his idea of the delusive power of our admiration for the great and powerful.

But otherwise the cause is hopeless. Intellectually, the 'two Smiths' view badly misunderstands his ideas and how they fit together. Sympathy in the crucial sense deployed in *The Theory of Moral Sentiments* is not the same thing as altruism, indeed it is not a motive for action at all: it is part of a process by which people are enabled to form moral judgements and achieve a degree of moral self-consciousness. There is thus no necessary contrast between it and self-interest. In factual terms as well, the argument never gets going. In his very early biographical note—which is, lest one forget, much the most authoritative independent major source we have on Smith—Dugald Stewart states that Smith was framing some of the leading ideas of *The Wealth of Nations* from at least 1755, and quotes from a paper of his at that time that 'Little else is requisite to carry a state to the highest degree of opulence from the lowest barbarism, but peace, easy taxes, and a tolerable administration of justice; all the rest being brought about by the natural course of things.' This was four years before the publication of the *Theory*. The *Lectures on Jurisprudence* reinforce this view, since they show that in his teaching in 1762 Smith was developing embryonic themes from *The Wealth of Nations*, just after completing revisions for the second edition of the *Theory*. Indeed the so-called *Early Draft of The Wealth of Nations*, apparently an attempt by Smith to write up parts of the lectures into a separate work on political economy, was most probably composed by April 1763, before he left for France.

There was, then, no conversion experience. When *The Wealth of Nations* was published, it contained an advertisement for the *Theory*; and the later editions of the *Theory* also contained the essay on the first formation of languages. This is what we should expect, given the broadly progressive and systematic way in which Smith developed his ideas. He spent the last decade of his life reviewing and revising the two books for successive editions, often during overlapping periods. And when at the close of his life he returned to his first book, he extended its argument without reference to *The Wealth of Nations*. There can be no doubt about it: Smith intended his two great works to be read alongside each other, and saw them as self-sufficient but deeply complementary and linked to other parts of a philosophically unified system. That system is built on the single idea of continuous and evolving mutual exchange: communicative exchange in language, exchange of esteem in moral and social psychology, market exchange in political economy.

This is not to say that Smith's thought does not evolve; or that there are no inconsistencies or differences of emphasis between the two works. They have different subjects, and they are very different in tone and character. *The Theory of Moral Sentiments* barely touches on commercial life, while *The Wealth of Nations* barely touches on sympathy, duty, prudence or any of the key themes of the earlier book. So it is hardly surprising that they have seemed to some like the products of different authors. Indeed, some modern writers have seen them as demarcating two different spheres of human life: one a tightly defined sphere of love and trust, including friends, family and immediate community, the other a vastly larger sphere of cooperation through which we tap, impersonally and anonymously, the economic and social benefits of extended civilization. On this view our moral norms do not and cannot extend to those we do not know; we simply interact with strangers, and accept their interactions with us, on the basis of self-interest, and it is self-interest, not love, that holds the trading system together.

In some ways this is a tempting line of thought, but it cannot be a correct reading of Smith, because it makes incoherent the logical relationships at the centre of his science of man. *The Theory of Moral Sentiments* does not demarcate a space of specifically moral interaction; it is intended to be an entirely general account of how moral norms and shared moral commitments arise within society. Yes, Smith believes that little more than self-interest, or rather 'self-love', is required among humans in order to explain the beneficent effects of well-functioning markets. But there is no evidence that he believed that moral values ceased to apply at all in the wider trading order described by *The Wealth of Nations*, and it would contradict the earlier book if he did. It would also contradict his overall theory, which is precisely that markets operate within a context of norms and trust which itself underwrites legal mechanisms of justice and enforcement. The reason why humans and not dogs can make a 'fair and deliberate exchange' of one thing for another is because such exchanges presuppose a shared context of fairness, and a human capacity to consider what to offer to exchange and for what, and what the other party would accept. Needless to say, the relevant moral norms may change, and as a psychological matter they will typically become more attenuated and less pressing in impersonal trading contexts; Smith is not a cosmopolitan in ethics. But Smith did not believe that the commercial world was *ipso facto* an amoral one. Nor did he believe that political economy was, or should or could ever be, a value-free science. Quite the opposite, as will become clear.

Myth 2: Adam Smith was an Advocate of Self-Interest

Understanding the true relationship between these two great works is important not merely insofar as it reveals Smith's overall view, but because it helps guard against the mistake of seeing *The Wealth of Nations* as his final word—as though he came to believe that economics always trumped ethics. The same is true of our second myth, the claim that Smith was in some way an advocate of self-interest. His famous line is often cited, that 'It is not from the benevolence of the butcher, the brewer or the baker that we expect our dinner, but from their regard to their own interest. We address ourselves, not to their humanity, but to their self-love, and never talk to them of our own necessities, but of their advantages.' In the famous words of the Nobel Prize–winning Chicago economist George Stigler, 'The Wealth of Nations is a stupendous palace erected upon the granite of self-interest.' And the idea that economics itself is, and perhaps should be, 'really' only about self-interest—indeed that the pursuit of self-interest is somehow definitive of human rationality itself—has long since become conventional wisdom.

It is undoubtedly true that *The Wealth of Nations* is in part an assertion of the legitimacy of commerce and capital accumulation, and a defence of their importance to the public good. It is also true that the notion of 'self-love' is crucial for Smith: it is one of the basic ideas, alongside such others as sympathy, the division of labour and the instinct to truck and barter, that hold his natural system of liberty together. But though Smith has a Newtonian desire to build his science of man on a small number of leading principles, he does not stake it on one idea only; in a different context he is critical of the Greek philosopher Epicurus for being too parsimonious in basing his own ethical system just on prudence, and his physics just on atomism. In effect, Smith would rather accept a degree of complexity in his assumptions than fail to do justice to the full range of the political-economic phenomena he is seeking to explain. He wants more than one string to his instrument, so that he can play a richer and more rewarding melody.

Indeed, Smith recognizes and discusses a multiplicity of human emotions, some of which—including wonder, pride and vanity—have little or nothing to do with personal advantage as such. Moreover, the emotions can and do combine in novel and unexpected ways in their actions: in the *Lectures on Rhetoric* he says:

> The different passions all proceed in like manner from different states of mind and outward circumstances. But it would be both endless and useless to go through all these different affections and passions in this manner. It would be endless, because though the simple passions are of no great number, yet these are so compounded in different manners as to make a number of mixed ones almost infinite. It would be useless, for though we had gone through all the different affections yet the difference of character and age and circumstances of the person would so vary the effects that our rules would not be at all applicable.

Again, the picture is dynamic and complex. Smith does not suppose there is a fixed or essential thing called 'human nature', though he takes certain instincts and desires as fundamental, and he accepts that people can have multiple identities. Humans have common characteristics, but they are formed by choice and circumstance within society. These factors, and this emotional complexity, help to render exact prediction difficult if not impossible within any science of man.

Moreover, the idea of self-interest, and the related idea of selfishness, is actually rather different from that of self-love. Smith only mentions self-interest as such once in *The Wealth of Nations*, in explaining the 'industry and zeal' of the Catholic clergy who, unlike their Protestant counterparts, have to depend upon gifts from their parishioners. He is perfectly clear that the common good should trump private self-interest: 'The wise and virtuous man is at all times willing that his own private interest should be sacrificed to the public interest of his own particular order or society. He is at all times willing, too, that the interest of this order or society should be sacrificed to the greater interest of the state or sovereignty, of which it is only a subordinate part.' Smith also attacked Hobbes and Mandeville for offering systems of thought based on self-interest. And the opening words of the *Theory of Moral Sentiments* specifically reject the idea of selfishness as the only source of human motivation: 'How selfish soever man may be supposed, there are evidently some principles in his nature, which interest him in the fortune of others, and render their happiness necessary to him, though he derives nothing from it except the pleasure of seeing it.'

This idea is the foundation stone for Smith's analysis of moral and social psychology—and it is specifically framed in terms of sympathy and in opposition to theories of self-interest. The point about the butcher, the brewer and the baker is not that they lack a moral sensibility, that they do not or should not have access to their emotions, that they are or should be actuated by self-love, or that this alone would constitute rational conduct. It is that no further motivation is required to explain how they in fact behave. To say that self-oriented behaviour can promote the common good may delimit the scope for virtue, but it is not to say that such behaviour is required, or that it can be justified in those terms.

Indeed, in line with the usage of the time, for Smith self-love is neither immoral nor even a particular term of opprobrium. Yes, it can lead people astray, in which case 'The natural representations of self-love can be corrected by the eye of the impartial spectator.' But David Hume had attacked the idea that self-love is the deep, hidden motivation for human action in an appendix to his *Enquiry Concerning the Principles of Morals* (1751), depicting it as an unnecessary and overly sophisticated attempt to explain everyday human actions. There is no reason to think Smith dissented from this view. But for Smith and for others of the time self-love had a positive moral dimension as well. It properly included aspects which went well beyond narrow economic self-interest, including a person's regard to their own well-being, and their property, family, dependants, friends and reputation. As a distinctively Stoic idea it also carried the moral connotation of a duty to attend to the proper care of one's own self and the cultivation of personal virtues; and this sits well alongside Smith's insistence that people, rather than governments, are best placed to judge their own self-interest. And finally, though it has its drawbacks, Smith sees the action of self-love through commerce as itself a civilizing force, which improves habits and channels human energy into sociability, thrift, hard work and investment. Even in the famous quote about the butcher, the brewer and the baker, the focus is in part on identifying and satisfying their interests, and on the mutual benefits of exchange.

Myth 3: Adam Smith was Pro-Rich

The Wealth of Nations was published at a time when Scotland was in the early stages of one of the longest and most rapid periods of national economic growth ever recorded. Vast fortunes were being made by Scottish merchants and industrialists, and the book serves in part not merely to explain but to ratify and defend emerging ideas of a commercial system based on free markets. As a result, Smith's name is often invoked today to justify extreme inequalities of wealth and income as the supposedly natural results of such a system.

Yes, *The Wealth of Nations* is a hymn to the possibility of 'universal opulence'—that is, material advancement for all sections of society. But Smith was in fact very far from being a believer in the importance of great wealth. 'All for ourselves, and nothing for other people,' he wrote in *The Wealth of Nations*, 'seems, in every age of the world, to have been the vile maxim of the masters of mankind.' As in his lectures on jurisprudence, he is extremely critical of institutions that allow the consolidation of property, such as inheritance laws, primogeniture and entails, which were used to tie up land over several generations. Nor does he defer to the rich. In *The Theory of Moral Sentiments*, as we have noted, he disparages the human instinct to admire the rich and powerful and despise the poor, and the fact that 'Wealth and greatness are often regarded with the respect and admiration which are due only to wisdom and virtue; and that the contempt, of which vice and folly are the only proper objects, is most unjustly bestowed upon poverty and weaknesses, has been the complaint of moralists in all ages.' But he sees value in it even so, for this self-deception 'rouses and keeps in continual motion the industry of mankind'.

Smith is also quite aware that wealth does not necessarily bring happiness. Indeed he is sceptical about consumption and the value of material possessions: 'How many people ruin themselves by laying out money on trinkets of frivolous utility?' And he cannot resist repeating that memorable phrase in considering how the rich man of folklore must reflect on his life in old age: 'It is then, in the last dregs of life, his body wasted with toil and diseases, his mind galled and ruffled by the memory of a thousand injuries and disappointments which he imagines he has met with from the injustice of his enemies, or from the perfidy and ingratitude of his friends, that he begins at last to find that wealth and greatness are mere trinkets of frivolous utility, no more adapted for procuring ease of body or tranquillity of mind, than the tweezer-cases of the lover of toys.' By contrast, 'In ease of body and peace of mind, all the different ranks of life are really upon a level, and the beggar, who suns himself by the side of the highway, possesses that security which kings are fighting for.' Even if wealth makes some difference to a person's happiness, a balanced outlook on life may count for more.

As this suggests, Smith is astonishingly egalitarian in outlook. When the interests of rich and poor clash, his instincts and arguments are almost without exception on the side of the poor. It is the poor, not the rich, who suffer from the restrictions on movement which he condemns. It is the worker and not the master who suffers from Parliament's decision to set an upper and not a lower limit on wages. According to Smith the control exercised on government by merchant interests means that a sympathetic hearing in law must always be given to workers' claims. Indeed value itself for Smith is ultimately to be understood in terms not of money or land, but of labour. But in talking of 'workers', 'masters' and 'ranks of life' he is not adopting a rigid Marxist-style class analysis. The picture he paints is far more fluid and dynamic than that. The reasons for favouring poor over rich are moral, yes, but they are also economic: to give the poor a fairer chance to compete, and to succeed.

MYTH 4: ADAM SMITH WAS ANTI-GOVERNMENT

Many of today's market libertarians like to see Adam Smith as the great prophet of *laissez-faire*, and the enemy of government and state intervention of any kind. But so too do those who seek to criticize Smith from the political left, for whom it is convenient to frame him as a straw man for their own views. For both sides, a canonical text is this: 'Every man, as long as he does not violate the laws of justice, is left perfectly free to pursue his own interest his own way, and to bring both his industry and his capital into competition with those of any other man, or order of men.'

On balance, however, the truth is rather different. Yes, there are numerous places where Smith deplores the impact of government, and specifically the effects of intrusive regulation on trade. As Dugald Stewart records, even in 1755 Smith said, 'All governments which thwart this natural course [of trade], which force things into another channel, or which endeavour to arrest the progress of society at a particular point, are unnatural, and to support themselves are obliged to be oppressive and tyrannical.' This was true not merely of national governments, but of the thickets of petty regulation and abusive official discretion to be found in eighteenth-century English and Scottish ecclesiastical and local government. *The Wealth of Nations* itself was a 'very violent attack . . . upon the whole commercial system of Great Britain'. And, as we have seen, Smith is brutal on the way in which governments permit or abet monopoly power and 'the corporation spirit', both at home and internationally through colonization.

But overall the view of Smith as anti-government seriously mistakes him. For one thing, Smith was not a believer in *laissez-faire*, if by that is meant the idea that markets should operate entirely independently of the state and with little or no regulation. The phrase 'laissez-faire' was adopted by Quesnay and the Physiocrats, but Smith nowhere uses it, and he explicitly rejected what he saw as the Physiocrats' utopian approach to economic policy. He was quite clear that markets—and indeed society as a whole—are generally sustained by trust and confidence, and that for these and other things they rely on external institutions, notably of law and government, for their viability. By contrast, if merchants are left entirely to their own devices, the result is corrosive: as we have noted, he robustly asserts that 'People of the same trade seldom meet together, even for merriment and diversion, but the conversation ends in a conspiracy against the public, or in some contrivance to raise prices.' No one who has read Smith closely can rationally believe he is an out-and-out free-marketeer.

Smith is also well aware that markets can underperform, and even of the point—emphasized above all by John Maynard Keynes in the 1930s—that a failure of market confidence can create a slump. In

Book I of *The Wealth of Nations*, Smith imagines what would happen if such a thing occurred in the labour market:

> Every year the demand for servants and labourers would, in all the different classes of employments, be less than it had been the year before. Many who had been bred in the superior classes, not being able to find employment in their own business, would be glad to seek it in the lowest. The lowest class being not only overstocked with its own workmen, but with the overflowings of all the other classes, the competition for employment would be so great in it, as to reduce the wages of labour to the most miserable and scanty subsistence of the labourer. Many would not be able to find employment even upon these hard terms, but would either starve, or be driven to seek a subsistence either by begging, or by the perpetration perhaps of the greatest enormities. Want, famine, and mortality would immediately prevail . . .

This is a near-perfect description of what Keynes would later think of as a sub-optimal equilibrium. So much for the idea that Smith believed that markets are always efficient and always maximize human welfare.

Moreover, the focus of Smith's 'system of natural liberty' is not on absolute market freedom, but on clearing away particular impediments to trade such as subsidies and tariffs; not on perfect markets but on market imperfections. Even in the canonical quotation above, Smith makes clear that he is talking specifically about the need to remove 'systems either of preference or of restraint'. Where a regulation has these negative effects, his instinct is to reject it. But he is aware that regulation can have positive effects as well, and emphasizes the importance of government in guaranteeing property rights, maintaining the rule of law and providing an institutional context of trust and predictability within which markets may flourish. As he remarks in *The Wealth of Nations*, 'Those laws and customs so favourable to the yeomanry have perhaps contributed more to the present grandeur of England than all their boasted regulations of commerce taken together.' That is, specific regulations can have value, for example in relation to banking, but custom and the rule of law are what really matter.

It is easy to forget just how wide a range of specific government interventions Smith was prepared to contemplate in his writings, at a time when the overall scope of government was vastly less than it is in developed countries today. They include: the Navigation Acts; taxing spirits more than beer to reduce the consumption of alcohol; the granting of temporary monopolies to stimulate overseas trade in remote or hostile regions; a duty in law to pay workers in cash rather than in kind, as protection against fraud; higher taxes on rents in kind than on money rents; the compulsory registration of mortgages; enforcement of building standards; sterling marks on silver plate and stamps on textiles, to show quality; special regulation of the banks, and of currency; and even a 5 per cent limit on the maximum rate of interest, as a protection against the wasteful activities of 'prodigals and projectors'. Smith comments approvingly on a moderate export tax on wool and moderate taxes on foreign manufactures, as likely to generate public revenue while giving domestic workers 'a considerable advantage in the home market'. And of course there is the wider role for government which Smith acknowledges: not merely the discharge of traditional functions such as defence and the administration of justice, but special institutions such as the Mint, and the improvement of general welfare through the promotion of commerce and education, street-cleaning, the prevention of disease and the construction of public works such as highways, bridges, canals and harbours.

Finally, the anti-government view wildly mistakes the character of Smith's overall approach to political economy. He is pragmatic not theoretical, concrete not utopian, a theorist of general rules not universal laws, concerned with specific remedies, not maxima and minima or attempts at one-size-fits-all solutions. He has an acute interest in how markets go wrong, through such things as poor communications, lack of security, economically irrational behaviour and asymmetries of information or power. Unlike many works of modern economics, *The Wealth of Nations* is packed with facts and historical material, and although Smith employs the 'let us assume' thought experiments characteristic of modern economics, his general instinct is to avoid abstractions. Instead he reaches for telling examples from history, or from other societies and cultures, to illustrate his point. He is much closer to David Hume's sage advice that when someone 'forms schemes in politics, trade, economy, or any business in life, he never ought to draw his arguments too fine, or connect too long a chain of consequences together. Something is sure to happen, that will disconcert his reasoning, and produce an event different from what he expected.'

MYTH 5: ADAM SMITH WAS FIRST AND FOREMOST AN ECONOMIST

The final myth is in a way the most revealing. Adam Smith is the father of economics, but he was not first and foremost an economist. Of course, in the eighteenth century an 'economist' was not a theorist or practitioner in economics, but someone who sought to make economies—that is, savings in expenditure. But even in the modern sense Smith was not principally an economist. This is not because he did not write academic papers, did not stud his works with mathematical formulae or had not mastered those prerequisites of respectable economics today, the integral and differential calculus, subjects at which he was in fact adept. No, it is because Smith was and saw himself as a philosopher, for whom political economy and its modes of thought were just part of a vastly wider science of man. And even that science is in Smith's hands more historical and less scientific, more oriented to explanation than to prediction, than is claimed for much modern economics.

Like others then and for decades afterwards, and in contrast to modern practice, Smith did not compartmentalize politics and economics. For him, one might say, there is no such thing as a purely political government, or a purely economic market. He sees the policies of the state as directed by 'the clamorous importunity of partial interests'. Far from being seen as separate domains, as often today, state and market were viewed as interdependent: hardly surprising, perhaps, in an age of corporate towns, licensed markets and chartered companies. In *The Wealth of Nations* Smith made a series of great attacks against established injustice: against the petty regulations of parish councils and church wardens; against the laws of settlement which impeded the free movement of the poor; against the restrictive practices of corporations and guilds, especially over apprenticeships; against the corruption of the East India Company and the other great incorporated trading companies; and against the subsidies, tariffs and bounties of the mercantile system. Only the latter might be thought mainly economic in character; and even to say that would separate it from the political lobbying that Smith regarded as a core part of its explanation.

Overall, Smith resists partial explanations, explanations which cut economic activity away from politics, from psychology and sociology, and from ethics; and his science of man is correspondingly wide-ranging. But even so he often analyses issues in recognizably economic ways. After all, he is seeking to explain large areas of human behaviour through the discovery or enunciation of general principles, such as the instinct to truck, barter and exchange; to bring those principles into reflective balance with data, and with his own observations, as in the division of labour, specialization and its relation to market size; and to apply his own tool kit of developed ideas to the analysis of market processes, as in his discussion of the corn trade. Smith does not use mathematical models in the modern style, to simplify and clarify what is at stake in economic problems. Such models did not then exist— though the extraordinary work of Condorcet shows that they were not too far off, at least in the related area of voting systems. But he was not afraid to question existing economic theories, or to extend what is clearly economic thinking to new areas.

There is, however, a serious caveat to be entered here. Adam Smith would almost certainly have been astonished by many of the achievements of modern mainstream economics. He would have marvelled at its theoretical sophistication and explanatory power, and he would have been amused to see how far *The Wealth of Nations* had the unintended but largely beneficent consequence in the nineteenth century of establishing political economy as an independent discipline. But he would also perhaps have entertained serious concerns about modern economics as well: about the narrowing process by which it came into being in the nineteenth and twentieth centuries, about the contrast between its professional self-confidence and its intellectual and practical limitations, and about the price, not least in public esteem, at which its achievements have been bought. For the modern world of economics—of rational economic man, general equilibrium theory and the Efficient Market Hypothesis, is one that has borrowed very selectively from Smith. It has quarried away at his thought not merely in the cause of better understanding and explanation of economic phenomena, but arguably in order to suit its professional and ideological purposes. And in so doing it has largely ignored the central feature of Smith's worldview—the embedding of market activity within a normative ethical and social framework.

The real Smith—the Smith of history, philosophy and political economy—still has a vast amount to teach us. In a wide range of areas, from markets to crony capitalism to inequality to the social foundations of our lives, there are profound lessons to be drawn from his thought, as we shall see. In the next chapter, we turn to his influence on economics itself.

CHAPTER 7

SMITH'S ECONOMICS

Тhink of it as an economic Just-So story. At the start of their highly successful economics textbook, the dauntingly entitled *General Competitive Analysis* of 1971, Kenneth Arrow and Frank Hahn acknowledged the importance of Adam Smith:

> There is by now a long and fairly imposing line of economists from Adam Smith to the present who have sought to show that a decentralized economy motivated by self-interest and guided by price signals would be compatible with a coherent disposition of economic resources that could be regarded, in a well-defined sense, as superior to a large class of possible alternative dispositions . . .
>
> Adam Smith's 'invisible hand' is a poetic expression of the most fundamental of economic balance relations . . . [But] Smith also perceived the most important implication of general equilibrium theory . . . Thus it can be maintained that Smith was a creator of general equilibrium theory, though the coherence and consistency of his work may be questioned.

The claim here is measured, the language guarded and semi-scientific. Decoded, however, its message is plain: Adam Smith was the first person to grasp, albeit vaguely, that individual self-interest working across different freely functioning markets under conditions of perfect competition can generate superior economic efficiency. It may not look like it, but this is a tribute to genius.

This idea was and remains arguably the central insight of mainstream modern economics. But for the lead author of the book, Kenneth Arrow, widely regarded as one of the greatest economists of all time, there was another and more personal reason to start with Smith. In 1954, with the brilliant French mathematical economist Gérard Debreu—and alongside Lionel McKenzie, working separately—Arrow had discovered what many saw as the philosopher's stone of modern economics. This was a rigorous mathematical proof that a general equilibrium could exist in a competitive market economy: that is, that there was a set of prices, perhaps more than one, at which the quantities supplied and demanded would be simultaneously equal across all markets.

In other words, out of the apparent chaos of billions of decisions to buy or sell, invest or save or spend could come—provably, via a formal mathematical demonstration—the unbidden windfall of economic order. And this came simply through the actions of individuals acting via the magic of self-interest or, in the jargon, 'maximizing their utility against a set of given preferences'. A massive coordinated outcome could arise, but with no overall coordinator, no overseer or supervisor, no central planner or directing organization—just simply through people buying and selling at known prices and on the basis of their own preferences. Indeed, not only did the operation of self-interest cause chaos to yield to order, it did so in a way that created both the greatest efficiency and, in a certain sense, the greatest public welfare, for it was later shown that such an economy maximizes the utility or benefit of the people in it. In particular, no one can be made better off without someone else being made worse off—a phenomenon known as Pareto optimality, after the Italian economist Vilfredo Pareto. On this view, Adam Smith's invisible hand thus creates not merely the greatest aggregate efficiency, but the greatest overall utility as well.

This discovery gave heart to those of a *laissez-faire* bent, who argued that it made the case for non-intervention in markets, at least—a crucial caveat—under ideal conditions. But paradoxically Arrow and Debreu's proof also inspired potential interventionists, because it was discovered that Pareto optimality was compatible in principle with widely varying distributional outcomes, and that the relevant equilibria could be reached by making lump-sum transfers between individuals and then allowing them to trade freely.

The 1954 proof launched what came to be known as general equilibrium theory, one of the landmarks of modern economics. In collaboration with Debreu, *General Competitive Analysis* suggested, Arrow had thus brought the key argument of *The Wealth of Nations* to a mathematically compelling modern resolution—a resolution which later figured heavily in the award of Nobel Prizes to both men, though not to McKenzie. But a reader of the book could be forgiven for thinking that for Arrow and Hahn Adam Smith's real genius lay not in what *The Wealth of Nations*—nor for that matter *The Theory of Moral Sentiments*, let alone his other writings—might have actually said, but in identifying a line of thought that anticipated their own general equilibrium proof itself. Smith's work was not quite coherent or consistent, they maintained, but he could nevertheless be considered a creator of general equilibrium theory, alongside Arrow and the others.

However, there was one small problem: as a reading of Adam Smith, Arrow and Hahn's great textbook was highly misleading. The use of Smith's name was apparently designed to give context and historical legitimacy to general equilibrium theory, but the implication that Arrow and Debreu's work somehow represented the culmination of Smith's thought is bogus. Their proof was undoubtedly a landmark in economics. But what Smith himself was actually saying ranged even wider, and was in many ways still more interesting.

'WELL-DEFINED QUESTIONS, PRESELECTED ASSUMPTIONS'

Fast forward thirty years. In the late 1980s, Vernon Smith and a group of ambitious younger economists in less well-known American universities were engaged on a project that seemed somehow both irrelevant and subversive to many of their older colleagues: to test under laboratory conditions, or as close to laboratory conditions as possible, whether and how far many of the key assumptions of mainstream economics were in fact true. The experiments took a wide variety of forms, including what have since become known as the Trust, Ultimatum and Dictator games, and a host of others.

What the experimenters found was baffling. According to the standard mainstream view, individual behaviour is defined as that of 'rational economic man', also known as *homo economicus*: a purely self-interested utility-maximizer. This idea has long been taken as the canon of economic rationality; it lay at the heart of general equilibrium theory, indeed of modern economics as a whole; and since economics has aspirations to explain all human behaviour, to that extent it could be thought of as definitive of rationality itself. Yet, as Vernon Smith and his co-workers found—in work that was later to win him a Nobel Prize, with Daniel Kahneman—it did not describe how individuals in fact acted under laboratory conditions. Economic theory implied, for example, that anonymous strangers who interacted once and only once with no history and no future expectations should act in an entirely self-interested way. With only one interaction there could be no reciprocal benefit, after all, and they would have nothing to lose from taking the maximum pay-offs, even if others did worse as a result. Yet again and again, in game after game and context after context, contrary results came back, with great robustness. People took the cooperative option, at personal cost; they respected norms of fairness, trust and reciprocity; they were cued by perceptions of propriety and legitimacy of ownership and a host of other moral, behavioural and cultural factors. And they were able to make their way to an efficient equilibrium even with only a few, ill-informed and incompletely rational participants. In Vernon Smith's words, this was 'good news for market performance, but not such good news for the scientific community because it demonstrates that we do not understand why markets work the way they do'.

In effect, the experimentalists' results raised questions about some of the deepest assumptions of mainstream economics. The issue was not so much that the mathematical models themselves were unrealistic; all models are simplifications to some degree. Nor was it that humans can act in self-interested ways; no one doubted that. Rather, it was a direct challenge to the central assumption of self-interest associated with rational economic man. This assumption was not some useful add-on, but sat at the very core of the standard theory. Yet it looked flawed and incomplete. Even within what could be called human economic behaviour, the results suggested that self-interest only captured part of a vastly wider and more diverse picture.

This in turn underlined a further point. Testing in the lab highlighted how formalistic mainstream economics had become; indeed that it was increasingly dissociated from the messy details of economic activity and increasingly preoccupied with the properties of the models themselves, with 'the accuracy of answers to well-defined questions posed with preselected assumptions', as another Nobel laureate, Amartya Sen, once put it. How people actually lived, how they actually traded with and treated each other, how their economic, social and moral lives interacted—these issues had somehow been left behind.

RATIONAL ECONOMIC MAN

But this in turn raises a series of important questions. How does mainstream economics relate to the political economy of *The Wealth of Nations*? What happened to economics in the intervening two centuries? Was Adam Smith the creator of rational economic man? To answer these questions, we need to review the history briefly, before turning to the present state of economics. We need to look not merely at the mainstream, but at what—and who—has been left out of the wider picture. The results are surprising, and highly significant.

The story starts around the time of Smith's death in 1790. In his *Introduction to the Principles of Morals and Legislation*, published in the previous year, Jeremy Bentham proposed that the moral goodness of an action should be defined not in terms of people's intentions or virtue or sense of duty, but only in terms of its consequences for people's happiness or pleasure, according to what he termed 'the principle of utility'. Bentham argued that pleasure and pain could be measured for this purpose along seven dimensions of a 'hedonic calculus': intensity, duration, certainty or uncertainty, propinquity or remoteness, fecundity, purity and extent. The attraction of this approach was its apparent potential to be objective and scientific: to reduce vague moral intuitions to objective facts about human psychology that could in principle be tested. 'Utility' became a catch-all for the satisfaction of human wants or preferences, and the general idea of a 'utility function', mapping an individual's consumption of goods to their utility, was born in embryo.

Less than a decade later, Thomas Malthus published his famous *Essay on the Principle of Population* (1798). There he predicted that, left unchecked, the world's population would grow geometrically, as in the series 1, 2, 4, 8, 16 . . . , while food production could only grow arithmetically, as in the series 1, 2, 3, 4 . . . , creating a gap with potentially catastrophic consequences. The *Essay* was more than simply a warning, however; it was a pioneering attempt to link what is recognizably proto-economic modelling to policy-making. For Malthus, a keen student of Adam Smith, the prediction served to invalidate radical and utopian ideas of the perfectibility of man, while also pointing to economic factors and policy measures that could limit population growth. Yes, population growth might lead to subsistence wages, pressure on the working poor and economic volatility; but public policies on later marriage and education, among other things, could soften and shape its effects.

Crucially, Malthus deliberately narrowed the scope of his analysis. He treated human beings in his theory as though they were simply subject to two fundamental drives. One was self-interest, but the other was not apparently economic at all: sexual passion. In his account these drives overwhelmed the dictates of reason, making other human attributes irrelevant to the basic analysis, though not to its remedies. The effect of this narrowing was to make the analysis simpler and more tractable; Malthus was able to theorize more generally by making radical assumptions about deep aspects of human nature and abstracting away from incidental features, anecdote and individual cases. Less than a decade after Adam Smith's death, he had taken a first step towards what we now think of as *homo economicus*.

A further step was taken twenty years later by David Ricardo. Ricardo is best known today for one very brilliant and counter-intuitive idea: the principle of comparative advantage. It is not hard to see how, if two countries each have lower costs in different areas of production, they can both gain from trading with each other: this is a basic Smithian insight. But Ricardo took the idea much further. In his *Principles of Political Economy* (1817), he pointed out that, in theory at least, it can be mutually advantageous for two countries to trade with each other even if one of them has lower costs than the other *in every single product*. In his simple worked example, if England is more efficient at producing cloth than wine, and Portugal more efficient at producing wine than cloth, then it can make sense for them to trade with each other, even if Portugal is in fact able to produce both cloth and wine at lower cost than England. Why? Because trading with each other frees up resources in both countries to produce more of the product in which it has a comparative advantage: in this case, cloth for England and wine for Portugal. Production in both countries is thereby maximized. In effect, Ricardo had taken the Smithian theory of exchange and looked more closely and systematically at its effects on production.

But, again, Ricardo's thought operates through processes of abstraction, at two levels. In the first place, perhaps surprisingly in a businessman, he is remarkably unconcerned with specific facts or individual cases. Indeed, he appears to have been the first major thinker to introduce the idea of class analysis self-consciously into British political economy, again generalizing an idea of Smith's, and of the Physiocrats before him. Since profits depended in part on wages, there was a natural conflict between the proprietors and owners as a class, on the one hand, and the workers on the other. Neither the point nor the wider analysis was lost on Karl Marx. Secondly, Ricardo thinks more in terms of categorical laws of political economy than in terms of flexible general rules: in his words, 'The principle of gravitation is not more certain.' The market mechanism becomes an operation of fixed and unchanging economic laws, regardless of place and circumstance. The effect is that Smith's cautious, empirical and qualified 'system of natural liberty' becomes transformed into 'a system of perfectly free commerce'. This capacity for radical generalization was a crucial source of the power of Ricardo's ideas: it is perhaps little wonder that the politician Henry Brougham thought of him as having dropped to earth from another planet.

However, it was not until 1836 that economic man first made his full appearance on the public stage, and even then not by name. That appearance came in John Stuart Mill's essay *On the Definition of Political Economy*. Mill was later to remark that '*The Wealth of Nations* is in many parts obsolete, and in all, imperfect'; for him, political economy had come of age only in his own time. He was himself quite aware of the multiplicity and variety of human life. But in Ricardian spirit he defined political economy by abstracting away from such detail: '[Political economy] does not treat of the whole of man's nature as modified by the social state, nor of the whole conduct of man in society. It is concerned with him solely as a being who desires to possess wealth and who is capable of judging of the comparative efficacy of means for obtaining that end.' What was that nature? Mill discarded Malthus's focus on sexual passion, and substituted a still narrower, and this time entirely economic, view: 'It makes entire abstraction of

every other human passion or motive; except those which may be regarded as perpetually antagonizing principles to the desire of wealth,
namely, aversion to labour, and desire of the present enjoyment of
costly indulgences.'

The Turn to Mathematics

Mill's utilitarian thinking was focused, like Bentham's, on outcomes
and consequences, on the maximization of utility irrespective of duties
and obligations, and it reflected the increasing preoccupation of political economists with physics and mathematics. For all his Newtonianism, Adam Smith had also been acutely aware that human beings were
not like physical bodies and did not behave as such, but in a dynamic
way that responded to incentive and circumstance; the purpose of *The
Theory of Moral Sentiments* is in part to set out an understanding of
these phenomena in potentially lawlike terms, but one also able to account for their dynamic character. These caveats about formal methods had found echoes in the work of Malthus and Mill, and there was
a body of nineteenth-century opinion that opposed the introduction of
mathematical methods into political economy as misleading, alienat-
ing and obfuscatory. When Alfred Marshall published his *Principles of
Economics* in the 1890s, he was careful to relegate his mathematical
workings to the end, so as not to deter the general reader.

However, as political economy became publicly established in the
middle decades of the nineteenth century, the drive to mathematize
it became more ambitious. In the 1870s, a set of new ideas came together in what has since become known as the Marginalist Revolution
in economics, and it too marked a further step in the creation of rational economic man. Three men stood at its centre: William Stanley
Jevons in Britain, Carl Menger in Austria and Léon Walras in Switzerland. They worked independently, but they were linked by an understanding that the incremental value or 'utility' of a good tended
to decline as the amount of it increased: what is now known as the
principle of diminishing marginal utility. As Jevons put it, 'Exchange

will . . . go on until each party has obtained all the benefit that is possible, and loss of utility would result if more were exchanged. Both parties, then, rest in satisfaction and equilibrium, and the degrees of utility have come to their level, as it were.' But this meant that, in a competitive market, prices would be set not by wages or other costs of production but by the marginal price at which the amounts supplied and demanded were equal. In Jevons's words, 'This point of equilibrium will be known by the criterion, that an infinitely small amount of commodity exchanged in addition, at the same rate, will bring neither gain nor loss of utility.' And he was able to show in principle how the mathematics of the differential calculus could be used to compute the point of equilibrium in such a case.

Jevons's work illustrated the potential power of mathematical formalization in the new economics, its claim to greater precision than ordinary language and its capacity to present complex ideas in simple form. Working independently in Lausanne, Jevons's French contemporary Léon Walras went further still. Walras thought of economics and equilibrium in what he took to be Newtonian terms. He had been taught by Antoine Augustin Cournot, who had pioneered the use of mathematics in political economy. As Cournot had argued, it was not controversial that individual markets could be in equilibrium, with supply equal to demand. But was it possible to prove that a whole economy could be in equilibrium across all its markets simultaneously? Walras's answer was Yes, and he offered a sequence of putative incremental proofs towards that conclusion. These proofs were and have since been much debated and contested. But what has not been contested is the research programme that Walras thereby laid down: the systematic investigation and development of different general equilibrium theories, which has proven to be hugely influential.

Over time, these ideas coalesced, expanded and developed into what later became the mainstream of modern microeconomics. Yet from the outset there were also competing views about how markets worked, and how they could reach equilibrium. Of these one of the most ultimately fruitful was that of Francis Ysidro Edgeworth. Edgeworth rejected Walras's approach, in which people traded with 'the market', rather than with each other, as overly formalistic. Rather, he defined a process of negotiation or—adopting a phrase of Smith's—'higgling' by which market participants reached agreement. With small numbers of people, this process was an indeterminate one, which allowed for inefficient bargains; but as numbers grew greater, so the market as a whole would progressively move towards a maximally efficient equilibrium. The ingenuity of Edgeworth's approach was that it plausibly related much more realistic descriptions of how people actually bargain to the mathematically idealized outcomes of perfect competition—it was in this sense more Smithian than Walrasian. Ignored for decades, his ideas were rediscovered and reinvigorated with the work of John Nash and others in the second half of the twentieth century, when they gave rise to important work in the theory of cooperative and non-cooperative games.

Game theory was yet another example of mathematics being incorporated into economics. But the core concept of man as a rational economic agent, *homo economicus*, lay at the centre of all this work; and as economics grew more mathematical, so the idea of *homo economicus* became progressively narrower. Classical political economists such as John Stuart Mill had thought in terms of general rules, to which numerous exceptions might exist; indeed, exceptions might exist even to the basic principle of free trade itself. For them economic man—and it always was a man—was a profit-seeker, but he had not lost touch with his social, institutional and cultural context. Rationality in political economy was but one kind of rational human behaviour. Political economy itself enshrined a link between the political and the economic, and left room for historical and social factors in its search for economic explanations. And purposive human activity of all kinds was seen as embedded in ethics: as conduct, that is, not merely as behaviour.

By the time of Walras, however, the political economists were in retreat. The term 'political economy' was starting to be replaced by 'economics', and 'economics' both dropped the reference to a 'polity' or political community and carried an air of being an intellectually self-sufficient subject in its own right alongside mathematics, aesthetics, ethics and politics. Indeed, economics went further: it aspired to be an exact science on the model of physics. That is, it was intended to be an entirely general theory, concerned with 'universal laws' that transcended any specific context or set of circumstances, and any given type or epoch of society. It was well defined, precise and increasingly mathematical, to the point of being unintelligible to the non-specialist. It was cast as a theory of individuals, rather than classes or groups. As with physics and the other 'hard' sciences, it regarded itself as value-free, as descriptive and empirical rather than normative in character. In transcending context and history, it had no space for institutions: for if profits are to be maximized, marginal cost must equal marginal revenue, all opportunities to reduce cost and all opportunities for advantageous exchange must have been taken, and all technological improvement adopted. The resulting allocation of resources will be efficient—this is purely a matter of mathematics.

In its basic form, such a theory never begins to ask about the nature of companies, families or other institutions—in its models they do not exist, and nor do human artefacts such as culture, history and tradition. Indeed, later it would come to see much if not all of politics itself as reducible to economics, even if not quite as an epiphenomenon or add-on, as some latter-day Marxists would have it. As with physics, it disdained psychology and sociology as irrelevant to its own concerns and methods. And as with physics, it purported to be memoryless; for what could the point be of memory or history in a hard science, where present results supersede past ones?

And the idea of *homo economicus* changed as well. As general equilibrium thinking moved to centre stage, individuals came to be seen increasingly not even as human at all, but as mere economic agents, atoms cut off from others, perfectly rational, operating in an exceptionless way in frictionless markets possessed of perfect information. The theory itself was highly abstract, not to say utopian—no such state of affairs existed or ever could exist in nature—and rather than reasoning from nature directly, it took perfect market conditions as its starting point. And it was static in character. Such was the effect of a general equilibrium that in theory any perturbation or change to even a single agent's marginal desire for a product would affect demand for that product and, potentially, the prices of every other product in the given economy, as the different equivalences worked their way mathematically through the system.

When Kenneth Arrow and Gérard Debreu gave their own widely celebrated general equilibrium proof in 1954, then, it was within this broadly neoclassical tradition, and that proof reinforced the school's claim to be a central part of the modern mainstream in microeconomics. Political economy had long since become economics, and economics had given birth to *homo economicus*. It is little wonder, then, that the name of Adam Smith is so often cited, not merely as the father of economics, but as an originator—perhaps even *the* originator—of this idea as well.

But the ironies were manifest. Mathematics was originally intended to be a tool of analysis. Instead it had moved to centre stage, increasingly shaping what questions could be asked, and expanding within the universities into a means by which economists established themselves in priestly professional hierarchies. *Homo economicus* originally developed over time as a useful fiction, whose purpose was to reduce complex questions down to the bare bones of mathematical structure—that is, to allow the simplifications necessary for mathematics to get some purchase on the problem. Instead it had been taken over by utilitarian thinking and marginalist mathematics, and transformed into a culturally significant meme shaping the development of economics itself, and eliciting a far-reaching political reaction from those concerned about the impact of 'neoliberal' economics on policy-making. Thus, too, was born in outline the popular caricature of economic man we see today: as wealth-maximizing, pleasure-seeking, greedy, calculating—and idle to boot.

Moreover, the work of Arrow and Debreu itself was swept up in this process as well, although a key part of the point of their work—as Arrow was at pains to make clear—was to clarify just how demanding were the conditions required to achieve a general market equilibrium. In other words, just as Malthus had used economic modes of thought to argue against utopian ideas of human perfectibility, so did Arrow use them more than a century later to highlight the imperfectibility of markets. The conditions he identified were so demanding, in fact, that such an equilibrium could never occur. In other words, the mathematics showed that markets by themselves could never be guaranteed to achieve optimal allocations of economic goods and welfare across an economy, or to adjust optimally for the effects of redistribution. There would always be scope, both in theory and in practice, for politics and government to make a difference, and that difference could be for good or ill.

As for Smith himself: he did not invent general equilibrium theory, or bargaining theory, or the theory of comparative advantage. There is no mention of rational economic man or *homo economicus* in his work, and in many ways the idea is foreign to his thinking. Moreover, many of the stock criticisms of contemporary economics do not apply to Smith himself; indeed many of those criticisms have echoes in his own work. His genius is, rather, to have set out the field of political economy with markets at its centre, in a way that remains startlingly relevant; to have used what are recognizably economic modes of thought in doing so; to have placed institutions and a historical sensibility at its centre; and to have filled the field with insights that continue to inspire economists across an astonishing range of fields today.

MAINSTREAM ECONOMICS

Before we can gauge the true magnitude of Smith's achievement, however, we need to go deeper into the nature of mainstream economics itself. What exactly *is* 'mainstream economics'?

This apparently straightforward question has proven to be rather contentious, for the word 'mainstream' can be used and misused for ideological or professional purposes to define and sideline others as unorthodox, narrow or irrelevant. It is conventionally identified with the work of Paul Samuelson, the third (1955) edition of whose best-selling *Economics* offered a mathematically rigorous but accessible synthesis combining 'foundations' in the microeconomics of companies and markets with a wider picture taken from the Keynesian macroeconomics of GDP, inflation, employment and the rest; it became over many editions the best-selling economics textbook of all time. But this conventional account greatly underplays the achievement of Keynes himself. Keynes saw his *General Theory of Employment, Interest and Money* (1936) as exactly that—a general theory, of which classical economics is supposed to be a special case—but it is of a radically different kind to those of the equilibrium theorists. Yes, Keynes argued, there can be points of equilibrium in an economy, but this may be precisely because markets, in particular labour markets, are *not* clearing: an economy can be trapped for long periods in high unemployment and low aggregate demand. And these can occur because of factors affecting the real economy—above all, radical uncertainty, hoarding and what Keynes called 'animal spirits' affecting confidence and morale—which appear nowhere in the standard economic models.

Keynes advertised the *General Theory* as a break from what he called the 'classical tradition'. But he traced the origins of that specific tradition, accurately, not to Smith but to Ricardo and the French economist J. B. Say. For Keynes, Smith stood above it; as he wrote in his *Essays in Biography*, 'Economists must leave to Adam Smith alone the glory of the Quarto, must pluck the day, fling pamphlets into the wind, write always *sub specie temporis,* and achieve immortality by accident, if at all.' And in his insistence on seeing man as a human animal, and on embedding markets within a social and normative context, Keynes was perhaps more Smithian than he acknowledged. Paul Samuelson later took Keynes's economics and—drawing on work by John Hicks—turned it into the crucially different 'Keynesian economics'. But in many ways that so-called 'neoclassical synthesis' would be better described as a Keynesian synthesis; and even that phrase does insufficient justice to Keynes's own creativity, realism and willingness to explore behaviour that others took to be economically irrational or mathematically intractable.

However it is described, this broad cluster of views remains the economic mainstream. It has arguably had policy disasters in recent decades, but it would be absurd to play down its achievements. It has proven to be of central importance in understanding human behaviour, in analysing economic activity, and in explaining, framing and guiding the decisions of individuals, households, corporations and governments. But mainstream economics has also grown in public stature from having three key features less closely connected to its intrinsic merits. The first is that it is often presented as an autonomous realm of public wisdom and social choice. This in turn can generate a powerful moral justification for the market, as the place where individuals' freedoms to choose find expression in transactions, are aggregated into a collective freedom for the multitude and have unexpected, unintended and yet beneficial social consequences overall.

The second feature is that economics itself is often seen as a putative theory of everything. One can see this in the growth of its definition over the decades. In 1844 John Stuart Mill had defined political economy as 'the science of the laws which regulate the production, distribution, and consumption of wealth'. Some ninety years later, Lionel Robbins described economics in 1932 still more generally, as 'the science which studies human behaviour as a relationship between given ends and scarce means which have alternative uses'. More recently,

1. Adam Smith's mother, Margaret Douglas, a portrait attributed to Conrad Metz (1749–1827). 'I certainly loved and respected [her] more than I shall ever love or respect any other person,' Smith said.

2. Smith's 'never-to-be-forgotten' teacher, Francis Hutcheson, by Allan Ramsay (1713–84).

3. David Hume, painted by Allan Ramsay in 1766. Smith said 'I have always considered him . . . approaching as nearly to the idea of a perfectly wise and virtuous man, as perhaps the nature of human frailty will permit.'

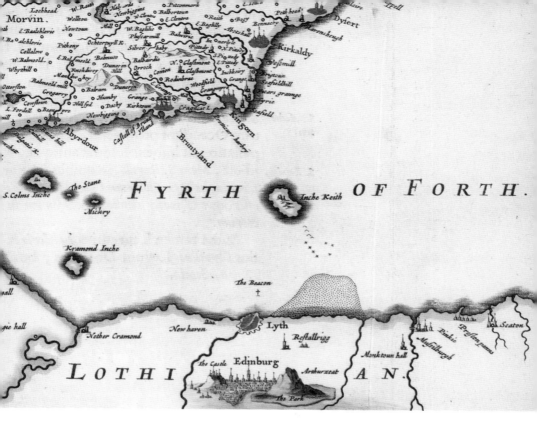

4. The Firth of Forth, showing Edinburgh, Leith and Kirkcaldy, from the Blaeu Atlas of Scotland, 1654.

5. View of Edinburgh from Arthur's Seat, by Wenceslaus Hollar, 1670.

6. Charles Edward Stuart, 'Bonnie Prince Charlie'; the so-called 'Lost Portrait' by Allan Ramsay, painted just before the Jacobite invasion of England, autumn 1745.

7. Adam Smith's pupil, patron and friend Henry Scott, 3rd Duke of Buccleuch, by Thomas Gainsborough, 1770.

8. Edmund Burke, studio of Joshua Reynolds, *c.* 1769. Smith reportedly said Burke was 'the only man, who, without communication, thought on [economic subjects] exactly as he did'.

9. Jean Jacques Rousseau, painted in his favourite Armenian costume by Allan Ramsay, 1766. The picture was a gift from Ramsay to David Hume, with whom Rousseau later violently fell out.

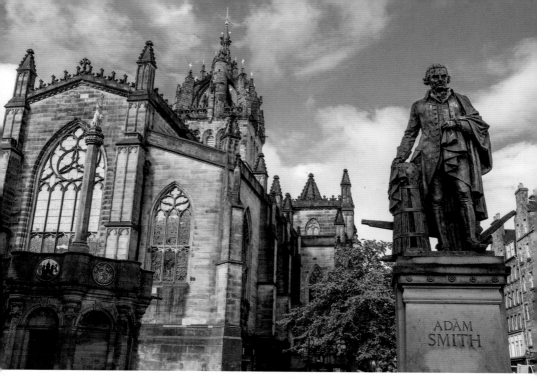

10. Adam Smith by Alexander Stoddart, in heroic pose in front of St Giles' Cathedral on the Royal Mile in Edinburgh …

11. … and David Hume as a Roman senator, also by Stoddart, on the other side of the Cathedral.

12. John Maynard Keynes with Henry Morgenthau, the US Treasury Secretary, at the Bretton Woods conference, 1944. Keynes said 'Economists must leave to Adam Smith alone the glory of the Quarto ... and achieve immortality by accident, if at all.'

13. Kenneth Arrow receiving the Nobel Prize for economics, 1972. No less than Keynes and Hayek, his work stands in dialogue with Smith.

14. Adam Smith on a medallion by James Tassie, 1787: the only surviving portrait from life.

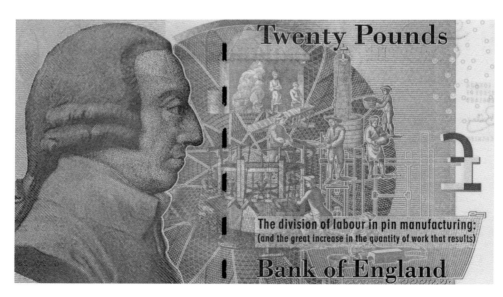

15. The Bank of England's £20 note, honouring Adam Smith, the father of economics.

the authors of the best-selling book *Freakonomics* have expressed the now fashionable view that 'Economics is, at root, the study of incentives: how people get what they want, or need, especially when other people need the same thing.' What is so striking about this progression is not merely the expansion of economics from wealth-creation and -distribution via behaviour to the maximally general study of incentives as such, presumably including incentives that appear to have nothing to do with economics: it is the way in which economics has been increasingly defined in terms not of subject matter but of methodology. This appears to be unusual, perhaps unique, among academic and policy disciplines. Historians study history, chemists study chemistry, lawyers study law. Economists study how incentives work. That makes economics a very general study indeed.

The idea that economics is or could be a—or even the—theory of everything as regards human behaviour has enhanced its prestige immensely. Indeed, so much so that as a subject it now exercises an often unquestioned dominance over policy analysis and policy tools in the minds of many politicians and officials around the world. And this in turn has been bolstered by a third factor: its forbidding technical demands. Though there have been welcome moves to open up economics further to public scrutiny and debate, the subject as a whole remains highly inaccessible to the non-specialist. This tendency has been greatly reinforced by the jargon, core theoretical assumptions and, in particular, mathematical formalism of mainstream economics, which offer formidable barriers to wider understanding and participation. These in turn have served to discourage lay scrutiny, endow the discipline as a whole with a certain mystique and promote a culture of academic dispute and intellectual logic-chopping which can impede outside challenge, interdisciplinary research and a more self-conscious awareness of its own assumptions.

The overall effect of these three features has been to build in a certain presumption in favour of economics over other disciplines. Subjects such as politics, psychology, sociology, anthropology, planning, design, even history, culture and the arts have had to with-stand the suggestion that they are at least partly derivative, or 'really' about economics all along. Traditions and practices, concepts, modes of thought developed in those areas can then supposedly be recon-strued in purely economic terms. Far from the claims of economics to be a purely descriptive science, offering neutral policy tools, these factors can nudge practitioners and experts towards a particular and rather narrowly individualistic and profit-seeking view of the world, as though its idealized models were desirable in themselves and could be made to happen in actual markets.

Beyond the Mainstream

Why does this matter? We can answer this by asking not just what mainstream economics assumes, but what it leaves out.

For one thing, it leaves out the rest of economics. Textbooks disagree on how to categorize the different modern schools of eco-nomic thought. But, at the risk of oversimplification, there are at least six identifiable, coherent and more or less active alternatives to the mainstream. In very rough chronological order, they include Marxism, focused on production, class conflict, capital accumula-tion, business cycles and technological change; Austrian economics, stressing limitations on human rationality, the importance of norms, spontaneous order, prices as signals, innovation and entrepreneur-ship; post-Keynesianism, emphasizing uncertainty and 'animal spirits', stagnation, unemployment and the scope for active government fiscal interventions; developmental economics, analysing the industrial link-ages which hinder or assist improvements in productive capabilities, protection and the role of policy in nurturing infant industries; insti-tutional economics, exploring how institutions shape individual and collective behaviour, and more recently the specific role of transac-tion costs; and monetarism, emphasizing the importance of the money supply and the influence of monetary factors on inflation, economic performance and national output. The boundaries are porous: many would argue, for example, that institutional economics or behavioural economics should now be considered part of the mainstream.

Mainstream economics thus represents one set of ideas elaborated from *The Wealth of Nations*. But it is far from clear that Smith would have endorsed many aspects of it. Such is the power of his original insights about the centrality of markets, and such is the range of his wider views, that every single other modern school of economics can with justice claim him as a progenitor as well. Indeed, two of them—Marxist economics and Austrian economics—have claims that are arguably at least as good as those of the modern mainstream.

Take Marxism, for example. Karl Marx was both a keen student and a trenchant critic of Adam Smith, but at first sight the idea that Marxist economics derives in any way from Smith may seem absurd. Surely Marxism is the very antithesis of free markets? How can the doctrines of the *Communist Manifesto* owe anything to *The Wealth of Nations*? These issues are too large to be debated properly here, but we can note some parallels and points of contact. In Marx's imagined future, history can only lead to the ultimate triumph of the proletariat, the abolition of private property rights and the common ownership of the means of production and exchange; at that point markets of any kind will cease to exist in favour of collective ownership and the administrative distribution of goods. But that historical process—indeed the course of history itself—is ultimately economically determined, according to Marx. His is a staged theory of a very broadly Smithian, though materialist and more broadly deterministic, kind.

For Marx, the iron logic of history is at root an economic logic, and in several key ways that economics too is Smithian. Marx's economic agents are not individuals but classes, and he extends Smith's outline categorization of landlords, workers and merchants into a full-fledged theory of class. He recognizes the focus Smith gives to the rights of workers, and adopts and develops Smith's labour theory of value. He accepts much of Smith's analysis of how markets work, but argues that markets have a tendency not towards equilibrium, but towards unavoidable instability and self-destruction. And he greatly extends the Smithian idea of the alienation caused by specialization and the division of labour, using it to mount a trenchant attack on the rapid industrialization of the mid-nineteenth century. So voracious was Marx's reading that his basic philosophy has a host of influences, and his policy prescriptions are his own and those of his collaborator Friedrich Engels. But much of his economic analysis comes, directly or indirectly, from reflection on Adam Smith, and so does that of Marx's modern successors.

The same is true, in a different way, for the Austrian school. Its founder, Carl Menger, was one of the creators of the so-called Marginalist Revolution, as we saw earlier. But his focus, and that of his great successors Ludwig von Mises and Friedrich Hayek, was very different from that of the neoclassical theorists of general equilibrium. The equilibrium theorists concentrated on states of the economy under ideal assumptions of perfect information and rationality, as we have seen: they used mathematics to analyse the conditions under which the quantities supplied and demanded would be equal in specific markets, and in an economy as a whole.

The Austrians rejected this approach. Instead they looked at the dynamics of markets; at how prices act as signals of relative scarcity and abundance; at how people could trade successfully with each other using limited information and partial rationality; at how, rather than constantly seeking to maximize utility, people often settled for less than optimal outcomes; and at how rules of thumb and maxims of action could act as 'heuristics'—psychological short-cuts—guiding such behaviour in the absence of hard-and-fast rules. They looked at institutions, which seemed to play such a significant role in shaping economic and social outcomes; at entrepreneurship and innovation; and above all at what von Mises called catallactics and Hayek catallaxy: how order could emerge spontaneously from the chaos of individual relationships and individual transactions. The link with the Smithian picture of the spontaneous emergence of moral and economic order is evident.

Arguably *The Wealth of Nations* is more Austrian than neoclassical in character. Indeed, in many ways mainstream economics gets Adam Smith exactly the wrong way round. It takes individuals as fixed and isolated vehicles for preferences, rather than as shape-shifting, dynamic and social, as Smith does. It takes their preferences as given, rather than as constantly changing, being ordered and reordered and formed dynamically by the disposition to truck, barter and exchange with others, as Smith does. Its conception of competition is as an end-state of equilibrium between traders, not as a continuous process of jockeying for advantage. And it is a closed and static theory, rather than an open-ended and evolutionary one, as is Smith's. Thus, far from being the culmination of Adam Smith's work, as Arrow and Hahn claimed, mainstream economics in general, and general equilibrium theory in particular, are at a deeper level actually in conflict with much of its central thrust.

LEAVING OUT HALF THE WORLD

But there is something else that mainstream economics and its conventional history have tended to leave out, something absolutely fundamental: the role of women. The point is not that *homo economicus* is a man, for the Latin word *homo* or 'man' is, like 'mankind', at root a species word, albeit a masculine one. Nor is it that the etymological link between economics and the Greek word *oikonomia* or 'household management' has been lost to view—and with it the original contrast with *political* economy, as the economics of the *polis* or city-state—and has diminished the contribution of women through the ages. No: the issue goes deeper than that. It is that this whole construct—of *homo economicus*, of mainstream economics, of equilibrium theory—tends to ignore ideas and expectations traditionally associated with women. These include the suggestion that people are fundamentally social animals, not atoms cut off from each other; that their behaviour is often not competitive, self-seeking and aggressive but fundamentally cooperative and altruistic; and that instead of being continuous calculating machines, they are often instinctive and empathetic. These associations may or may not be correct, but they point to what is missing. In highlighting them, the discipline of feminist economics is not a mere branch of the subject, let alone a quaint or esoteric sideline; it is in part a critique of the foundations of economics itself.

In fact, far from the supposed culture of *homo economicus*, for centuries before the modern era the dominant representation of nature as a whole was a female one. In ancient Greek mythology the earth was Gē or Gaia, who brought forth Ouranos the Sky and gave birth to the gods, the titans and Cyclopes. In ancient Rome, the gods associated with productive nature, nature as bringing forth crops, were almost invariably female: Ceres (crops), Feronia (wildlife), Flora (flowers), Ops (fertility), Pomona (orchards), Terra (earth). Nature and womanhood were linked through ideas of fertility, of nurturing, bounty and reproduction, and associations of seasonality and life cycle. The cosmos was seen as living, animate, with a mind/soul of its (or her) own, and able to react against those seeking to harm it.

Correlatively, the rise of science and its use in technology was accompanied by the idea that nature was not supremely powerful and all-embracing, but subordinate: something that could and should be managed, or indeed conquered, tamed, dominated and perhaps exploited. For that purpose natural phenomena should be observed and measured, but in a detached, scientific way. Nature was feminine, unruly, wilful and subjective, while science was objective, orderly, calm and masculine. As Francis Bacon himself wrote in his *Temporis Partus Masculus* or *The Masculine Birth of Time* (1602), 'I am come in very truth leading to you Nature with all her children to bind her to your service and make her your slave.' It was only a short step to identify science with rationality and reason and the male, by implication rendering the female emotional and irrational. And since science was purportedly value-free, it appeared as though this was not a result that could properly be judged or criticized. It was simply the way the world was.

As the sciences became professionalized and tied into the

academic, government and military establishments of many Western countries in the late nineteenth and early twentieth centuries, it was in ways whose effect was largely to exclude or marginalize women. The same was true as classical political economy mutated into mainstream economics. One might have expected that the detachment of the discipline from the Millian focus on the production, distribution and consumption of wealth might have opened up the field to a vastly wider array of possible subjects; and all the more so given the power and range of the marginalists' new mathematical tools. In fact, however, the subject became still further detached from real life. Yes, it still focused on the traditional, and traditionally male, area of exchange in public markets and, later, on the macroeconomy, but it moved away from production and towards consumption and, as we have seen, it increasingly ignored the actual experience of real individuals—or, in time, real households and real firms—making real choices. In his *Principles of Economics*, Alfred Marshall defined the subject as 'the study of men as they live and move and think in the ordinary business of life'. The phrase concealed a double irony: not only was economics itself not merely about men, even as he presented it; his book was not, despite his rhetoric and his own genuine misgivings, about the ordinary business of life in any concrete sense at all.

The same was true within the profession itself. In 2014 just 12 per cent of American economics professors were women, and there was just one female Nobel laureate, the late Elinor Ostrom. It was not until decades after the Second World War that areas of important public concern, but supposedly only or mainly related to women, were addressed by economists. And even then, as in the pioneering work of Gary Becker, it was in ways that drew on and reinforced the impact of mainstream economics. These hidden topics included such economically, politically and culturally central matters as the household itself as an institution; families; marriage; the nature of work and in particular unpaid work; care and the caring professions; discrimination; and the experience of women in the workplace.

The focus on market exchange also meant that for a long time mainstream economics tended to ignore much one-way human activity, such as personal giving and philanthropy, and the work of non-governmental organizations. These subjects were apparently viewed as 'soft'—a telling word—or as mere 'sociology in disguise'. Alongside this went a view that, again, saw the economy as 'the economy': as a distinct entity, apart from society and many of the usual norms of society. The economy was independent, self-sufficient, a place of business where the rules were set by law—both economic and juristic—and where there was, specifically, no room for ethics. Indeed, the argument was sometimes heard that all but minimally ethical behaviour was positively inappropriate to business. Markets were subject to impersonal 'market forces' and—the language here is often deterministic, almost Marxist—supposedly followed an iron logic of their own that could not be bucked. Within this dog-eat-dog competitive environment, what mattered was survival of the fittest. Any sense of responsibility to others, to nature or to ethical principle that went beyond strictly legal requirements applicable to all would impose unnecessary costs, and so undermine a person or company's competitiveness and efficiency. And with reduced efficiency went reduced economic growth. These arguments were made especially loudly in the worlds of finance and banking.

By contrast, as the economist Julie Nelson has argued, the household has been implicitly seen in ways akin to older views of the environment: as an unlimited source of human value, a place of nurturing and love, governed not by greed and profit-maximization but by norms of cooperation, care and altruism. These oppositions between economy and household and male and female have sometimes, it appears, been reinforced by economic statistics. To take a notorious example, the official calculation of GDP in the UK and USA and many other countries around the world is based on measuring the number and size of transactions for payment. It therefore fails to account, quite literally, for housework, for caring for the elderly and for other unpaid work that still falls mainly on women, reflecting and further reinforcing stereotypes about gender. More recent work has found that the standard modelling assumption of raceless and genderless economic agents has serious practical drawbacks.

Instead of the usual textbook definitions, Nelson has offered a definition of her own: economics is 'about how societies organize themselves to support human life and its flourishing—or about how they fail to do so'. This places economics squarely within society; it is subject-oriented and not procedural, and inclusive of the hidden topics mentioned earlier; and it does not beg the question as to issues of scarcity or abundance, market or non-market interaction, exchange or one-way activity, or the role of government. Alongside this, she has advocated an idea of husbandry in economics, in an old sense of 'careful cultivation, tending and management', and equally applicable to both men and women. 'Husbandry' suggests, not economic agents conforming to a single model of rationality and utility-maximization, but people embedded in society and respectful of the natural forces around them. As she points out, the antonyms of 'to husband' include to 'blow, dissipate, fritter (away), lavish, misspend, run through, squander, throw away, waste'. In her words, '"Economic man" dissipates. "The good husbandman" does not . . . The good husbandman, whether executive or worker, tends and cultivates. The good husbandman does a good, responsible day's work for a good day's pay.' And overall: 'Men who neglect their capability to care are less fully men.' It is a provocative and arresting thought.

SMITH ON WOMEN

How does all this bear on Adam Smith, and he on it? The answer is that the idea of rational economic man or *homo economicus* has not merely shaped modern economics; it has had a profoundly distorting effect on the public understanding of economics, and of Smith himself. In recent years Smith himself has come under attack from feminist writers and economists, who see his work as a key source of the marginalization of women both in and outside economics. In her recent book *Who Cooked Adam Smith's Dinner?*, for example, the journalist Katrine Marçal has suggested that Smith was the originator of the idea of economic man, indeed that Smith was a strict Newtonian who saw individuals as independent particles driven in a mechanistic, clockwork way by the laws of nature. According to Marçal, he believed that love was a scarce resource, marginalized women in his own writings and encouraged a belief in the supposedly separate spheres of home and work that has undermined women ever since. And, in doing all this while relying on his mother and on Janet Douglas nearly all his life, he was a hypocrite as well.

Marçal's book makes some very valuable points about the importance of 'women's work', the reasons for its historically low status and the marginalization of women, in economics and elsewhere. But unfortunately in relation to Adam Smith it offers a hopeless and slapdash caricature. None of these claims is true. Yes, Smith does not discuss women at length, and occasionally speaks of them in language that would be considered patronizing today. Yes, he sometimes analyses women and men in rather different terms, especially in *The Theory of Moral Sentiments*; indeed, one might expect such an attempt to recognize differences between men and women in a work of moral psychology and sociology. Yes, he barely writes about people's private lives, or household work, and in his own time he was not an advocate of the then radical causes of votes and political rights for women. But what is surprising overall is not how far Smith conforms to, but how far he departs from, conventional views of women, then and since. And Smith's intensely loving and respectful feelings for his mother and Mrs Douglas are clear from his letters. As Dugald Stewart said of his mother, 'He enjoyed the rare satisfaction of being able to repay her affection, by every attention that filial gratitude could dictate, during the long period of sixty years.' There is no conflict here with what Smith says about women elsewhere.

In the *Lectures on Jurisprudence*, Smith makes clear his view of the link between male power and the treatment of women: 'The laws of most countries being made by men, generally, are very severe on the women, who can have no remedy for this oppression.' Indeed, far from being committed to inequality between the sexes, Smith specifically associates the different stages in his stadial theory of social and economic development with a rise in the status of women, from 'the age of hunters', to those of shepherds, agriculture and commerce. He thus ties the increased refinement and sophistication of society directly to increased respect for women. And he is highly critical of the pre-Christian treatment of women, of double standards in relation to the law of adultery, and of the unfairness of the underlying power relations. Asking why women were punished more severely for infidelity than men, he says, 'The real reason [was not the fear of what he terms "spurious offspring" but] . . . that it is men who make the laws with respect to this; they generally will be inclined to curb the women as much as possible and give themselves the more indulgence.'

The absence of women is most noticeable in *The Wealth of Nations*. But even there Smith recognizes the value both of women's wage-earning and of their unpaid work. Women spinners and knitters must often cross-subsidize their work with employment in domestic service, he says, and their work 'never enters the public registers of manufactures', prefiguring present-day issues of low pay and the calculation of GDP. Overall, 'Thus far at least seems certain, that, in order to bring up a family, the labour of the husband and wife together must, even in the lowest species of common labour, be able to earn something more than what is precisely necessary for their own maintenance.' Far from denying women status, as did so many of his contemporaries and successors, Smith specifically recognizes their role as economic and moral agents.

Smith has also been faulted for his supposedly bourgeois view of women's education. He says that 'Every part of [women's] education tends evidently to some useful purpose; either to improve the natural attractions of their person, or to form their mind to reserve, to modesty, to chastity, and to economy; to render them both likely to become the mistresses of a family, and to behave properly when they have become such'—words which grate harshly on modern ears. But Smith's characteristically pragmatic if rather condescending view is that its very usefulness is what makes women's education superior, not inferior, to that of men. As he puts it, with a touch of asperity in both directions, 'There are no public institutions for the education of women, and there is accordingly nothing useless, absurd, or fantastical in the common course of their education. They are taught what their parents or guardians judge it necessary or useful for them to learn, and they are taught nothing else.' And when he advocates state support for public education, he talks generally not of 'men' but of 'the common people'; there is no reason to think his proposals for public education excluded women.

Indeed, as some feminist writers have contended, far from marginalizing women, Smith arguably lays the groundwork for a moral reorientation that does the reverse: that inhibits marginalization as such. The moral world Smith argues for is a profoundly egalitarian one, and acutely aware of the possibility of oppression; it is notable that Mary Wollstonecraft drew from *The Theory of Moral Sentiments* in writing her own *Vindication of the Rights of Women*. It is a world of sympathetic mutual recognition, which places the philosopher and the street porter on a level, which acknowledges the importance of injury and dignity and self-respect in its system of justice, and which emphasizes the quiet private virtues of sociability and love.

THE RETURN TO REALITY

So Marçal's criticisms miss their target. Indeed, the whole wider construction, this whole massively influential modern picture of Adam Smith—of Smith as, in effect, a 'neoliberal' economist in embryo—is quite wrong. First, as we have seen, Smith did not originate the idea of economic man, and he was scathing about human greed. Indeed, far from adopting the modern paradigm of self-interested economic rationality, in *The Wealth of Nations* he identifies a host of areas, now familiar from modern behavioural economics, in which people do not behave in supposedly economically rational ways. These include loss aversion, where people react much worse to the loss of something than they do positively to its acquisition; a very marked preference for short-term over long-term gains, or what are referred to today as hyperbolic discount rates on future gains; and overconfidence in assessing risky options. This is what we should expect, for where there are obvious mistakes of perspective and judgement, it is the function of the impartial spectator within Smith's system to correct for them. And as some have pointed out, there is ample scope for further work now in behavioural economics along lines already laid out by Smith, including people's desire to be well regarded by posterity; their negative reactions to being misjudged; their mistaken belief in the objectivity of tastes; and their sympathy for the rich and great. No less that he is for economics as a whole, Smith is the father of behavioural economics.

Secondly, any such simple account of motivation runs directly contrary to Smith's very nuanced understanding of human psychology. He does not think of people as individual atoms at all. Contrary to the modern picture, the idea of an individual as somehow 'given', independent of others, is entirely foreign to him; indeed it is unintelligible within his thought. Rather, the exact opposite is true: within his system, individuals cannot be given independent definition; they are seen as continuously dynamically defined and redefined through their relations with others.

Finally, Smith is empirical and not rationalistic in his methods. He generally dislikes abstractions, and he specifically rejects the use of highly idealized and artificial assumptions in economic policy-making, insisting that practical experience is more valuable in political economy than abstract theorizing. As he put it, 'If a nation could not prosper without the enjoyment of perfect liberty and perfect justice, there is not in the world a nation which could ever have prospered.' Substitute 'markets' for 'justice', and it is a point Kenneth Arrow would have been proud of.

It is this Smithian seam of inquiry that Vernon Smith and his fellow workers in experimental economics found themselves mining so successfully when they started to test mainstream assumptions about economic rationality under laboratory conditions. They found that their subjects' behaviour could not be adequately explained by the simple assumption of utility-maximization. On the contrary, it was deeply influenced by specific norms of reciprocity and fairness, by force of habit and by desire to preserve reputation. In other words, the people they were studying inhabited the real world, which blends norms of cooperation and trust with competition and rivalry.

Indeed, they found that, far from being adjuncts to economic activity, norms are what make that activity possible at all. This is close to Smith's view, for he specifically identifies the role of norms of fairness and justice in human interactions: 'Nature has implanted in the human breast, that consciousness of ill-desert, those terrors of merited punishment which attend upon its violation, as the great safeguards of the association of mankind, to protect the weak, to curb the violent, and to chastise the guilty.' It is only that collective norm or sense of justice that keeps the structures of market exchange in place: 'If it is removed, the great, the immense fabric of human society . . . must in a moment crumble to atoms.'

For Adam Smith, there is no such thing as an economics hermetically sealed from history, sociology or philosophical reflection. His is a spacious and inclusive view of political economy, not a reductive one. It does not seek to apply a single mode of thinking to every area it addresses, and its intended audience is anyone able to read *The Wealth of Nations*. Yet at the same time the very idea of political economy for him involves a self-conscious recognition of the embedded and value-freighted nature of economic theorizing. Norms of fairness, reciprocity and justice pervade all human dealings, personal and impersonal, exchange and non-exchange. Those norms may differ from market to workplace to home, and they may operate differently at the different levels of individual, institution and society, but they are always available. Within a commercial society, they are generally enforced in law and reinforced in culture by norms of justice whose effect is to apprehend, punish and bring back into line those who cheat. And since people like to exchange information and gossip as much as they do goods, those norms are supported, in places from the water cooler to TripAdvisor, by inexpensive means to sanction and reward behaviour. Trust is widespread, and the society flourishes. This is the world of the modern market economy.

CHAPTER 8

ADAM SMITH AND MARKETS

Meet Mr Market. If you have any exposure to the finan-cial markets—if you have a pension or a mortgage, or just need currency for a holiday abroad, for example—then whether you know it or not, Mr Market is your business partner. He is a friendly, obliging fellow, who turns up every weekday, except on bank holidays, and tells you what he thinks your shares or bonds or currency, or a host of other things, are worth. And not only that: Mr Market is almost endlessly willing to buy your shares or bonds or currency or whatever at present prices, or to sell you some of his to add to what you already have.

But alas the poor man is not well. Indeed, Mr Market is subject to appalling mood swings. At times he is wildly exuberant, and offers sky-high prices at which you can sell to or buy from him. At others he is deeply pessimistic, and so sunk in gloom that he values what you have at close to nothing, and his prices, buy or sell, are at rock bottom.

Mr Market is the metaphorical creation of a great investor, Benja-min Graham, and is regularly discussed by a legendary one, his student Warren Buffett. The metaphor contains a deep underlying point. Mr Market's moods are not rational; indeed in Buffett's colourful words, 'He's kind of a drunken psycho.' His prices may be right from time to time, or indeed for long periods, but the wise investor treats them with extreme care. As Buffett puts it, 'Mr Market is there to serve you, not to guide you . . . If he shows up some day in a particularly foolish mood, you are free to either ignore him or to take advantage of him.' It follows that the intelligent investor, in the title of Graham's famous book, must have some independent and more fundamental way to assess long-term value, as well as the patience to wait till Mr Market is foolish enough to offer them an opportunity, and the financial where-withal to grab it.

THE EFFICIENT MARKET HYPOTHESIS

But there is another view of markets, which is often contrasted with the Graham–Buffett view. This is the so-called Efficient Market Hy-pothesis. It does not date from the dawn of political economy; rather, it was first developed by Eugene Fama, an economist at the University of Chicago, in the late 1960s. It comes in different varieties: strong, semi-strong and weak. But at their heart these varieties all have two key ideas: what the behavioural economist Richard Thaler has aptly called 'The Price is Right' and 'No Free Lunch'. The Price is Right is the idea that the prices in financial markets reflect all available in-formation about the assets being traded, so that capital allocations through financial markets are economically efficient. No Free Lunch is the idea that market prices are impossible to predict, so that any in-vestor will struggle to beat the market, after adjusting for risk.

In principle, for a market to be efficient it must encompass myr-iads of anonymous buyers and sellers, each of whom is too small to have an influence on the market price, while the goods traded must be homogeneous and interchangeable, such as stocks and shares, foreign exchange, commodities and the like; this is one reason why securi-ties markets have been central to the development of efficient market theory. Such markets supposedly react instantly to any new informa-tion; there are no processes that take place over time, and no frictional costs. When prices move, they move towards equilibrium, so that dis-turbances are self-correcting. Because these markets are constantly in equilibrium, or moving towards equilibrium, they have a tendency to be docile. There may be external shocks, which reset market expectations about future supply or demand, and so affect prices, perhaps sharply; but competitive markets instantly adjust to the changed circumstances so as to restore their equilibrium.

These assumptions are idealized, of course. But just considered on their own terms, they raise significant questions. For one thing, it is not even clear that the theory can be stated without circularity: if markets reflect all available information, then they reflect consumers' preferences and expectations, which are themselves taken to be rational—that is, to be those of a utility-maximizing agent operating on . . . the available information. But, if that is so, the theory is assuming the claim it wishes to prove. Moreover, in its strongest form the theory contradicts itself. For if markets always contained all available information, no one would or could have an incentive to find out more—similarly, if all technological insights were immediately available to others, no inventor would have an economic incentive to innovate, and innovation would rapidly decline. Perfect informational efficiency and market equilibrium would thus, paradoxically, inhibit competition from taking place at all.

According to the Efficient Market Hypothesis, financial asset prices are always right. It follows from this that there can be no such thing as an asset price bubble or market overshoot: since asset prices always reflect fundamental value, rapidly inflating asset prices can only reflect rising expectations of future returns. Because there can be no market bubbles, moreover, there can be no role for central banks to prick or deflate them; indeed some economists—including Milton Friedman—have suggested that central banks should be abolished altogether. But the Efficient Market Hypothesis goes further. It means, in effect, that markets are memoryless. If past events played any role in predicting price movements, then a sufficiently savvy investor could in principle game the market and make a riskless profit. But the theory's insistence on informational efficiency makes this impossible. If an asset's price is too low, given new information, investors will buy the asset; if too high, they will sell it. Prices are therefore deemed to follow what statisticians call a random walk. They move up and down according to no discernible pattern, and at any given moment there is as much chance that a price will go down as up, and vice versa. There are no free lunches, no riskless profits to be gained, and no investor, however expert or naive, can do better over time than the market.

The Efficient Market Hypothesis has been hugely influential in the development of modern finance theory; its early impact was such that in 1978 the economist Michael Jensen roundly stated, on the basis of considerable research, that 'there is no other proposition in economics which has more solid empirical evidence supporting it than the Efficient Market Hypothesis.' In effect, it allows analysts to construct recognizable mathematical distributions of the probability of future price movements. These are then used to create the risk-allocation models that underlie banks' balance sheets, investors' portfolios, corporate and bond credit ratings and regulators' rules and interventions. And out of financial analysis has come financial engineering, and so the pricing of such exotic modern instruments as derivatives, collateralized debt obligations (securities backed by mortgages or other assets) and credit default swaps (a kind of loan loss insurance). Thousands of banks and institutional investors around the world use models that rely on the workings of the Efficient Market Hypothesis every day, whether they know it or not—and so do the regulators, who also demand such models from banks and investors in order to do their work. The livelihoods of hundreds of millions, perhaps billions, of people around the world—not just people who work in financial markets or banks but people with pensions, people with mortgages or mutual funds or investments—hang directly or indirectly on it.

The overall line of thought is clear: that financial markets are unmatched in their capacity to gather and distribute information and to allocate capital efficiently. They possess a collective wisdom that exceeds anything available to governments, companies or individuals; by making them as frictionless as possible, by chopping up cash flows and repackaging them into an ever-expanding range of financial instruments, banks lower the cost of capital for companies, while the financial system becomes not just richer but healthier, and the economy gets stronger. Far from Benjamin Graham's emphasis on the value of fundamental analysis, the Efficient Market Hypothesis suggests that such analysis has no value at all.

So which view of markets is right? Is it the drunken lurching of Mr Market, or the smooth imperturbability of the Efficient Market Hypothesis? In fact, there are two questions here, corresponding to Thaler's earlier distinction. Do markets always get prices right—that is, are markets economically efficient? And are there any free lunches—that is, are there any riskless profits to be made? Oceans of academic ink have been spent on these questions, and a full answer lies outside the scope of this book. But one way to address it is to ask whether the ideas of Adam Smith can shed any light. It turns out that they can.

But before we get to Smith himself, we need to notice one further thing. This is the astonishing degree to which the Efficient Market Hypothesis has become central to the public understanding of economics itself. As the financial markets go, so, it is often thought, go markets in general. With the growing prominence of financial economics has come a growing tendency to see financial markets—and in particular the vast, and vastly liquid, global foreign exchange market—as the perfect exemplar of the market mechanism itself. In effect, then, a specific thesis about financial markets has been adopted alongside the idea of *homo economicus* as the *de facto* defining public features of modern economics, with the ideas of Adam Smith supposedly at their centre. Both have become the stand-out targets of the wave of popular anger, hostile commentary and expert diagnosis that followed the financial crash of 2008. In the process, economics itself has been financialized in the public mind.

THE CASE OF SLAVERY

How, then, does Smith understand markets? We can answer this in three parts: by looking at his overall approach; by analysing in detail what he says about one extreme example in his own time, that of slavery; and by seeing how his ideas play out in today's vastly more ramified and developed global market economy.

As we saw from his critique of François Quesnay and the Physiocrats, Adam Smith rejected the use of highly idealized and artificial assumptions in political economy. His focus in *The Wealth of Nations* is more concrete, more historical, more closely informed by data and more policy-oriented. He tends to see markets first and foremost as specific places of business, though he is quite aware of the wider idea of a disembodied market, which was familiar from international trade. The analysis of market exchange is intellectually central, but it is not idealized, and it is subordinate to his wider purposes. It is striking that nowhere in his 'Introduction and Plan of the Work', summarizing the five books of *The Wealth of Nations*, does Smith mention either markets or prices.

As we have seen, there is no general treatment of the 'invisible hand' in Smith's writings; he does not idolize the market mechanism or see market exchange as a panacea for economic ills; and he is aware that much economic activity does not operate through markets at all. Having outlined what he takes to be the key drivers of economic growth, in the course of the work he looks, closely or glancingly, at numerous different markets, from capital and land to wool and herring. Far from being unconcerned with the messy detail, Smith is happy on occasion to plunge himself and the reader into long paragraphs of careful analysis and factual description.

In examining specific markets, Smith's main interest lies in how, and how well, they function. In the vast majority of the markets of his time, that functioning involved a degree of external intervention, manipulation or regulation—and sometimes a high degree, whether by guilds, city corporations, producer cartels, the Church or government. As we shall see in the next chapter, Smith reserves some of his choicest invective for attacking these restrictive practices, with their tendency to support monopolies and cartels. But he also recognizes that markets do not in fact always tend towards equilibrium; and that when they do, that equilibrium can be, not socially beneficial, but actively harmful.

Smith also has a clear grasp of many other ways in which markets can underperform. Small markets function less well than big ones, because they are less productive, supporting less specialization and so less investment. Cities are more specialized and productive than rural areas, and rich towns than poor ones. Because markets are dependent on communication between buyers and sellers and, often, the physical transport of goods, markets in ports generally function better than those inland. And just as he is acutely aware of the potential for producers to form cartels against consumers, so he is aware of structural flaws in labour markets, especially the asymmetries of power and information that undermine the negotiating position of workers and help employers to keep wages down.

As we have seen, for Smith people do not cease to be social beings because they enter into economic transactions, and so for him any analysis of individual behaviour or market functioning that is purely economic can only be partial at best. By the same token, markets do not function independently of human society; they are embedded in it. They are not mathematical abstractions, but human artefacts with specific histories and particular norms and values. As *The Theory of Moral Sentiments* makes clear, those norms and values can and do vary from one context to another: from time to time and place to place. They develop and evolve, as human societies themselves do.

We can see Smith's thought here in action by focusing on it in relation to one specific issue: slavery and the slave trade. It is sometimes suggested that Adam Smith cynically condoned slavery, or that slavery is the inevitable result of a Smithian 'natural system of liberty'. And it is sometimes suggested that in a perfectly free market there can be no impediment in principle to people selling themselves into slavery, just as it is sometimes suggested there can be no impediment in principle to their selling their body parts. After all, such markets are supposedly secured by private property rights and, the argument goes, if people have private property rights those must include rights over their bodies and the product of their future labour. Yet this view of Smith is a direct inversion of the truth: Adam Smith despised slavery and the slave trade, and he argued with enormous force that, far from resulting from natural liberty, both were abetted by mercantilism and monopoly.

Britain banned the slave trade across the British Empire by Act of Parliament in 1807, and abolished slavery itself in 1833. But already when *The Wealth of Nations* was published, slavery and the slave trade were—at last—becoming a highly emotive and contentious issue. British involvement had dated back at least 200 years to the 1560s, when Sir John Hawkins had plied the notorious triangle trade in sugar, goods and slaves between Britain, West Africa and the Caribbean. By 1672 the trade was so well established that the chartered Royal African Company was granted a monopoly over slaves across 2,500 miles of West African coast from the Sahara to the Cape of Good Hope. In 1713 Spain granted Britain a thirty-year contract to supply slaves and goods to its colonies under a notorious agreement known by its Spanish name as the *Asiento*. In 1778 the Court of Session, Scotland's supreme civil court, had freed a slave of the name of Joseph Knight, following a similar decision of 1772 in *Somersett's Case* in England, and established that slavery was not recognized in Scottish law. In a famous judgment Lord Auchinleck, the father of James Boswell, had asked 'Is a man a slave because he is black? No, he is our brother; and he is a man; though not of our colour; he is in a land of liberty, with his wife and child. Let him remain there.' Yet only nine years earlier an advertisement had appeared in the *Edinburgh Evening Courant*: 'To be sold: a black boy, about 16 years of age, healthy, strong, and well-made, has had the measles and small pox, can shave and dress a little . . . For further particulars inquire at Mr Gordon bookseller in the Parliament-close, who has full powers to conclude a bargain.'

The slave trade, and the related sugar and tobacco trades, were extremely lucrative for the merchants involved, and despite the long-standing and vigorous opposition of Quakers and other dissenters, it had amassed a formidable body of parliamentary support; more than a few MPs of the time had made their money directly or indirectly from the slave trade. And slavery had also received a degree of intellectual backing. The natural law theorists of the seventeenth century rejected Aristotle's view that some men were by nature slaves. But they argued that slavery was nonetheless a natural phenomenon, and so they thought a defensible one; that involuntary servitude could be justified with the taking of captives in time of war, especially where the alternative was execution; and that voluntary servitude was justifiable by agreement as a form of self-preservation. No less a figure than John Locke, celebrated today as a philosopher of individual rights, was an investor in the Royal Africa Company and believed that masters exercised an 'absolute dominion and arbitrary power', even 'a legislative power of life and death', over slaves taken in a just war.

Nor was the acceptance of slavery restricted to slaves abroad. Locke's contemporary, the renowned republican Andrew Fletcher of Saltoun, claimed that slaves should be made of 'all those who are unable to provide for their own subsistence'. Even Adam Smith's teacher Francis Hutcheson held that 'perhaps no law could be more effectual to promote a general industry, and restrain sloth and idleness in the lower conditions, than making perpetual slavery . . . the ordinary punishment of such idle vagrants as . . . cannot be engaged to support themselves and their families by any useful labours.' In holding the views he did, and as early as he did, Smith was quite unusual.

Smith discusses slavery mainly in the *Lectures on Jurisprudence*, focusing on rights and law, and in *The Wealth of Nations* in relation to mercantilism and colonization. If he were, as the caricature has it, preoccupied with conditions of absolute freedom to trade, or if he regarded respect for property rights alone as the prerequisite to market exchange, then he might be expected to have a degree of sympathy for the slave trade. All the more so, perhaps, given his engagement with the natural law tradition. But in fact it is perfectly clear that he will have no truck with slavery whatsoever.

The first thing to note is the extent of Smith's knowledge of slavery, and the use he makes of his characteristic comparative method to examine it in different times and places. He notes that 'We are apt to imagine that slavery is entirely abolished at this time . . . not remembering that all over Muscovy and all the eastern parts of Europe, and the whole of Asia, that is, from Bohemia to the Indian Ocean, all over Africa, and the greatest part of America, it is still in use.' Britain and a few other European countries are thus a special case. In the course of his discussions Smith ranges from ancient Rome to feudal England, from Africa and Germany to the Caribbean colonial settlements, making detailed comments on the deforming social and economic effects of slavery. The British, for example, are judged to be less 'illiberal and oppressive' as colonists than the Spanish and Portuguese, but their slave-owners harsher than the French ones.

Secondly, in relation to slavery Smith's indignation and moral egalitarianism are evident, and of a piece with his general admiration for the bravery of 'savage nations'. In *The Theory of Moral Sentiments*, for example, he says:

There is not a negro from the coast of Africa who does not [in his contempt of death and torture] possess a degree of magnanimity which the soul of his sordid master is too often scarce capable of conceiving. Fortune never exerted more cruelly her empire over mankind, than when she subjected those nations of heroes to the refuse of the jails of Europe, to wretches who possess the virtues neither of the countries which they come from, nor of those which they go to, and whose levity, brutality, and baseness, so justly expose them to the contempt of the vanquished.

These are very strong words, and highly controversial for the time.

Yet, thirdly, Smith was careful to focus his attack where he thought it would have most practical effect: not so much on the morality as on the economics of slavery and the slave trade. He deployed a battery of arguments to show that, contrary to appearances, slavery was more economically costly than waged labour to slave-owners, as well as imposing costs on wider society. Voluntary servitude existed in societies where it was impossible for the poor to make a living—societies such as ancient Rome, where manual trades were dominated by the slaves of the rich. Slaves could not own property and therefore had no incentive to produce more than a subsistence return. But slavery as a whole was sustainable, he argued, only because of colonization and the mercantile system: the slave-owners and merchants could afford the inefficiency of slavery because, and only because, they traded sugar and tobacco at prices kept exorbitantly high by cartel.

For Smith the slave trade was not driven by economic self-interest. But if not that, then by what? Smith is unequivocal: it was on tyranny, on human passions and the 'love of domination and authority', all of which were and had long been abetted by weak government. Weak government had failed to prevent the emergence of slavery, or actively exploited it; and no government of any stripe would ever get rid of it entirely, Smith believed, because 'To abolish slavery . . . would be to deprive the far greater part of the subjects, and the nobles in particular, of the chief and most valuable part of their substance. This they would never submit to, and a general insurrection would ensue.' Only the countervailing powers of monarchy and clergy had caused slavery to die out in Britain, Smith says, and in a few other European countries. But these were the exception: 'Slavery therefore has been universal in the beginnings of society, and the love of dominion and authority over others will probably make it perpetual.'

Smith's gloomy prediction still has great force, for slavery in its many forms remains a very serious problem across the world today. But, as regards his own views, the facts are plain. Far from cynically condoning slavery, he emphatically rejected it; and his opposition to it was heartfelt, carefully thought through and based on grounds both of morality and of political economy; indeed, he is among the earliest writers to have explored the economics of slavery in any detail. Moreover, his rejection of slavery dates from at least the late 1750s, when he was composing *The Theory of Moral Sentiments* and developing the *Lectures on Jurisprudence*. That is two decades or so before British public opinion started to turn, energized by the American War of Independence, in which many black Americans fought on the British side. And it comes some three decades before Thomas Clarkson's great essay against slavery of 1786, and the foundation of the Committee for the Abolition of the Slave Trade in the following year. In his opposition to slavery, then, Smith was early, original, vigorous and right.

How Markets Work

Adam Smith's treatment of slavery is not merely important in itself; it vividly illustrates a host of characteristic Smithian themes and ideas that bear on markets. Some of these are already familiar, including his view of markets as embedded in society, his critique of colonial oppression and his analysis of the generally adverse effects of monopoly. But we can add that it also more subtly illustrates his balancing of a general theory with detailed analysis of specific cases; his awareness of the dangers of weak government; his belief that artificially high profits carry both economic and moral dangers; and his understanding that markets can be dominated by greed and tyranny and become separated from—and sometimes directly oppose—the public interest.

The conflict here is stark, because for Smith markets and moral behaviour are generally mutually enabling. Commerce has moral value because it generates wealth, which allows people to live and thrive in increasing numbers and with a standard of living unimaginable in other places and times. As he says at the outset of *The Wealth of Nations*, 'The accommodation of an European prince does not always so much exceed that of an industrious and frugal peasant, as the accommodation of the latter exceeds that of many an African king, the absolute master of the lives and liberties of ten thousand naked savages.' But commerce is also morally valuable because it creates freedom, relieving people from the burdens of dependency and war: 'Commerce and manufactures gradually introduced order and good government, and with them, the liberty and security of individuals, among the inhabitants of the country, who had before lived almost in a continual state of war with their neighbours, and of servile dependency upon their superiors. This, though it has been the least observed, is by far the most important of all their effects.' That freedom in turn enhances morality, since it permits people to exercise an uncoerced moral judgement. Our norms of justice are based on such judgements, and justice and law are what hold markets and commerce together.

This is not to say that commercial society is in any way perfect or in some state of grace—far from it. It too has its weaknesses and its discontents, some of them very serious ones, as we shall see; Smith is far too much of a realist to think otherwise. His point is one about history and development. Commercial society is in certain ways not merely economically but morally superior to the feudalism of medieval Britain; and it is both economically and morally superior to the mercantilism still practised at that time by European nations around the world—and indeed by Britain.

Imagine, then, that we are looking at the modern world, and that we want to analyse normal and legitimate market behaviour through Smithian eyes. What do we see? First of all, there is something obvious but often unrecognized, with a touch of paradox about it. Think of your day yesterday. You woke up, got dressed; perhaps you had breakfast and another meal or two later on, perhaps you greeted members of your family, went to work, used public transport, drove a car, did some shopping off- or online, looked after children or elderly relatives, played a sport or went to a bar with friends in the evening. You almost certainly used electronic media, perhaps a lot: a study found that the average use of all electronic media by Americans over eighteen in 2015 was over eleven hours a day. Your work might involve trading of some kind, of course; and from time to time you doubtless enter the labour market, in switching from one job to another. But how much of your time overall was spent in market-based activity? An hour or two at most? And yet—here is the paradox—it is likely that almost everything you did, saw, heard, smelled, tasted or touched was shaped by, or was the direct result of, the operation of markets. Your home, your possessions, the town or city or countryside you live in, the bike or bus or train or car you use, your places of work or play, the music you listen to, your friend's aftershave or perfume, the skin lotion and toothpaste they use—almost everything.

The point is not merely that markets play a crucial role in people's lives, but that they do so in the background. Vastly more of people's time is spent interacting with each other in non-market than in market contexts, such as in sports, hobbies or entertaining, travelling, conversing, phoning, messaging or using social media; and even shopping has a heavily social component, as any retailer will tell you. Not only that: market exchange is just a part of our overall economic activity, much of which is engaged in cooperative work in teams or in small or large groups. That activity takes place not merely in companies, but within and through institutions which are more social than economic, and in particular within the family, which for most people in history has been by far the most important risk-sharing mechanism they have.

To look at people's lives in purely market terms or even in terms of economics more widely is, therefore, to miss another and larger part of what makes lives meaningful—not merely less market-oriented work, or work such as caring for others that the market arguably does not value enough, but the non-market activities of socializing and volunteering and playing and giving. These can be economically valuable, and they too are shaped by norms, including market norms of course, and they shape those norms in turn: norms of friendship and reciprocity and trust. In this sense *The Theory of Moral Sentiments* has an even wider breadth and scope of explanation than does *The Wealth of Nations*.

Secondly, when pundits talk grandly of free markets, they sometimes forget—as Smith does not—that in the modern world there are few if any entirely free markets, in the sense of a market that does not rely on any external rules and regulations at all. Even the most devout free-market theorists recognize that property rights need to be clear, public and enforceable, and that generally means law, police, courts and other institutions of the state. Indeed, some will actively argue for patent, copyright and other laws protecting intellectual property, although these are themselves in fact significant infringements on market freedoms.

But this catalogue merely scratches the surface. Take the many things that generally cannot be legally bought and sold at all: people, body parts, hard drugs, votes, court decisions, public qualifications, the outcome of sporting contests. Then there are items that in many countries can be sold only under licence: guns, alcohol, many medicines. There are regulations on who is allowed to work: on child labour, on immigration, on the professions and the qualifications needed to enter them. There are regulations on organizational form: companies, associations, partnerships, mutuals, cooperatives, employee-owned firms, charities. There are entry requirements for some industries, such as tests on ownership, capital and track record in banking. There are rules on product safety, on weights and measures and on conditions of trade, such as the right to a refund. The global foreign exchange markets are often thought of as the nearest thing to a perfectly free market. It is true that they are astonishingly large and astonishingly liquid—the most recent estimate of the Bank for International Settlements is that trading averaged $5.1 trillion a day in April 2016—but they are also very closely bound by rules and regulations.

Even private property rights themselves—in the modern sense of free and clear legal title to dispersed ownership—are a far more recent creation than is often recognized. The effect of the Norman invasion of 1066 was to appropriate all real property in Britain and bring it under the ownership of King William, as catalogued in Domesday Book; in the feudal system this land was not privately owned, but merely held under a tenurial relationship with the Crown, conditional on payment of tax or a commitment of military service or other work in kind to a superior. This system broke down with the passage of time, but the principle that official records should be kept of property ownership, records which could be used to decide between conflicting claims, did not. And what could be counted as property, and how it could be used, bought and sold, has constantly changed in law as wider social norms and laws have changed. In Britain wives were treated in law as their husbands' property until the nineteenth century. More recently, for example, musical recordings that used to be physically possessed in record or compact disc form have become licensed for online use under elaborate legal agreements. Internet domain names, landing slots and radio spectrum are all modern forms of property. And this is before once considers that certain markets cannot function at all without specific state interventions designed to prevent participants from, for example, dumping costs such as pollution on others.

Thirdly, the desire to see all markets as operating according to a single equilibrating mechanism misses the point that not all markets are the same. Smith is well aware of this, as he shows through his examination of specific markets such as those for corn or labour or bills of exchange. Today, in part for regulatory reasons, markets differ from each other far more than is commonly supposed. Markets for food products are very different from asset markets; financial markets differ radically from labour markets; markets in primary goods are different from secondary or resale markets in those goods; markets in risk are different from markets in real estate; markets in regulated areas such as water, gas and electricity are different again. To take a few examples: in product markets buyers know fairly precisely what they are getting in advance—not so in labour markets, despite the best efforts of recruitment consultants. In financial markets the edge for participants generally lies not in serving some need in the real economy, but in knowing what their competitors are doing and second-guessing them. The British housing market has evolved into a form of proxy savings vehicle in which price inflation, far from being despised, is actively welcomed by owners keen to see their properties increase in value, to the detriment of new buyers; the existing owners' reliance on mortgage finance makes them preternaturally sensitive to interest-rate changes, conditioning both domestic politics and central bank monetary policy. The German housing market, by contrast, is dominated by rental and leasehold properties, reducing both political tolerance of and economic exposure to house price inflation. And so on.

Fourth, as with property rights, and for similar reasons, markets are constantly changing and evolving. Today market changes are often seen to be driven by shifts in technology, in a way that was perhaps not so evident in the eighteenth century, and is certainly not well recognized by Smith. Take the capacity to communicate in writing: thousands of years ago hominids could draw on sand with their hands or with sticks, or scratch marks on stone; then came stylus and ink on papyrus, quill pens, pencils, the fountain pen, the ballpoint pen, the typewriter, the desk printer, the keyboard, the keypad, predictive text and automated speech recognition. The self-sufficient provision of one's own writing tools yielded to markets, competition, specialization, huge falls in cost, rapidly accelerating product lifecycles and almost universal availability. But even in Smith's day, with a much slower pace of change, markets changed and evolved in response to wider economic conditions, seasonal factors, government interventions, consumer or producer pressure, competition, taste, fashion and social norms, among a host of other things. Again, from a Smithian perspective this makes it hard to speak of markets in any fixed or static way. They are always coming into being.

Fifth, markets require infrastructure. Even in ancient Greece, marketplaces evolved into designated public areas or *agorai*. The Forum in Rome was a marketplace which developed civil, legal and religious functions; other fora arose across the city to buy and sell meat, fish, vegetables and wine. In medieval times cities across Europe had marketplaces at their core, such as the magnificent Rynek Główny in Kraków, rebuilt in 1257 after the Mongol invasion of 1241, and used as a centre for the cloth trade. As in Rome, markets could take on specialized uses, such as Edinburgh's Grassmarket, situated immediately below the castle and used for livestock sales from the fifteenth century. Londoners still think of different parts of the city by their original markets: Covent Garden for fruit and vegetables, Smithfield for meat, Billingsgate for fish. Fairs, too, proliferated in the thirteenth and fourteenth centuries, as periodic public occasions for people to trade and compete in jousting and other tournaments. But markets need scale to support growth, specialization and innovation, as Smith reminds us in Book I of *The Wealth of Nations*. In the modern era that has meant a requirement for infrastructure, especially for energy, communications and transport. Some of these projects can be funded by user charges, as Smith recommends; others may be of such size, complexity or risk that forms of collaborative or state-assisted funding may be required if they are to be built at all. But either way today's markets typically need the active cooperation of the state— or at the very least its presence and passive support—to secure the rights, access and interconnectivity required for them to succeed.

Finally, how markets function is not independent of the state of mind of their participants. Markets do not merely shape our homes, our possessions and the music we listen to. They shape our expectations of others, our manners and our capacity to trust; and those things in turn shape them. They are not merely antiseptic objects of expert study, or neutral tools of public policy, and the people who trade in them are not economic automata operating purely in accordance with financial incentives. On the contrary, markets are subject to 'animal spirits': the human passions of confidence or pessimism in the face of the unknown, but also the human instinct to be moved by stories and narratives, and to react to unfairness or corruption. Smith is acutely conscious of these phenomena, whether in the form of the desire to dominate of slave-owners, the popular clamour to invest in new mines, the ambition of the would-be entrepreneur or the trust on which public credit relies.

So what do these points amount to? Simply this. Markets may be, in Adam Ferguson's words, 'the result of human action, but not the execution of any human design'. But they are not purely natural, in the sense of arising simply from God or nature; when Smith talks about the simple and obvious system of natural liberty, he is describing free markets not as some naturally preordained system, but as one which gives scope to, and should respect, the human instinct for freedom, itself in part a social construct. Far from always being choked back by rules and law, markets vividly illustrate how personal freedom and prosperity can be enlarged by them. Their economic value both feeds off and enhances social and moral value, for Smithian reasons that we have noted.

In sum, therefore, markets constitute not a purely natural but a created, constructed order—indeed an order which shapes its own participants. They exist because they have economic value to those who take part in them, and because they almost always confer wider spillover benefits as well. Wise states and wise officials have recognized this over the years, and have sought to enable and support markets for that reason. Far from being intrinsically opposed, states and markets rely on and benefit from each other. Indeed, they rely on each other more and more today, as competition increases pressure on public resources, private property rights become more contested, globalization drives the need for enforceable international standards, and infrastructure requirements grow more complex. Some markets are set up for a public purpose. Many others, perhaps the vast majority, just arise out of the human instinct for barter and exchange. But provided they are legitimate and legal, markets generally have public as well as private value; and in the modern era the state almost always plays an indirect part, and very often a direct part, in creating and sustaining both private and public value. The old bromide that 'the private sector makes the money and the public sector spends it' misses a deeper and far more interesting truth.

The fact that markets are a constructed order has a further implication. In theorizing about actual markets, economics can never achieve the objectivity of the exact sciences. This does not at all make economics uninteresting or unfruitful. There will always be value to the creation and testing of different models. But there is no theoretical state of nature for markets, and there never was a historical one. Markets have no natural or scientifically determinable boundaries; they are human constructs. Their boundaries are ultimately what we, as consumers and as citizens, say they are. And correlatively, in relation to actual markets, there is no such thing as a market system, or a theory of one, that can stand independent of history and human values. There is only political economy: a discipline which seeks such limited perspectives as its subject matter and methods afford; which acknowledges its own tacit normative assumptions; which thinks of markets instrumentally, as a means to generate social value and address social evils, and tries to understand them each on their own terms, not simply in terms of a single abstract model; and which recognizes the degree to which they are conditioned, for good and ill, by history, culture and politics, and shaped through social and moral norms.

THE LIMITS OF MARKETS

A more rounded Smithian view of markets thus stands in sharp and salutary contrast to the idea that markets always know best or are always beneficial, let alone fitting a one-size-fits-all template based on the financial markets. Specifically, it suggests a different response to the two sides of the Efficient Market Hypothesis: that in markets, even financial markets, the price may sometimes not be right, whether or not it is true that there are any free lunches.

Far from endorsing the Efficient Market Hypothesis, in fact much of economics, in and out of the mainstream, has also rejected the idea that markets always know best. Indeed, economists have spent a substantial portion of the past half-century trying to get clear on the very different ways in which markets actually operate, and how they go wrong. Much of the analysis has probed what the implications are, not of insisting on perfect information, perfect rationality and perfect liquidity, but of relaxing these very strong assumptions in different ways, through models focusing on imperfect or asymmetric information, bounded rationality and the impact of transaction costs. The best of this work has been rewarded with a hatful of Nobel Prizes.

The career of Kenneth Arrow is again a case in point. For one thing, Arrow himself did a great deal of work to explore and explain the negative effects of asymmetric information in the US healthcare insurance market, and how that market might be made to function better. But in 1953 he had also produced what was in effect an impossibility theorem for finance, by asking under what conditions the concept of general equilibrium could be extended to include financial markets. To do this he postulated the competitive creation of what later became known as 'Arrow securities', financial instruments putatively covering all contingent future risks in every market at every specific possible future time and state of the world—a mind-bogglingly large total. The effect of this theory was to show that the general equilibrium could hold equally well in principle for finance, but again only under impossibly stringent conditions. The Efficient Market Hypothesis was in part a competitive response within the academic establishment itself: an attempt to rebut Arrow's argument, by claiming that prices in continuously trading financial markets reflected all available current information; but without the demonstration that the necessary range of Arrow securities in fact existed.

The ironies are manifest. After the financial crash of 2008, public attention rightly focused, not merely on the foolishness, bad incentives or misbehaviour of the banks and their staff, but on the economics of the global financial system. Financial economics, which had come of age not in university economics departments but in the business schools, and which had grown massively during the boom of the previous two decades, now fell under the spotlight. Overreliance by the banks and brokers on the Efficient Market Hypothesis was all but required by the regulators, it was convenient, it was essential to their professional *raison d'être* and expertise, and it was—and remains—highly profitable. But it was hardly regarded within the economics profession as a core piece of mainstream economics, let alone as an explanation for the ways in which many markets actually worked, even before the crash. It did not codify the idea of rational economic man, which had originated more than a century earlier and was of far wider application within economics. And it was only indirectly related to the factors—communications, technology, development and specifically the opening up of India and China and other new markets under the free-market 'Washington Consensus'—which drove the globalization of trade over the same period. The critique of 'neoliberalism' had real force in places, but in its desire for a sweeping and condemnatory overall narrative it mistook much of what was really going on. It reinforced the caricatures, rather than dispelling them. And it had and retains the potential to make matters considerably worse, by abetting a populist politics that turns countries away from markets altogether. That would be a catastrophic result.

And Adam Smith? Well, it should be clear by now that both the Efficient Market Hypothesis and the criticisms of Smith as a supposed 'neoliberal' are far removed from what he actually thought and wrote. But we can go further. A Smithian viewpoint can give us a different and deeper understanding of what went wrong in the economic crisis of 2008. And it is arguable that if the leading players had known and absorbed what Smith actually believed, at least some of the crisis could have been averted or softened in its impact. For one key reason why the crisis occurred is that asset markets—and, in particular, the markets for credit and housing—did not behave as almost all the economists and regulators expected. Those people were in the grip of an economic ideology, a *déformation professionnelle* which meant that they failed to attend to or understand what was really happening.

Few if any markets are the same, or work in exactly the same way, as we have noted. But, for key types of market at least, Smith's basic analysis is an astonishingly successful one. About 75 per cent of US private spending—gross domestic product minus government spending—goes on normal consumer products, that is non-durable goods and services, in what are sometimes called 'haircuts and hamburger' markets. These items are not resold but are made, sold and used, and new ones made, sold and used again in an endlessly repeating process. Once used, the products disappear from the market. The buyers generally have a fixed or natural end-use for the goods—the trips get made, the meals get eaten, the holidays get taken—and so they do not generally switch roles to become sellers depending on price. The selling mechanism is generally a single sale price as in supermarkets, not the bid–offer spreads seen on foreign exchange kiosks at airports, or one of a large range of other possible price mechanisms. On the whole, these markets work in the way canonically attributed to Smith on the model of the so-called 'invisible hand', with supply and demand tending towards competitive equilibrium, and they work extremely well.

Another way of thinking of these markets is that they exhibit what has become known as the 'wisdom of crowds', and they do so because they satisfy four conditions: those involved are diverse in their access to information and in their opinions; they are independent, each person exercising his or her own view and not deferring to others; they are decentralized, so that they can specialize or draw on local knowledge; and there is a means—a market mechanism—to aggregate or gather their private judgements or choices together into a collective decision. There is a great deal of evidence to suggest that these markets are highly efficient in allocating resources effectively, and highly generative of economic wealth and welfare. What is still more surprising is that they appear to work this well even when the demanding theoretical conditions imposed by mainstream economics are relaxed—that is, even when there are relatively few people involved, and they are operating under limited information and using limited human rationality. As we have seen, Smith himself noted the point, in saying, 'If a nation could not prosper without the enjoyment of perfect liberty and perfect justice, there is not in the world a nation which could ever have prospered.' Part of the genius of these markets is precisely that they can be rather imperfect—rather short of information, rationality and participants—and still work extremely well.

As we saw in the last chapter, in some ways Smith is better thought of not as a neoclassical in embryo but as a proto-Austrian economist. He is interested in the dynamics of markets, he can see that not all markets work in the same way, and he is punctilious in seeking to explain their differences. In particular, he singles out the conflicting effects of the human disposition to admire the rich and powerful. This he recognizes as a core driver of competitive behaviour, of the desire of people to get on; but he also sees wealth and greatness as deceptive, as a snare and delusion that can never truly yield human happiness. In identifying the man who misses what matters in life by questing after 'trinkets of frivolous utility', Smith shows his awareness that markets can be driven by human passions as well as by human calculation. Today we might describe some such items as 'Veblen goods'. Named after the great Norwegian-American economist Thorstein Veblen, Veblen goods are those of 'conspicuous consumption', for which demand does not lessen when the price rises, as the standard theory would predict. Instead, demand for the good increases, as consumers see the price rise as a signal of relative scarcity or status, making the good still more desirable. Often the result is orderly, as in everyday markets for jewellery and luxury cars. But, as the history of bubbles, manias and crashes attests, sometimes it is not; sometimes these markets can rise and fall vertiginously.

Asset markets often have these and related Veblen-type features.

Not all are the same, of course, but they have common characteristics, and they are very different from 'haircuts and hamburger' non-durable goods markets. In asset markets, markets such as those for real estate, credit, derivatives and other so-called securities, the goods are durable, they are traded and re-traded; and for securities in particular, their buyers and sellers are generally not fixed but switch from side to side depending on price. The market mechanism is generally by bid–offer prices, not a single take-it-or-leave-it selling price. As a result, asset markets function very differently from product markets. As Keynes once famously noted, in comparing professional investment to a newspaper beauty competition, the quest for fundamental value yields to ever-more complex processes of second-guessing the other participants.

As this suggests, investment managers of mutual, hedge and pension funds—the overwhelmingly predominant *de facto* owners of financial securities—do not in general constitute a 'wise crowd', because although their potential information sources are indefinitely many, in practice they tend to act on the same or similar ones, reducing their diversity; and because they are not independent in their behaviour. On the contrary, they jostle and herd together in mutual- and self-awareness. Their public incentives are typically asymmetrical, in that while there is some glory in making above-average gains, making above-average losses can quickly be terminal. The result is that, notwithstanding a handful of mavericks, few wish to be seen as unusual or apart from the others.

The behaviour of these markets is often dominated by 'momentum' investors, who trade based not on any estimate of fundamental or intrinsic value, but on the rate of rise or fall in the asset's price. As with Veblen goods, high share prices come to be seen as a mark of underlying value, and rapid or extended price rises as signals of lack of supply, stimulating demand and causing investors to crowd in. Conversely, price falls are read as signals of over-supply, causing investors to sell heavily in turn. But these rises and falls can also occur in apparently autonomous ways, as investors simply cue their behaviour off each other, rather than for any more fundamental reasons.

The effect of this combination of factors is to give asset markets, far more than product markets, a pronounced tendency towards boom and bust. Far from moving towards equilibrium, these markets are often subject to destabilizing forces which operate through, and are worsened by, channels specific to them. In the banking system, the most basic form of this is a bank run. In normal times banks operate by taking savers' deposits, which can generally be withdrawn at will, and then lending them out for weeks or months, sometimes years, at a time. If savers all seek their deposits at once, however, the bank cannot meet the demand from cash on hand; and if the bank is not large enough, or cannot borrow enough in time from the money markets for other reasons to cover the shortfall, it will quickly fail. This is what happened with the collapse of Northern Rock in the UK and Washington Mutual in the US in 2008. Almost exactly the same process can operate with the failure of money market funds; and of bank lending to businesses against collateral, or trading on margin. A relatively small initial market movement can quickly become a rout, as occurred with the failures of the investment banks Bear Stearns and Lehman Brothers.

Our understanding of these channels of destabilization has greatly improved in recent years, in part due to the pioneering work of Hyman Minsky. It does not require us to make any unusual assumptions about human behaviour. Within each channel lie specific internal incentives for investors to act as they do. But what about asset markets as a whole? They do not operate independently of the wider economy, as mainstream economics often seems to suggest. On the contrary, the two sides interact in several causally interconnected ways. When asset prices rise, their effect is to create additional paper value on bank balance sheets, value which can in turn be used as security within the banking system for new loans to purchase further assets. To the outside eye, the loan remains well covered by its security, as long as prices keep rising; leverage ratios may even fall. So the bank's credit committee, charged with making secure loans and sustaining the creditworthiness of its overall portfolio, will be happy. If the loans are then gathered together in an asset-backed bond such as a mortgage-backed security, the ratings agencies will look benignly on it. And because banks are so often not merely lenders but also sellers of financial products, they have a specific incentive to get investors to buy more products, with still more implicit leverage, using the fees to pump up their profits despite the evident threat to credit quality and the clear conflict of interest involved. But if at any point market sentiment changes, and investors take a less rosy view of the future—as they inevitably do from time to time—the same processes can rapidly unwind in the other direction. Falling profit expectations feed into lower asset valuations, weaker demand and reduced growth, in a self-fulfilling cycle. The result can quickly be catastrophe.

There are, then, both specific and general channels within asset markets which link asset price inflation, credit growth and profitability. These make asset markets intrinsically unstable, this instability can lead to dangerously self-reinforcing cycles of boom and bust, and these can in turn inflict horrendous damage on the wider economy. This is exactly what happened in the 2008 crash. This was a 'balance-sheet' recession: not a recession of the more frequent and familiar kind, driven by falling profitability across the business cycle, but a fundamental shift in asset values, triggered by a collapse in the housing market and in due course spreading from the US and UK to affect much of the wider global economy.

The signs were there. In the US, as with the Great Crash of 1929, there was a rapid rise in asset markets in the preceding years, in particular in housing. Real estate values rose rapidly after 1997 to surpass in 2001 their previous high of 1989, then rose again; and this latter rise was at an accelerating pace, signalling the presence of momentum investors in a huge market ramp. This rise was fuelled by an extraordinary increase in mortgage credit, assisted by an easing of terms: in 2005, some 45 per cent of first-time home-buyers made no down payment at all. The effect of this rise was that from 1997 to 2006 overall inflation-adjusted equity in US real property—that is, the equity people owned in their homes and so in general their main source of wealth—more than doubled to $13 trillion. But by the end of 2011 this had fallen some 58 per cent to $5.6 trillion, a level not seen since 1983. More than $7.4 trillion of value had been wiped out, thrusting millions of home-owners into negative equity. The housing market was, it appears, both a cause and a leading indicator of the catastrophe; there was a marked fall in new housing starts and housing expenditure in 2006–8, before the crash, even while equity and other financial asset markets continued to rise.

THE ECONOMIC CONSEQUENCES OF FORGETTING SMITH

This brief and inevitably schematic account of a highly complex set of events illustrates all of our key themes. First of all, it underlines the deep difference between markets for products, many of which can readily be understood in terms of a tendency to equilibrium and the so-called invisible hand, and asset markets, which have a different price mechanism, a different internal logic and an embedded tendency to boom and bust. The 2008 recession vividly highlighted the contrast between the different kinds of markets: US consumption of non-durable goods and services had a maximum decline of 1.7 per cent; but that of housing fell by nearly 60 per cent. This is an astonishing difference.

Secondly, it allows us to return to the question with which we started: the adequacy or otherwise of the Efficient Market Hypothesis. Of its two key claims, the idea that there is No Free Lunch—that is, that market prices are impossible to predict—has stood up to much detailed scrutiny. The Price is Right—the idea that prices in financial markets reflect all available information—is a different matter. It is notoriously hard to test—what to compare it with?—but it looks untenable. As the fund manager and author George Cooper has noted, 'There were analysts who believed that the Nasdaq Composite Index was correctly priced at 1,140 in March 1996, again correctly priced at 5,048 in March 2000 and still correctly priced in October 2002 when it fell back to 1,140.' In effect, the hypothesis seeks to explain too much with too little. It is easy to explain to non-experts, and taken in a general sense it can have real explanatory power. But in its simplicity and generality it blurs crucial distinctions between markets, and encourages a one-size-fits-all view which appears to have caused legislators, policy-makers and regulators to ignore the effects of excessive credit-creation and housing asset inflation in the US and UK. Instead, in the decade before 2008 they were encouraged to indulge in the potentially ruinous asymmetry of believing that measures of restraint should be avoided not merely during the economic bad times, but during the good times as well. And there is the non-trivial point that if the price is not right, if markets do not in fact reflect all available information, then the core theory of capital allocation and efficiency at the heart of the world's financial system is very seriously flawed. The implications of that thought are horrendous.

Thirdly, there is nothing irrational about the tendency of asset markets towards instability. These booms and busts are not what are sometimes referred to as 'fat tail' or 'black swan' events—that is, events so far outside the normal probabilities as to be all but mathematically impossible. On the contrary, they are the results of positive feedback loops working through specific market channels, whose effect is to magnify and compound instability. That is why they—and their cousins, rapid market over- and undershoots—occur with such alleged statistically improbable regularity. It is why 'boom and bust' has been such a regular feature of the world's economy ever since monetary flows were liberalized after the collapse of the Bretton Woods Agreement in 1971; and why a tendency to 'boom and bust' is likely to remain for the foreseeable future. And it is the central insight which lies behind Benjamin Graham's memorable metaphor of the friendly but deranged Mr Market.

And finally, there is reason to think that, had those in positions of public authority before 2008 genuinely read and absorbed the ideas of Adam Smith on political economy, they could have mitigated such problems. In a very influential essay of 1953, 'The Methodology of Positive Economics', Milton Friedman issued a challenge to critics of economics as science: 'The relevant question to ask about the "assumptions" of a theory is not whether they are descriptively "realistic", for they never are, but whether they are sufficiently good approximations for the purpose in hand. And this question can be answered only by seeing whether the theory works, which means whether it yields sufficiently accurate predictions.' Friedman's challenge expressed his grand expectations of economics, many of whose practitioners have recently discovered the predictive limitations of their discipline once again through bitter experience. But it has also had the effect of diverting attention from the need to examine markets in their specifics. That is a test that economists and policy-makers collectively failed before 2008.

Smith, by contrast, has more than one theory of markets. In discussing money and capital in Book II of *The Wealth of Nations*, he analyses the collapse in 1772 of the Ayr Bank, as we have seen. There he notes the need for reserves to be prudently held against risky loans; the importance of knowing one's customer well in order to be able to judge their creditworthiness; the effects of market hyperbole on sentiment; the rapid acceleration in the early 1770s in the circulation and kiting of bills of exchange that resulted; the detachment of this booming market from real and productive investment; the resistance and public lobbying of borrowers and 'projectors' to any attempts to restrain their issuance; the disastrous underlying economics of these transactions for the Ayr Bank; and the effect of the boom in magnifying the subsequent bust. Each of these has its direct counterpart in our analysis of the 2008 crash.

In the course of that discussion, Smith makes clear that the 'natural system of liberty' he favours does not license a free-for-all; and in so doing he shows the limits of the modern invisible-hand theory that has been elaborated from his writings. He specifically entertains the claims made on behalf of *laissez-faire*: 'To restrain private people, it may be said, from receiving in payment the promissory notes of a banker, for any sum whether great or small, when they themselves are willing to receive them; or, to restrain a banker from issuing such notes, when all his neighbours are willing to accept of them, is a manifest violation of that natural liberty which it is the proper business of law, not to infringe, but to support.' But he rejects those claims, and the terms of his rejection are emphatic and prescient: 'Such regulations may, no doubt, be considered as in some respect a violation of natural liberty. But those exertions of the natural liberty of a few individuals, which might endanger the security of the whole society, are, and ought to be, restrained by the laws of all governments; of the most free, as well as of the most despotical. The obligation of building party walls, in order to prevent the communication of fire, is a violation of natural liberty, exactly of the same kind with the regulations of the banking trade which are here proposed.'

We can only regret such party walls did not exist in 2008.

Part Three

IMPACT

CHAPTER 9

CAPITALISM AND ITS DISCONTENTS

S NAPSHOTS OF A MODERN AMERICA:
In 2004, following an intense period of corporate lobbying, the US Congress passed a law permitting corporations to repatriate offshore income at a tax rate of 5.25 per cent, rather than the usual 35 per cent. This was supposedly designed to stimulate growth in jobs and investment, and any use of the money for share buybacks or executive compensation was expressly prohibited by law. In fact, as a National Bureau of Economic Research study found, the new law made no material impact on employment, investment or R&D. What it did do, however, was to allow 843 corporations to repatriate some $362 billion, at less than one-sixth of the usual tax cost. Between 62 and 90 per cent of every dollar returned went on payouts to shareholders. According to one estimate, the return on the cost of lobbying involved was a tidy 22,000 per cent, or $220 for every dollar spent.

In 1980, the top 1 per cent of Americans received 10 per cent of total annual income. In 2014 it was 20 per cent.

In 2015 an unusually wide-ranging national survey found that 79 per cent of Americans believed that their government was 'run by a few big interests looking out for themselves', compared with just 29 per cent in 1964. Nearly two-to-one believed their 'vote does not matter because of the influence that wealthy individuals and big corporations have on the electoral process'. Large majorities of both Democrats and Republicans held that 'our economic system unfairly favours the wealthy,' and attended 'very well' or 'somewhat well' to the interests of the wealthy and those of big corporations.

In 2016, in the case of *McCutcheon* v. *Federal Election Commission*, the US Supreme Court held by a 5–4 majority that a law passed by Congress was unconstitutional because it limited the total amount of money that one person could give to all federal candidates and party committees combined in one election cycle. Concluding his lead opinion, Chief Justice Roberts invoked no less an authority than Edmund Burke, and quoted Burke's famous line that a representative should be in 'the strictest union, the closest correspondence, and the most unreserved communication with his constituents'. However, Roberts neglected to mention two things: first, that Burke would never have accepted the equation of 'constituents' with 'campaign donors', and indeed spent much of his own life in severe debt, in part due to his unwillingness to accept financial inducements; and secondly that the *McCutcheon* case precisely concerned donations from *outside* the representative's own district, so that no constituents as such were involved at all. On the case itself, Justice Breyer led the dissent, writing of the decision that 'It creates a loophole that will allow a single individual to contribute millions of dollars to a political party or to a candidate's campaign. Taken together with *Citizens United* v. *Federal Election Commission* . . . today's decision eviscerates our Nation's campaign finance laws, leaving a remnant incapable of dealing with the grave problems of democratic legitimacy that those laws were intended to resolve.'

REGULATION, RENT-EXTRACTION, AND PERIODIC CRISIS

For many people, this toxic combination of political lobbying, anti-competitive regulation, egregious executive pay, escalating inequality and loss of public trust is the natural result of the market system. On this view, far from being of general benefit, free trade simply serves to worsen economic inequality, while capitalism itself tends to encourage corruption and greed. And all the more so, the argument goes, in an increasingly globalized world: a world in which capital is liquid, companies are multinational and effectively able to choose where they pay tax, labour is offshored to low-cost jurisdictions with few rights or union protections, while the rich are mobile and can relocate as and where they see fit. This in turn supports an emergent global value system which exalts material success and tacitly despises national cultures and local values and institutions. The runaway success of Thomas Piketty's recent book *Capital in the Twenty-First Century*, with its argument that the past thirty years have been conspicuous for the imbalance between the economic returns accruing to capital and to labour, is just one token of a much deeper and wider sense of malaise. But as with economics, as with financial markets, so some would go further still, and place the ultimate blame for these failures of capitalism on Adam Smith himself. Are not Smith and his ideas at the heart of the causes of global populism and the revolt against the elites of the early twenty-first century?

Particular attention has rightly focused on the excesses of the banking system. In the words of the financial commentator Martin Wolf, 'Banking seems inefficient, costly, riddled with conflicts of interest, prone to unethical behaviour, and, not least, able to generate huge crises.' The world of international banking operates as a semi-cartel, in which regulation designed to prevent malfeasance and abuse is used to restrict competition, support established players and deter new entrants. As such, it positively thrives on enormous amounts of new and increasingly complex rules, which generate asymmetries of power and information that insiders can exploit. Banks have both lobbied against new regulation and proven adept in exploiting it to their own advantage. Officials and politicians have been remarkably naive, to put the matter kindly, in deregulating an industry long known to be subject to periodic crises.

These trends have, if anything, significantly worsened since the financial crisis of 2008. Thus the Basel I rulebook governing international bank capital requirements, published in 1988, was 30 pages long; the Basel II rulebook of 2004 was 347 pages long; the Basel III rulebook of 2010 came in at 616 pages. In the USA, a key piece of post-Depression legislation, the Glass–Steagall Act of 1933, was 37 pages long; the Dodd–Frank Act of 2010 was no fewer than 848 pages long—and that ignores more than 400 pieces of associated further rule-making which could take Dodd–Frank as a whole up to a mind-boggling 30,000 pages of regulation. And regulation begets regulators. In the UK, the number of bank regulators has risen since the late 1970s by a factor of forty. As Andy Haldane, the Chief Economist of the Bank of England, has pointed out, 'In 1980, there was one UK regulator for roughly every 11,000 people employed in the UK financial sector. By 2011, there was one regulator for every 300 people.'

The effect of these trends has largely been to reduce competition, drive up costs and further disconnect the banking system from the public interest. Thus the unit cost of US financial intermediation has not fallen in a hundred years, as Haldane shows, despite astonishing breakthroughs in technology and immense cost reductions in other service industries. In the UK, far from commercial banks supporting business growth, only around 10 per cent of bank lending goes towards company and enterprise investment outside commercial property. Meanwhile, some 10 million US households and 1.5 million UK adults still have no bank account at all. In this context, it is hardly surprising that public trust in the banks is so low.

As with banks, so with much of the wider financial sector. Moreover, there is a growing body of research, by the International Monetary Fund and others, to suggest that in some countries the financial sector can be 'too large' for the economy, and actually detrimental to growth. An IMF paper of 2012 identified two key potential causes: the increased probability of large financial crashes, and the misallocation of capital induced by a finance-dominated economy more oriented to exploiting differences in information in financial markets than to assessing commercial risk and reward for businesses. But to these we might add a key further and related factor: the extraction of 'rents'—unearned income received, over and above the returns generated in competitive markets—by the banks from the wider economy. The banks' rent-extraction has been turbo-charged in recent decades by the growth of the sector as a whole, and the emergence of a large tier of 'Too Important to Fail' banks. Since these institutions cannot be allowed to fail, they benefit from an implicit bailout subsidy from the taxpayer, and that subsidy appears to have been gigantic; according to the IMF, virtually all the earnings of the major US banks in 2013—some $80 billion—may have been due to subsidy rather than to productive activity. In the UK, estimates of the implicit subsidy from taxpayers to the banks have ranged from an astonishing £150 billion in 2009 to a still substantial £10 billion in 2013.

Such numbers suggest that the banking sector may be generating little or no net real economic value, even before its wider effects are taken into account. And bank lobbying has been found to correlate with laxer credit standards, higher levels of securitization, faster-growing mortgage loan portfolios and worsened returns during the 2008 crisis. This in turn implies that vigorous lobbying may have encouraged such lenders to take more risks in order to generate greater private gains—gains for staff and other insiders—in the belief they would be bailed out in the event of failure, at what proved to be vast cost to the public welfare.

Yet if the banks' capacity to extract rents has been remarkable, so too has been the ability of their employees to extract rents from the banks themselves, in the form of pay and bonuses. A 2009 study found that as much as half of the unexpectedly high wages accruing to the US financial sector since the late 1990s could be accounted for by rents, that is income over and above competitive levels, even when controlling for such factors as risk of unemployment, wage volatility and education. And this disproportionate level of pay appears to have fed into wage inequality at the top end of the income spectrum. Between 1979 and 2007, the top decile of wage-earners increased their share from 28.4 per cent to 42.6 per cent of total income; the top per-centile took two-thirds of these gains; and roughly 60 per cent of the top percentile's gains went to those working in the financial services sector. On this view, a general reduction in pay and bonuses across the sector to levels closer to those of other similarly skilled industries, if it could be achieved, would transform the profitability of the banks, and the returns to shareholders.

CRONY CAPITALISM AND 'THE MERCANTILE INTEREST'

Lobbying, rent-extraction, very high pay, growing inequality . . . the pattern seems clear. Yet, although it is especially evident in the bank-ing sector, one should not ignore the wider picture. For this is just one extreme example of a much more general phenomenon: crony capitalism.

What is crony capitalism? It has no single settled definition. But for present purposes we can usefully think of it as having two key fea-tures. The first is that business activity loses any relation to, and often clashes with, the wider public interest; the second is that business merit is separated from business reward. These features then feed off and into a culture in which values of decency, modesty and respect are disregarded, and short-termism and quick returns come to domi-nate long-established norms of mutual obligation, fair dealing and just reward. It becomes evident that extraordinary payoffs can be had by spending relatively small amounts of money to lobby government for subsidies or favourable changes of regulation. In theory at least, some lobbying—that is, 'informational' lobbying as opposed to the peddling of influence—can be both an important part of the democratic pro-cess and economically valuable as a direct means to hear from groups potentially affected by public policy, be they companies, unions, char-ities or others. Often those involved suggest that their own lobbying is not merely permissible but actively required as a counterweight to other lobbying. Some go still further and argue that it is morally right for a company to seek out legal subsidies and political favours, on the grounds that its management are under an obligation to maximize profits in the interests of shareholders.

Crony capitalism comes in different varieties. *Monopoly capitalism* flourished in the USA at the end of the nineteenth century. At that time individuals such as Cornelius Vanderbilt and John D. Rockefeller were able to amass enormous wealth by agglomerating new industries such as railroads and oil into 'trusts', which exercised monopoly or oligopoly market power within markets, before they were regulated or broken up by Theodore Roosevelt using the Sherman Act. *Licence capitalism* flourished in India after 1947 under the so-called Licence Raj. The Nehru government and its successors attempted to establish a planned economy, but ended up throttling economic growth and stimulating corruption through a vast array of licences, regulations and red tape, a system only finally dismantled nearly fifty years later. *Franchise capitalism* developed in Russia during the 1990s. A generation of so-called oligarchs emerged, working alongside and through the official apparatus of the state, much of whose wealth derived from state-created and -directed lucrative natural resources franchises in oil and gas. *Khaki capitalism* has taken root in countries such as Egypt and Pakistan, where the armed forces have become large economic actors in their own right. In Egypt, for example, the army runs roughly 10 per cent of the economy. *Narco-capitalism* has been seen in recent decades in countries such as Mexico and Colombia. The drugs trade created enormous illicit profits; as it became a substantial part of a local or regional economy, it was further entrenched through corruption and money-laundering, further complicating and undermining efforts to suppress it.

This list is hardly exhaustive, and these varieties can coexist in a given country or society. Some, such as narco-capitalism, are illegal; others may be corrupt but not actually illegal; all exploit the absence of law or law enforcement, market mechanisms or culture which in other times and places act as constraints on individual self-enrichment.

Over time, the winners become significant interest groups in their own right, and seek to exercise influence over government in order to extract favourable regulation, subsidies and low oversight. Again and again, the same pattern—of lobbying, rent extraction, very high rewards for insiders and, often, reduced economic growth and higher inequality—emerges. It differs in its degree and effects in different countries; some have proven quite resistant to it, others very vulnerable.

But it would be a serious mistake to regard this pattern as confined, either sectorally to the banks and financial markets or geographically to the developing world. US corporate spending on lobbying in 2008 alone was estimated at $3.2 billion, according to an OECD study. One lobbying group alone is cited there as having generated $1.2 billion in government contracts and assistance to its clients in a single year, for just $11 million in fees: a return of over $100 for every $1 spent. An investment index based on the intensity of lobbying by American firms was reported in 2016 to have beaten the S&P 500 benchmark for the eighteenth consecutive year, with returns for much of that period, according to *The Economist*, 'comparable to [those of] the most blistering hedge fund'.

Overall, then, this is a damning indictment, and it raises issues that run far beyond the scope of this book. But do the charges stick in relation to Adam Smith? Is he the cause of our present discontents? How far should we see him as implicated in the rise of crony capitalism?

The first point to note is the difficulty of making worthwhile judgements across more than two centuries and in such vastly different circumstances. Smith was writing at a time when the Western world was making a transition from a long period of warring kingdoms and principalities to a recognizably modern era of globally competing commercial states. It was far from obvious then that, or why, trade would gradually supplant war as the principal mode of state-to-state interaction, or that economic issues would increasingly bulk so large as to change the basic terms of theorizing itself from statecraft, royal or other, towards political economy, let alone to change them again into the separate disciplines of politics and economics seen in the twentieth century. These are, precisely, trends that Smith in his own time was seeking to understand and explain.

Furthermore, if we think of capitalism as the combination of open markets and of industrial corporations functioning as independent institutions and controlling autonomous pools of capital, then capitalism itself did not come into existence until the second half of the nineteenth century, eighty years or so after the publication of *The Wealth of Nations*. The term 'capitalism' appears nowhere in Smith's writings. Indeed, it is a striking fact about Smith that he did not in any deep way foresee industrialization as an economic phenomenon, despite a few early signs of it around him, or indeed the rise of the joint-stock company, which prefigured the modern corporation. But in any case his interest runs wider even than capitalism was to stretch, to the nature and causes of commercial society.

So we should hesitate to give too much credit either to Smith's foresight or to our own hindsight. It would be absurd to blame or credit Smith for all the twists and turns that market economies, and market economics, have taken since his death. Even so, these views are sufficiently widely held and trenchantly expressed to deserve careful reflection and examination, and all the more so in a world now particularly prone to believing facile soundbites. All successful modern economies are, to greater or lesser degree, market economies. So the question whether the market system as such breeds inequality, corruption and unethical behaviour goes to the heart of the legitimacy of modern commercial society itself—all the more so because of the growing body of evidence that extreme or entrenched inequality is not only morally indefensible but harms educational and job opportunities, reduces economic growth and undermines social trust. Tackling this central question can give us a better understanding both of Smith and of the underlying issues themselves, and how they can be addressed.

Let us start, then, not with 'Adam Smith' the bogeyman or caricature, but with Smith as he actually was. As we have seen, the real Adam Smith was not an advocate of self-interest, did not believe rational behaviour was constituted solely by the pursuit of profit, was not a believer in *laissez-faire* and was not pro-rich. Nor was he anti-government, though he shows a deep understanding of its limitations and scope for possible abuse. Smith did not think that all markets behaved the same way, let alone that they behaved as some financial markets now do, or that markets form a kind of self-regulating system that might obviate the need for the state. He recognizes the role and significance of capital accumulation, but he is not a theorist of capitalism as such; indeed, he misses some of its central features. Far from glorifying consumption for its own sake, Smith deprecates it, both in his writings and in his life; far from exalting material success, he sees its pursuit as inevitably bound up in processes of economic development and worthwhile only insofar as it permits greater human well-being and freedom. It is precisely because of his belief that commercial society reflects and can assist the development of 'natural liberty', and can enable human well-being and freedom to flourish—indeed to flourish better than other forms of political-economic self-organization permit—that Smith values commercial society.

Yet Smith is also acutely aware of the strengths and weaknesses of commercial society, and of its vulnerability to the 'mercantile system' and the 'exclusive corporation spirit'. As noted earlier, he is excoriating in his criticism of the adverse economic effects of monopolies, bounties, duties and other restraints of trade. But he is also alive to the way in which the mercantile interest can clash more generally with the wider public interest. 'The interest of the dealers, however, in any particular branch of trade or manufactures, is always in some respects different from, and even opposite to, that of the public.' The merchants are 'an order of men, whose interest is never exactly the same with that of the public, who have generally an interest to deceive and even to oppress the public, and who accordingly have, upon many occasions, both deceived and oppressed it'. The interest of companies once established is to ensure their own survival, and so to inhibit or prevent competition and the entry of new players into the market. This is directly contrary to the public interest in ensuring free competition and open entry. Free markets can be not the exemplar but the antithesis of corporate capitalism; and where they conflict Smith is on the side of the markets.

Moreover, the merchants have huge political influence, which they exercise aggressively to defend their own interests and suppress competition: 'Were the officers of the army to oppose with the same zeal and unanimity any reduction in the number of forces, with which master manufacturers set themselves against every law that is likely to increase the number of their rivals in the home market . . . to attempt to reduce the army would be as dangerous as it has now become to attempt to diminish in any respect the monopoly which our manufacturers have obtained against us.' And, extending the military metaphor, Smith argues that such a degree of influence threatens government itself: 'This monopoly has so much increased the number of some particular tribes of them, that, like an overgrown standing army, they have become formidable to the government, and upon many occasions intimidate the legislature.' For this reason, they should be treated by politicians and officials with extreme suspicion: 'The proposal of any new law or regulation of commerce which comes from this order, ought always to be listened to with great precaution, and ought never to be adopted till after having been long and carefully examined, not only with the most scrupulous, but with the most suspicious attention.'

Smith specifically rebukes the 'prodigals and projectors' who, he claims, hurt the public interest by crowding worthwhile investments out from access to credit with their own fanciful schemes. But his strongest criticism is, of course, directed at the effects of the mercantile system in distorting domestic markets for goods and capital and promoting colonial trade, which is both exploitative and inefficient; and at the East India Company and its competitors in particular. At

267

their worst, such manipulations are nothing less than catastrophic: 'The drought in Bengal, a few years ago [in 1770], might probably have occasioned a very great dearth. Some improper regulations, some injudicious restraints imposed by the servants of the East India Company upon the rice trade, contributed, perhaps, to turn that dearth into a famine.' In this he prefigures influential modern arguments that famines do not occur in democracies, where governments are subject to the constraints of free speech, public criticism and re-election.

However, in the spirit of Montesquieu, Smith also suggests that different economic arrangements can affect not merely the wallets, but the values and moral character of a country's people. Thus he welcomes the way in which the emergence of commercial society in Britain served to curb hitherto ingrained habits of subordination and deference by recasting social relationships in a market context, creating 'liberty and security' in place of 'continual war' and 'servile dependency'.

As so often with Adam Smith, then, the truth is in many ways not so much a controversion as a direct contradiction of the popular caricature. There was a kind of crony capitalism in Smith's own day, long before the advent of capitalism itself in its full form, which—just as today—linked political lobbying, anti-competitive regulation, egregious financial returns, growing inequality and loss of public trust. This was what Smith called the 'mercantile system', exemplified by the East India Company; and far from embracing it, he denounced it in the most vigorous terms. Given his specific friendships and connections with the great merchants of Glasgow, it may well have taken a degree of personal bravery for him to do so.

Indeed, Smith appears to have been the first person to present a comprehensive analysis of what crony capitalism amounts to, and why it is damaging to business and government alike. In doing so he opened up and made prominent three sets of ideas which, further refined and developed, have become analytic tools of lasting significance. The first of these is the idea of rent-seeking. 'Rent' in this sense, or 'economic rent', is not quite the same thing as the rent received on land or property, though the ideas are related. We can refine the description given earlier—as unearned income received, over and above the returns generated in competitive markets—by thinking of it as the difference between the market price and the lowest price a seller would accept. In the perfectly competitive markets of economic theory, there are no brands or products with an established public reputation—indeed there are no brands at all—and no participant has a large enough market presence to have any effect on pricing. So rents never arise; they are competed away. In the real world, however, successful businesses can often sustainably charge more than others in the marketplace for good reasons, because of their brands or their product quality or service; in economic terms, they generate higher rents. Sometimes, as with Hoover or Xerox, their brands can be so well known that they even enter the language as synonymous with the product.

The problem comes when businesses seek to raise their returns not through better performance in the marketplace, not by innovating, building new brands or by raising product quality or service, but by non-competitive means: by colluding with each other, or by using political influence to win unfair grants, subsidies or exemptions, build monopoly power or impose costs and barriers to market entry on other competitors. Smith does not have a theory of economic rent as such—the first steps towards one were taken in 1777, a year after publication of *The Wealth of Nations*, in a work by his contemporary and critic James Anderson of Hermiston—and as a result he appears to underestimate the possibility that companies can build up 'good' rents and thus sustainable competitive advantage by entirely legitimate means. But, as we have seen, Smith is acute in identifying and characterizing the special interests of his time, and the interrelated issues of rent-seeking, collusion, lobbying and their effects; and the wider links he draws between mercantilism and colonization are bold and illuminating.

The second important idea in analysing crony capitalism is that there can be asymmetries of information and power between players in a market. Merchants can readily hoodwink politicians, as we have seen; and in commerce, far from believing that an invisible hand inevitably works to create conditions of equal competition in markets, Smith is alive to the possibilities for some market players to exploit and derive unfair advantage over others. As well as highlighting the tendency for merchants' meetings to end in 'a conspiracy against the public, or in some contrivance to raise prices', he castigates trade regulations that have the active effect of facilitating such meetings, and thereby promote 'conspiracies' that would struggle to get going in freer markets.

Smith is equally alive to the potential for employers or 'masters' to drive unfair bargains with their workers through 'a constant and uniform combination, not to raise the wages of labour above their actual rate'. They are a compact group, while their workers are dispersed, so that 'The masters, being fewer in number, can combine much more easily,' and this compactness allows them to punish any defecting employers who might wish to pay more: 'To violate this combination is everywhere a most unpopular action, and a sort of reproach to a master among his neighbours and equals.' Finally, they also have more power because they can hold out for longer in a short-term dispute: 'A landlord, a farmer, a master manufacturer, or merchant, though they did not employ a single workman, could generally live a year or two upon the stocks which they have already acquired. Many workmen could not subsist a week, few could subsist a month, and scarce any a year without employment.' Smith notes that 'in the long run the workman may be as necessary to his master as his master is to him; but the necessity is not so immediate.' But the structure of the market does not allow workers to take financial value out of their long-term importance to employers.

The third is what has since become known as the principal–agent problem: the problem that someone charged with carrying out a task may have a conflict of interest, an agenda of their own which affects their judgement or performance. Smith comes to this by discussing the difference between 'joint-stock' companies such as the East India Company, whose shares could be traded and which often had many passive outside shareholders, and partnerships or 'copartneries', whose members or shareholders have unlimited liability and so an interest in the company that is far more closely tied to its fortunes. In theory, at least, the directors of a joint-stock company, then as now, were the trusted agents of the shareholders, but 'being the managers rather of other people's money than of their own, it cannot well be expected, that they should watch over it with the same anxious vigilance with which the partners in a private copartnery frequently watch over their own.' This leads to sloppiness and underperformance: 'Like the stewards of a rich man, they are apt to consider attention to small matters as not for their master's honour, and very easily give themselves a dispensation from having it.' And, as Smith recognized in *The Theory of Moral Sentiments*, a similar phenomenon exists within government: 'Sometimes . . . the interest of the government; sometimes the interest of particular orders of men who tyrannize the government, warp the positive laws of the country from what natural justice would prescribe.' The modern theory of interest groups, and the 'public choice' theory of James Buchanan and Gordon Tullock, which sees government itself in effect as an interest group, spring from this.

So Smith does not endorse what we would now consider crony capitalism; he attacks it. Indeed, he does not merely attack it; he offers a deep critique of it as a pathology of commercial society, and lays down the intellectual foundations of modern approaches to this topic, including the key ideas of rent-seeking, of asymmetrical market information and power and of agency which have become standard tools of political and economic analysis.

But there is something else going on here that is perhaps even more interesting. Earlier on we saw how Smith is no friend to inequality or to poverty; the emphasis in his memorable phrase 'universal opulence' is more on 'universal' than on 'opulence', and for reasons both of economics and of equity he associates a nation's worldly success with high, not low, wages, contrary to the orthodoxy of the time. But Smith's subversive idea seems to go much further: it is not simply that the 'system of natural liberty' that he advocates is not compatible with great inequality; rather, it is one in which it is hard for great inequalities of wealth to come into being at all.

In the first place, Smith takes it that in the most advanced economies the ability to generate profits is heavily constrained by competition. For him, as already noted, 'The rate of profit does not, like rent and wages, rise with the prosperity, and fall with the declension of the society. On the contrary, it is naturally low in rich, and high in poor countries, and it is always highest in the countries which are going fastest to ruin.' In Holland, widely seen as the most advanced commercial economy in Europe, 'the ordinary rate of clear profit would be very small, so the usual market rate of interest which could be afforded out of it, would be so low as to render it impossible for any but the very wealthiest people to live upon the interest of their money.' In such an economy, the suggestion is, large concentrations of capital were less like to arise than in an economy—such as, notoriously, that of eighteenth-century France—that was less competitive and more cronyistic. Moreover, when put to the question Smith's preference is to rebalance public revenue in favour of the poor and against the wealthy through the tax system, again for characteristic reasons of both economic productivity and fairness. He acknowledges, for example, that 'A tax upon house-rents . . . would in general fall heaviest upon the rich.' But this fact does not count against it. On the contrary: 'It is not very unreasonable that the rich should contribute to the public expense, not only in proportion to their revenue, but something more than in that proportion.' Equally, Smith condemns taxes that 'fall much heavier upon the poor than upon the rich', and is opposed to taxes on necessities, which the poor have no option but to pay out of their limited incomes.

What about existing concentrations of capital or wealth? Smith's view combines realism and principle. For him some inequality is the inevitable counterpart of the emergence of agricultural surpluses and the development of private property rights, which undergird commercial society. But Smith is no friend to inequality as such. He sees the rich in every age as having a tendency to dissipate their fortunes through vanity and self-love. But, as we have seen, he also condemns primogeniture and entails, which had the effect of preserving and concentrating wealth over time. For Smith these are the unwanted remains of feudal government, whose effect is to undermine the productive use of land. And by the same token he recognizes the value of inheritance taxes which encourage wider—and fairer, and more productive—ownership. Taken together, these views amount to a vigorous critique of the class structure of British society.

Any suggestion that Smith is somehow a founding father of crony capitalism is, then, wildly mistaken. Indeed, Smith's idealistic vision of an economy according to the 'natural progress of liberty'—a vision for Great Britain 'as absurd as to expect that an Oceana or Utopia should ever be established in it'—specifically inhibits people from amassing large concentrations of wealth. Profits are competed away; wages are high; land is widely distributed; inheritances are shared; and taxes, equitably applied, can in principle be onerous. Meanwhile government acts to support education, improve public works and prevent market-manipulation and rent-extraction. This is not crony capitalism, in any of its many varieties, but its antidote.

CAPITALISM AND EQUALITY

A better understanding of Adam Smith and his thought does not merely serve to refute some of the wilder allegations made about him. We can also use it to review the achievements of the modern market economy, to trace the arguments over free trade since Smith's death and to examine new forces helping to drive crony capitalism today.

One point is absolutely fundamental, and bears restating: that markets are the greatest tool of economic development, wealth-creation

and social advance ever known. They enable the owners of intellectual, financial or human capital to earn a profit through the exercise
of their property rights as a reward for putting that capital to use. This
is one half of capitalism. The other is the pooling of capital, risk and
knowledge made possible by the emergence of the corporation. These
two elements of capitalism together create wealth. Historically, they
are a key part of the wider liberalization since the late eighteenth
century that the economist Deirdre McCloskey has called the Great
Enrichment, a period in which real per capita income—beginning in
north-western Europe and spreading out to North America and the
Far East—rose by an astonishing thirty times, or 3,000 per cent. More
recently, one may compare the development of Western democracies
with that of communist countries after 1945. In 1990 per capita GDP
in capitalist West Germany was over 60 per cent higher than that of
communist East Germany, and this estimate almost certainly under-
states the true picture.

The same is true for developing countries. As a result of the war
of 1950–1953, Korea was split into two countries, north and south.
Thirty years after the Korean War, GDP per capita in capitalist South
Korea was five times that of communist North Korea; in 2009 it was
sixteen times greater. China's economic growth started to accelerate
only in the 1980s, when it opened up special economic zones and
started to implement market-oriented reforms; India's growth did the
same after its reforms in 1991. Technology-enabled trade, far more
than aid, is pulling countries across Africa out of poverty after decades of stagnation.

The second point is no less fundamental: overall, global inequality
is falling, not rising. Indeed, it is falling at an astonishing rate, and
it is falling because of the growth of open, freely trading markets.
In the twenty years between 1988 and 2008, the cumulative gain in
real income for over 60 per cent of the world's population was between 40 and 75 per cent; this is the so-called global emerging middle
class, mainly from Asian countries such as India, Thailand, Vietnam,

Indonesia and especially China. The bottom decile have made real gains, albeit at a slower rate. Deciles eight and nine—mainly the middle classes of Europe and the US—have seen little or no growth, creating potentially severe cost-of-living issues in these countries.

In the top decile within many countries it is a different story altogether, however, and this has helped to fuel anger at inequality more generally. There we see rapidly rising inequality between the top 1 per cent, the top 0.1 per cent and the top 0.01 per cent and the rest—that is, at the very high end of the income spectrum—and this is in part the result of crony capitalism. But the overall picture is that global inequality is falling, especially between nations, and it is falling because of the spread of markets. This confirms the point already made: that crony capitalism is a specific pathology, a disease of capitalism rather than capitalism itself.

The capacity to create human prosperity is a human good, so the case for capitalism is not just one about wealth-creation. As Smith reminds us, it is also one about the value of a society which gives scope for freedom and the cultivation of human capabilities. One might go further, in similar spirit: a properly functioning capitalist system thrives on personal freedom, hard work, creativity, enterprise and thrift. It encourages institutions of social as well as economic exchange, and traditions and practices by which intellectual, financial and human capital can be shared and deployed to best effect. It relies on the family to share risks across the generations, and on the rule of law to protect property rights. But capitalism can encourage people to behave in socially productive or unproductive ways: to devote their energies to building homes or finding new tax loopholes, to developing life-saving drugs or running offshore sweatshops. It can stimulate fruitful investment, or the search for unwitting clients to be ripped off. It can lead people to astonishing human achievements in science, technology and engineering, or systematically feed and exploit known human weaknesses. When capitalism is working well, it engenders trust, cooperation and innovation. When those virtues are missing, it is a sign that something deeper is going wrong with capitalism itself.

THE USES OF TRADE

Contrary to popular belief, however, even in the Western world reasonably free-market policies have largely been the exception, not the rule, in the two centuries and more since Smith's death. In continental Europe the leading free-trade nations at that time were the Netherlands, as Smith had noted, and Switzerland. As for the USA, in the words of the doyen of American business historians Alfred Chandler, the century after the end of the Civil War in 1865 consisted of 'ten years of competition and ninety years of oligopoly'. Nor was the USA a free-trade country before then. The early nation was broadly split between 'Jeffersonians' and 'Hamiltonians'—that is, between the agrarian interest and the proto-industrial interest, between the followers of Thomas Jefferson from the agricultural slave states of the South, who sought free markets for their cotton, and the followers of Alexander Hamilton from the manufacturing states of the North, who wished to impose tariffs on competing imports. In his *Report on the Subject of Manufactures* of 1791, Hamilton, then the US Treasury Secretary, had argued that tariffs were necessary to support American manufacturing until it could be strong enough to withstand the full blast of foreign competition. This theme was taken up by the leading Whig politician Henry Clay after the War of 1812, and later by his great admirer Abraham Lincoln at the time of the birth of the Republican party; and the tariff lobby remained in the ascendant until it fell into disrepute during the Depression, after passage of the notorious Smoot–Hawley Tariff Act of 1930.

Only after the Second World War, once the USA had achieved a role as global commercial leader and rule-setter, did a drive towards lowering trade barriers really begin, albeit heavily conditioned by the Cold War and other US foreign policy interests. Even today, the idea that the USA is a bastion of the free market is distinctly quaint, as anyone will know who has dealt with its labour laws, immigration rules, agriculture, many remaining manufacturing tariffs and laws on foreign investment and ownership. In 2016, the USA ranked just 36th out of 177 nations listed in the Heritage Foundation's *Index of Economic Freedom*, and 22nd out of 136 nations in the World Economic Forum's *Enabling Trade Index*.

The UK took a rather different path, but with a similar underlying rationale. The drive for free trade did not really get under way until the 1840s, and reached its zenith during the high Victorian period. Domestically, it took the form of the repeal of the Corn Laws by Peel's government in 1846, pressed by the radical Liberals Richard Cobden and John Bright, followed by William Gladstone's pioneering budget of 1853, which abolished 123 duties and reduced a further 133. The move towards free trade gave Adam Smith a kind of sanctified official status. But it had not always been so. Indeed, Walter Bagehot, legendary editor of the free-trade paper *The Economist*, remarked at the centenary of *The Wealth of Nations* in 1876 that 'It is difficult for a modern Englishman, to whom "Free Trade" is an accepted maxim of tedious orthodoxy, to remember sufficiently that a hundred years ago it was a heresy and a paradox.'

Overseas, British policy was far more imperial than free trade in character. The Cobden–Chevalier Treaty of 1860 between Britain and France picked up the threads of Pitt's pioneering efforts of the 1780s and reduced tariffs on British manufactures and French wines and spirits; it can claim to be the first true free-trade agreement. But, as the British Empire expanded, military power increasingly trumped diplomacy and negotiation. Notoriously, Britain had forced open five major Chinese ports to trade—much to its own advantage—and seized control of Hong Kong, in the Treaty of Nanking of 1842, which concluded the first Opium War. The growth of the East India Company, supported by dozens of former company men and shareholders in Parliament, was followed by great-power conflict across central and southern Asia, the Company's collapse after the Indian Mutiny in

1857, direct British control of India and a series of British thrusts into inland Africa in pursuit of trading opportunities and mineral wealth. Egypt was annexed in 1882, giving Britain outright control of the Suez Canal and so of the direct trade links to the Indian Ocean and the Far East. Trade was important, indeed vital, but it was an integral part of the structure and demands of empire. People may approve or disapprove of different aspects of the British Empire, a topic which remains fiercely contested today. What is harder to dispute is that, as with the USA, it was only once Britain was achieving hegemony in its chosen markets, by industrialization, technology or growth of empire, that it really encouraged free trade—and even that was designed to serve political as much as economic ends.

As we have seen, Adam Smith deplored the tendencies to monopoly and colonial exploitation, the anti-competitive effects of trade restrictions, privileges and tariffs, and the distortion of domestic politics created by the great mercantile lobbies—the national and international forerunners of today's crony capitalism. And there can be little doubt he would have denounced many of these later developments. He was a committed believer in the wisdom of freeing up trade as between willing partners, but he was also acutely aware of the evil effects of colonial exploitation, and was hostile to the use of coercion to open up trade.

What about Hamilton's temporary protections for infant industries? The argument was taken up and developed by Friedrich List and John Stuart Mill in the 1840s; and it has become a live one in recent years, as some economists have argued in favour of 'Hamiltonian' policy measures as part of a general critique of libertarian views of trade. The suggestion is that much of British eighteenth-century economic success was in fact based on a system of selective tariffs and other restrictions on trade, particularly developed by Sir Robert Walpole in the 1720s and buttressed by the Navigation Acts; and that infant-industry protection has been a key policy lever for South Korea, Indonesia, China and other highly successful developing nations.

As we have seen, Smith's views on trade are hardly those of many modern libertarians. His discussion of import restraints in Book IV of *The Wealth of Nations* suggests that he accepted that retaliatory tariffs might be temporarily necessary, provided that their goal was to induce another nation to drop tariffs of their own. Infant-industry protection is a different thing, however. In Book II Smith considers how countries with limited access to capital should best employ the capital they have. His answer is that rather than spreading their capital too thinly, they should favour agriculture over manufacturing, and manufacturing over trade, on the grounds that this approach will best promote 'the quantity of productive labour which it puts into motion within the country', and 'the value which its employment adds to the annual produce of the land and labour of the society'.

Smith is unequivocal that agricultural preference—to be clear, a form of protectionism—has been the source of American economic success hitherto, and he goes on to draw the general lesson for the colonies, in a characteristically clear and vigorous passage:

> Were the Americans, either by combination or by any other sort of violence, to stop the importation of European manufactures, and, by thus giving a monopoly to such of their own countrymen as could manufacture the like goods, divert any considerable part of their capital into this employment, they would retard instead of accelerating the further increase in the value of their annual produce, and would obstruct instead of promoting the progress of their country towards real wealth and greatness.

Does this mean Smith ruled out infant-industry protection in all circumstances? Actually, it is far from clear that it does. Over the long term, Smith was clearly wrong to think that agriculture could outstrip manufacturing in value. But the logic of his argument is that it is permissible to favour one sector of a developing economy over another, and that countries with limited capital resources should use what they have to promote areas of greatest added value. For the American colonies at that time, that meant agriculture; but more widely for Smith it included 'productive labour', which he allowed for in manufacturing and trade, and so presumably what would today be called intellectual capital, as well as other factors of production.

Thus Smith did not fully grasp, as Hamilton did, the extraordinary productive potential of industrialization, in America or elsewhere. But, if he had, it is not hard to imagine that he might have backed the use of scarce capital in that developing country for new manufacturing industries in nascent markets over existing agriculture, on the grounds of its greater added value—despite his clear dislike of interference in established markets.

CRONY CAPITALISM: THE NEXT FRONTIER

From a Smithian viewpoint, then, the case for freely trading markets is overwhelming, but the idea that the modern world has enjoyed a glorious history of free trade over the past two centuries, in Britain, continental Europe or the USA, is largely a myth. The West enjoyed the benefits of commercial society, but it also continued to deploy the weapons of mercantilism or crony capitalism to extract value from other countries. This is quite at odds with the radical critique of Smith as the supposed originator of the ills of global capitalism.

Yet a Smithian viewpoint also enables us to look forward: at new forms of crony capitalism, and how they can be addressed. For there is every reason to fear the continued growth of crony capitalism. First, the economics of lobbying continue to be enormously enriching, especially to the global corporations which dominate it. Secondly, the consolidation of many industries through takeovers and mergers in recent decades has created a set of international oligopolies in sectors from semiconductors to pharmaceuticals and brewing. This in turn has reduced competitive pressure between the largest companies, while further increasing their domestic lobbying power and putting extra pressure on companies lower down their supply chains. *The Economist* reported in September 2016 that the share of nominal US GDP created by the Fortune 100 largest American companies had risen from 33 per cent to 46 per cent—a rise of more than one-third—in just twenty years. The revenues of the median listed public company have risen by three times over that period, with profit margins to match.

At the same time, a recent report by the US Council of Economic Advisers and other expert studies have found a significant rise in market power, and not merely among financial institutions. In 2014, the average US firm charged prices 67 per cent over marginal cost, compared to 18 per cent in 1980; there is a growing concentration of power among the top fifty firms in leading industries, a huge increase in profitability and evidence of a decline in the number of new firms each year. These factors may help to explain a host of other troubling recent phenomena: relatively low rates of industrial investment, despite low interest rates; sluggish productivity growth; and rising inequality of incomes. There is thus every reason for concern about the loss of effective competition in many advanced economies, and so the loss of economic value to consumers and to the public interest, a loss of value not reflected in share prices, which have become increasingly disconnected from improved economic performance. Within firms, as Robert Solow has argued, the tacit understandings that historically governed the allocation of value between labour and capital may be coming under threat, not least from capture by management. If this is true, then in fundamental ways it seems that capitalism itself may be starting to struggle.

But by far the most significant development has been the increasing impact of technology. With more technology has come rapidly increasing complexity in markets, as choices proliferate for the consumer. Behind this technology sits the awesome potential of big data, for good or ill—potential which often translates into increased power for those who hold it over technology-users. Supposedly free services are of course not in fact free: they are markets in which users' time and attention are traded for advertising and sales. The businesses that offer these services—Google, Apple, Facebook and the like—are modern titans which bestride their markets as completely as the old oil and railway trusts. Google has a 70 per cent market share in search services; Google and Apple together provide the operating systems of 90 per cent of smartphones; Facebook has 2 billion active users every month. These companies manage technology platforms that are private and proprietary, their inner workings opaque to public scrutiny. They are highly scalable, and benefit from so-called 'network effects' by which new members increase the value of connectivity for all, and growth in data equates to super-growth in economic value. The introduction in recent years of feedback methods that allow buyers and sellers to evaluate each other, reducing informational gaps and improving incentives on both sides to perform well, has only added to the platforms' extraordinary market power. And they have proven to be highly effective in identifying, and destroying or purchasing, potential competitors. In the words of the online investor and entrepreneur Peter Thiel, 'Competition is for losers.'

These companies have grown through brilliant innovations in technology and business processes, which they have used to offer new services of immense value to individual and corporate consumers. The possibilities for future social benefit are far-reaching, from artificial intelligence to smart manufacturing to the deep integration of machines into human biology. Yet the possibilities for abuse are arguably no less great.

Public attention has rightly focused so far on apparently egregious uses of intra-company transfer pricing and other devices to reduce tax payments to a minimum. But there is another issue that may ultimately cast a still longer shadow. These companies enjoy gigantic and increasing asymmetries of power and information versus the individual consumer. These asymmetries often allow them the scope to exploit their consumers, both in specific segments or in groups and individually, in ways that run counter to established norms of fair dealing and justice. They are hard for government or regulators to scrutinize, because they are closed systems. But at the same time their status as networks means the normal armoury of regulatory tools against market monopoly or oligopoly is far less effective. Compare: the Standard Oil Company could be and was broken up after 1911 under the Sherman Act into a host of smaller (but still enormous) oil and gas companies, including what would become Exxon, Amoco, Chevron, Conoco, Mobil and Sohio (later bought by BP). But few if any people seriously believe that, say, Google could be effectively broken up into different regional or business units, or that to do so would generate economic value.

Alongside these technology titans sits a tier of more traditional companies in areas such as broadband communications, energy and insurance, in which technological change has increasingly tilted power towards insiders—the company and its employees and shareholders—and against the customer. Their products are not free—far from it—but the sheer number and complexity of them can make it next to impossible for the normal customer to exercise effective choice. Typically, these 'bent markets' have four features: the products involve large expenditures by the customer; the companies are able to differentiate between 'savvy' and 'non-savvy' customers; there are plenty of non-savvy customers; and the negative impact of bad behaviour on the companies' brands or reputation is not enough to prevent them from doing it. Information overload is a recognized and widespread human phenomenon: people, especially the less well-off, struggle to make choices when faced with more than a few options. At the limit, the difficulty and cost for the fallible, time-pressed and often poorer human customer of searching for the best product becomes so high that they remain inert. So the basic recipe can be as simple as: create lots of different products that are hard to compare with each other; separate out those customers that can find the best deals from the much larger number that cannot; and raise prices for the latter. Ignore any relevant traditions or ethos of public service, brush off the inevitable opprobrium and consumer complaints, and encourage regulators and the press to blame consumers for being insufficiently active. Then enjoy large profits. The UK's retail electricity markets are a case in point.

A third tier consists of more traditional products and services that digital technologies are rendering less intelligible, and so potentially more harmful, to consumers. Take Volkswagen, for example, a company that made its name as a mass manufacturer of cars for the people, as its name implies. In 2015, the company was found to have deliberately evaded emissions regulations on its diesel cars through the creation of a 'defeat device', a piece of software specifically designed to suppress emissions during tests but not when on the road. In other words, it was using technology in a plainly dishonest way in order to break the law without appearing to do so, knowing that the effect would be to reduce air quality and damage public health. In June 2016 Volkswagen agreed to settle what had become the largest consumer class-action suit ever in the USA, for $15.3 billion. There was an international outcry at its behaviour—was this what German engineering excellence had come to? But what was less noted was that the use of defeat devices in the America auto industry is at least forty years old; as technology developed, so did the scale and sophistication of the cheating, and the difficulty of its detection by consumers.

The contrast between these 'black box' cases and normal well-functioning markets—markets like those for food, where competition generally drives prices down and quality up and consumers have a very wide choice, immediate availability of products and little or no burden of calculation in making choices—is evident. Yet as technology spreads, there are increasing dangers of the proliferation of a new tech-enabled crony capitalism: a self-reinforcing cycle in which greater insider power encourages the development of bent markets; these in turn create popular demands for more government regulation, creating more complexity and opportunities for lobbying, a further boost to the power of insiders, and so on. The result would almost certainly be to increase inequalities of information and market power and further damage public trust in free and open markets. That is a bleak prospect indeed.

So what can be done? Old-style legal and regulatory measures to improve competition and reduce monopoly run up against serious difficulties here, in part for the reasons noted, in part because of a systematic modern tendency to construe competition policy exclusively in terms of consumers' economic detriment. Not only that: price-comparison websites, often hailed as a means for consumers to lower costs and switch between providers, have had an unhappy tendency to add fees of their own and restrict competition, as UK regulators have found. There is huge scope to increase transparency and improve public accountability and effectiveness in the boardrooms of these companies. But another kind of approach offers greater prospects of success, and it comes straight from the thought of Adam Smith. As we have seen, Smith identifies asymmetries of power and information between masters and workers, and supports measures to increase the bargaining power of workers. In a similar way, there is huge scope to make big data portable, and enhance the power of consumers in relation to the great tech giants of today by putting more computing power at the service of the consumers themselves. Human consumers can be supported by *algorithmic consumers*—that is, by pieces of software able to compare and contrast different offers in the digital marketplace, and make choices on the human consumer's behalf. Imagine trying to choose the best home insurance in such a world; instead of poring for hours over dozens of sites and hundreds of products, or using potentially costly price-comparison sites, you could have your personal online assistant do it for you, in its own time and using networked computational power.

It has been rightly said that entrepreneurship is mostly the discovery of a hidden cost, and many of these costs are hardly hidden. Over time, such online assistants are likely to become commonplace; still more so if data comes to be seen as a public good, as something created by individuals, not simply accumulated by companies. These digital agents could in principle make automatic purchases subject to individual guidelines, negotiate transactions and even build coalitions with other digital consumers automatically in order to get keener prices or elicit new products. Indeed, there is no reason why an array of new businesses should not be established to enable this levelling of the playing field to take place. It would require careful regulatory interventions, to disable online terms of contract which prevent consumers from shopping around, to require the seller to offer neutral access to price and product information which the digital agents can use, and to enable more consumer control over what advertising is shown to them; and these kinds of measures will have to be adapted further so that digital agents can be used within Facebook and on other platforms and environments. But there is no reason to think that any of this is impossible. These can potentially be the new trading and trust-busting standards of the digital future.

Once again we can see here the enduring importance of the thought of Adam Smith. It reminds us that no two markets are the same; that markets have no divine right to exist, but serve a public as well as a private function; that regulation may be required to ensure their effective and competitive operation, but that regulation itself carries potential costs; that the lobbying power of corporate interests is a serious risk both to effective markets and to legitimate government; that crony capitalism flourishes where markets are not competitive; that crony capitalism can be understood in terms of the three key ideas of economic rent-seeking, asymmetries of power and information, and agency costs; and that unless active measures are taken, there is a serious risk that it will escalate.

Yet a Smithian viewpoint carries with it at least three wider implications for understanding our modern world as well. First, Smith's economic egalitarianism anticipates recent academic work which suggests that great inequality, far from creating incentives that boost economic growth, can actively undermine it. Secondly, Smith underlines the degree to which different forms of modern mercantilism—the strategic use of trade surpluses and tariff and non-tariff barriers, the hollowing out of labour markets in developing countries as their most mobile talent is drawn into advanced economies, the competitive withdrawal by nations from shared environmental costs—can be read not merely in terms of a retreat from the responsibilities of a globalizing world but as the plain old-fashioned pursuit of political power by a form of economic nationalism, a modern 'jealousy of trade', in Hume's memorable phrase.

Finally, Smith highlights the missing dimension to much debate about globalization, which is a moral one. It is increasingly clear that it is not enough for the winners from globalization simply to seek to pay off the losers. What is at stake here is not merely money, but meaning: the capacity of those affected to lead worthwhile and meaningful lives with fulfilling work, with dignity and the respect of others, and in the fullest possible discharge of their capabilities. Moreover, as inequalities of power, status and information proliferate, and the exercise of market power becomes increasingly hidden behind a technological veil, so the importance not merely of effective public institutions and norms but of public-spirited individual leadership of both companies and nations becomes greater than ever. A purely economic analysis—of malfunctioning markets, of globalization, of capitalism itself—mistakes both the diagnosis and the possible cure. As the next chapter shows, what are ultimately at stake are culture, identity and meaning; and they are fundamental to any policy measures aimed at redress and renewal for those who are left behind.

CHAPTER 10

THE MORAL BASIS OF COMMERCIAL SOCIETY

IN 1761 JEAN CALAS WAS A PROSPEROUS HUGUENOT MERCHANT, sixty-three years of age, a husband and the father of six children, and the owner of a shop specializing in calicoes and printed cloths in Toulouse. On the night of 13 October, his eldest son Marc-Antoine was found dead at the family home. Calas declared that the young man had been murdered by an intruder, but a medical investigation determined that he had been 'hanged whilst alive, by himself or by others'. A sudden rumour went round the city that the family had killed him to prevent his conversion to Catholicism, and Calas himself was arrested. In prison, he changed his story: they had found Marc-Antoine hanging, he said, but were afraid of what would happen if the truth came out, because under prevailing law the bodies of suicides could be stripped and dragged naked through the streets.

There was a mockery of a local trial, which featured the conflicting testimonies and hearsay of more than 100 people, but no eye-witnesses and little hard evidence. No Catholic confessor for the supposed convert could be found, but the dead man was nevertheless given a full Catholic funeral, attended by thousands of people. Calas was quickly found guilty of murder, with the formal support of the Church, and the verdict was referred to the Toulouse *parlement*, the local legislative body which also served as an appeal court, where on 9 March 1762 it was upheld.

Calas was then publicly interrogated and tortured. Under the so-called *Question Ordinaire*, he was placed on a rack and his limbs slowly pulled apart. There being no confession, the magistrate moved on to the *Question Extraordinaire*. Calas's mouth was forced open and covered with a cloth, a funnel placed in it, his nose pinched and pitchers of water poured down his throat. This too was unavailing. He was then taken to the main square and fixed to a cross. His legs and arms were broken and his abdomen crushed by repeated blows of an iron rod. This done, he was strapped to a wheel and left in the sun, face up, still protesting his innocence, then finally strangled and burned.

A FRAGILE WORLD

By the time Adam Smith arrived in Toulouse, less than two years later, the intervention of Voltaire had already made the Calas case into a national scandal and a byword for administrative and judicial injustice. Smith and Voltaire had a good friend in common, Dr Théodore Tronchin, and it is inconceivable that they did not discuss the case when they met—five or six times, according to John Rae—at Voltaire's retreat at Ferney in the following year. Smith was an enthusiastic admirer of the great *philosophe*, and is reported to have remarked that 'He has done much more for the benefit of mankind than those grave philosophers whose books are read by a few only. The writings of Voltaire are made for all and read by all.' For Smith as for Voltaire, the case seems to have had considerable resonance, and he evidently admired Calas as an exemplar of moral character, for he added to *The Theory of Moral Sentiments* Calas's haunting final words to a monk sent to hear his confession: 'My Father . . . can you yourself bring yourself to believe that I am guilty?'

The Calas case had implications for the nature of society itself. Though Calas's punishment was severe, it was hardly unusual, on either side of the Channel—there had been over fifty British sentences of hanging, drawing and quartering for high treason in 1746 in the name of the Crown after the Jacobite Rebellion. Rather, the case revealed the vivid contrast between the French legal system and the legal independence and due process of the English and Scottish judiciaries. And legal torture had not been seen, in England at least, for well over a century: it had fallen into disuse after 1600 and finally been abolished in 1640. Indeed, Voltaire himself had rather bravely celebrated the peculiarly English blend of tolerance, liberty, law and trade in his book *Letters Concerning the English Nation*—published first in England in 1733, and then the following year in France, where it was quickly and predictably suppressed.

But the treatment of Calas was a reminder of just how close violence could lie to the surface of even an apparently sophisticated city. Violence had come with similar speed to the polite professional classes of Edinburgh from the Jacobite Rebellion of 1745: as Smith put it, 'four or five thousand naked unarmed Highlanders took possession of the improved parts of this country without any opposition from the unwarlike inhabitants.' But that was from without: Toulouse showed how swiftly popular anger, aroused by heavy taxes and stoked by religious panic, could boil over into bloodshed from within.

Finally, it was evident at the time that a key cause of Calas's incrimination, torture and death was a moral panic driven on by Catholic fear of his outsider status as a Huguenot, a panic which the legal institutions of Toulouse had not merely failed to contain under the rule of law, but actively abetted. Smith had written in his final additions to *The Theory of Moral Sentiments* in 1789 that 'Of all the corrupters of moral sentiments, therefore, faction and fanaticism have always been by far the greatest': the Calas case was a perfect case study of that faction and fanaticism in action. And it can only have further reinforced the emphasis already present in Smith's jurisprudence lectures on the importance of public institutions, practices and norms as shapers of human conduct.

Seen in this light, commercial society was an astonishing phenomenon, which demanded investigation and explanation; but the Calas case showed that it was also a specific, complex and potentially fragile human achievement, and one which differed in strength between Britain and France. The political, financial and economic contrasts between the two countries are a key theme in *The Wealth of Nations*, and Smith was apparently quite familiar with the resistance of the regional French *parlements* to central authority, and the autocratic interventions from Versailles which impeded France's commercial development and helped to set the scene for the violence of 1789. There was a strong contrast with the constitutional containment of the British monarchy since 1688, which had greatly assisted both the creditworthiness of the Crown and the growth of the independent commercial classes.

Today, in a world yearning for genuine sources of intellectual authority, Adam Smith has been recruited to, or disparaged by, a vast range of different economic, political or social viewpoints. But he remains little read, and that little reading has tended to focus on *The Wealth of Nations*. The result, as we have seen, has been a series of caricatures: Smith as economic libertarian, Smith as apologist for *homo economicus*, Smith as high priest of capitalism. Underlying them is often the idea—shared by many across the political spectrum, from libertarians to Marxists—that what 'really' matters is economics: that culture is irrelevant, that material economic forces of production and consumption will always predominate within society, and that all that is required for economic success is to set those forces free. Alongside this has sat the idea that much of politics, sociology, psychology, anthropology and the like are ultimately derivative of and reducible to economics.

In fact, however, even within economics much of the best analysis of the past thirty years or more has questioned these assumptions, and begun to assert and explore the centrality of culture in its models. Moral and social norms, in particular—the tacit rules of society that structure our lives—are coming more and more into the spotlight. The effect, ironically, is to return inquiry almost to its starting point. For in the work of Adam Smith, from the earliest essays to *The Theory of Moral Sentiments*, the *Lectures on Jurisprudence* and *The Wealth of Nations* itself, what we would call 'culture' is in several different aspects an absolutely central concern. Yes, much of Smith's thought concerns how liberty enables commerce, and the economic benefits that do or would flow from his 'natural system of liberty'. But he was also preoccupied with the opposite phenomenon: with how commerce sustains liberty and the values of liberty. What is the nature of commercial society? How does it shape human norms and human personality?

THE CIVILIZING PROCESS

Montesquieu's famous idea of *doux commerce*, of the softening effects of trade, had helped to stoke an intense debate on the nature of commercial society among eighteenth-century writers and intellectuals. In *The Spirit of Laws*, Montesquieu had remarked that 'the spirit of commerce is naturally attended with that of frugality, economy, moderation, labour, prudence, tranquillity, order and rule.' The idea was not merely that commerce and markets had benefits—in particular for Montesquieu in constraining monarchical power—that went beyond the strictly economic: it was that they were agents of civilization for society, and for the individual as well in polishing previously barbaric manners. Others had fretted that commerce served to undermine aristocratic virtue or civic order or the quest for religious salvation. But for Montesquieu commerce was a direct force for social improvement. As he put it, 'Commerce is a cure for the most destructive prejudices; for it is almost a general rule, that wherever we find agreeable manners, there commerce flourishes; and that wherever there is commerce, there we meet with agreeable manners.'

David Hume too had written in a splendid essay, 'Of Luxury', later retitled 'Of Refinement in the Arts', about the advantages of the industriousness, knowledge and humanity derived from commercial society, of how commerce brought people together, and of the spillover effects of these advantages in improving the well-being of others in society. Contrary to much republican theorizing, luxury did not automatically lead to moral decadence or political enervation. But Smith goes further still. His general four-stage analysis of development—from hunting to shepherding to agriculture and finally to commerce—ties manners, property, law, politics and government into a single, overarching dynamic theory. As we saw in Chapter 3, in the most primitive hunting society, according to Smith, men can have only what they kill; there is virtually no private property, and so no special source of authority beyond personal attributes of strength and skill. Private property emerges in the second or shepherd stage, in the possibility of owning herds beyond one's own needs; and property rights are then extended in the agriculture stage to ownership of surplus produce and land. In the fourth stage of commerce, property rights are continuously extended as markets and trade proliferate. Each stage marks, in effect, a further development of the division of labour and of the instinct to truck, barter and exchange, as well as the transition to an increasingly complex and ramified society. At the same time, the scope of an individual's ambition and responsibilities is progressively extended from mere possession of a few necessities of life to the ownership of animals, of grain stores, of land and ultimately of abstractions such as money and credit which can arise only through shared public trust. The theory is not merely materialist or economic, but social and cultural as well.

As property rights develop, so does the wealth of property-holders and of those around them. And so too does inequality—and, in Smith's words, 'avarice and ambition in the rich, in the poor the hatred of labour, and the love of present ease and enjoyment'—and the forms of authority required to maintain the social order. The result is that wealth and noble birth become the basis for political authority in the agricultural stage; in Britain this resulted in feudalism, Smith argues, since the principal use for a magnate's surplus income was to pay and house his retainers and militias. But with the advent of commercial society these forms of personal subordination yield to economic relationships of interdependence. As Smith says, 'Every man thus lives by exchanging, or becomes, in some measure, a merchant,' as people autonomously create mutual obligations with each other. Cities, trade, manufactures and commercial contracts come to the fore, together with the banks and lending networks required to finance them. Legal institutions emerge to adjudicate on and protect claims to property rights, and then rights more generally. The nature of criminal justice changes from direct individual or familial redress and compensation to a focus on the impact of crime on society as such, with a growing state monopoly of adjudication and enforcement. The collective demand for society to be orderly becomes of central importance. As the needs of society grow stronger, so too do society's demands on the state.

But human manners, morals and character also change, and become more complex. Commerce creates wealth and economic freedom, but it also brings people together in voluntary and mutually beneficial exchanges of every kind. Commercial society is a society of rhetoric, of negotiation, of trucking and bargaining as much as of material gain. Its surpluses pay via taxation for courts and judges. In less developed societies, Smith says, the 'heroic and unconquerable firmness' demanded of the 'savage', who lacks any system of justice, prevents him from yielding to soft emotions on pain of being thought weak. But 'a humane and polished people, who have more sensibility to the passions of others, can more readily enter into an animated and passionate behaviour, and can more easily pardon some little excess.' Softer, more polished commercial societies may lack both the martial virtues and the economic incentives to sustain militias; but they have the financial wherewithal to afford a standing army, and in the British case the political and legal institutions needed to stop such an army from becoming oppressive. And the softening effects of commercial society are not merely domestic: over time, European nations under its sway have an increasing interest to compete not on the battlefield, but in the marketplace.

Smith is far from uncritical about commercial society, as we saw in the last chapter; and he acknowledges, indeed argues, that the actual course of history can vary within this simplified account. His general theory is one in which the expansion of trade increases economic freedom and encourages innovation and specialization. But these developments themselves demand, and feed off, an evolving legal and constitutional order which protects property rights, suppresses violence and inhibits the state from making predatory interventions.

If people change and are changed by commercial society, the same is true for institutions. The separation of powers within government itself functions as a kind of division of labour, allowing increased specialization within public institutions, while limiting the extraction of rents. This in turn sustains further commercial expansion, in a virtuous and expanding cycle of growth. The legitimacy of government is grounded in considerations of utility and evolved authority, not in natural law, revelation or social contract.

Smith's picture is thus of a social, economic and political order bootstrapping itself into existence over time, the product not of any individual mind or minds or initial founding act, but evolving as the unintended consequence of endlessly repeated social interactions. The result is a dynamic theory of political and economic development, which anticipates—and often sets the terms for—the work of a host of distinguished modern writers, from Norbert Elias and Steven Pinker on the decline of violence, to Deirdre McCloskey on the bourgeois virtues and Daron Acemoglu and James Robinson on 'extractive' and 'inclusive' institutions as causes of national economic failure and success.

A THEORY OF NORMS

But if commercial society emerges as a co-evolved system of institutions, laws and manners, this in turn raises questions about the source of the moral values and behaviour that underlie it. What ultimately binds such a society together? More deeply still: how is it that different people are able to inhabit a broadly shared moral world? How can they come to have shared assumptions and moral values at all?

For Thomas Hobbes, the answer subordinated individual morality to sovereign authority. According to the theory advanced in his masterpiece, *Leviathan,* civil society—and so the possibility of moral behaviour over and above self-interest and the basic human need for security—derived from a social contract by which individuals gave up a portion of their sovereign freedom in favour of government. This idea proved to be hugely influential. But, among other objections, it was vulnerable to a brilliant argument of Hume's: how could human society derive from the promise contained in a social contract if people did not *already* accept a norm that promises should be honoured? And if they already accepted the validity of promises, how could a social contract be the foundation of society, as Hobbes claimed? Indeed, why was it necessary to posit a social contract at all? It is a devastating attack.

It is also an attack that points the way to a quite different approach: to start not from on high with sovereign authority, but from below with norms themselves. This is what Smith does, via his idea of the 'impartial spectator' in *The Theory of Moral Sentiments.* As we have seen, this is not, and is not designed to be, in the first instance a substantive theory of moral values such as 'the good' or 'the right', though moral judgements and ideas of virtue may flow from it. It is naturalistic and descriptive, not prescriptive—almost a theory of moral and social causation in its own right. It does not offer a specific criterion or rule of moral action, like the utilitarian rule that one should act so as to maximize the greatest good for the greatest number. Nor is it intended as a detached, Olympian account of universal moral principles to which any rational being is supposed to subscribe, in the style of Kant. Indeed, for those schooled to such expectations, the relativity that comes from Smith's insistence on moral community is a serious weakness. But it is also the book's strength: it offers what is, perhaps, the earliest detailed theory of the formation of moral norms.

On Smith's view, as we have seen, moral self-awareness comes from the bottom up and from the outside in: we assess the moral value of an action not by consulting religious texts, a 'moral sense' or our own faculty of reason, but by imaginatively putting ourselves in the place of others, and asking how they would view it in context 'if the whole circumstances of our conduct were known'. But to do that is to locate oneself in a world of reciprocity, of mutual recognition and obligation, of potential approbation or rebuke: to recognize one's own status as an object of scrutiny, and as a potential spectator of others. Given the nature of human fallibility, and the specific circumstances involved in each case, there is no objective standard or absolutely independent viewpoint to be achieved here, and we may not even succeed in having our actions and motivations well understood by others. Even so, we can ask what they find 'lovely'—worthy of their approbation—and since 'Man naturally desires, not only to be loved, but to be lovely; or to be that thing which is the natural and proper object of love,' this generates general rules which can function as norms of conduct. There may be multiple general rules in play at any given time: for example, that lying is always wrong; or that lying about the tooth fairy or to enemies or to protect a friend is acceptable, or a host of other things. There is then what would now be described as selection pressure in favour of norms which are deemed most widely acceptable within a given context, even if they may be disobeyed in specific instances. Once again moral norms emerge, tacitly or explicitly, as the outcome of human action but not of human design.

David Hume had pointed out in his *Treatise* that social agreement did not require a social contract. It could arise naturally, without any specific decision or design, on both the smallest and the largest scale: 'Two men who pull the oars of a boat, do it by an agreement or convention, although they have never given promises to each other. Nor is the rule concerning the stability of possessions the less derived from human conventions, that it arises gradually, and acquires force by a slow progression . . . In like manner are languages gradually established by human conventions without any promise. In like manner do gold and silver become the common measures of exchange.' This account works well for conventions, such as which side of the road to drive on, where everyone immediately benefits from the adoption of a rule. Matters are less clear in relation to social and moral norms, such as whether it is permissible to drop litter or right to repay a favour, where it can often be in a person's individual interest to disobey. The brilliance of Smith's theory is that it gives an explanation of how such norms can arise naturally, and yet have moral force once they have been established. In effect, Smith generalizes Hume's hint, and his own work on linguistic exchange, from the grammar of language to 'the grammar of society'.

This overall approach has potential political implications, which Smith does not explore. In the first place, politicians no less than others will seek to be 'lovely' in the eyes of their voters, and may compete to influence public opinion both directly and in relation to the norms to be applied to themselves and to their rivals. Secondly, and more deeply, the processes of norm-formation themselves can be highly sensitive to the starting conditions, and in particular to the allocation of power among those involved. Smith leaves scope for causal factors to have a role in establishing specific norms, such as, in our own day, Presidential decrees, Acts of Parliament, local regulations, mass movements, religious campaigns, personal crusades and the like. But his theory applies in principle at any level: from great macro-norms about equal treatment and non-discrimination within society to tiny shifts of expectation within specific circumstances. It applies to norms that are not necessarily in themselves *ethical* norms—norms about good and evil, justice and the like—but which are moral or social in the looser sense of having a bearing on what people value and how they behave. And, since norms are the product of continuously evolving mutual agreement, it underlines the difficulty of treating them within economics as part of a set of preferences that are both static and individualized.

As we shall see, Smith's theory of norms has such pervasive applicability as to cover a vast range of human behaviour. Inevitably, in what is a huge, rich and still far from settled area of research, it is difficult to do more here than sketch an overall line of thought. Nevertheless, it is striking how many lines of scientific and social scientific research on these themes have begun to converge in recent years. These include the work of Frans de Waal and others on norms of reciprocity in primates; of Joe Henrich and others on the evolutionary selection of social norms in different populations; and of Giacomo Rizzolatti and others on the activity of 'mirror neurons'—neurons that fire both when a monkey or human performs an action and when they see another monkey or human doing a similar action. Some people have seen a potential grounding in neuroscience for Smith's idea of 'sympathy'.

Perhaps most striking of all is the degree to which game theory has developed and illuminated ideas to be found in Hume and Smith. From this perspective, norms are a central mechanism by which people come to coordinated solutions to social problems. These solutions can often be formally modelled as 'Nash equilibria'—that is, as stable states of affairs in which each participant knows the strategies of the others and cannot improve their own strategy as a result. Moreover, norms can be treated as the product of evolutionary processes, or simply of numerous repeated interactions, and both approaches fit the Smithian picture well. But repetition is not required for Smith's account to bite. It provides a psychologically plausible account of a core norm of fairness, of 'putting oneself in another's shoes' and seeing things from their perspective—the kind of norm that underlies, for example, the well-known theory of justice developed by the philosopher John Rawls. Overall, the use of game theory enables the idea of norms to be integrated into the equilibrium models beloved of economists. But this is also its weakness, for as a purely formal treatment it operates at a single moment or repeated succession of moments in time. It thus misses the continuous, energetic and ever-changing understanding of human interaction to be found in Smith.

As game theory reminds us, far from being irrelevant or subordinate to economics and commercial activity, norms bear directly upon them. Take the issue of how to raise economic productivity, a problem that has bedevilled Western economies in recent decades, and especially since the 2008 crash. One notable feature is that within a wide range of industries the difference in productivity between the top and bottom 10 per cent of firms is enormous: in the US, the top firms are on average twice as productive *with the same measured inputs* as the bottom ones; in India and China they are five times as productive. This points to the possibility that within each nation social and cultural factors are playing an important role alongside purely economic ones.

Much other research supports this suggestion. For example, a study of forty-one operating units of a US commercial food company producing nearly identical products for similar consumers found that 'even after controlling for such factors as local labour market characteristics, size of the local market, unionization, capital vintage, product quality, and local monopoly power, the top-ranked unit was still twice as productive as the bottom-ranked unit.' How can this be? The answer appears to be that the best firms operated according to a set of established tacit understandings between and among management and employees that went far beyond specific contractual requirements. These were reinforced by norms that emphasized fair treatment, respect for others' viewpoints and rewards for innovation. The result was greater trust and greater productivity. The point has long been known to any union shop steward: simply 'working to rule'—that is, to the letter of a contract—is a recipe for commercial disaster. What matters are the unwritten agreements and understandings, the norms and trust, that sit alongside and around the formal agreements. A better understanding of culture and norms within companies thus comes to seem, not irrelevant to economics, but central to it—indeed, a deep prerequisite to improved economic productivity.

IDENTITY, PROPERTY AND LANGUAGE

The ideas at the core of Smith's moral theory can be taken much further. When someone comes to understand what the right thing to do is, they generally also acquire a belief about what they ought to do. But they can acquire, or take a step towards acquiring, further beliefs too: about their identity, about the kind of person they are, and how they came to be that person. Indeed, the idea of identity is at root a shared or group concept, which links a person with other people or with their past or future selves. And it is implicit in the very idea of Smith's impartial spectator, since the question there is always how one's own conduct compares or would compare with that approved by the spectator. In general, according to Smith, the desired identity is of someone who is 'lovely . . . or the natural and proper object of love', and the judgement by the impartial spectator of what is lovely will always be as in the eyes of others.

But what happens when such a person does something at odds with their identity—something that they know is not lovely in the eyes of others? The result, according to the great American social psychologist Leon Festinger, is cognitive dissonance: that is, a feeling of discomfort which encourages the individual to rationalize their action as having somehow been right all along. For Smith, this is seen in the excuses offered for infanticide in ancient Greece, that it 'is commonly done, and they seem to think this a sufficient apology for what, in itself, is the most unjust and unreasonable conduct'. Festinger predicted—and his findings have been widely replicated—that the greater the dissonance, the more extreme the need for self-justification. Examples of this abound, in private behaviour and public policy. To take a recent example, when it was shown that weapons of mass destruction did not exist in Iraq in 2003, and therefore that the stated rationale for the US-led invasion of Iraq had been groundless, supporters of the invasion generally did not accept this; instead they insisted that the war had been a success anyway, was justified for other reasons, had brought peace, had increased international security and the like.

Festinger's work on cognitive dissonance, and his earlier work on social comparison, sit at the heart of much modern social psychology; and they revisit ideas to be found in Adam Smith. But Smith's work also hints at a deeper explanation for these phenomena. Recall that for Smith someone's reputation or public character is part of their personal property, under what he calls the *jus sincerae aestimationis*, or right to an unspoiled reputation. Indeed for Smith the greatest happiness lies in a good reputation, which may be the result of considerable investment over a long period of time and serve as a source of both private satisfaction and posthumous renown, in the manner of the ancients. But the opposite can also happen, of course: a man's reputation can be destroyed posthumously by others. After Hume's death William Strahan had wished to publish his letters, but Smith had urged him against the idea, saying that unscrupulous men 'would immediately set about rummaging the cabinets of those who had ever received a scrap of paper from him. Many things would be published not fit to see the light to the great mortification of all those who wish well to his memory.' If we are seeking an explanation for Smith's own caution in destroying his notebooks of unfinished work, and in refusing to publish Hume's *Dialogues Concerning Natural Religion*, the answer surely lies here, as well as in his personal modesty.

But, by the same token, someone's sense of their identity can also be an asset acquired with considerable sacrifice. For Smith the idea of the human self is a social one: it is formed, pre-rationally as well as via rational processes, through human interaction. As he says, 'By nature a philosopher is not in genius and disposition half so different from a street porter, as a mastiff is from a greyhound.' In moral terms the self may reflect an accumulation of individual judgements by comparison with the views of an impartial spectator, judgements that may be psychologically costly because they cut against the person's deepest needs and desires. And of course, it may also reflect a person's specific conscious judgement about who they want to be. In each case the result may be that they have, so to speak, an internal reputation to protect and defend as well as an external one. This private internal reputation can be a hugely useful asset in supporting someone's belief in their value in the world, their will to make things happen and their resilience in the face of adversity. But it also leads directly to the patterns of defensive self-justification described by Festinger.

Treating people's core beliefs and moral identity as property assets, perhaps hard-won, in Smithian fashion makes it easier to understand their reluctance to give them up in the face of cognitively dissonant behaviour. But this approach can also help to explain many other kinds of behaviour as well. People who see themselves as rich in the assets of moral identity tend to behave in a more entitled way. They are more likely to 'coast', that is, to give themselves licence to misbehave in later situations, while those who see themselves as depleted may take up worthy causes: privately in an effort to renew their identity capital, or publicly to renew their reputation with others. There are 'treadmill effects', whereby people who are heavily invested in a specific identity, often through their work, invest at a high or perhaps pathological rate in order to maintain that capital, to the detriment of their families, colleagues and themselves. There is a recognized tendency for people to screen out information that might threaten such an identity in which they have a lot at stake. New immigrants, who may not feel they carry with them enough of the identity-conferring assets of knowledge and culture of their country of origin, but have not accumulated enough from their adopted country either, exhibit special vulnerability to new and undermining identities, including perhaps identities of extremism. There is a recognized tendency for those who may feel their identities overshadowed or relatively depreciated by the good deeds of others to seek in some way to punish them, as often happens to whistleblowers. And more generally, one might highlight the tendency of some young people to move through different identities, like investors looking for a suitable home for their savings.

Language can be a clue: words such as 'invested', 'entitled', 'depreciated', 'valued' suggest that the idea of property here may be more than metaphorical. The line of thought sketched above shows how this might be so in Smithian fashion, and how to situate much modern thinking in this area within a wider theory of norms. Such a contextual approach has its limits: for example, it struggles to explain the functioning of taboos, which invoke a sense of the sacred—the unconditional, of what is not to be done no matter what—that is less subject to human appraisal and calculation. But, strikingly, it pushes us towards a more dynamic understanding of everyday human identity, in which the beliefs that function as its core assets are seen as more mutable, more exchangeable, as continuously tested, adopted and cast off in the face of others' behaviour. Identity becomes what it is in reality, even among the old and apparently established: emergent, unsettled, forward-looking, with the question of *who one is* somehow always in play.

THE ECONOMY OF REGARD

Smith, then, offers a rich analysis of this—to us—most familiar and yet extraordinary thing, commercial society; and he does so in terms not merely of economics, but of jurisprudence, sociology and indeed moral philosophy. Markets are sustained not merely by incentives of gain or loss, but by laws, institutions, norms and identities, and without those things they cannot be adequately understood. We are reminded of the astonishing ambition of Smith's project. What we think of now as different disciplines may contribute to it and offer deep insights, but each is inevitably partial in the perspectives it can offer and so they must be brought together in order to give a unified picture. Ultimately, however, there is just one world, the human world.

How, then, does a modern market economy influence human activity beyond the strictly economic? We can think of it as doing so in three ways. The first lies in the sometimes overworked contrast between the private and the public sectors: between the behaviour of markets and the activities of the modern state. Economically, these include buying in goods and services; commissioning, building and managing infrastructure; running public services and distributing benefits.

The state is subject to market pressures, both narrowly in its buying, procuring and commissioning activities—in some of which, like defence, it may hold monopoly power—and globally through the bond and currency markets. It has huge economic effects on others, and in this sense is an economic actor. But it also shapes human behaviour and society in a host of other ways: through the legal system and its enforcement, through its administrative priorities, through legislation, through the wider political process, through the 'bully pulpit', through the (often conflicting) tacit and explicit priorities of government.

A second dimension would contrast present economic activity with the hard-to-price 'further future'—that is, a time perhaps fifty or more years in the future. This includes, for example, some of the long-term economic effects of climate change or population growth and decline, which fall outside the normal time horizons of most if not all public and private investors. But this fact creates a problem. Normally future income and expenditure are discounted relative to the present, to reflect the human preference for the near over the longer term. This is the so-called time value of money, and it is one of the basic foundations of economic analysis. But at any normal discount rate the effect of discounting over such long periods is to reduce the present value of such further future payments to close to zero. Yet long-term projects such as dams and other infrastructure can obviously have continuing value, and their operating lives may run for a century or more; even today much of London's sewage system is based on pipes, wells and drains constructed in the Victorian era. Not only that, but some of the most vital issues facing humankind—population growth, climate change—have precisely this long-term character. Excluding them from economic analysis courts short-termism of a potentially catastrophic kind. It is an important challenge for political economy to give these considerations weight within public policy even so.

The third dimension is arguably no less interesting, and it is directly germane to the present discussion. This is what Avner Offer has called the *economy of regard*. Much of the behaviour of markets in goods and services, especially of consumer non-durable 'haircuts and hamburger' markets, can be explained by an assumption of self-regard, as we have seen; and the miracle of these markets is not just that they are autonomous, unplanned and self-correcting, or that they generate a continuous stream of innovations, but that they yield socially valuable outcomes without regard to the moral character of the participants.

But alongside these is the economy of personal, face-to-face or small-group interaction, of gift-giving, reciprocity and volunteering: the economy of regard. As Offer says, 'Regard takes many forms: attention, acceptance, respect, reputation, status, power, intimacy, love, friendship, kinship, sociability.' But by the same token, to withhold regard from someone is to keep them at a distance, and to withdraw reward is to punish or reject. In the first instance, the economy of regard is centred on the family and on kinship and friendship groups, and just that aspect by itself is vast in scale: the household economy is not captured in standard national accounts, but it alone generates an estimated 25–35 per cent of gross national product in countries such as the US, the UK and Australia. Over and above this, the intergenerational exchange of value in bequests from old to young and in unpaid care for the elderly is hard to measure but without doubt of enormous size. For example, just under half of all adults in the UK do some kind of formal or informal volunteering once a month or more. Offer's theory suggests that including these vital activities—many of them traditionally seen as somehow more 'female' in character, as we noted in Chapter 7—implies a much wider reorientation of economics within political economy.

To monetize regard is to destroy it. But the market economy and the economy of regard are not two separate islands, each entire of itself. On the contrary, the market economy is also saturated with regard. Normal commercial transactions rely on the rhetoric of persuasion, and so on courtesy. Services provided are often rewarded with tips, whose value is not merely financial but as tokens of regard. Company team-building, personal contacts, the business lunch and relationship-selling all involve gifts or exchanges of regard. The same is true across the world, from corporate hospitality in the USA to 'bread and butter' thank-you letters in Britain to *guanxi* practices of gift-giving and reciprocity in China.

At the margin, the economy of regard is subject to different forces. On the one hand, there is increasing pressure from public authorities to bring gifts and other informal transactions under the aegis of taxation, to make them formal parts of the recorded economy. On the other hand, there is pressure from both private and public interests to use regard for their own purposes: 'say it with flowers' is one example, stigmatizing smoking is another. But overall the rapid expansion of services in developed and developing countries alike, the trend towards increasing personalization, and above all the explosive growth of internet commerce and friendship or contact networks through social media, all point to the escalating importance of the economy of regard. We live in an age of instant feedback and opinion, an age of 'likes' and 'follows', an age in which TripAdvisor comments on a new restaurant can matter more than newspaper reviews, an age where a supermarket's buying team can track a specific punnet of blueberries back to the field in Chile where it was grown, and send a personal message of thanks and recognition to the farmer.

The economy of regard is a central part of modern human economic activity. But as an idea, it comes straight out of the pages of *The Theory of Moral Sentiments*. Once again, we are back at the dawn of political economy, rediscovering insights advanced by Adam Smith over 250 years ago. And the word 'regard' itself is well chosen: first, because it captures both aspects of the Smithian impartial spectator, that of seeing someone's behaviour, and that of evaluating it; and secondly because it nicely counterpoints the core idea of *self*-regard that underlies both of Smith's great published works. As Smith recognized, there are personal market transactions, with people we trust; and there are market transactions that are utterly impersonal, between counterparties unknown—but normally knowable—to each other, sustained by our generalized trust in market norms and the reliability of human self-love. But there are also non-market transactions of regard, sustained by the human desire to love and be lovely to others. And there is an infinite array of human exchanges that combine both characteristics.

ANTI-SOCIAL MORALITY

But even this is only half the story. Where there is regard, there can also be disregard; where there is respect, there can also be disrespect; where there is reputation, there can also be notoriety and infamy. While regard serves to strengthen moral community, these factors can work in the opposite way, to undermine and destroy it.

So far, we have taken Smith's theory in the spirit in which it is mainly offered: in modern terminology, as an explanation for the positive moral norms and values that knit society together, and, in parallel, for the outside-in moral development of the individual. But it is not hard to see how the same mechanism working in a different direction could work to generate anti-social norms. Take littering, for example. In pure cost-benefit terms, individual and group well-being do not coincide over littering: an individual who drops a soft-drink can in the street is saved the cost of disposing of it properly and is relatively unlikely to be caught and punished. Yet the costs of litter, to the environment and the public purse, are collectively vast. By the same token, the value of an effective norm against littering is also vast: it is not merely the awareness of the social cost of littering that restrains people from doing it, but the awareness that they are subject to the observation and judgement—and so the disapproval—of others if they do, an awareness that cuts across the desire to be lovely in the eyes of others. Over time this norm is internalized into a value for each individual which operates independently of any external scrutiny. Costs are minimized; and no law, or even much enforcement, may be required. Overall, this can be a stable, economically efficient, socially beneficial state of affairs.

So far, so Smithian. But the opposite can happen as well: people can keep littering, and for a number of different reasons. First, the norm may just not be strong enough compared to the incentive to litter; in the jargon of game theory, the individual may 'defect'. Secondly, the norm-formation mechanism may not operate, because the person may not in fact wish to be lovely or seek others' approbation at all; they may be asocial in some way. Thirdly, the mechanism may operate, but in reverse: the individual may actively wish to court disapproval, perhaps as a member of a gang whose approval they do seek. Or fourthly, the norm may simply be displaced by another and more dominant norm. Of course more than one of these factors may be in play at the same time. Graffiti, for example, can be the result of an artistic calling; a heedless act irrespective of the beliefs or interests of others; a deliberate attempt to annoy and provoke; or it can reflect a principled belief that a particular public space should be contested in some way. The result may be a stable but inefficient and anti-social equilibrium. The well-known 'broken windows' theory reflects the insight that minor disorder tends to escalate unless tackled, and (more controversially) claims that serious crime can be prevented as a result.

Different subcultures can vary widely in the norms they obey. In October 2002, the Clinton–Schumer Amendment allowed the city of New York to tow illegally parked diplomatic vehicles, revoke diplomats' United Nations parking permits and deduct 110 per cent of the total amount of any fines due from US aid given to the country of origin. Between November 1997 and the end of 2002, however, diplomats in New York City from 146 countries around the world had accumulated over 150,000 parking tickets, and outstanding fines of more than $18 million, none of which was paid due to the recipients' diplomatic immunity from demands for payment. As a well-known paper by Raymond Fisman and Edward Miguel pointed out in 2006, this was in effect a unique natural experiment testing the effects of different norms in relation to corruption, which they defined in a rather eighteenth-century way as 'the abuse of entrusted power for private gain'. These were all 'government employees from different countries, all living and working in the same city, all of whom [could] act with impunity in (illegally) parking their cars'.

What did Fisman and Miguel discover? First, in this case at least, that the standard economic theory of crime did not apply. With no enforcement, the theory went, there should have been rampant unpaid parking violations across the board. Instead, they found substantial differences in behaviour among the diplomats: even when everyone could get away with it, those from some countries had accumulated zero unpaid parking charges collectively over a three-year period, while others had over a hundred unpaid violations each on average. Furthermore, even allowing for outliers and a few surprises, there was a strong correlation between the countries with the most violations and those scoring highly on standard international measures of corruption. In the words of Fisman and Miguel, 'The worst parking violators—the ten worst are Kuwait, Egypt, Chad, Sudan, Bulgaria, Mozambique, Albania, Angola, Senegal, and Pakistan—all rank poorly in cross-country corruption rankings.'

By contrast, countries such as Japan, the UK and Canada ranked highly on both counts, for parking payments and for low corruption. Fisman and Miguel concluded that some cultural or social norms related to corruption were persistent and hard to shift: 'Even when stationed thousands of miles away, diplomats behave in a manner highly reminiscent of officials in the home country. Norms related to corruption are apparently deeply engrained, and factors other than legal enforcement are important determinants of corruption behaviour.' Another way to put this is that socially beneficial local norms of obeying the law, paying for parking tickets and not imposing costs on others were respected by some but defeated by other already internalized but anti-social national norms and cultures; and those anti-social norms and cultures could, once again, form stable long-term equilibria.

We can clearly see how well this fits with the Smithian description of norm-formation. So too does another phenomenon, on which the evidence is also clear: corrupt norms have a tendency once engrained to replicate themselves, and to feed into other corrupt norms. In one set of studies in Holland, the mere introduction of graffiti into a given situation more than doubled the number of people littering and stealing a small amount relative to a control; in effect, it seems to have given them permission, or perhaps a cover story, to do so. In another study, based on evidence gathered from twenty-three countries across the world, Simon Gächter and Jonathan Schulz found a systematic relationship between subjects' willingness to profit by cheating on a simple die-rolling exercise and a wider index for each country compiled from independent studies of known political fraud, tax evasion and corruption. As in Festinger's research, people are found to have a strong underlying desire to maintain a positive self-image, which limits the amount of cheating. When they see others behaving corruptly, especially when those people are in positions of authority, they are more likely to do so themselves. Rather than clearly break a norm or established standard, however, they tend to bend rules and stretch the truth as far as their identities permit. As Smith insists, they benchmark themselves against others, because they wish to love, and to be lovely in the eyes of others. Again, there can be equilibria for corrupt norms, perhaps multiple equilibria in each case, and these may be strong enough to resist selection pressures for more positive alternatives. In these cases, the only way forward may be through political intervention or social action.

This brings us to the hardest question of all. What about commercial society itself? What happens when commercial values themselves appear to corrupt society?

COMMERCIALIZING SOCIETY

In 2009 Air New Zealand hired thirty people to act as 'cranial billboards'. Their heads were shaved and given temporary tattoos with the words 'Need a change? Head down to New Zealand'. The price for two weeks of cranial advertising was a round trip ticket to New Zealand worth $1,200, or alternatively $777 in cash.

How should we feel about this? Is this perfectly fair, a straight market transaction, or has something gone wrong here? If cranial billboards are OK, how about prison-cell upgrades? In Santa Ana, California, as of 2012, non-violent offenders could reportedly pay for a clean quiet cell away from the non-paying inmates. The price? A mere $82 per night. Or how about paying someone to stand in line for a Congressional hearing (c. $60) or to stand in line for a free ticket to see Shakespeare in Central Park (up to $125)? Or paying students to do well in exams, or HIV-carrying mothers to have long-term contraception? Or fighting foreign wars by proxy, through the private security contractors which came to outnumber American troops after the invasions of Iraq and Afghanistan?

These examples all come from the American philosopher Michael Sandel, who has carefully highlighted the myriad ways in which different aspects of life, and indeed death, in the USA have become subject to corporate and market values, and specifically subject to being priced, bought and sold. As he points out, public spaces, public institutions such as schools, libraries and universities and instruments of public power such as the police and fire services have become increasingly filled with corporate advertising, product placements and sponsorship.

These corporate intrusions may be benign in their immediate effects or not; there is plenty of evidence to suggest, for example, that corporately sponsored educational materials are often heavily slanted towards the sponsor's interests or viewpoint. But, as Sandel emphasizes, that is not the point: the point is that education in the full sense is not about learning to be a better consumer; it is about learning to be a self-aware and critically reflective human being. Whether or not public spaces, or indeed human identity, should be colonized in this way, what is gained or lost individually and collectively by such transactions, and who should undertake them—these are just the kinds of questions a good education should equip its recipients to raise and consider.

The wider result of this commercialization, Sandel argues, has not merely been to upend existing cultural norms and expectations; it has fed into, and in turn been fed by, what he sees as the increasing difficulty in having an intelligent public conversation about serious issues. In his words, 'At a time when political argument consists mainly of shouting matches on cable television, partisan vitriol on talk radio, and ideological food fights on the floor of Congress, it's hard to imagine a reasoned public debate about such moral questions as the right way to value procreation, children, education, health, the environment, citizenship and other goods . . . The problem with our politics is not too much moral argument, but too little. Our politics is overheated because it is mostly vacant, empty of moral and spiritual content. It fails to engage with big questions that people care about.' In Sandel's view, corporate and market values have a tendency to overwhelm other values, especially moral values; to enervate public debate about what people can and should care about; and to encourage a purely instrumental view of others, and of the natural world. The question becomes not 'Is this the right thing to do?' but 'How much does this cost?' Not 'Who is this person, what do they care about and how can we respect that?' but 'What can they do for me?' Not 'What is there here to delight in, what landscapes, what natural resources, what communities, to feed, engage and sustain us all, now and in future generations?' but 'What scope is there for commercial gain?' It is quite a charge sheet.

Now, a straightforward and often expressed response is: well, so what? It's a free country, and this is the modern world. People are free to act as they please, provided they obey the law, and if they choose to tattoo their heads or pay someone to stand in line for them, that's their business. Similarly, if a school's board of governors chooses to have corporate-sponsored textbooks, that's up to them in the legitimate, and often democratic, exercise of their duties. In both cases, the money gained can be used for other purposes, so these activities may also be economically efficient. What's not to like?

There is a clash between different worlds of value here: between different perceptions of what matters; between what the cultural psychologist Richard Shweder has called the ethics of autonomy, of community and of divinity and a sense of the sacred. Whether or not these are on some level reconcilable, the clash is a subtle reminder of the norm-mediated nature of all human interactions, however sterile, professionalized and value-neutral they may appear. And the question remains: are these commercial activities and values a kind of corruption? People of all ages, all walks of life and all political opinions, from reactionaries to Marxists and anarchists, have thought so, and the critique cannot be readily defused by distinguishing between corporate and market behaviour, since the two so often operate in tandem. The facts are undeniable, and rarely contested: in developed and developing nations across the world, many areas of human life that were until recently far removed from corporations and markets have become full of, and arguably overtaken by, their values, assumptions, concepts and language. Moreover, there is now a wide body of evidence to suggest that in some specific countries, notably the UK and USA, the commercialization and materialism of modern society may also be contributing to 'affluenza', social anxiety, insecurity and illness. The key question is not whether this is happening, but what it means, and what if anything can or should be done about it.

This very rapid growth of market and corporate norms within society is a relatively modern phenomenon. But worries about the corrupting effects of commercial society are as old as commercial society itself. Rousseau, Ferguson and Jefferson were among those who in different ways offered scorching criticisms of the evil effects or potential of manufacturing and commerce and the capacity for private gain to subvert the public good, and who looked back to classical antiquity for models of republican virtue or case studies of vice and dissipation.

There were concerns in the eighteenth century about inequality, about the effects of 'luxury' in increasing greed and envy, about the potential for malfeasance and despotism in a world where property was no longer fixed but tradable. And Montesquieu himself pointed to the usurpation of traditional values by commercial values and exchange, saying 'We see, that in countries where the people move only by the spirit of commerce, they make a traffic of all the humane, all the moral virtues: the most trifling things, those which humanity would demand, are there done, or there given, only for money.'

Lying behind these disagreements is a deeper question about the nature of freedom. Is it a privilege or a right? Is it something that is achieved, as the tradition of civic republicanism had it; something that confers status and responsibility on people as citizens of a moral and political community, and that requires constant attention to institutions and public virtue to sustain it? Or is it a space in which people can act as they please, purely as individuals, subject only to law and their own self-created moral principles—a space which gives vast scope to human personality and emotions but needs little more than the exercise of their own prudence and self-love to sustain it commercially and socially?

As we have seen, Adam Smith was one of the great defenders of the emergent commercial society of his day. For him what existed then fell some way short of his preferred 'system of natural liberty', but he celebrated such a society even so: as an antidote to the servility and personal dependency of feudalism, for the way in which it often improved morals and manners, and above all for its capacity to create 'universal opulence', that is general wealth and prosperity. In relation to civic republicanism, Smith's celebration of commercial society is, precisely, a repudiation of slavery and the classical idea that a virtuous citizenry could be built upon slavery. Far from generating corruption, markets often reduced it; far from increasing power, they often dispersed or bridled it. 'Each tradesman or artificer derives his subsistence from the employment, not of one, but of a hundred or a thousand different customers. Though in some measure obliged to them all, therefore, he is not absolutely dependent upon any one of them.' The rhetorical strategy is clear, and highly effective: to take the central concerns of republicanism about corruption, and argue, often without directly engaging with them, that what has been perceived as evil is in fact beneficial. The 'so what?' argument above is a modern variant of the same approach.

Yet Smith well understood the ways in which commercial society could be corrupting, in the classical republican sense that set private interest against public virtue. For one thing, of course, he inveighs against the 'mean rapacity' and 'monopolising spirit' of the merchants. But he also devotes a section of his unpublished *Lectures on Jurisprudence* to a much wider understanding of corruption as a rotting or undermining of the human mind or spirit. He concludes: 'These are the disadvantages of a commercial spirit. The minds of men are contracted and rendered incapable of elevation, education is despised or at least neglected, and heroic spirit is almost utterly extinguished.' And he specifically emphasizes the coercive effects which commerce can have on education: the fact that a boy of six or seven in a commercial centre such as Birmingham can earn sixpence a day means his parents put him to work: 'Thus [his] education is neglected. The education which low people's children receive is not indeed at any rate considerable; however, it does them an immense deal of service, and the want of it is certainly one of their greatest misfortunes.'

He returns again in *The Wealth of Nations* to the threats he sees from commercial society to people's minds. He fears, first, for the mental mutilation of those performing endlessly repetitive manufacturing tasks within the division of labour, tasks which did not allow the working man to 'exert his understanding, or to exercise his invention in finding out expedients for removing difficulties which never occur'. Secondly, he worries about the loss of martial spirit. And finally, he denounces the 'disposition to admire, and almost to worship, the rich and the powerful', and its counterpart, the instinct 'to despise, or, at least, to neglect persons of poor and mean condition', as we have seen. It is notable that, for all his dislike of religious fanaticism, Smith praises moderate religious observance on occasion specifically because it stimulates the mind. Children from poor families should, he says, receive 'the benefit of religion, which is a great advantage, not only considered in a pious sense, but as it affords them subject for thought and speculation'.

For Smith, then, commercial society can have a tendency to suppress education, mental energy and understanding among the general population, and to divert some into the delusive pursuit of the lifestyles and possessions of the rich and powerful. Why do these things matter to him? Not merely for their immediate ill effects, but because the one destroys the moral imagination, the other distorts it. Without moral imagination it becomes impossible to put oneself in any genuine way in another's shoes, to persuade them or to empathize with them. In such a world there can be no exchange, no regard, no public debate or deliberation, no shared identity, no consent, no genuine basis for government. There is no room for the stories or narratives that can rouse human energies and emotions, and the capacity to seek collective social change. Above all, there is no scope for the work of the impartial spectator. And without the impartial spectator, moral community, the basis for humanity itself, comes under threat.

So there is every reason to think that Adam Smith, quite possibly the most vigorous and effective defender of commercial society in any age, would nevertheless sympathize with modern concerns about its potentially corrupting effects. Nor, though Smith's thought is complex and incomplete, is it impossible to see the outlines of a Smithian response. After all, a theory of norms is, precisely, a theory about how people unconsciously but collectively create a space of shared value that sits between the freedom of the individual and the laws and coercive power of the state. That is a space of what ought not to be done, even thought it may not be against the law—a space of civility and trust.

As we have seen, Smith's system of thought rests on a recognition of the absolutely fundamental importance of the 'harmony' or interdependence of humans within a society. It is this recognition that underlies the emphasis on perspicuous language in his early lectures on rhetoric, on resentment in his jurisprudence, on 'sympathy' and the operation of the impartial spectator in his moral theory and on the instinct to truck, barter and exchange in *The Wealth of Nations*. It is this that underlies both his egalitarianism and his conception of political leadership: the wise and virtuous individual is a person of 'humble modesty and equitable justice', who is 'at all times willing that his own private interest should be sacrificed to the public interest of his own particular order and society'. Political power is necessary, but must be self-limiting.

In terms of personal morality, Smith's view is that people's practical capacity to identify with others is limited by time, place and circumstance. The capacity to recognize personal injury, and the reactions injury elicits, may be almost universal, but Smith is not in his writings a cosmopolitan believer in the value or inevitability of a universal moral community. No: communities are built up from below through human interaction and exchange, and it is that free exchange that gives them commercial, social and moral value. Yet in the final analysis Smith never quite cuts his moral worldview away from the workings of providence. He struggles to supply a wholly naturalistic basis for his theories either of norms or of justice, and one does not sense in him Hume's astonishing equanimity at the idea of a disenchanted world.

But if Smith's evolutionary account cannot ultimately escape a broadly Christian moral ethos, there are at least other potential sources of moral inspiration available. Within this context, his egalitarian outlook demands in principle that all voices should be able to be heard, and as communications expand, so too does the Smithian capacity for sympathy. Norms may flourish and have value in a restricted social context, but they are always potentially subject to review, via the impartial spectator, in a context that is broader, more equal or more free. Human society and the institutions that compose it deserve respect, but this does not insulate particular societies from criticism for practices that are or would be condemned more widely. A degree of mutual recognition is not a moral free-for-all.

For Smith, the benefits of spontaneous and evolving order—linguistic, legal, moral, economic—depend on the freedoms of the individual afforded within society. So he supported, and would doubtless support today, measures that lift human capabilities and improve the capacity for human interaction, communication and mutual recognition: better education, free and independent institutions, the rule of law, but also, by his example, personal courtesy and the moderate virtues of tolerance and mutual respect. In short, not merely private freedoms but a free and educated public realm, filled with the conversation of civil, honest and independent minds. A world that Jean Calas deserved to live in, but did not.

CONCLUSION

WHY IT MATTERS

Death and Hermes of late in Elysium made boast,
That each would bring thither, what earth valued most:
Smith's Wealth of Nations Hermes stole from his shelf;
Death just won his cause—he took off Smith himself.

Agricola (now thought to be Robert Burns),
'On the late Death of Dr Adam Smith', 1790

IN HIS MONUMENTAL WORK *THE GREAT TRANSFORMATION* (1944), KARL
Polanyi examined the spread of market-based beliefs and practices
during the nineteenth century. Traditional patterns of reciprocity and
local redistribution had been overtaken by impersonal market exchange, he argued, causing the market economy and the nation-state
to become fused into 'market society'. The system of *laissez-faire* had
taken control, and 'a self-regulating market demands nothing less than
the institutional separation of society into an economic and a political
sphere.' The result had been to diminish the importance of politics
and unleash uncontrollable economic forces, which led to the successive crises of war, Depression and renewed war between 1914 and
1939.

Polanyi's polemical thesis causes him to overstate the case against
nineteenth-century capitalism, and underrate the importance of

imperial over-extension, nationalism, weak political leadership, rotten policy and sheer bad luck. But the fundamental questions he raises are the right ones. Capitalism is losing its legitimacy as an engine of wealth-creation and personal freedom. Growth is sluggish, productivity stagnating, the future unclear and insecure. We are living in a new Gilded Age, in which extreme wealth and deference to wealth and celebrity coexist with escalating public concern about the stability and fairness of our political and economic systems.

There are good reasons to be optimistic about the long-term future; more people around the world are living longer, richer and healthier lives than ever before. Yet there has rarely been greater public disenchantment with capitalism itself. The modern corporation has increasingly proven to be an 'externalizing machine', adept at pushing costs on to others while raising prices, limiting competition, suppressing wages and erecting barriers to market entry for others. At the same time, open and freely trading markets have come to seem simultaneously inevitable and impossible: inevitable, because no remotely plausible alternatives exist as a large-scale means to allocate goods efficiently and create wealth; and impossible, because they so often seem to bring as their consequence escalating inequality and a coarsening of moral norms and values. This dilemma is only aggravated if, as has been argued, the rates of long-term economic and social gains from technology, and of secure, good-quality job-creation, are falling. Meanwhile the benefits of globalization have been dispersed and gradual, its costs often focused, sharp and unexpected. The result has been deep social anger and frustration at the results of the market economy, so much so as to call into question its very status and legitimacy. And that anger and frustration have come amid times of economic growth and booming markets; think what they might be in a serious recession.

To make matters still worse, after the fall of the Berlin Wall in 1989 there was remarkable complacency across the political spectrum about the status of capitalism, especially in the UK and USA.

History had supposedly ended. Since then, the centre-right has not found it necessary to make the case for the market economy in any serious way, let alone to develop the kind of systematic account of its strengths and weaknesses that might enable it to combat the spread of crony capitalism. Until recently, the centre-left has neglected to offer any serious critique either, let alone to prepare for or address the negative effects of globalization. Little wonder, then, that the way has been open to more radical arguments and movements; little wonder that extreme schemes of nationalization, expropriation and state control are gaining public currency. But the idea of open markets, as with any political idea, must be challenged, revised and renewed to remain legitimate. If it is not challenged by those who believe in it, then it will be challenged by those who wish to destroy it.

The financial crash of 2007–8 not only wiped out a vast amount of economic value: it wiped out much of the public credibility of economics itself, and pushed the public understanding of economics into a general critique under the heading of 'neoliberalism' or 'market fundamentalism'. This conflation has been convenient. It is easy for policy-makers to understand, it creates a simple public narrative out of a far more complex underlying reality, and it gives immediate scope for often justified criticism of banks, financial markets, regulators and indeed politicians and capitalism itself. Yet the ideas that there was effective competition in the banking sector, that this made deregulation possible and that that deregulation could be economically and socially valuable formed the critical intellectual backdrop to the 2008 financial crisis. What is so striking about that crisis in retrospect is not, even, the egregious self-enrichment of the previous decade, or the specific failures of policy, law and enforcement involved. It is the intellectual grip which the language of free markets held on almost all the parties concerned, regardless of the often very different reality. It is hard not to link that grip to the remarkable facts that, in the UK at least, no properly comprehensive and independent review of the 2008 crash ever took place, and virtually no one was genuinely held to account for what had happened.

There is a serious intellectual error hidden here, which disfigures policy-making and undermines public debate. As we have seen, markets often differ from each other in crucial ways, few more so than those for land, labour and capital. Moreover, economies are not just about markets, and *laissez-faire* is not the same thing as market competition. Many of the best economists around the world have spent the last few decades trying to think through the limitations of markets— imperfect information and rationality, transaction costs, preferences, linkages and the rest—and to understand how different markets, from housing to healthcare, actually work. As an ideology, neoliberalism is dead. But the debate we need to have, the debate about what markets are and should be for, about the limitations of the idea of 'market failure' and the need to ensure effective competition, and about norms and culture and the role of the state, has been left by the wayside.

Economics itself needs to own up to its limitations. It is hard not to conclude that the profession itself would greatly benefit from a little less incumbency and a little more accountability and competition. Its claims to scientific status are in disarray, with leading economists unable to agree even on whether it can or should be used to make predictions, let alone relied upon to make them correctly. In Friedmanite fashion, it has long been overly preoccupied with its own models rather than with the real-world phenomena they are supposed to represent. It is still struggling to tackle even such basic theoretical issues as how human preferences should be modelled or aggregated. It encourages politicians to persist in the responsibility-abrogating technocratic fantasy that economics trumps politics and can itself solve issues of justice, fairness and social welfare. The North Korean economy could in principle be in a Pareto-optimal position, incapable of improving the position of anyone without worsening the position of someone else— but few would regard it as worthy of imitation.

What is to be done? How can the benefits of markets be safe-guarded and extended, and their ill-effects contained? How can public trust be regained for markets and the market system? How can we protect this qualified but still priceless inheritance?

We need a new master-narrative for our times. We need better frameworks of public understanding, better explanations, better shared identities, through which we can come to terms with these issues. But, to create them, we must return to the dawn of our economic modernity, and to Adam Smith himself. Not to Smith the caricature one-note libertarian alternately celebrated by his partisans and denounced by his detractors, but to what Smith actually thought, across all his writings, from ethics to jurisprudence to political economy. Even among economists, few read beyond Books I and II of *The Wealth of Nations*, if they read that far at all. Yet in many ways Smith's problems are our problems, and his work is a trove of neglected insight and wisdom.

The real Smith was not an intellectual turncoat who switched from altruism in *The Theory of Moral Sentiments* to egoism in *The Wealth of Nations*. He was not a market fundamentalist, an economic libertarian, or in that strong sense a *laissez-faire* economist. He was not an advocate of selfishness, pro-rich or a misogynist, the creator of *homo economicus* or the founder of predatory capitalism. And he certainly did not condone the slave trade. But he was—and still is and will always be—a thinker of remarkable depth and power. He is rightly called the father of economics, conceptually because he was the first to put markets squarely at the centre of economic thought, and practically because there are few if any economists since Smith—including both Marx and Keynes—who do not stand in his intellectual debt. But his political economy ranges far wider than economics alone, and he could with equal justice be considered one of the founding fathers of sociology. The implications of his Newtonian philosophy of science, which receives its greatest modern exploration, alongside much else, in the work of the American philosopher Charles Sanders Peirce, are still far from fully understood.

For many people Smith's political economy will always hold centre stage: both as a model of economic analysis and for his specific insights into human behaviour, markets, trade, specialization and the division of labour, taxation and the negative effects of subsidies, bounties and protection. Others will admire his moral egalitarianism, his feeling for the underdog, his belief in the importance of dignity and respectability to people's status and sense of self, the way he minimizes inequality within his 'natural system of liberty', his devastating attack on crony capitalism, his stadial theory of human development, his historical analysis of the supersession of feudalism by commerce and his extremely subtle exploration and defence of commercial society—an exploration far more subtle than Polanyi's later analysis of 'market society'. Still others will recognize the foundational importance of his theory of moral and social norms, and his jurisprudence.

But to look at Smith in parts is to miss the power and coherence of the whole. For Smith, 'The state of property must always vary with the form of government,' and since both property and government rely on norms and patterns of social consent as they have evolved, both have a grounding in humans' moral sentiments. It is, therefore, ultimately impossible to separate politics and economics from each other, or either from moral evaluation. There can be no such thing as a value-free economics; and while we can theorize about human action in economic or political or moral terms, to do so reflects our appetite for intellectual convenience, not a deep partition in nature.

A new narrative, then, must start with a new political economy. Such an enterprise will be the work of many hands, and lies beyond the scope of this book. But we can anticipate some of its substance, perhaps, by drawing out six lessons from Smith's thought.

The first is that we must distinguish capitalism from commercial society. For Smith, as we have seen, the emergence of commercial society is the moment when 'every man . . . becomes in some measure a merchant'. It marks the historic transition from feudalism to what we now think of as economic modernity: a society, not a clan or tribe; of people trading freely with each other under law; inclusive, at least in principle, of all and spreading wealth and opportunity to all; generating surpluses that can be used to protect the vulnerable; working with the grain of human instincts and human nature; and held together not by force, class hierarchy or rank but by mutual moral and social obligation.

Seen in this way, commercial society is an achievement of extraordinary value, which it is our duty to protect and enhance. It has had enormous resilience, because—at least in its democratic form—it has had a unique capacity to command the allegiance of citizens, and to sustain its legitimacy by increasing their prosperity and freedom. In Smith's astonishingly comprehensive and illuminating account, that allegiance comes in different ways: from history, from shared identities and narratives and the norms that underlie them, from public institutions, and from competition and economic interest, all deriving fundamentally from the human desire to love and be lovely, and from the instinct to truck, barter and exchange. As recent events have shown, commercial society is also fragile and, in a world of just-in-time interdependence, especially vulnerable to threats including financial crisis, terrorism and natural disaster. But the alternatives, of war over trade, of religious autocracy, authoritarian communism and nationalism over democracy, or indeed of empty economic materialism over the benefits of *doux commerce*, are not to be contemplated. There can be no decent human future in turning away from effective, well-functioning markets and an international trading order. If the preservation of commercial society requires the reform of capitalism, then reform it we must.

But, secondly, commercial societies need states that are resilient, modest, strategic and strong. Markets rely on wise laws, well enforced, and moral communities rely on people who are not merely legally free but free in the full exercise of their capabilities. Amid Smith's concerns to relieve trade of the baleful effects of pettifogging regulation and subsidy, it is easy to forget the central importance of the state in his thought, as protector of the nation, adjudicator and enforcer of justice, treaty signatory, guarantor of trade—even including support for the Navigation Acts—provider of public works, infrastructure and local schools, and, yes, as regulator of markets. To these we might add such enabling functions of the modern state as the provision of risk-insurance, redistribution of income across and between generations, and macroeconomic stabilization, to say nothing of the creation of new markets, such as in space and cyberspace, where regulation alone allows the clear definition of property rights, and the effective allocation of commercial risk and reward. The demands on states have become more complex as the complexity of markets, business, social needs and international relationships has grown, and this creates serious political challenges. But the idea that 'the private sector earns the money and the public sector spends it' misses the point: both require each other to function effectively.

Thirdly, successful commercial societies have strong states not merely because they need to have them, but because they can: because they have the independent institutions and the pluralism to withstand the potential for state domination. Above all, they have the legitimacy, the consent, the culture, the trust required—for the whole system, markets and government alike, relies on trust. Legitimacy matters in the first instance because it reflects and enables social trust, and the reciprocity and patterns of mutual obligation without which a society cannot hold together. At a practical level, social trust enables taxation. Britain had comparatively high levels of taxation throughout the eighteenth century in part because government, for all its imperfections, had enough social trust and legitimacy to levy it. When the financial crisis of 2007–8 struck, the immediate solution did not lie in international institutions or multilateral organizations, but in the established national taxing and spending powers that enabled the UK, the USA and other countries quickly to underwrite and bail out their failing banks. The crisis itself was ruinous not merely for its economic consequences but for its destruction of social capital, that is of trust. The global financial sector has a unique ability to damage trust, because of its size, because of the pervasive importance of money and credit, and because perhaps more than any other sector it is based on trust, and on fiduciary relationships. And as Smith recognized, finance requires 'party walls' to prevent its periodic crises from becoming generally disastrous, as they did in 2007–8.

But, fourth, as well as specific vulnerabilities, commercial society has its own intrinsic weaknesses. Because markets are all different from one another, they carry with them their own pathologies. Their purpose is to facilitate trade, to allocate goods, services and capital efficiently, to stimulate innovation and thereby to serve the best interests of the public. As Smith shows, magnificently, in well-functioning markets these different interests are generally aligned. But, as he also shows, those interests can come apart when markets cease to function well: through a tendency to monopoly, through poor regulation, through loss of animal spirits and more widely through crony capitalism enabled by rent-seeking, asymmetries of information and power, and conflicts of interest between owners and managers. Crony capitalism is a general blight, because it damages the economy, corrupts politics, tends to increase inequality and invalidates and delegitimizes markets and commercial society itself. It flourishes where companies and markets lose their connection to the public good, and where business rewards float free of underlying business merit. These things undercut the core rationale for market exchange: that it should be what Smith sees in his system of natural liberty, a source of 'universal opulence', that is of general prosperity, not the enrichment of a few.

However, a fifth lesson is that crony capitalism is far from the only challenge facing modern commercial society. The deepest threats are those which directly affect the idea of human value itself. One is the continuing commercialization of the public realm. Another is the impact of new technologies, which have the capacity to worsen crony capitalism by tilting the playing field still further towards insiders and away from citizens and consumers. The spread of social media also raises profound questions of public accountability and legitimacy. These go to such issues as the effects of social media on vulnerable and other teenagers, and their impact on the workings of democracy itself, through their contagious capacity to manipulate public opinion. That is the lesson of Facebook's '61-million-person experiment in social influence and political mobilization' during the 2010 US Congressional elections, to say nothing of more recent revelations about the sector's political power, over and above its capacity to extract rents and exclude competitors.

Adam Smith gives a powerful explanation of how we live in a world whose values are formed through human interaction: vertically, through the disposition to admire the rich and powerful and the potential inhibition by commercial society of sympathy, especially for the poor; and horizontally, through the tendency to compare ourselves with others, and our desire 'not only to be loved, but to be lovely'. The apparently insatiable desire of the present age for social comparison, and the status anxiety it creates, are beautifully diagnosed by Smith. They sit at the heart of social media—to the increasing cost of young people in mental illness—and exploiting them is a core part of the rationale and business models of those media. From a Smithian perspective, the key questions are not merely about public accountability and the legitimate exercise of power; they are about who we conceive ourselves to be. And they go to the issues of whether our values themselves are being shaped not through dispersed social interaction, or democratically through the election of chosen leaders, but by very small numbers of people operating in the shadows and subject to little genuine accountability—and whether anyone is really watching.

A final lesson is that commercial society constantly evolves, and constantly poses new challenges. Today, the nature of commercial society is arguably changing faster than ever before. Artificial intelligence, robotics and automation are transforming the world of work. Globalization is drawing the most productive workers from around the world into countries that already enjoy the benefits of commercial society, and threatening to impoverish those they leave behind. Even within industrialized countries there are sharp and increasing divergences of mortality and health between different regions and different groups within society. The polarization of income creates incentives for the very rich to remove themselves mentally, physically and financially into private gated communities, both actual and virtual, potentially weakening the incentives to pay tax and pool risk that lie at the centre of the modern welfare state. Vast amounts of liquidity and risk are traded every day in under-regulated ways through shadow banking networks. The rules-based system of trade founded after the Second World War has become increasingly ineffective as trading blocs have grown. The 200-year historical anomaly of relative Asian economic weakness has ended. A growing number of the largest and most technologically advanced companies apparently have the capacity to bully cities, perhaps nations and even in time peoples, in their own interests. Commercial society itself, in the typically Western combination of capitalism and democracy, is under increasing ideological threat from models of state-first capitalism led by China.

A new Smithian narrative must, therefore, take shape amid wrenching and divisive forces of change. These astonishing developments demand of us the most vigorous intellectual and practical renewal. Politics, political deliberation and political understanding need to be reclaimed and re-energized. The consent on which modern commercial society relies, consent given freely by people who believe it will enable them to prosper, is starting to break down. The so-called developed countries do not have answers to globalization, because they have not thought much beyond the boundaries of ideology and self-interest. We have had, not the end of history, but the end of ideas. Instead, we must reflect far more deeply and specifically about societies, cultures and economics, in order to ask ourselves what we are and what we can become.

Renewal must start with the intellect, with ideas. For economists, that means greater awareness of the nature and limitations of economics itself, greater humility among its practitioners and an end to grandiose claims of scientific objectivity. In particular, the rationalist dream of making economics into a value-free science is a futile one, and the project of separating economics from politics, sociology and ethics can never succeed, even in principle. Economic theorizing is of great importance, but so is an effective working economics that uses models for insight, education, communication and practical policy-making, in bad times as well as good, rather than for display or, worse, some illusion of accuracy and accountability. In Smith's time, regulations largely existed to protect insider interests, and so liberalization tended to benefit the wider mass of people. Today, matters are often more nuanced. In any case, much of what we think we know about the benefits of free markets loses its core economic rationale once the realities of imperfect information, limited human rationality, preference-formation and transaction costs are acknowledged. That acknowledgement must sit within a wider conception of political economy that better grasps the realities of crony capitalism, the insufficiency of pure 'market failure' explanations, the central facts of uncertainty and dynamic interaction within human life, the relevance of other disciplines and the importance of norms, values, identities and trust alongside and within economic explanations. The arguments for markets must be made again and again, but in context and on their own terms.

There must also, in true Smithian spirit, be social renewal. That means a degree of humility among those who exercise power, and a wider acceptance that success is often the result of where you start— of families, culture and capabilities—and what luck you have on the way. It means a recognition that achievement of almost any kind is dependent on the efforts of others and on the strength of society, not merely victory in some dog-eat-dog struggle in which only the fittest survive. It means a Smithian focus on human dignity and human capabilities, and on how a well-functioning society can help all its members to flourish in their lives. But it also involves a shared recognition that there is a space in every society that lies outside what is measurable or governed principally by law. That is the space of cultural values, of existing practices and habits, of reasonable social expectations, of norms of conduct, the space of what is 'done' and 'not done'. It is not always benign, for what is 'done' and 'not done' in a society can offer scope to repression and discrimination. That space is under threat today, perhaps especially from commercial values: what's wrong with paying to upgrade your prison cell, or to have someone stand in line for a public event? But a good society will find ways to defend that space of norms. Without it all that counts is law, and the dynamics of the marketplace, and these by themselves can never be enough. With it can come greater social trust, and the potential to strengthen the institutions and public standards that restrain crony capitalism.

Finally, there must be political renewal. In effect, Smith's ideas pose challenges to the outer flanks of both the left and the right: to give up extreme aspirations and start to recreate a political middle ground, a shared sense of the common good, by engaging once more with the real, complex, messy issues of reforming capitalism and defending and developing the benefits of commercial society.

Adam Smith himself belonged to no political party, and he is not the property of any one ideology or political movement. Many of his political views remain obscure. In eighteenth-century terms he combined a characteristically Scottish Enlightenment belief in the possibility of personal improvement with a generally Whiggish commitment to the idea of social progress. But he was no radical: he did not adopt key radical policies of the day, such as a universal male franchise or annual parliaments, and he avoided radical positions on such issues as militias, the American colonies and public debt. He rejected utopian thought and explanations from any supposed state of nature; he preferred the local to the global; he despised 'faction and fanaticism' in both politics and religion, and he excoriated the 'the man of system' who tries to control people and suppress human individuality and freedom. He repeatedly emphasized the importance of 'slow and gradual' change, and of reform over revolution; he reasoned more from cases than from first principles. He was realistic about the importance of the state, and about its weaknesses. As he wrote, 'No government is quite perfect, but it is better to submit to some inconveniences than make attempts against it.' In modern terms he is neither libertarian nor socialist nor social democrat, but probably on balance a moderate small-c conservative. Indeed, he and Burke can be read together as setting the terms for different but overlapping kinds of a humane and moderate conservatism.

Needless to say, to reassert the importance of politics and political economy is not to seek to hand over our affairs to a group of Soviet-style commissars. There are many more or less efficient ways to organize an economy; the question is what you value, how you wish to get there and who should lead, and these are political questions. The old certainties are over, and the task for politicians of every stripe is this: to acknowledge the complexity of these issues, and address, explain and lead on them in public as clearly and simply as they can. Modern states have the capacity not merely to destroy but in some cases to improve the functioning of markets through careful interventions. Markets themselves almost always have effects and impacts that go beyond the strictly economic, so they can never be an entirely politically or morally neutral means for the allocation of goods and services. At the same time, their growing complexity often gives more opportunities for insiders to rip off outsiders, while imposing formidable demands, both in practice and in principle, on those seeking to guide or constrain them. And all around is a commercial society which must deal not merely with the astonishing challenges of the coming century, but with the forms of liberalism and individualism on which it is itself presently based, while preserving the public domain through which decent, mutually respectful debate and human exchange can flourish. We must rise to these challenges, or our open society will consume itself.

Smith had harsh words on occasion for politicians, attributing trade retaliations and other such short-term expedients to 'that insidious and crafty animal, vulgarly called a statesman or politician, whose councils are directed by the momentary fluctuations of affairs'. But his 'science of man' is also part of the science of the statesman or legislator, 'whose deliberations ought to be governed by general principles which are always the same'. Such a legislator will have a sense of civic purpose and a commitment to public service over private interest that allow them to be held to account for failure, at personal cost. He or she will value law, institutions and policy, will respect individual freedom and above all will enforce justice, because justice properly determined, administered and enforced is the legitimating bedrock of commercial society. What ultimately matters are not rewards or status but those norms of justice, integrity, reciprocity and fairness themselves, the moral character and virtue that the internalization of norms creates and the public institutions and habits of public service that they support. For Smith, as for Burke, a politician should be a 'philosopher in practice'.

Like Burke, Adam Smith was at core a philosopher, but of a more theoretical stamp. He believed in the workings of providence, of harmony, of order. But for him human society—not divine revelation, rational intuition or the individual will—is the ultimate source of our moral life. His whole emphasis is on communication and community, on what free people have in common between them. In his great project, his Humean science of man, mutual recognition—working through sympathy and tempered by the impartial spectator—generates social and moral norms small and large that constantly evolve and proliferate, rise and fall, are superseded or survive. By this means Smith opens the door to a potentially unified understanding of a vast range of human activity, in all its glorious diversity. Premised as they are on free exchange, in commercial societies these norms demand the same basic things of us all, wherever and whoever we are: awareness of others, courtesy, open-mindedness, consideration, tolerance and respect. In the course of his life Smith applied this core set of ideas again and again, refining it as he went: from his early essays and work on rhetoric, through *The Theory of Moral Sentiments* and the unpublished, little-known but crucial *Lectures on Jurisprudence* to *The Wealth of Nations*. That is, he took it from the basis of communication itself to the foundation of moral psychology to the pursuit of scientific inquiry to the administration of justice to market exchange; and if more time had been permitted to him, he might have gone on to include artistic creation and politics too. Embedded in it all is a dynamic, future-oriented and ever-unfolding sense of human possibility.

It is a colossal achievement, whose proper measure has still never been taken. Today, in a world of uncertainty, extremism and misunderstanding, we need Adam Smith, and the wisdom to follow his thought through in its full implications, now more than ever.

ACKNOWLEDGEMENTS

THE OXFORD HISTORIAN ROHAN BUTLER MEMORABLY CONCLUDED THE first volume of his biography of the Duc de Choiseul on page 1078, with the ominous words: 'The diplomatic and political career of the Duke of Choiseul had begun.'

Alas, we will never know what Butler thought of that career—or of Choiseul's singular unhelpfulness to Adam Smith and Buccleuch in 1764—since he did not live to complete a second volume, let alone a projected third. But even at the much shorter length of this book, history has its perils. Academic wisdom teaches us to shun the three wicked witches of anachronism (the projection of one time onto another), prolepsis (the assumption that later events had been foreshadowed) and teleology (the unfolding of history towards a goal). But a brief biography of any kind finds itself constantly at risk of falling under the witches' spell. There is no space to explore the sheer uncertainty and contingency of events, or the contemporary contexts and languages that make that contingency come alive. The choice of subject generally assumes his or her relevance to the reader and to current matters of public interest. A life, especially told in its novelistic form, implies a narrative arc. We know, or think we know, in advance how it will go and how it will end.

This biography can hardly be exempt from such concerns; but its structure can help to guard against them. Building on that adopted with *Edmund Burke: Philosopher, Politician, Prophet* (2013), it starts with Smith's life before moving on to examine his thought and its impact. Such an approach requires delicate handling, because it involves a series of modal shifts, from what Smith in his lectures on rhetoric and belles lettres calls the narrative to the didactic and on to the persuasive style, across a range of fields including history, economics and philosophy. The pay-off is that it allows the book to address a much wider range of audiences: the general reader looking for a short and lively biography of Smith; the student seeking an engaging but, I hope, wide and authoritative introduction to Smith's ideas; someone in business hoping to grasp Smith's influence on present-day economics and politics; the concerned citizen asking of modern capitalism and society 'How did we get here?' and 'What can we do about it?' There can be few thinkers from any period whose work continues to be as relevant, and useful, to such a wide range of readers.

Standard biographies usually end, naturally enough, with the end of their subject. In this case, however, Smith's natural death becomes the stepping-off point for an analysis of his afterlife. And here too the wicked witches of historiography can be frustrated, at least to a degree. Fact and value cannot be entirely distinguished. But keeping a life and its appraisal separate allows the author to be more self-conscious about the difference; to tell the history more on its own terms; and to acknowledge that the present reflects the legacies and continuities of the past, without using the present as a criterion for the past.

Adam Smith has been very fortunate in the quality of his biographers over the years, and in the scholarly literature he has attracted; and my immense debt to both will be evident. But such is the range and depth of his ideas, and their living force, that it would have been impossible for me to write about him without the amazing generosity of many people and institutions. First and foremost, I thank the great heroes who read and commented on part or all of the text at various stages. They include Angus Armstrong, Lee Auspitz, Tim Besley, Kate Bingham, Richard Bourke, Paul Collier, Tony Curzon-Price, Armand d'Angour, Claudia Daventry, Knud Haakonssen, Bob Klitgaard, John Lucas, Bob Monks, Leonidas Montes, Julie Nelson, Casey Norman, Craig Smith, Romesh Vaitilingam and Amy Woolfson.

Many others have been extremely kind in sharing their ideas and insights in conversation and/or by email, whether recently or over many years, including Daron Acemoglu, Kate Auspitz, John Cairns, Vince Crawford, Simon Green, Andy Haldane, Ran Halévi, Ian Harris, James Harris, Oliver Marc Hartwich, Joe Henrich, Anya Hurlbert, John Kay, Colin Kidd, Deirdre McCloskey, Neil MacGregor, Nell Minow, Bobby Monks, Mary Morgan, Avner Offer, the late Nick Phillipson, David Rand, Matt Ridley, Dani Rodrik, Ignacio Briones Rojas, Martin Sandbu, Michael Sandel, Lucia Santa Cruz, Paul Seaward, Adam Tomkins, John Vickers, Richard Whatmore, Jo Wolff, David Womersley, Adrian Wooldridge and David Wootton. Chris Watkins very kindly showed me around Panmure House during its early restoration, and gave me a sense of what it must have been like in Smith's time. There are numerous others in and around the modern world of politics and political economy whom I will not embarrass by naming.

Various institutions have been no less kind. I was very fortunate to be able to work on the book during a Visiting Fellowship at All Souls College, Oxford in 2016–17, for which I warmly thank the Warden and Fellows; and I have learned a vast amount from two series of seminars on political economy which Tim Besley and I have since held at the college. I have also been privileged to take part in several extremely stimulating seminars hosted by the Liberty Fund on different aspects of seventeenth- to nineteenth-century thought. Finally, I have given talks based on this book at the National Institute for Economic and Social Research, and at the British Academy; and, more widely, at the Universidad Adolfo Ibañez in Santiago, Chile, and the Australian Catholic University in Sydney. Again, I thank them all.

Three people have played pivotal roles in the creation of this book: Lara Heimert at Basic Books, who originally suggested I should write about Adam Smith; Stuart Proffitt, my magnificent publisher at Allen Lane, whose blue pen worked wonders; and my agent Caroline Michel, whose inspiration and support have been unflagging. I am grateful to the excellent team at Penguin, and to my peerless copy editor, Peter James, and indexer, Christopher Phipps.

Finally, I am hugely obliged to my past and present staff in Hereford and London, including Tom Hirons, Tom Kennedy, Pindie Kuzvinzwa, Susie Macleod, Georgina Miller, Freddie Mitchell, Gill Rivers, Wendy Robertson, James Sibley, Rosie Turner and Amy Woolfson, whose professionalism allowed me to combine my parliamentary and constituency work with writing and research.

The astonishing kindness and tolerance of my wife Kate Bingham and our children, Sam, Nell and Noah Norman, somehow enabled them to live with me during the writing of this book.

I grew up discussing the Smithian subjects of economics, law, politics, history, art, literature and psychology with my father, Torquil Norman, and my late mother, Anne Norman. It is to them that this book is dedicated.

Hereford,
March 2018

NOTES

Here, as in the main text itself, eighteenth-century idiosyncrasies of spelling and grammar have been silently corrected. Page numbers are included to hard-copy versions consulted.

ABBREVIATIONS

CAS: *Correspondence of Adam Smith*, ed. Ernest Campbell Mossner and Ian Simpson Ross, Liberty Fund 1987

ED: *An Early Draft of Part of The Wealth of Nations*, in *LJ*

EPS: *Essays on Philosophical Subjects*, ed. W. P. D. Wightman and J. C. Bryce, Liberty Fund [1795] 1980

LAS: *Life of Adam Smith* [by various authors]

LJ: *Lectures on Jurisprudence*, ed. R. L. Meek, D. D. Raphael and P. G. Stein, Liberty Fund [1762–4] 1982; includes both lecture series *LJ(A)* and *LJ(B)*

LRBL: *Lectures on Rhetoric and Belles Lettres*, ed. J. C. Bryce, Liberty Fund [1762–3] 1985

Strahan: *Letter from Adam Smith, LL.D. to William Strahan, Esq.*, in David Hume, *Essays, Moral, Political, and Literary*, ed. Eugene F. Miller, Liberty Fund [1777] 1987

TMS: *The Theory of Moral Sentiments*, ed. D. D. Raphael and A. L. Macfie, Liberty Fund [1759–90] 1982

WN: *An Inquiry into the Nature and Causes of the Wealth of Nations*, ed. R. H. Campbell, A. S. Skinner, and W. B. Todd, 2 vols., Liberty Fund [1776] 1981

INTRODUCTION

ix 'The textbook on contemporary capitalism': from Naomi Klein, Sydney Peace Prize Lecture 2016, excerpted in *The Nation*, 14 November 2016. Smith is also deemed to be the origin of 'Selfish Capitalism' by the psychologist and writer Oliver James in his *Selfish Capitalism*, Random House 2008

x   Survey of economists: William L. Davis, Bob Figgins, David Hedengren and Daniel B. Klein, 'Economics Professors' Favorite Economic Thinkers, Journals, and Blogs (along with Party and Policy Views)', *Econ Journal Watch*, 8.2, May 2011; JSTOR survey, see Avner Offer and Gabriel Söderberg, *The Nobel Factor*, Princeton University Press 2016, Ch. 5

x   Pushkin: *Eugene Onegin*, I.7

x   Banknotes: in 2016 it was announced that Smith's image would be succeeded on the £20 note by that of J. M. W. Turner

x   Mrs Thatcher on influence of Smith: Speech to Scottish Conservative Conference, City Hall, Perth, 13 May 1988. See also Charles Moore, 'Margaret Thatcher and Capitalism', 2012 Adam Smith Lecture, Pembroke College, Cambridge, 6 February 2012, on www.margaretthatcher.org

xi   Greenspan on 'emanations' affecting Gordon Brown: Adam Smith Memorial Lecture, St Bryce Kirk, Kirkcaldy, 6 February 2005

xi   Gordon Brown on Smith: Hugo Young Memorial Lecture, Chatham House, 13 December 2005. To support the idea of a helping hand, Brown also invoked a supposedly Smithian spirit of neighbourliness. 'Intellect-enhancing emanations' or no, however, both suggestions 'bear no relation to the writings of the eighteenth-century political economist', according to Richard Bourke, 'Visible Hands', *Times Literary Supplement*, 18 January 2008. One of Smith's most subtle and sophisticated modern interpreters, the economist and historian Donald Winch, also rejects readings of *TMS* in terms of charity or benevolence in 'Science and the Legislator: Adam Smith and After', *Economic Journal*, 93.371, 1983

xii   Viner on Smith's catholicity: Jacob Viner, 'Adam Smith and Laissez Faire', *Journal of Political Economy*, 35.2, April 1927

xii   Viner's most famous student: Viner's later students also notably included Donald Winch

xii   Friedman article: Milton Friedman, 'Adam Smith's Relevance for Today', *Challenge*, March–April 1977; the article was based on a paper delivered to the Mont Pelerin Society in August 1976

xiii   Contra Friedman on Smith: not a radical, see D. D. Raphael, *The Impartial Spectator: Adam Smith's Moral Philosophy*, Oxford University Press 2007, Ch. 13 pp. 124ff.; did not believe sympathy required economizing, see Avner Offer, 'Self-Interest, Sympathy and the Invisible Hand: From Adam Smith to Market Liberalism', *Economic Thought*, 1.2, 2012

xiv   Whiggish outlook: with the specifically Scottish twist that turned Whigs north of the border away from sixteenth- and seventeenth-century resistance to overbearing monarchy and more towards a wider critique of feudal and aristocratic society

xiv   Smith's appetite for privacy: Dugald Stewart, *LAS*

xiv   Recent biographers: see the Bibliography

xv   Adam Smith on Burke: see Robert Bisset, *Life of Edmund Burke*, 2 ed., 2 vols, George Cawthorn 1798, ii p. 429. A further apocryphal story in *The Bee, or Literary Weekly Intelligencer* for 11 May 1791 hints at Smith's view of Burke: 'I mentioned a story I had read of Mr Burke having seduced and dishonoured a young lady, under promise of marriage. "I imagine," said [Smith], "that you have got that fine story out of some of the magazines. If any thing can be lower than the Reviews, they are so . . . As to Mr. Burke, he is a worthy honest man. He married an accomplished girl, without a shilling of fortune."'

xvi   Smith as the hinge of economic modernity: compare Ronald Coase in his bicentennial lecture: 'What Adam Smith did was to give economics its shape . . . From one point of view the last two hundred years of economics have been little more than a vast "mopping up operation" in which economists have filled in the gaps, corrected the errors and refined the analysis of *The Wealth of Nations*'. *Essays on Economics and Economists*, University of Chicago Press 1994, p. 78

CHAPTER 1: KIRKCALDY BOY, 1723–1746

3   For detailed citations supporting the facts of Adam Smith's life, see in particular Ian Simpson Ross, *LAS*

3   Gipsy encounter: John Rae, *LAS* Ch. 1

3   'Preserving to the world a genius': Stewart, *LAS* Section 1

6   Boswell on Smith's supposed military ambitions: James Boswell, *London Journal 1762–3*, William Heinemann 1950, entry for 25 April 1763

7   Infant mortality: Ian D. Whyte, *Scotland before the Industrial Revolution: An Economic and Social History c. 1050–c. 1750*, Routledge 2014, p. 117

7   'Very much straiten'd': Simpson Ross, *LAS* Ch. 2

8   Miller and Stoicism: Nicholas Phillipson, *David Hume: The Philosopher as Historian*, rev. edn, Penguin Books 2011 offers a Stoical reading of Smith's schooldays. This is interesting, and plausible given Smith's later expressed views, but there is almost no direct evidence for it

10   'Round, schoolboy hand': see Rae, *LAS* Ch. 3

11   Scotland before and after Union: see e.g. T. M. Devine, *The Scottish Nation 1700–2000*, Allen Lane 1999; Christopher Whatley, *The Scots and the Union: Then and Now*, rev. edn, Edinburgh University Press 2014.

Scottish unionism: Colin Kidd, *Union and Unionisms*, Cambridge University Press 2008. Recent political arguments have often ignored or underplayed the balance of historical analysis on the process of union itself: in Whatley's words (p. xiii), 'The long-held and popular notion that the Scots were bought and sold for English gold seems not to stand up to close scrutiny.' As Colin Kidd has emphasized, adopting a very long historical perspective, 'Unionism was very much a Scottish coinage,' not an import from England (p. 8). Far from unionism and nationalism being polar opposites, as modern political mythology would have it, Scottish unionism was often seen as enabling the expression of a distinctively cultural—and especially religious—sense of Scottish nationhood

15   Extent of smuggling: Devine, *The Scottish Nation*, p. 57. Devine insists that the Union was not a cause of, but merely gave an economic context to, Scottish growth in the eighteenth century. But it is surely more likely that the Union was both cause and context

16   Defoe on Glasgow: Daniel Defoe, *A Tour Thro' the Whole Island of Great Britain*, G. Strahan 1724–6

21   Utilitarianism: Francis Hutcheson, *An Inquiry into the Original of our Ideas of Beauty and Virtue*, J. Darby, London 1725, III.8

22   Gibbon on Magdalen College, Oxford: Edward Gibbon, *Memoirs of my Life*, A. Strahan, T. Cadell Jun. and W. Davies 1795–1815

24   Contrast between stipend and fee income: as noted, it was at Balliol that Smith first saw the difference that economic incentives could apparently make to academic outcomes, an argument he made vigorously in the *Wealth of Nations*, and for the rest of his life. Arguably, then, Balliol should be considered the true intellectual home of today's tuition fees

24   'Extravagant fees': letter to William Smith, 24 August 1740. Unless otherwise indicated, all letters to and from Smith cited in these Notes can be found in *CAS*

25   'Violent fit': letter to Margaret Smith, 29 November 1743

25   Inability to write: letter to Margaret Smith, 2 July 1744

25   Tar water: George Berkeley, *Siris: A Chain of Philosophical Reflexions and Inquiries Concerning the Virtues of Tar Water*, W. Innys, C. Hitch and C. Davis 1744

26   Oxford acquaintances: letter from Alexander Wedderburn, 20 March 1754

26   'The gift of an interval': Michael Oakeshott, 'The Idea of a University', in his *Rationalism in Politics*, Methuen 1962

27   Smith reading Hume's *Treatise*: review of *EPS*, *Monthly Review*, 22, 1795; see Simpson Ross, *LAS* p. 71

CHAPTER 2: 'THE MOST USEFUL, HAPPIEST AND MOST HONOURABLE PERIOD OF MY LIFE', 1746–1759

30   Jacobitism and the rebellions: in addition to the general histories of the period, see e.g. Daniel Szechi, *The Jacobites: Britain and Europe 1688–1788*, Manchester University Press 1994. It is notable that the British government was recruiting loyal and highly effective regiments of highlanders to fight for the Crown within a few years of the '45 rebellion

38   Hume on Kames: James Boswell, *Boswell's Edinburgh Journals 1767–1786*, ed. Hugh Milne, Mercat Press 2001, rev. edn 2013

39   Maclaurin's 'disrelish of affected ornaments': see Alexander Fraser Tytler, Lord Woodhouselee, *Memoirs of the Life and Writings of the Honourable Henry Home of Kames*, T. Cadell & W. Davies 1814

40   'And all because I am a Scotsman': letter from Hume to Gilbert Elliot of Minto, September 1764, in Hume, *Letters of David Hume*, ed. J. Y. T. Greig, Oxford University Press 1932

40   Smith's pronunciation: obituary notice from *The Times*, 24 July 1790, quoted in C. R. Fay, *Adam Smith and the Scotland of his Day*, Cambridge University Press 1956, p. 33. See also Rae, *LAS* Ch. 3. A letter of 1757 from Hume to Gilbert Elliot says we 'are unhappy, in our accent and pronunciation, [and] speak a very corrupt dialect of the tongue which we make use of', quoted *LRBL* p. 7. As Rae noted, 'We know the pains taken by great writers like Hume and Robertson to clear their English composition of Scotch idioms, and the greater but less successful pains taken by Wedderburn to cure himself of his Scotch pronunciation, to which he reverted after all in his old age.'

41   Hume's 'Of Eloquence': in his *Essays Moral, Political and Literary*, ed. Eugene F. Miller, Liberty Fund [1752] 1985

41   Millar on importance of literature: quoted in Stewart, *LAS* Section I

43   Smith and Newton: my argument here is much indebted to Leonidas Montes, 'Newtonianism and Adam Smith', in Christopher J. Berry, Maria Pia Paganelli and Craig Smith (eds.), *The Handbook of Adam Smith*, Oxford University Press 2013, Ch. 2; see also his 'On Adam Smith's Newtonianism and General Economic Equilibrium Theory', in Leonidas Montes and Eric Schliesser (eds.), *New Voices on Adam Smith*, Routledge 2006

43   Development of belles lettres: cf. Marcelo Dascal, 'Adam Smith's Theory of Language', in Knud Haakonssen (ed.), *The Cambridge Companion to Adam Smith*, Cambridge University Press 2006

44   Scots and English literature: Robert Crawford (ed.), *The Scottish Invention of English Literature*, Cambridge University Press 1998

44   Early precursors of leading ideas in Smith: see Donald Winch's entry on

Adam Smith in the *Dictionary of National Biography*, Oxford University Press 2004

46 Rule 4: Isaac Newton, *Principia Mathematica Philosophiae Naturalis*, Jussu Societatis Regiae 1687

48 'I am too old, too fat, too lazy and too rich': quoted in the *New Evening Post*, 6 December 1776

49 'I should prefer David Hume': letter to William Cullen, November 1751

49 Hume on the Faculty of Advocates' library: Hume, *The Life of David Hume, Esq. Written by Himself*, W. Strahan and T. Cadell 1777

49 First letter: David Hume to Adam Smith, 24 September 1752

50 Smith as teacher, Boswell as student: Stewart, *LAS*; Boswell, *Correspondence of James Boswell and John Johnston of Grange*, ed. R. S. Walker, William Heinemann 1966

51 Review of Johnson's *Dictionary*: *Edinburgh Review*, 1, 1755

52 Johnson on Smith: from James Boswell, *Dr Johnson's Table Talk*, J. Mawman 1807

54 Smith's happy days in Glasgow: letter to Archibald Davidson, 16 November 1787

54 Miss Campbell: Harold Thompson, *A Scottish Man of Feeling: Some Account of Henry Mackenzie . . . and of the Golden Age of Burns and Scott*, Oxford University Press 1931

54 Smith's private life as 'a footnote in the history of sublimation': Simpson Ross, *LAS* p. 228

54 *The Theory of Moral Sentiments* as 'problem child': J. K. Galbraith described it as 'a work now largely forgotten and largely antecedent to [Smith's] interest in Political Economy', in *A History of Economics: The Past as the Present*, Penguin 1989. This dismissal contrasts vividly with the enthusiasm of Gilbert Harman, who calls it 'one of the great works of moral philosophy' in his 'Moral Agent and Impartial Spectator', The Lindley Lecture, University of Kansas 1986. D. D. Raphael soberly reviews some of the contrasting views in *The Impartial Spectator: Adam Smith's Moral Philosophy*, Oxford University Press 2007, Ch. 6, and argues for the philosophical superiority of Smith's ethics to Hume's, and its psychological superiority to Freud's. For a charming and insightful reading of Smith as contemporary moralist, see Russ Roberts, *How Adam Smith Can Change Your Life*, Penguin 2014

55 Smith and Kant: it is worth noting that Smith's focus on what he takes to be actual processes of moral reasoning reflects his wider critique of previous moral systems: that they are constructed in overly narrow terms and so fail to account for how people in fact reach moral judgements. See Craig Smith, 'Adam Smith, the Scottish Enlightenment, and

"Realistic" Philosophy', INET Edinburgh Conference, October 2017, available through www.ineteconomics.org. Edmund Burke seems to have felt the same way: in a letter to Smith of 10 September 1759 he commented that 'I have ever thought that the old systems of morality were too contracted and that this science could never stand well upon any narrower basis than the whole of human nature. All the writers who have treated this subject before you were like those Gothic architects who were fond of turning great vaults upon a single slender pillar. There is art in this, and there is a degree of ingenuity without doubt; but it is not sensible, and it cannot long be pleasing.'

55 Review of Rousseau: 'A Letter to the Authors of the *Edinburgh Review*', *Edinburgh Review*, 2, 1756. For an approach emphasizing points of commonality between Smith and Rousseau, see Istvan Hont, *Politics in Commercial Society*, Harvard University Press 2015

59 'To judge of ourselves . . . ': *TMS* III.i.2, from the first edition

59 Mutuality of sight: I owe this important point to Knud Haakonssen

62 'It is because mankind are disposed to sympathise . . . ': *TMS* I.iii.2

63 'There is an affinity between vanity and the love of true glory': *TMS* VII.ii.4

63 'All the members of human society stand in need of each other's assistance': *TMS* II.ii.3

65 'Every savage . . . is in continual danger': *TMS* V.ii.9

65 Continuous exchange: Knud Haakonssen, *The Science of a Legislator: The Natural Jurisprudence of David Hume and Adam Smith*, Cambridge University Press 1981. James Otteson has importantly elaborated this line of thought into a fully fledged theory of a 'marketplace of morals' in *Adam Smith's Marketplace of Life*, Cambridge University Press 2002. But the idea of exchange itself is surely more fundamental, and it lacks the connotations of buying and selling normally associated with markets; Smith's theory of *market* exchange is then a natural offshoot of the wider theory

66 Hume on Burke's 'pretty treatise': letter from David Hume to Adam Smith, 12 April 1759

66 Burke's review of *TMS*: *Annual Register*, 1759

66 Burke's letter of thanks: letter from Edmund Burke to Adam Smith, 10 September 1759

CHAPTER 3: ENLIGHTENED INTERLUDE, 1760–1773

70 'You would not know your country again': letter from Horace Walpole to Sir Horace Mann, 23 July 1761

70 National debt and GDP: John Brewer, *The Sinews of Power: War, Money and the English State 1688–1783*, Harvard University Press 1988; and B.

R. Mitchell, *British Historical Statistics*, rev. edn, Cambridge University Press 2011

71 'My very advanced age': advertisement to *TMS*, 6th edn

74 Scottish natural law jurisprudence: on the wider cultural significance and long-lasting effects of the Scottish natural jurisprudence tradition, see Knud Haakonssen, 'Natural Jurisprudence and the Identity of the Scottish Enlightenment', in Ruth Savage (ed.), *Philosophy and Religion in Enlightenment Britain*, Oxford University Press 2012

76 'The offices of prudence, of charity . . .': *TMS* III.vi.9

76 'Justice is violated when': *LJ(A)*, 24 December 1763

77 'It in reality serves no purpose': *LJ(B)*, Introduction

78 'Four distinct states which mankind pass through': *LJ(A)*, 24 December 1763; on Smith's stadial theory generally, see Ronald L. Meek, *Social Science and the Ignoble Savage*, Cambridge University Press 1976, and Donald Winch, 'Adam Smith's "Enduring Particular Result": A Political and Cosmopolitan Perspective', in Istvan Hont and Michael Ignatieff (eds.), *Wealth and Virtue: The Shaping of Political Economy in the Scottish Enlightenment*, Cambridge University Press 1986

82 'The greatest man of this age . . . if he had had but common truth, common sincerity, common honesty, common modesty, common steadiness, common courage and common sense': Horace Walpole, Earl of Orford, *Memoirs of the Age of King George III*, Richard Bentley 1845, Vol. III, p. 100

82 'Honours which the most exorbitant vanity could wish or desire': letter from David Hume to Adam Smith, 28 October 1763

82 'But Mr Smith was not to be bent from his purpose': Tytler, *Memoirs*, quoted by Rae, *LAS* Ch. 11

83 Jean Calas: see e.g. Edna Nixon, *Voltaire and the Calas Case*, Victor Gollancz 1961; Frederic Maugham, *The Case of Jean Calas*, William Heinemann 1928. Voltaire's celebrated response came in his *A Treatise on Religious Toleration*, T. Becket and P. A. de Hondt 1764

84 'The progress we have made': letter to David Hume, 5 July 1764

85 Smith on the Physiocrats: see *WN* IV.ix generally. The 'nearest approximation to the truth' is at IV.ix.38

86 'The exact regimen': *WN* IV.ix.28

86 'Three moderate tea-cupfuls of blood': letter to Charles Townshend, 6 p.m., 27 August 1766

87 'Most terrible calamity': letter to Lady Frances Scott, 19 October 1766

87 'I long passionately to rejoin my old friends': letter to Andrew Millar, undated, October 1766

87 'Call me simply Adam Smith without any addition': letter to William

Strahan, undated, winter 1766–7

87 'My business here is study': letter to David Hume, 7 June 1767

89 Failure of the Ayr Bank: Henry Hamilton, 'The Failure of the Ayr Bank 1772', *Economic History Review*, 8.3, 1956

89 Commercial growth of Scotland after 1750: see e.g. T. M. Devine, *The Scottish Nation 1700–2000*, Allen Lane 1999. There is a substantial literature on the wider causes—material, technological, cultural—of British economic growth during the industrial revolution. See e.g. Robert Allen, *The British Industrial Revolution in Global Perspective*, Cambridge University Press 2009, Joel Mokyr, *The Enlightened Economy: Britain and the Industrial Revolution 1700–1850*, Yale University Press 2009, and the works of McCloskey and Hoppit listed in the Bibliography

92 'Their own distress': *WN* II.ii.72 and ff.

94 'Solicitous for a publication': letter from Kames to Daniel Fellenberg, 20 April 1773, quoted in Simpson Ross, *LAS* p. 262

94 Pomade: Simpson Ross, *LAS* p. 251, quoting Robert Chambers's *Picture of Scotland*, 1827

94 'Eighteen thin paper folio books': letter to David Hume, 16 April 1773

CHAPTER 4: 'YOU ARE SURELY TO REIGN ALONE ON THESE SUBJECTS', 1773–1776

97 'As dull a dog as he had ever met with': from James Boswell, *Boswell: The Ominous Years, 1774–1776*, ed. Charles Ryskamp and Frederick A. Pottle, McGraw-Hill 1963. The antipathy between the two men may have spilled out into outright insult. Many years afterwards Sir Walter Scott recounted a story of John Millar's in a letter to the Irish writer and politician John Wilson Croker: 'Upon closer examination, it appeared that Dr. Johnson no sooner saw Smith than he brought forward a charge against him for something in his famous letter on the death of Hume. Smith said he had vindicated the truth of the statement. "And what did the Doctor say?" was the universal query: "Why, he said—he said", said Smith, with the deepest impression of resentment, "he said—'You lie!'" "And what did you reply?" "I said, 'You are a son of a b—h!'" On such terms did these two great moralists meet and part, and such was the classic dialogue betwixt them.' Croker, *The Croker Papers*, ed. Louis J. Jennings, John Murray 1884, 1:430, 10 January 1829

97 'Have you ever seen Brentford?': James Boswell, *The Life of Samuel Johnson*, Henry Baldwin, for Charles Dilly, London 1791 and 1793, 30 March 1783

97 'It is not hypocrisy, but madness': cited in Amicus, 'Anecdotes Tending to Throw Light on the Character and Opinions of the Late Adam Smith,

LLD', *The Bee, or Literary Weekly Intelligencer*, 11 May 1791, included in *LRBL* Appendix I

98 'A man must have extensive views': Boswell, *Life of Johnson*, 15 March 1776. The range of sources behind those views is sometimes forgotten: Smith lived in six important cities—Glasgow, Oxford, Edinburgh, London, Paris and Toulouse, as well as staying in Geneva, Bordeaux and Montpelier; he was a member of a wide range of clubs and societies, including the Royal Society and the Edinburgh Royal Society, and was a regular guest at the great salons while in Paris; he had a very broad professional, business, scholarly and political acquaintance; and, at over 3,000 volumes, a large library; see R. H. Hartwell's 'Comment' in Thomas Wilson and Andrew S. Skinner (eds.), *The Market and the State: Essays in Honour of Adam Smith*, Oxford University Press 1976

98 'The best seminaries of learning': letter to William Cullen, 20 September 1774

99 'Do these events anywise affect your theory?': letter from David Hume, 27 June 1772

102 Positive reaction in Parliament to Townshend's budget of 1767: report of James West to the Duke of Newcastle, quoted in *CAS*, note 21 to the letter from Charles Townshend to Smith below

102 'I will add to these a *real* American Revenue': letter from Charles Townshend, undated, probably in October–December 1766

102 Smith as tax adviser: blaming Smith, C. R. Fay claimed that 'It was professorial advice which lost us the first empire' in *Adam Smith and the Scotland of his Day*, Cambridge University Press 1956, p. 116. For a detailed rebuttal, see Iain McLean, *Adam Smith, Radical and Egalitarian*, Edinburgh University Press 2006, pp. 16–17

104 National wealth as 'the annual produce of the land and labour of any nation': *WN*, 'Introduction and Plan of the Work'

104 'Science of a legislator': *WN* IV.ii.39. On this important idea, see Knud Haakonssen, *The Science of a Legislator: The Natural Jurisprudence of David Hume and Adam Smith*, Cambridge University Press 1981; Donald Winch, 'Science and the Legislator: Adam Smith and After', *Economic Journal*, 93.371, 1983; Edward S. Cohen, 'Justice and Political Economy in Commercial Society: Adam Smith's "Science of a Legislator"', *Journal of Politics*, 51.1, 1989

105 The pin factory: *WN* I.i.3

105 'Propensity to truck, barter and exchange': *WN* I.ii.1

105 'Nobody ever saw a dog make a fair and deliberate exchange': *WN* I.ii.2. Compare this passage, a few lines further on: 'Whoever offers to another

a bargain of any kind, proposes to do this. Give me that which I want, and you shall have this which you want, is the meaning of every such offer; and it is in this manner that we obtain from one another the far greater part of those good offices which we stand in need of.'

106 'Desire of bettering our condition': *WN* II.iii.28–36

106 Cooperation required to produce a woollen coat: *WN* 1.i.4, also discussed in *ED*

106 Man 'becomes, in some measure, a merchant': *WN* I.iv.1

106 'It is not from the benevolence of the butcher': *WN* I.ii.2

107 Division of labour limited by the extent of the market: see *WN* I.iii

107 Labour as real measure of value: *WN* I.v.1

107 'The universal instrument of commerce': *WN* I.iv.11

108 'It is not by augmenting the capital of the country': *WN* II.ii.86

108 'The natural price, therefore, is, as it were, the central price': *WN* I.vii.15

109 'The rate of profit does not . . . fall with the declension of the society': *WN* I.xi, 'Conclusion of the Chapter', para 10

109 'People of the same trade seldom meet together': *WN* I.x, Part 2, para 27

109 'We rarely hear . . . of the combinations of masters': *WN* I.viii.13

109 'Consumption is the sole end and purpose of all production': *WN* IV.viii.49

110 'The wages of idleness': *WN* II.iii.20

111 Servants whose 'services generally perish in the instant of their performance': *WN* II.iii.1

111 The sovereign as 'unproductive labourer': *WN* II.iii.2

111 Parsimony as 'the immediate cause of the increase of capital': *WN* II.iii.16

111 'Every prodigal appears to be a public enemy': *WN* II.iii.25

111 'Great nations are never impoverished': *WN* II.iii.30

111 'The highest impertinence and presumption': *WN* II.iii.36

111 'The very violent attack . . . upon the whole commercial system of Great Britain': letter to Andreas Holt, 26 October 1780

112 'The great object of the political economy of every country': *WN* II.v.31

112 'The rude produce of the land': *WN* IV.ix.10

112 'The wealth of nations as consisting . . . in the consumable goods annually produced': *WN* IV.ix.38

113 'The proposal of any new law or regulation of commerce': *WN* I.xi, 'Conclusion of the Chapter', para 10

114 'Whenever the legislature attempts to regulate the differences': *WN* I.x, Part 2, para 61

114 'A great empire has been established': *WN* IV.viii.53

114 'It cannot be very difficult to determine': *WN* IV.viii.54

115 'Nothing . . . . can be more absurd than this whole doctrine of the balance

of trade': *WN* IV.iii, Part 2, para 2

115 'The obvious and simple system of natural liberty establishes itself': *WN* IV.ix.51

116 Duties of the sovereign: *ibid.*

116 Cost of war 'laid out in distant countries': *WN* IV.i.26

116 'Civil government . . . is in reality instituted for the defence of the rich against the poor': *WN* V.i, Part 2, para 12

117 'No society can surely be flourishing and happy': *WN* I.viii.36

118 Smith on militias: *WN* V.i, 'Of the Expense of Defence'. There is an acute analysis of the main issues in Leonidas Montes, 'Adam Smith on the Standing Army vs. Militia Issue: Wealth over Virtue', in Jeffrey T. Young (ed.), *The Elgar Companion to Adam Smith*, Edward Elgar 2009

119 'The extraordinary duties of my office': letter to Andreas Holt, 26 October 1780

120 Smith on churches and religious competition: *WN* V.i, 'Of the Expense of the Institutions for the Instruction of People of All Ages'

122 Smith's four principles of taxation: *WN* V.ii, Part 2

123 Strahan on Smith's and Gibbon's books: National Library of Scotland, Hume MSS vii.67, quoted in Simpson Ross, *LAS* p. 287.

123 'Much less abused than I had reason to expect': letter to Andreas Holt, 26 October 1780

124 'You have given me full and complete satisfaction and my faith is fixed': letter from Hugh Blair, 3 April 1776

124 'You have formed into a regular and consistent system': letter from William Robertson, 8 April 1776

124 'You are surely to reign alone on these subjects': letter from Adam Ferguson, 18 April 1776

125 Burke's review of *WN*: *Annual Register*, 1776. Burke's insight is well highlighted by James Buchan in his biographical essay in Ryan Patrick Hanley (ed.), *Adam Smith: His Life, Thought, and Legacy*, Princeton University Press 2016

CHAPTER 5: WORKING TO THE END, 1776–1790

126 'In point of health and spirits I never saw him better': letter from Adam Ferguson, 2 September 1773

126 Hume on cooking: letter to Sir Gilbert Elliot, 16 October 1769

126 'If you delay much longer, I shall probably disappear altogether': letter from David Hume, 8 February 1776

127 'He has been declining several years': letter from Joseph Black, undated, April 1776

128 'And yet I have no enemies; except . . . ': Henry, Lord Brougham, *Lives of*

Men of Letters and Science, Who Flourished in the Time of George III, Vol. II, Richard Griffin, London and Glasgow 1855, p. 200

128 'Poor David Hume is dying very fast': letter to Alexander Wedderburn, 14 August 1776

129 'Nothing could have made it better': letter from Joseph Black, 26 August 1776

130 'I now reckon upon a speedy dissolution': Hume, *The Life of David Hume, Esq. Written by Himself*, W. Strahan and T. Cadell 1777, p. 30

130 'He submitted with the utmost cheerfulness': in *Strahan*

130 'Have a little patience, good Charon': *ibid.*

132 Horne's denunciation of Hume: George Horne, *A Letter to Adam Smith LL.D. on the Life, Death, and Philosophy of His Friend David Hume Esq. by One of the People Called Christians*, Clarendon Press 1777

132 'Is this not an age of daring effrontery?': Boswell, *Life of Johnson*, 9 July 1777

132 'A single, and, as I thought, a very harmless sheet of paper': letter to Andreas Holt, 26 October 1780

133 'His Grace sent me word by his cashier': *ibid.*

133 Panmure House: for the history and restoration of Panmure House, see www.panmurehouse.org

134 Charles James Fox on *WN*: Rae, *LAS* Ch. 18

135 'Thoughts on the State of the Contest with America': reprinted in *CAS*

136 'There is trade enough in the world': letter from Henry Dundas, 30 October 1779

136 'To crush the industry of so great and so fine a province': letter to Henry Dundas, 1 November 1779

136 'A very slender interest of our own manufacturers': letter to Lord Carlisle, 8 November 1779

136 'I wished to set an example and burnt them all': letter to William Eden, 3 January 1780

137 'The familiar and social converse of these illustrious men': from John Playfair's 'Life of Dr James Hutton', in *Transactions of the Royal Society of Edinburgh*, 10 January 1803

137 'He generally contented himself with a bold and masterly sketch of the object': Stewart, *LAS* Section V

138 '*Principia* to the knowledge of politic operations': *A Letter from Governor Pownall to Adam Smith*, 25 September 1776, in *CAS*. In fact Smith appears to have made few changes in response to Pownall

138 'This edition will probably see me out': letter to William Strahan, 22 May 1783

138 'The difference between light and darkness through the best part of my

life': letter of 1795 from Lord Shelburne to Dugald Stewart, quoted in Note I to Stewart's *LAS*

138 Smith and Burke: for a fuller though still only partial exploration of the relationship between Smith and Burke, their key differences of view and the rather tortured resulting historiography, see Donald Winch, 'The Burke–Smith Problem and Late Eighteenth-Century Political and Economic Thought', *Historical Journal*, 28.1, 1985. There has been a recurrent tendency to try to put intellectual and political distance between Smith and Burke, with mixed success; cf. Emma Rothschild, 'Adam Smith and Conservative Economics', *Economic History Review*, 45.1, 1992, recapitulated in her *Economic Sentiments: Adam Smith, Condorcet, and the Enlightenment*, Harvard University Press 2001. As their correspondence attests, in the 1780s at least there can be little doubt of the two men's very warm personal feelings for each other

139 'A full exposition of the absurdity and hurtfulness of almost all our chartered trading companies': letter to William Strahan, 22 May 1783

139 'Debauched me from my proper business': letter to Thomas Cadell, 7 December 1782

141 'By a perpetual monopoly': *WN* V.i.119

142 'The weather is fine, my villa at Wimbledon a most comfortable healthy place': letter from Henry Dundas, 21 March 1787

143 'Two other great works upon the anvil': letter to the Duc de La Rochefoucauld, 1 November 1785

143 'Chronic obstruction in his bowels': Stewart, *LAS* Section V

144 'This year I am in my grand climacteric': letter to Bishop John Douglas, 6 March 1787

144 '[I] fear that the machine is nearly worn out': letter from Peter Elmslie to Edward Gibbon, 10 June 1787, quoted in C. R. Fay, *Adam Smith and the Scotland of his Day*, Cambridge University Press 1956, p. 141

144 'No preferment could have given me so much real satisfaction': letter to Dr Archibald Davidson, 16 November 1787

145 'As I consider my tenure of this life as extremely precarious': letter to Thomas Cadell, 15 March 1788

146 'I am a slow a very slow workman': *ibid.*

146 'The great and most universal cause of the corruption of our moral sentiments': *TMS* I.iii.3

147 'Man naturally desires, not only to be loved, but to be lovely': *TMS* III.ii.1

147 'We do not love our country merely as a part of the great society of mankind: we love it for its own sake': *TMS* VI.ii.2

148 'The interest of that great society of all sensible and intelligent beings': *TMS* VI.ii.3

149 'A certain spirit of system is apt to mix itself with that public spirit': *TMS* VI.ii.2

150 '[The] book is now at last perfectly finished to the very last sentence': letter to Thomas Cadell, in Heiner Klemme, 'Adam Smith an Thomas Cadell: Zwei neue Briefe', *Archiv für Geschichte der Philosophie*, 73.3, 1991

151 'Of all the corrupters of moral sentiments': *TMS* III.iii.3

151 '[She] seems to die with satisfaction and contentment': letter to Dr James Menteath, 16 September 1788

151 'She will leave me one of the most destitute and helpless men in Scotland': letter to Lord Porchester, 23 September 1788

151 'I can bear no fatigue': letter to Robert Cullen, 9 February 1790

151 'My progress to recovery is so very slow': letter to Thomas Cadell, 25 May 1790

152 'Perfectly patient and resigned': quoted in Robert Kerr, *Memoirs of the Life, Writing and Correspondence of William Smellie*, John Anderson 1811, p. 295

152 'Dr Black hated nothing so much as error, and Dr Hutton nothing so much as ignorance': John Playfair, quoted in Rae, *LAS* Ch. 21

154 'I am a beau in nothing but my books': William Smellie, *Literary and Characteristical Lives of J. Gregory, M.D., Henry Home, Lord Kames, David Hume, Esq., and Adam Smith, LL.D.*, n.p. 1800, p. 297

154 'A legacy to my family and Posterity, if it should ever please God to grant me any': letter to Lord Stanhope, 8 May 1777

155 'Without the slightest disagreement or coolness': Buccleuch, quoted in Stewart, *LAS*

CHAPTER 6: REPUTATION, FACT AND MYTH

159 Two statues: the statues were erected in 1996 (Hume) and 2008 (Smith); both are by Alexander Stoddart

160 Scottish portraits: see especially Mungo Campbell, *Allan Ramsay: Portraits of the Enlightenment*, Prestel 2013

161 'Mainstream' economics: note that mainstream economics is sometimes distinguished, following Kenneth Boulding, from a supposedly more enduring economic 'mainline', also originating from Smith. See Peter J. Boettke, Stefanie Haeffele Balch and Virgil Henry Storr, *Mainline Economics: Six Nobel Lectures in the Tradition of Adam Smith*, Mercatus Center, George Mason University 2016

161 Smith's early impact in the American colonies: see Samuel Fleischaker, 'Adam Smith's Reception among the American Founders, 1776–1790', *William and Mary Quarterly*, 59.4, 2002. As Fleischaker notes, 'Smith wrote extensively, after all, on some of the central issues debated in America

during the 1780s—the role of banking, the relative merits of militias vis-à-
vis standing armies, the adverse effects of slavery and primogeniture, the
proper relationship between church and state, as well as tax policy and the
regulation of commerce.'

162 Smith's death, Stewart and the separation of politics from economics: cf.
Emma Rothschild, 'Adam Smith and Conservative Economics', *Economic
History Review*, 45.1, 1992

168 Smith and evolution of common law in Scotland: see John W. Cairns, 'Legal Theory', in Alexander Broadie (ed.), *The Cambridge Companion to the
Scottish Enlightenment*, Cambridge University Press 2003 and 'The Influence of Smith's Jurisprudence on Legal Education in Scotland', in John W.
Cairns, *Enlightenment, Legal Education, and Critique*, Edinburgh University Press 2015

168 Smith's likely influence on Darwin: see Matt Ridley, 'The Natural Order
of Things', *Spectator*, 11 January 2009

170 'The result of human action, but not the execution of any human design':
Adam Ferguson, *An Essay on the History of Civil Society*, n.p. 1767, III.ii

172 Different readings of the invisible hand:, see William D. Grampp, 'What
Did Smith Mean by the Invisible Hand?', *Journal of Political Economy*,
108.3, June 2000; for its history and uses prior to Smith, especially in Calvinist and generally providential theology and in natural science, see Peter
Harrison, 'Adam Smith and the History of the Invisible Hand', *Journal of
the History of Ideas*, 72.1, January 2011. As Mark Blaug points out, Smith's
idea of competition is 'a process conception, not an end-state conception'.
Blaug, *Economic Theory in Retrospect*, 5th edn, Cambridge University
Press 1997, p. 593

172 First mention of the invisible hand: in his *History of Astronomy* essay,
Smith says, 'Fire burns, and water refreshes; heavy bodies descend, and
lighter substances fly upwards, by the necessity of their own nature; nor
was the invisible hand of Jupiter ever apprehended to be employed in those
matters. But thunder and lightning, storms and sunshine, those more irregular events, were ascribed to his favour, or his anger . . . And thus, in
the first ages of the world, the lowest and most pusillanimous superstition
supplied the place of philosophy' (*EPS* III.2). In this case, the invisible
hand is being invoked as an external force within a putatively pre-scientific
and personalized explanation for individual, often adverse, events. The
contrast with modern views of the invisible hand as a scientific, law-like,
iterated and collective explanation for benign market phenomena is evident, and reinforces the suggestion that Smith has no overall theory of the
invisible hand. See Eugene Heath, 'Metaphor Made Manifest: Taking Seriously Smith's "Invisible Hand"', in David F. Hardwick and Leslie Marsh

(eds.), *Propriety and Prosperity: New Studies on the Philosophy of Adam Smith*, Palgrave Macmillan 2014, pp. 169 ff.

173 Corn laws: see Avner Offer, 'Self-Interest, Sympathy and the Invisible Hand: From Adam Smith to Market Liberalism', *Economic Thought*, 1.2, 2012. There is a very thoughtful analysis of Smith's views in relation to the corn supply given the prevailing political and economic context in Donald Winch, 'Science and the Legislator: Adam Smith and After', *Economic Journal*, 93.371, 1983

174 Political economists before Smith: see William Letwin, *The Origins of Scientific Economics*, Methuen 1963, and Terence W. Hutchison, *Before Adam Smith: The Emergence of Political Economy 1662–1776*, Basil Blackwell 1988. Angus Maddison, *Contours of the World Economy 1–2030 AD*, Oxford University Press 2007 contains a fascinating personal survey of econometricians before and after Smith's time

174 Late eighteenth-century economic life: see e.g. Ha-Joon Chang, *Economics: The User's Guide*, Pelican Books 2014

174 Supposed errors and omissions in Smith: failure to foresee industrialization: Charles Kindleberger, 'The Historical Background: Adam Smith and the Industrial Revolution', in Thomas Wilson and Andrew S. Skinner (eds.), *The Market and the State: Essays in Honour of Adam Smith*, Oxford University Press 1976; the same collection of essays contains a vigorous defence of Smith by R. M. Hartwell; see also Hiram Caton, 'The Preindustrial Economics of Adam Smith', *Journal of Economic History*, 45.4, 1985. For a defence of Smith on monetary economics, see David Laidler, 'Adam Smith as a Monetary Economist', *Canadian Journal of Economics*, 14.2, 1981. Smith considers inflation, the contrast between money and real prices and what would later become known as purchasing power parity at some length at the end of Book II of *WN* in his 'Digression Concerning the Variations in the Value of Silver During the Course of the Four Last Centuries'

175 Smith's supposed lack of originality: Joseph Schumpeter, *History of Economic Analysis*, Routledge [1954] 1987. A far more dismissive, and indeed manifestly unfair and inaccurate, critique is offered by Murray Rothbard, for whom 'The mystery is the enormous and unprecedented gap between Smith's exalted reputation and the reality of his dubious contribution to economic thought . . . The problem is that he originated nothing that was true, and that whatever he originated was wrong'. Rothbard, *Economic Thought before Adam Smith: An Austrian Perspective*, Edward Elgar 1995. An interesting specific counterclaim is that Smith was the first economist to argue that a normal rate of profit on 'stock' was a necessary constituent of price; cf. Ronald L. Meek, *Studies in the Labour Theory of Value*,

Lawrence & Wishart 1956. For a much more detailed and balanced overall assessment, see Hutchison, *Before Adam Smith*. Jacob Viner's verdict still stands: 'Smith's major claim to originality . . . was his detailed and elaborate application to the wilderness of economic phenomena of the unifying concept of a co-ordinated and mutually interdependent system of cause and effect relationships.' Viner, 'Adam Smith and Laissez Faire', *Journal of Political Economy*, 35.2, April 1927

176   Smith's attitude to his predecessors: one notes Karl Marx's acid comment, 'The Scottish proverb that if one has gained a little it is often easy to gain much, but the difficulty is to gain a little, has been applied by Adam Smith to intellectual wealth as well, and with meticulous care he accordingly keeps the sources secret to which he is indebted for the little, which he turns indeed into much', in *A Contribution to the Critique of Political Economy*, ed. Maurice Dobb, Lawrence & Wishart [1859] 1971

178   The 'Adam Smith problem': there is a useful overview of the often rather labyrinthine debate on this issue, and its historical background, in Leonidas Montes, '*Das Adam Smith Problem*: Its Origins, the Stages of the Current Debate, and One Implication for our Understanding of Sympathy', *Journal of the History of Economic Thought*, 25.1, February 2003. For an important restatement of the problem following the 1976 Smith bicentennial, see Richard Teichgraeber III, 'Rethinking *Das Adam Smith Problem*', *Journal of British Studies*, 20.2, Spring 1981. For a new Adam Smith problem, see James R. Otteson, *Adam Smith*, Bloomsbury 2011. For the modern ideological and policy implications of a 'two Smiths' view, see Matthew Watson, 'Gordon Brown's "Adam Smith Problem"', *Renewal*, 16.3–4, 2008

180   Two spheres: Friedrich Hayek, *The Fatal Conceit*, University of Chicago Press 1988. It is far from clear that Hayek in fact ever read *The Theory of Moral Sentiments*

181   'Granite of self-interest': George Stigler, 'Smith's Travels on the Ship of the State', *History of Political Economy*, 3.2, Fall 1971. Stigler does not mention *The Theory of Moral Sentiments*, or indeed any of Smith's writings apart from *The Wealth of Nations*, in this article

183   Smith's anti-utopianism: Smith's thoroughgoing resistance to views he considered overly generalized or utopian is borne out by recently discovered letters between him and the Count of Windischgrätz in 1785–8. The Count had written to solicit Smith's support for a prize he was proposing to provide a unified—and as it appears mathematically tractable—account of property transfers. Smith replied courteously but firmly that in his view the range of property forms and types of transfer was far too wide to be captured in a formal theory; that there was no one qualified to undertake the work; and that a prize would merely encourage charlatans, so that the

Count would do better to save his money. He also added, tellingly, 'I never suffer my name to appear in a newspaper when I can hinder it, which, to my sorrow, I cannot always do.' See José M. Menudo and Nicolas Rieucau, 'A Previously Unpublished Correspondence between Adam Smith and Joseph Nicolas de Windischgrätz', *History of Political Economy*, 49.1, 2017

183 Self-interest, selfishness, self-love: see Pierre Force, *Self-Interest before Adam Smith: A Genealogy of Economic Science*, Cambridge University Press 2003. Note that David Hume made a similar point about attributed motivation in relation to politics in his essay 'Of the Independency of Parliament': 'It is, therefore, a just political maxim, that every man must be supposed a knave'

184 'The natural representations of self-love can be corrected by the eye of the impartial spectator': *TMS* III.iii.4. This occurs alongside a well-known passage in which Smith compares the natural concern someone might have for the loss of a little finger with their reaction to a disastrous earthquake in China: 'The most frivolous disaster which could befall himself would occasion a more real disturbance. If he was to lose his little finger to-morrow, he would not sleep tonight; but, provided he never saw them, he will snore with the most profound security over the ruin of a hundred millions of his brethren, and the destruction of that immense multitude seems plainly an object less interesting to him, than this paltry misfortune of his own.' This has sometimes been read as underlining the centrality of self-interest to Smith's worldview. In fact it is part of an argument to precisely the opposite conclusion: Smith's point is that a sense of moral obligation is compelling enough to overcome the dictates of self-love: 'It is not the soft power of humanity, it is not that feeble spark of benevolence which Nature has lighted up in the human heart, that is thus capable of counteracting the strongest impulses of self-love. It is a stronger power, a more forcible motive, which exerts itself upon such occasions. It is reason, principle, conscience, the inhabitant of the breast, the man within, the great judge and arbiter of our conduct.'

185 Rich and poor: see Deborah Boucoyannis, 'The Equalizing Hand: Why Adam Smith Thought the Market Should Produce Wealth without Steep Inequality', *Perspectives on Politics,* 11.4, December 2013. As Boucoyannis herself points out, there is an interesting parallel here with modern ideas of 'predistribution', in which policy changes are designed to inhibit certain inequalities from emerging in the first place, as opposed to seeking to rectify them once they have occurred; see Jacob S. Hacker, 'The Institutional Foundations of Middle-Class Democracy', Policy Network, May 2011

186 The beggar, who suns himself: Thomas Martin has suggested that this is a concealed reference to a famous fictional encounter from Dio Cassius, in

which Diogenes the Cynic dismisses Alexander the Great for blocking the sunlight. See 'The Sunbathing Beggar and Fighting Kings: Diogenes the Cynic and Alexander the Great in Adam Smith's "Theory of Moral Sentiments"', *Adam Smith Review*, 8, 2015

186 *Laissez-faire*: see e.g. Viner, 'Adam Smith and Laissez Faire'

186 Criticism from the left: see e.g. Joseph Stiglitz, 'Monopoly's New Era', *Project Syndicate*, 13 May 2016, where Stiglitz tries to distinguish between 'two schools of thought . . . about how the economy functions': one emphasizing competitive markets, which he associates with Adam Smith and nineteenth-century liberal political economists, and one which, 'cognizant of how Smith's brand of liberalism leads to rapid concentration of wealth and income, takes as its starting point unfettered markets' tendency toward monopoly'. But this argument misreads Smith as a *laissez-faire* economist, ignores the important differences between Smith and his nineteenth-century liberal successors and mistakes the thrust of Smith's attack on monopolies and crony capitalism; for which see Chapter 9 below

186 'Every man . . . is left perfectly free': *WN* IV.ix.51

188 'Those laws and customs so favourable to the yeomanry': *WN* III.ii.14

190 'Something is sure to happen, that will disconcert his reasoning': David Hume, 'Of Commerce', in his *Essays Moral, Political and Literary*, ed. Eugene F. Miller, Liberty Fund [1752] 1985

190 Compartmentalization of state and market: I am indebted for these points to Emma Rothschild, *Economic Sentiments: Adam Smith, Condorcet, and the Enlightenment*, Harvard University Press 2001

191 Economic models before mathematics: David Hume gives a clear early example of informal economic modelling in his essay 'Of the Balance of Trade', in his *Essays Moral, Political and Literary*

Chapter 7: Smith's Economics

193 Use of economic models: for a sophisticated and pluralistic modern treatment of the function, use and abuse of economic models, see Dani Rodrik, *Economics Rules*, Oxford University Press 2015; and the very stimulating but more technical 'On the Future of Macroeconomic Models' by Olivier Blanchard, in *Oxford Review of Economic Policy*, 34.1–2, 2018

193 Kenneth Arrow and Frank Hahn: *General Competitive Analysis*, Holden-Day 1971. I owe this example to Mark Blaug, 'No History of Ideas, Please, We're Economists', *Journal of Economic Perspectives*, 15.1, Winter 2001

197 Vernon Smith on good and bad news: overall, see his 'Constructivist and Ecological Rationality in Economics', Nobel Prize lecture, 8 December 2002, extended in *Rationality in Economics: Constructivist and Ecological Forms*, Cambridge University Press 2008. Vernon Smith has himself been

an extremely illuminating interpreter of Adam Smith; cf. e.g. 'The Two Faces of Adam Smith', Distinguished Guest Lecture, Southern Economic Association, 21 November 1997, and 'What Would Adam Smith Think?', *Journal of Economic Behavior and Organization*, 73, 2010. For the spill-over effects of prosocial environments, and the importance of institutions in shaping persisting habits, see Alexander Peysakhovich and David G. Rand, 'Habits of Virtue: Creating Norms of Cooperation and Defection in the Laboratory', *Management Science*, Articles in Advance, 2015

197 Experimental economics: Robert Sugden has suggested that David Hume should be considered one of the originators of experimental economics. In the *Treatise* Hume argues that the workings of the human mind should be investigated by 'careful and exact experiments, and the observation of those particular effects, which result from its different circumstances and situations' (*A Treatise of Human Nature*, ed. L. A. Selby-Bigge, rev. edn, P. H. Nidditch, Oxford University Press 1978, pp. xv–xvii). See Robert Sugden, 'Hume's Non-Instrumental and Non-Propositional Decision Theory', *Economics and Philosophy* 22. 3, 2006

197 Perils of formalism: see Amartya Sen, 'Rational Fools', *Philosophy & Public Affairs*, 6.4, Summer 1977

199 Nineteenth-century economics: there is a large literature on this topic; a fascinating but idiosyncratic overview is Mark Blaug, *Economic Theory in Retrospect*, 5th edn, Cambridge University Press 1997. See also his 'No History of Ideas, Please, We're Economists'. As Blaug notes, 'Actually, history of economic thought is in many ways more difficult, more subtle, less capable of being cloned on a master mold than standard mainstream economics.'

199 Development of *homo economicus*: see e.g. Mary Morgan, 'Economic Man as Model Man: Ideal Types, Idealization and Caricatures', *Journal of the History of Economic Thought*, 28.1, March 2006. It is interesting to note that Michel Foucault associates '*homo oeconomicus*' as a cultural phenomenon with Ricardo and not Smith, and with a post-Kantian awareness of human limitations and the fact of scarcity: '*Homo oeconomicus* is not the human being who represents his own needs to himself, and the objects capable of satisfying them; he is the human being who spends, wears out, and wastes his life in evading the imminence of death.' Foucault, *The Order of Things: An Archaeology of the Human Sciences*, repr. Routledge 2002

199 Principle of Comparative Advantage: David Ricardo, *On the Principles of Political Economy, and Taxation*, John Murray 1817, Ch. 7, 'On Foreign Trade'

201 Jevons on market exchange and equilibrium: W. S. Jevons, *The Theory of Political Economy*, Macmillan 1888, Ch. 4

203 'Higgling': see *WN* I.v.4; for Edgeworth's overall critique of Walras, see his 'Review of Léon Walras, *Éléments d'économie politique pure*', *Nature*, 40.1036, September 1925

204 Transformation of political economy into economics: although Alfred Marshall is often credited with the shift in name, it is worth noting that he and Mary Paley Marshall had already scouted the change eleven years earlier, in their book *The Economics of Industry* of 1879

204 Effect of mathematical and physical models on economics: see Philip Mirowski, *More Heat than Light*, Cambridge University Press 1989

204 Politics as epiphenomenon: the exact relations between politics and economics in Marx's thought remain a matter of scholarly debate. In the words of Ralph Miliband, 'Marx and Engels explicitly rejected any rigid and mechanistic notion of "determination" . . . But one must not protest too much. There remains in Marxism an insistence on the "primacy" of the "economic base" which must not be understated.' See his *Marxism and Politics*, Oxford University Press 1977, p. 8. G. A. Cohen, *Karl Marx's Theory of History*, Princeton University Press 1978 explores these issues in detail and with great clarity and sophistication

204 Loss of institutions as a result of development of economic theory: see e.g. Peter Boettke, 'Hayek's Epistemic Liberalism', *Liberty Fund Review*, September 2017. See also Murray Milgate and Shannon C. Stimson, *After Adam Smith: A Century of Transformation in Politics and Political Economy*, Princeton University Press 2009, Ch. 13

206 Critique of 'neoliberalism': see e.g. Naomi Klein, *The Shock Doctrine*, Penguin 2008, and Paul Mason, *Postcapitalism: A Guide to our Future*, Penguin 2015. For a vigorous defence and reclamation of the word 'neoliberal', see Madsen Pirie, *The Neoliberal Mind: The Ideology of the Future*, Adam Smith Institute 2017. For initiatives to create a more inclusive public understanding of capitalism, see the work of the Coalition for Inclusive Capitalism, www.inc-cap.com

207 Keynes and uncertainty: the fundamental impact of distinguishing uncertainty from risk and treating uncertainty as a radical part of nature is explored within Keynes's work by Hyman P. Minsky in *John Maynard Keynes*, McGraw-Hill [1975] 2008

208 Different definitions of economics: as 'the science which studies human behaviour as a relationship between given ends and scarce means', see Lionel Robbins, *An Essay on the Nature and Significance of Economic Science*, Macmillan 1932; as the study of incentives, see Steve Levitt and Stephen Dubner, *Freakonomics: A Rogue Economist Explores the Hidden Side of Everything*, HarperCollins 2005

210 Centrality of institutions to economic life: for the firm as economic

institution, see Ronald Coase, 'The Nature of the Firm', *Economica*, 4.16, 1937. More widely, see e.g. Douglass North, 'Institutions', *Journal of Economic Perspectives*, 5.1, Winter 1991, which includes North's own sketch of a stadial history of market evolution, and analysis of non-evolution. For an argument that economic ideology has corrosive effects on institutions, see Stephen Marglin, *The Dismal Science: How Thinking Like an Economist Undermines Community*, Harvard University Press 2008

211 Smith and Marx: see e.g. Spencer Pack, 'Adam Smith and Marx', in Christopher J. Berry, Maria Pia Paganelli and Craig Smith (eds.), *The Oxford Handbook of Adam Smith*, Oxford University Press 2013, Ch. 25

214 Feminist economics: overall, see e.g. Nancy Folbre, *Greed, Lust and Gender: A History of Economic Ideas*, Oxford University Press 2009

215 Marshall's definition of economics as 'the study of men as they live and move and think in the ordinary business of life': see Michèle A. Pujol, *Feminism and Anti-Feminism in Early Economic Thought*, Edward Elgar 1992, Ch. 8

217 'Human life and its flourishing': Julie A. Nelson, 'Poisoning the Well, or How Economic Theory Damages Moral Imagination', in George DeMartino and Deirdre McCloskey (eds.), *The Oxford Handbook on Professional Economic Ethics*, Oxford University Press 2016. It is notable how far mainstream economists have started to draw on this wider cluster of ideas, as e.g. in two recent books by Nobel laureates: Edmund Phelps, *Mass Flourishing: How Grassroots Innovation Created Jobs, Challenge, and Change*, Princeton University Press 2013; and Jean Tirole, *Economics for the Common Good*, Princeton University Press 2017

217 Inadequacy of genderless and raceless economics: Margherita Borella, Mariacristina De Nardi and Fang Yang, 'The Aggregate Implications of Gender and Marriage', *Journal of the Economics of Ageing*, 2017; Tomaz Cajner, Tyler Radler, David Ratner and Ivan Vidangos, 'Racial Gaps in Labor Market Outcomes in the Last Four Decades and over the Business Cycle', Washington DC, Federal Reserve System 2017

217 Husbandry: Julie A. Nelson, 'Husbandry: A (Feminist) Reclamation of Masculine Responsibility for Care', *Cambridge Journal of Economics*, 40, 2016. The inversion of values since Smith's time is striking; in the second half of the eighteenth century it was often commerce, with its connotations of luxury and consumption, that was contrasted with war and pejoratively seen as unmanly and effeminate. To base an account of commercial society on the social glue of human sentiment, as Smith did, might be thought to reinforce this view; cf. e.g. Karen O'Brien, *Women and Enlightenment in Eighteenth-Century Britain*, Oxford University Press 2009, esp. Chs. 1–2

220 Wollstonecraft and Smith: interestingly, Wollstonecraft refers to Smith as a 'respectable authority' (Ch. 8), engages with and sometimes echoes the arguments of *TMS* and also takes aim at Rousseau (and arguably Mandeville)

221 Behavioural economics: see Nava Ashraf, Colin F. Camerer and George Loewenstein, 'Adam Smith, Behavioral Economist', *Journal of Economic Perspectives*, 19.3, Summer 2005

Chapter 8: Adam Smith and Markets

224 'He's kind of a drunken psycho': Warren Buffett, quoted on Benzinga.com, 6 January 2015

225 Benjamin Graham: *The Intelligent Investor*, Harper & Bros. 1949

225 Efficient Market Hypothesis: Richard Thaler, 'Markets can be wrong and the price is not always right', *Financial Times*, 4 August 2009. On the theory, see e.g. Andrei Shleifer, *Inefficient Markets*, Oxford University Press 2000. A highly readable overview of the history is Justin Fox, *The Myth of the Rational Market*, Harriman House 2009

225 Information incentives and efficient markets: see Sanford J. Grossman and Joseph E. Stiglitz, 'On the Impossibility of Informationally Efficient Markets', *American Economic Review*, 70.3, 1980

227 'There is no other proposition in economics which has more solid empirical evidence': Michael Jensen, 'Some Anomalous Evidence Regarding Market Efficiency', *Journal of Financial Economics*, 6.2–3, 1978. Jensen's views have since undergone considerable modification; see Fox, *The Myth of the Rational Market*, Ch. 15 ff.

230 Slave trade and Scotland: the old view that Scotland had little to do with the slave trade has now been exploded. Glasgow was not a centre for the triangle trade, but some slaves were imported into Glasgow, including by John Watt, the father of James; early Scottish industrialization was supported by revenues from slave economies; and the Scots were a significant force in the management and financing of the trade. Scotland also had a notably higher proportion of absentee slave-owners than England, and received a disproportionately high level of compensation when slavery was finally abolished. In the words of Tom Devine, 'There was full and enthusiastic Scottish engagement at every level of the trade, even if direct trading from Scottish ports was minuscule'; see his *To the Ends of the Earth: Scotland's Global Diaspora 1750–2010*, Allen Lane 2011; the essays in Devine (ed.), *Recovering Scotland's Slavery Past: The Caribbean Connection*, Edinburgh University Press 2015; and the work of the Scottish Centre for Diaspora Studies at the University of Edinburgh

230 Smith's alleged cynicism over slavery: see e.g. Johann Hari,

'What if the anti-slavery campaigners had listened to the carp-
ing cynics?', *Independent*, 6 July 2005 and Blake Smith, 'Slavery
as Free Trade', Aeon Essays, 29 June 2016 https://aeon.co/essays/
why-the-original-laissez-faire-economists-loved-slavery

232　Enlightenment thinkers on slavery: see, generally, Domenico Losurdo,
Liberalism: A Counter-History, Verso 2011; John Locke, *Two Treatises of
Government*, ed. Peter Laslett, Cambridge University Press [1689] 1967,
11.7.85–6; Fletcher of Saltoun, see his speech of 1698 to the Scottish
Parliament, quoted in Karl Marx, *Capital: Critique of Political Economy*,
Penguin [1867–83] 2004, I.8.27; Francis Hutcheson, *A System of Moral
Philosophy*, 2 vols., A. Millar and T. Longman 1755, Vol. II, p. 202. John
Cairns has described the opposition of Smith and John Millar in the 1760s
as 'essentially lone voices crying in the wilderness'. 'Slavery in Scotland'
podcast, *How Glasgow Flourished* exhibition 2014. There was a significant
reaction by pro-slavery advocates to adverse legal judgments in the 1770s,
especially following the publication of Edward Long's *History of Jamaica*
in 1774, which argued for the fundamental inferiority of black Africans;
while Scottish anti-slavery petitions only really got going in the late 1780s

233　'We are apt to imagine': *LJ(A)*, 15 February 1763

233　'There is not a negro from the coast of Africa': *TMS* V.ii.9

234　'A general insurrection would ensue': *LJ(A)*, 16 February 1763

235　Smith's analysis of the economics of slavery: there is also a pithy summary
of Smith's views in *ED*, which is dated to before April 1763. See also e.g.
John Salter, 'Adam Smith on Slavery', *History of Economic Ideas*, 4.1–2,
1996, pp. 225–51, and Barry Weingast, 'Adam Smith's Theory of the Per-
sistence of Slavery and its Abolition in Western Europe', Stanford University 2015. The wider economics of slavery, especially in the American
South, remains much debated

235　Balancing general theory with specific cases: cf. Thomas Schelling: 'In
my own thinking, they have never been separate. Motivation for the purer
theory came almost exclusively from preoccupation with (and fascination
with) "applied" problems; and the clarification of theoretical ideas was absolutely dependent on an identification of live examples.' Schelling, *The
Strategy of Conflict*, Harvard University Press 1980, vi

235　'The accommodation of an European prince': *WN* I.i.11

236　'Commerce and manufactures gradually introduced order and good government': *WN* II.iv.4

236　Morality and markets: Maria Pia Paganelli, 'Commercial Relations: From
Adam Smith to Field Experiments', in Christopher J. Berry, Maria Pia
Paganelli and Craig Smith (eds.), *The Oxford Handbook of Adam Smith*,
Oxford University Press 2013, Ch. 16. Paganelli looked at some of the

recent literature testing whether market dealings increase or decrease the human willingness to trust others, exploring ways in which trust fosters economic growth and vice versa, and finding support for Smith's views in both respects

238 Size of the global foreign exchange markets: *Triennial Central Bank Survey: Foreign Exchange Turnover in April 2016*, Bank for International Settlements

239 Smith on labour markets: *WN* I.viii.51

241 Smith on animal spirits: slave-owners, see above; new mines, *WN* IV.vii.18; ambition, see below; public trust *WN* V.iii.7

243 Markets' structure and histories: see e.g. Alex Marshall, *The Surprising Design of Market Economies*, University of Texas Press 2012

244 Arrow securities: see K. J. Arrow, 'The Role of Securities in the Optimal Allocation of Risk-Bearing', *Review of Economic Studies*, 31.2, 1964 (original in French, 1953). Bruce Greenwald and Joseph Stiglitz importantly extended the same overall line of argument in their paper 'Externalities in Economies with Imperfect Information and Incomplete Markets', *Quarterly Journal of Economics*, 101.2, 1986. This showed that the effect of imperfect information was to break the link between equilibrium models and any presumption of efficiency. The formal conditions of market failure were thus all but inevitable in any real-world situation, with imperfect information, incomplete markets and a host of other frictional factors at work. In such cases—that is, in virtually every case—policy interventions could in principle be made that generated improvements in welfare. In other words, market failure is endemic, and can never be the sole justification for policy interventions; and there can be no escape through economic theory from the need for political economy. I am very grateful to Tim Besley for this point; see especially his 'The New Political Economy', *Economic Journal*, 117.524, 2007. See also Roman Frydman and Michael D. Goldberg, *Imperfect Knowledge Economics*, Princeton University Press 2007

246 Wisdom of crowds: cf. James Surowiecki, *The Wisdom of Crowds*, Doubleday Books 2004

247 Veblen goods: see Thorstein Veblen, *The Theory of the Leisure Class: An Economic Study in the Evolution of Institutions*, Macmillan 1899. In his essay on the imitative arts (in *EPS*) Smith memorably analyses the phenomenon of topiary in Veblenian terms: 'It was some years ago the fashion to ornament a garden with yew and holly trees, clipped into the artificial shapes of pyramids, and columns, and vases, and obelisks. It is now the fashion to ridicule this taste as unnatural . . . In the cabbage-garden of a tallow-chandler we may sometimes perhaps have seen as many columns

and vases, and other ornaments in yew, as there are in marble and por-
phyry at Versailles: it is this vulgarity which has disgraced them. The rich
and the great, the proud and the vain, will not admit into their gardens an
ornament which the meanest of the people can have as well as they.'

247 History of manias, bubbles and crashes: there is considerable controversy
as to the correct explanation for different bubbles or manias. See e.g.
Charles P. Kindleberger, *Manias, Panics, and Crashes*, 4th edn, John Wiley
2000; Robert Shiller, *Irrational Exuberance*, Princeton University Press
2000; Peter Garber, *Famous First Bubbles: The Fundamentals of Early Manias*, MIT Press 2000; and for finance, Carmen Reinhart and Kenneth
Rogoff, *This Time is Different*, Princeton University Press 2011

248 Keynes's beauty competition: J. M. Keynes, *The General Theory of Employment, Interest and Money*, Macmillan 1936

249 Asset markets and credit creation: see George Cooper, *The Origin of Financial Crises*, 2nd edn, Harriman House 2010

249 Hyman Minsky: see his *Stabilizing an Unstable Economy*, Yale University
Press 1986. Minsky's insistence on radical uncertainty, on the centrality of
the financial sector to the modern economy and on the pro-cyclical nature
of market dynamics is especially noteworthy

250 US housing market and the 2008 crisis: Steven D. Gjerstad and Vernon
Smith, *Rethinking Housing Bubbles: The Role of Household and Bank Balance Sheets in Modeling Economic Crises*, Cambridge University Press
2014

252 Pricing of the Nasdaq Composite Index: Cooper, *The Origin of Financial
Crises*

253 Friedman on economic methodology: 'The Methodology of Positive Economics', in his *Essays in Positive Economics*, University of Chicago Press
1953

CHAPTER 9: CAPITALISM AND ITS DISCONTENTS

257 NBER study of 2004 buyback: Dhammika Dharmapala, C. Fritz Foley and
Kristin J. Forbes, 'Watch What I Do, Not What I Say: The Unintended
Consequences of the Homeland Investment Act', MIT Sloan Research
Paper No. 4741-09, available at SSRN: https://ssrn.com/abstract=1337206

257 Top 1 per cent share of national income: see the widely respected World
Wealth and Income Database www.wid.world

257 National attitudes survey: see Robert P. Jones, Daniel Cox, Betsy Cooper and Rachel Lienesch, 'Anxiety, Nos-
talgia and Mistrust: Findings from the 2015 American
Values Survey', Public Religion Research Institute 2015, http://www
.prri.org/wp-content/uploads/2015/11/PRRI-AVS-2015-1.pdf

258 *McCutcheon* v. *Federal Election Commission*: US Supreme Court (12-536), 2 April 2014

258 *Citizens United* v. *Federal Election Commission*: US Supreme Court (08-205), 24 March 2009

259 Inefficiency and conflicts in UK banking: Martin Wolf, 'Good news—fintech could disrupt finance', *Financial Times*, 8 March 2016. Also see Andy Haldane, 'Finance Version 2.0?', Bank of England/London Business School 2016

259 Increase in bank regulation and regulators: Andy Haldane, 'The Dog and the Frisbee', Federal Reserve Bank of Kansas City 366th Economic Policy Symposium, Jackson Hole, Wyoming, 31 August 2012

260 Effects of large financial sectors: Jean-Louis Arcand, Enrico Berkes and Ugo Panizza, 'Too Much Finance?', IMF Working Paper 2012

261 Implicit subsidy to banks: IMF, *Global Financial Stability Report*, April 2014; Andy Haldane, 'Who Owns a Company?', Speech, Bank of England 2015

261 Lobbying and moral hazard: Deniz Igan, Prachi Mishra and Thierry Tressel, 'A Fistful of Dollars: Lobbying and the Financial Crisis', IMF Working Paper 2009

261 Bank employee rents and effects on inequality: Thomas Philippon and Ariell Reshef, 'Wages and Human Capital in the U.S. Financial Industry: 1909–2006', NBER Working Paper 14644, 2009; Brian Bell and John Van Reenen, 'Bankers' Pay and Extreme Wage Inequality in the UK', CEPR 2010

262 Banking culture and honesty: in one study, bank employees were not on average shown to be less honest than other employees. When reminded of their occupational role, however, they were significantly less honest on average than their colleagues in a control group; and this finding was not replicated in other industries. See Alain Cohn, Ernst Fehr and Michel André Maréchal, 'Business Culture and Dishonesty in the Banking Industry', *Nature*, 19 November 2014

262 Lobbying returns: 'Lobbyists, Government and Public Trust: Promoting Integrity by Self-Regulation', OECD 2009; 'Money and Politics', *The Economist*, 1 October 2011

263 Varieties of crony capitalism: cf. Jesse Norman, 'The Case for Real Capitalism', Working Paper, www.jessenorman.com 2011. A tour de force on crony capitalism is Luigi Zingales, *A Capitalism for the People: Recapturing the Lost Genius of American Prosperity*, Basic Books 2012

264 Corrupt business relations with government: see former FEC Chairman Trevor Potter's speech to the Chatauqua Institution at http://www.campaignlegalcenter.org/sites/default/files/Chautauqua%202016%20Final.pdf

265 Trade and business before modern capitalism: see Fernand Braudel, *Capitalism and Material Life 1400–1800*, Weidenfeld & Nicolson 1973, and more recently Martha C. Howell, *Commerce before Capitalism in Europe 1300–1600*, Cambridge University Press 2009; it is notable that Angus Maddison dates the 'capitalist epoch' after 1820

265 Negative social and economic effects of inequality: see e.g. Era Dabla-Norris, Kalpana Kochhar, Nujin Suphaphiphat, Frantisek Ricka and Evridiki Tsounta, 'Causes and Consequences of Income Inequality: A Global Perspective', IMF Staff Discussion Note, June 2015

267 'Prodigals and projectors': in a long letter, written as part of his *Defence of Usury* and sent from his travels in Russia in March 1787, Jeremy Bentham took Smith to task for his dismissive remarks about 'prodigals and projectors', arguing that Smith's 'projectors' were in fact 'adventurous spirits' given to innovation and improvement. Smith was said to have admired Bentham's letter, but he would have been highly aware from the Ayr Bank disaster that many 'projectors' were no such thing, and there is no direct evidence that he changed his mind. See CAS, Appendix C. On Smith's contrast between prodigality and prudence, see Craig Smith, 'Adam Smith, the Scottish Enlightenment, and "Realistic" Philosophy', INET Edinburgh Conference, October 2017, available through www.ineteconomics.org

267 East India Company: on the Company, and Smith's wider ambivalence about globalization, see e.g. Sankar Muthu, 'Adam Smith's Critique of International Trading Companies: Theorizing "Globalization" in the Age of Enlightenment', *Political Theory*, 236.2, 2008

268 The drought in Bengal: *WN* IV.5 'Digression Concerning the Corn Trade and Corn Laws', para 6. On the relation between famines and democracy, see Amartya Sen, *Poverty and Famines*, Oxford University Press 1981; and more recently, Cormac Ó Gráda, *Famine: A Short History*, Princeton University Press 2009

268 Rent-seeking: this idea was first specifically developed by Gordon Tullock in 'The Welfare Costs of Tariffs, Monopolies and Theft', *Western Economic Journal*, 5.3, 1967. It was further developed, and the term 'rent-seeking' coined, by Anne Krueger in 'The Political Economy of the Rent-Seeking Society', *American Economic Review*, 64.3, 1974. See also Roger D. Congleton and Arye L. Hillman (eds.), *Companion to the Political Economy of Rent-Seeking*, Edward Elgar 2015

269 James Anderson on rent: see *An Enquiry into the Nature of the Corn Laws*, 1777. I am very grateful to John Kay for this reference. J. H. Hollander, 'Adam Smith and James Anderson', *Annals of the American Academy of Political and Social Science*, May 1896, summarizes what is known of the

relationship between the two men. Smith was evidently aware of Anderson's criticism, but never addressed it in later editions of *The Wealth of Nations*

269 Information and power asymmetries: Deborah Boucoyannis, 'The Equalizing Hand: Why Adam Smith Thought the Market Should Produce Wealth without Steep Inequality', *Perspectives on Politics*, 11.4, December 2013

271 Government as interest group: see James Buchanan and Gordon Tullock, *The Calculus of Consent*, University of Michigan Press 1962

274 The 'Great Enrichment': see Deirdre N. McCloskey, *Bourgeois Equality: How Ideas, Not Capital or Institutions, Enriched the World*, University of Chicago Press 2016; and more broadly the work of Angus Maddison, e.g. *Contours of the World Economy 1–2030 AD*, Oxford University Press 2007; there is a very vigorous debate on all sides of this issue. On progress and inequality—and the dynamic ebb and flow between them—see Angus Deaton, *The Great Escape: Health, Wealth, and the Origins of Inequality*, Princeton University Press 2013

274 GDP disparity between West and East Germany: *CIA World Factbook*, 1990

275 Incentives within capitalism encouraging rip-offs and exploitation: see George A. Akerlof and Robert J. Shiller, *Phishing for Phools: The Economics of Manipulation and Deception*, Princeton University Press 2015

277 '"Free Trade" is an accepted maxim of tedious orthodoxy': Walter Bagehot, 'Adam Smith and our Modern Economy', reprinted in *Economic Studies*, ed. R. H. Hutton, Longman, Green 1895

278 Hamiltonian arguments for managed trade: cf. John Stuart Mill, *Principles of Political Economy*, John W. Parker 1848; Friedrich List, *The National System of Political Economy*, J. B. Lippincott 1856. More recently, see Ha-Joon Chang, *Kicking Away the Ladder: Development Strategy in Historical Perspective*, Anthem Press 2002. There has been a substantial modern academic literature on this issue; see e.g. the somewhat question-beggingly entitled 'When and How Should Infant Industries be Protected?' by Marc J. Melitz, *Journal of International Economics*, 66.1, 2005

280 On the wider implications of Smith's failure to recognize the impact of industrialization: cf. Hiram Caton, 'The Preindustrial Economics of Adam Smith', *Journal of Economic History*, 45.4, 1985

281 Rise in share of nominal US GDP created by largest companies: Adrian Wooldridge, 'The Rise of the Superstars', *The Economist*, 17 September 2016

281 Recent increase in market power: overall, see Martin Sandbu, 'America's Threadbare Capitalism', *Financial Times*, 21 April 2016. For the Obama White House's critique of market power, see 'Benefits of Competition

and Indicators of Market Power', US Council of Economic Advisers Issue Brief, May 2016; Jan de Loecker and Jan Eeckhout, 'The Rise of Market Power and the Macroeconomic Implications', NBER Working Paper 23687, August 2017. On the erosion of real wages and the loss of trust within firms, see Robert Solow, 'The Future of Work: Why Wages Aren't Keeping Up', *Pacific Standard*, 11 August 2015

282　Scalability of technology platforms: this is just one aspect of the economic effects of investment in intangible assets, which now outstrips investment in tangible assets in the US and UK. For a pioneering analysis see Jonathan Haskel and Stian Westlake, *Capitalism without Capital: The Rise of the Intangible Economy*, Princeton University Press 2017

282　'Competition is for losers': Peter Thiel, *Wall Street Journal*, 12 September 2014

283　Effects of information and choice overload, especially on the poor: see Sendhil Mullainathan and Eldar Shafir, *Scarcity: The True Cost of Not Having Enough*, Allen Lane 2013

284　Consumer detriment from UK retail electricity market: UK Competition and Markets Authority, *Energy Market Investigation: Final Report*, 24 June 2016

284　Volkswagen scandal: see Frank Dohmen and Dieter Hawranek, 'Collusion between Germany's Biggest Carmakers', *Der Spiegel*, 27 July 2017, and Jack Ewing, *Faster, Higher, Farther: The Inside Story of the Volkswagen Scandal*, Bantam Press 2017

285　Limits of competition policy: recent arguments, and disparate US and EU views, are explored by John Vickers in 'Competition Policy and Property Rights', *Economic Journal*, 120.544, 2010

285　Hidden costs of price comparison websites: see e.g. 'Costly Comparison', *The Economist*, 9 July 2015

285　Algorithmic consumers: I owe this idea to Tony Curzon-Price. There is a rapidly increasing literature on this topic; see e.g. Michal Gal and Niva Elkin-Koren, 'Algorithmic Consumers', *Harvard Journal of Law and Technology* (forthcoming). A good overview, including a discussion of the potential for collusion and the difficulty of creating transparency, is 'When Algorithms Set Prices: Winners and Losers', OXERA Discussion Paper, June 2017, www.oxera.com

CHAPTER 10: THE MORAL BASIS OF COMMERCIAL SOCIETY

288　Calas: see Nixon, *Voltaire and the Calas Case* and Maugham, *The Case of Jean Calas*; final words, *TMS* III.ii.11. For the wider social and religious context, see David D. Bien, 'The Background of the Calas Affair', *History*, 43.149, 1958

289 'The writings of Voltaire are made for all and read by all': Barthélemy Faujas Saint-Fond, *Travels in England, Scotland and the Hebrides*, 2 vols, J.
Ridgway, London 1799, Vol. II

290 Smith on the violence of 1745: *LJ(B)* pp. 331–2

290 'Faction and fanaticism have always been by far the greatest': *TMS* III.
iii.43

292 Montesquieu: *The Spirit of Laws*, 2 vols., J. Nourse & P. Vaillant 1750, Bk
V.vi

293 'Avarice and ambition in the rich': *WN* V.ii.2

294 'A humane and polished people': *TMS* V.ii.10

296 Smith and Kant: the relationship between the thought of Smith and Kant
is unclear and of great interest. Although their philosophical projects are
different, it is now fairly clear that Kant was aware of *TMS*, as well as *WN*,
and drew on some of its ideas, notably that of the impartial spectator, rendered in German as *unparteiische Zuschauer*. See e.g. Samuel Fleischaker,
'Philosophy in Moral Practice: Kant and Adam Smith', *Kant-Studien*, 82.3,
1991, which usefully summarizes the scattered evidence across the corpus of Kant's writings. Smith's sympathy-based psychology appears rather
closer to Kant's notion of the 'forms of intuition' than is Hume's more passive theory of 'impressions' and 'ideas'

297 Hume on conventions: *A Treatise of Human Nature*, ed. L. A. Selby-Bigge,
rev. edn, P. H. Nidditch, Oxford University Press 1978, Bk III.2 'Of Justice
and Injustice'; as Peyton Young has pointed out, this section brilliantly
captures three core ideas about norms: that they can be equilibria in repeated games; that they can evolve through a dynamic learning process;
and that they underpin many wider forms of social and economic order.
Cf. also H. Peyton Young, 'The Evolution of Social Norms', Oxford Department of Economics Discussion Paper 726, October 2014. Modern
debate on the exact nature and proper philosophical characterization of
convention largely derives from David Lewis's work in *Convention*, Harvard University Press 1969

298 Norms as 'grammar of society': see Cristina Bicchieri, *The Grammar of
Society: The Nature and Dynamics of Social Norms*, Cambridge University
Press 2006. For a wide-ranging and provocative essay on norms in relation
to self-interest, see Jon Elster, 'Social Norms and Economic Theory', *Journal of Economic Perspectives*, 3.4, 1989

299 Scientific views on reciprocity, social norms and mirror neurons: see e.g.
Frans de Waal, *Our Inner Ape: The Best and Worst of Human Nature*,
Granta Books 2006; Jean Ensminger and Joseph Henrich (eds.), *Exper-
imenting with Social Norms: Fairness and Punishment in Cross-Cultural
Perspective*, New York, Russell Sage Press 2014; Giacomo Rizzolatti and

Laila Craighero, 'The Mirror-Neuron System', *Annual Review of Neuroscience*, 27, 2004. For a contrary view (less contrary than the title implies), see Gregory Hickok, *The Myth of Mirror Neurons*, W. W. Norton 2014. On the supercharging effect of culture within evolution, see Joseph Henrich, *The Secret of our Success*, Princeton University Press 2016

299 Smith and Rawls: See John Rawls, *A Theory of Justice*, Harvard University Press 1974. The game theorist and economist Ken Binmore has very fruitfully explored the relationship between Humean social conventions and Rawls's 'Original Position', and much else, in his book *Natural Justice*, Oxford University Press 2005. Amartya Sen has argued that 'Smith's analysis of "the impartial spectator" has some claim to being the pioneering idea in the enterprise of interpreting impartiality and formulating the demands of fairness which so engaged the world of the European Enlightenment'. Sen, 'Adam Smith and the Contemporary World', *Erasmus Journal for Philosophy and Economics*, 3.1, Spring 2010

300 Productivity differences: Robert Gibbons and Rebecca Henderson, 'What Do Managers Do? Exploring Persistent Performance Differences among Seemingly Similar Enterprises', Working Paper, Harvard Business School, August 2012

301 Identity and economics: overall, on identity as non-pecuniary source of motivation, see George A. Akerlof and Rachel E. Kranton, 'Identity and the Economics of Organizations', *Journal of Economic Perspectives*, 19.1, 2005, and their *Identity Economics*, Princeton University Press 2010. For the importance of 'mission' (and its implications for theories of agency), especially in non-profits, educational organizations and public-sector bureaucracies, see Timothy Besley and Maitreesh Ghatak, 'Competition and Incentives with Motivated Agents', *American Economic Review*, 95.3, 2005. For a general framework integrating identities, narratives and norms into economic analysis, see Paul Collier, 'The Cultural Foundations of Economic Failure: A Conceptual Toolkit', *Journal of Economic Behavior & Organization*, 126, November 2015

301 Leon Festinger: see Leon Festinger, Henry W. Riecken and Stanley Schachter, *When Prophecy Fails*, University of Minnesota Press 1956, and Festinger, *A Theory of Cognitive Dissonance*, Stanford University Press 1957; and more generally, Carol Tavris and Elliot Aronson, *Mistakes Were Made (But Not by Me)*, Mariner Books 2015, and Dan Ariely, *The (Honest) Truth about Dishonesty: How We Lie to Everyone—Especially Ourselves*, HarperCollins 2012

302 'Not in genius and disposition half so different from a street porter': *WN* I.ii.5

302 Self as formed by human interaction: cf. Kenneth Boulding, 'Economics as

a Moral Science', *American Economic Review*, 59.1, 1969: 'It was . . . Veblen's principal, and still largely unrecognized, contribution to formal economic theory, to point out that we cannot assume that tastes are "given" in any dynamic theory' (my added inverted commas). As Boulding notes, when he was a student at Cambridge University this understanding of economics was still reflected in its status as part of the (now defunct) Moral Sciences Tripos

303 Beliefs as property: Roland Bénabou and Jean Tirole, 'Identity, Morals, and Taboos: Beliefs as Assets', *Quarterly Journal of Economics*, 126. 2, 2011

304 The economy of regard: see Avner Offer, *The Challenge of Affluence: Self-Control and Well-Being in the United States and Britain since 1950*, Oxford University Press 2006, Ch. 6; and 'Self-Interest, Sympathy and the Invisible Hand: From Adam Smith to Market Liberalism', *Economic Thought*, 1.2, 2012

309 Parking tickets in New York: Raymond Fisman and Edward Miguel, 'Cultures of Corruption: Evidence from Diplomatic Parking Tickets', NBER Working Paper 12312, 2006. On wider relationships between intrinsic honesty, rule violations and institutional strength across twenty-three countries, see Simon Gächter and Jonathan F. Schulz, 'Intrinsic Honesty and the Prevalence of Rule Violations across Societies', *Nature*, 531, 2016

311 Norms of littering in Holland: Kees Keizer, Siegwart Lindenberg and Linda Steg, 'The Spreading of Disorder', *Science*, 322, 2008

311 Corrupt local equilibria: Robert Klitgaard, 'On Culture and Corruption', unpublished paper, June 2017

311 Influence of public fraud and corruption on individuals: Gächter and Schulz, 'Intrinsic Honesty and the Prevalence of Rule Violations across Societies'

311 Growth of market and corporate norms: Michael Sandel, *What Money Can't Buy: The Moral Limits of Markets*, Penguin 2012; on the crowding out of non-market norms, see his 'Market Reasoning as Moral Reasoning: Why Economists Should Re-Engage with Political Philosophy', *Journal of Economic Perspectives*, 27.4, 2013

314 Types of moral community: Richard Shweder, Nancy Much, Manmohan Mahapatra and Lawrence Park, 'The "Big Three" of Morality (Autonomy, Community, Divinity) and the "Big Three" Explanations of Suffering', 1997, reprinted in Richard Shweder, *Why Do Men Barbecue? Recipes for Cultural Psychology*, Harvard University Press 2003

315 Smith and civic republicanism: recent debates among historians on civic republicanism, its classical antecedents and specifically humanist strand have been complex and highly nuanced. In relation to Smith, see Istvan Hont and

Michael Ignatieff (eds.), *Wealth and Virtue: The Shaping of Political Economy in the Scottish Enlightenment*, Cambridge University Press 1986

318 Smith and cosmopolitanism: see Fonna Forman-Barzilai, *Adam Smith and the Circles of Sympathy*, Cambridge University Press 2010

CONCLUSION: WHY IT MATTERS

320 'On the late Death of Dr Adam Smith': *Gentleman's Magazine*, 60, September 1790. The attribution to Burns is made by Andrew Noble and Patrick Scott Hogg (eds.) in *The Canongate Burns*, Canongate Books 2001

320 Karl Polanyi: *The Great Transformation*, Farrar & Rinehart 1944

321 Growing global longevity, wealth and health: for a vigorous exposition and analysis of these trends, see Stephen Pinker, *Enlightenment Now*, Allen Lane 2018

321 The corporation as an 'externalizing machine': for this brilliant phrase, and a deep critique, see Robert A. G. Monks and Nell Minow, *Power and Accountability*, HarperCollins 1991, and Robert A. G. Monks, *Corpocracy: How CEOs and the Business Roundtable Hijacked the World's Greatest Wealth Machine—and How to Get It Back,* John Wiley 2007

321 Arguments for falling rates of gain from technology: see Robert J. Gordon, *The Rise and Fall of American Growth*, Princeton University Press 2016

321 Absence of critique: debate on the nature of capitalism has been hugely reinvigorated by Thomas Piketty's book *Capitalism in the Twenty-First Century*, Allen Lane 2014. In many ways rightly so, for it offers a very important analytical window into data on wealth and incomes, a simple but comprehensive theory of their long-term evolution and an overdue focus on the distributional consequences of the key trends involved. It is, moreover, framed as a work of political economy, conscious of the limitations of economics as such and infused by an awareness of the importance of norms and institutions. There are many points of potential critique; see e.g. Heather Boushey, J. Bradford DeLong and Marshall Steinbaum (eds.), *After Piketty: The Agenda for Economics and Inequality*, Harvard University Press 2017; and, emphasizing the importance of supply-side responses and human capital formation, Deirdre McCloskey's review essay in the *Erasmus Journal for Philosophy and Economics*, 7.2, Autumn 2014. What is striking from the present perspective is that *Capitalism in the Twenty-First Century* is far more successful as an aggregate historical analysis than in its claim to diagnose in Marxist fashion the 'central contradictions' of capitalism

322 2008 crisis: It has sometimes been suggested that Alan Greenspan set Federal Reserve policy as though a full set of Arrow Securities in fact existed

322 Lack of UK independent review into the 2008 crash: by contrast, the US Congress established the Financial Crisis Inquiry Commission, which reviewed millions of pages of documents, interviewed more than 700 witnesses and held nineteen hearings across the country before publishing its report in January 2011. In addition, the US Senate Permanent Subcommittee on Investigations conducted an entirely separate but similarly painstaking investigation, reporting in April 2011

323 Inadequacy of 'market failure' explanations: see in particular John Kay's magisterial essay, 'The Failure of Market Failure', *Prospect*, 1 August 2007; and the note on Arrow Securities above

325 Charles Sanders Peirce: see in particular the lectures by Peirce published as *Reasoning and the Logic of Things*, ed. Kenneth Laine Ketner, Harvard University Press 1992. By far the best short introduction to Peirce's philosophy remains Josiah Lee Auspitz, 'The Greatest Living American Philosopher', *Commentary*, December 1983; see also Auspitz's 'The Wasp Leaves the Bottle', *American Scholar*, 63.4, 1994. The overlaps in thought between Smith and Peirce are of great interest and importance. Smith's subtle Newtonianism and open-ended view of scientific advance anticipate Peirce's emphasis on the fixation of belief, on abductive theorizing and on truth as the limit of inquiry. Smith's emphasis on sympathy, communicative exchange and the impartial spectator finds an echo in Peirce's radical anti-Cartesianism, public theory of mind and triadic semiotic theory. For a broadly if unconsciously congruent psychology of human reason, see Hugo Mercier and Daniel Sperber, *The Enigma of Reason: A New Theory of Human Understanding*, Harvard University Press 2017

325 'The state of property must always vary with the form of government': Part 1, 'Of Justice', *LJ(B)*; this is one of the key lessons of the stadial theory

329 Facebook and vulnerable teenagers: 'Leaked document reveals Facebook conducted research to target emotionally vulnerable and insecure youth', *The Australian*, 1 May 2017; response by Facebook on https://newsroom.fb.com /news/h/comments-on-research-and-ad-targeting/. A further 700,000-person study showed how the Facebook newsfeed can be manipulated to influence users' moods via 'emotional contagion'; see Adam D. I. Kramer, Jamie E. Guillory and Jeffrey T. Hancock, 'Experimental Evidence of Massive-Scale Emotional Contagion through Social Networks', *Proceedings of the National Academy of Sciences USA*, 24, June 2014. Interestingly, the journal included an Expression of Concern that, as the study was conducted internally by Facebook, it was not fully compliant with accepted consent and privacy rules for research of this kind

329 'A 61-million-person experiment in social influence and political mobilization': Robert M. Bond, Christopher J. Fariss, Jason J. Jones, Adam D. I.

Kramer, Cameron Marlow, Jaime E. Settle and James H. Fowler, *Nature*, September 2012

329 Smith on status anxiety: see Ryan Patrick Hanley, *Adam Smith and the Character of Virtue*, Cambridge University Press, 2009, esp. Ch. 1. On modern status anxiety and its causes, see e.g. Alain de Botton, *Status Anxiety*, Hamish Hamilton 2004

329 Impact of social media on children's well-being: see e.g. Emily McDool, Philip Powell, Jennifer Roberts and Karl Taylor, 'Social Media Use and Children's Wellbeing', IZA Institute for Labor Economics Discussion Paper 10412, December 2016. As Nobel laureate Herbert Simon presciently remarked, 'What information consumes . . . is the attention of its recipients. Hence a wealth of information creates a poverty of attention', in 'Designing Organizations for an Information-Rich World', in Martin Greenberger (ed.), *Computers, Communication, and the Public Interest*, Johns Hopkins Press 1971

330 Movement of skilled workers: see Dani Rodrik, 'Premature Deindustrialization', NBER Working Paper 20935, 2015

330 Modern divergences in mortality and health: cf. Anne Case and Angus Deaton, 'Mortality and Morbidity in the 21st Century', *Brookings Papers on Economic Activity*, Spring 2017

330 Gated communities: see Branko Milanovic, 'The Welfare State in the Age of Globalization', http://glineq.blogspot.co.uk/2017/03/the-welfare-state-in -age-of.html

330 Capacity of companies to bully cities, states: Cf. e.g. Olivia Solon, 'How Uber conquers a city in seven steps', *Guardian*, 12 April 2017; Deborah Haynes and Marcus Leroux, 'Boeing has power to turn off planes say British military chiefs', *The Times*, 28 September 2017

331 Limitations of economics: two projects aiming to address different limitations are the Rebuilding Macroeconomics Network at the UK's National Institute of Economic and Social Research, and the CORE Economics Education programme directed by Wendy Carlin (http://www.core-econ. org). For a very rich analysis from a range of perspectives, including a critique of the dominant DSGE macro models, see the Rebuilding Macroeconomic Theory Project essays in the *Oxford Review of Economic Policy*, 34.1–2, 2018

331 Impossibility of a value-free economics: see e.g. Kenneth Boulding, 'Economics as a Moral Science', *American Economic Review*, 59.1, 1969; and more recently the papers in Hilary Putnam and Vivian Walsh (eds.), *The End of Value-Free Economics*, Routledge 2011

331 Failure of rationalism in economics: Mark Blaug goes still further: 'No idea or theory in economics, physics, chemistry, biology, philosophy and

even mathematics is ever thoroughly understood except as the end-product of some slice of history, the result of some previous intellectual development.' Blaug, 'No History of Ideas, Please, We're Economists', *Journal of Economic Perspectives*, 15.1, Winter 2001

332   Human dignity and capabilities: inspired by Amartya Sen and Martha Nussbaum, there is now a large literature exploring how a focus on human capabilities can be the centre of a non-utilitarian approach to welfare economics, and the policy implications of such a view: cf. Amartya Sen, *Development as Freedom*, Oxford University Press 2001, and Martha Nussbaum, *Creating Capabilities: The Human Development Approach*, Harvard University Press 2011. For a more radical philosophical critique of conventional approaches to equality, see Elizabeth Anderson, 'What's the Point of Equality?', *Ethics*, 109.2, 1999; and, in relation to Adam Smith, her 'Adam Smith on Equality', in Ryan Patrick Hanley (ed.), *Adam Smith: His Life, Thought, and Legacy*, Princeton University Press 2016

333   'No government is quite perfect, but it is better to submit to some inconveniences than make attempts against it': *LJ(B)* p. 435

333   Smith as small-c conservative: in addition, Smith's emphasis on such things as the role of sentiment and the unbidden benefits of markets betokens a deep awareness of the limits of human reason, and of the need for reason to scrutinize and prune back its own claims—an awareness that is Humean, realistic and rather small-c conservative. See Sheldon S. Wolin, 'Hume and Conservatism', *American Political Science Review*, 48.4, 1954, who describes Hume's as 'a conservatism without benefit of mystery', arising from a desire to dissolve the claims of natural law and natural science independent of human nature, by means of reason itself

333   A humane and moderate conservatism: this is at least the ambition of my book *The Big Society*, University of Buckingham Press 2010; and, in Smithian style, *Compassionate Economics*, Policy Exchange 2008, online at www.jesse norman.com

334   'That insidious and crafty animal, vulgarly called a statesman or politician': *WN* IV.ii.39

334   Rewards and status vs. norms and character: for a rather Smithian exploration of public and private virtue, and the beautifully named 'résumé' and 'eulogy' virtues, see David Brooks, *The Road to Character*, Allen Lane 2015

BIBLIOGRAPHY

WORKS BY ADAM SMITH

Correspondence of Adam Smith, ed. Ernest Campbell Mossner and Ian Simpson Ross, Liberty Fund 1987

An Early Draft of Part of The Wealth of Nations, in *LJ*

Essays on Philosophical Subjects, ed. W. P. D. Wightman and J. C. Bryce, Liberty Fund [1795] 1980

An Inquiry into the Nature and Causes of the Wealth of Nations, ed. R. H. Campbell, A. S. Skinner and W. B. Todd, 2 vols., Liberty Fund [1776] 1981

Lectures on Jurisprudence, ed. R. L. Meek, D. D. Raphael and P. G. Stein, Liberty Fund [1762–4] 1982

Lectures on Rhetoric and Belles Lettres, ed. J. C. Bryce, Liberty Fund [1762–3] 1985

Letter from Adam Smith, LL.D. to William Strahan, Esq., in David Hume, *Essays, Moral, Political, and Literary*, ed. Eugene F. Miller, Liberty Fund [1777] 1987

The Theory of Moral Sentiments, ed. D. D. Raphael and A. L. Macfie, Liberty Fund [1759–90] 1982

SELECTED BIOGRAPHIES OF ADAM SMITH

Buchan, James, *Adam Smith and the Pursuit of Perfect Liberty*, Profile Books 2006

Campbell, R. H. and A. S. Skinner, *Adam Smith*, Croom Helm 1982

Otteson, James, *Adam Smith*, Bloomsbury 2011

Phillipson, Nicholas, *Adam Smith: An Enlightened Life*, Penguin 2010

Rae, John, *Life of Adam Smith*, Macmillan 1895

Raphael, D. D., *Adam Smith*, Oxford University Press 1985

Simpson Ross, Ian, *The Life of Adam Smith*, 2nd edn, Oxford University Press 2010

Stewart, Dugald, *Account of the Life and Writings of Adam Smith, LL.D.*, n.p. 1794

COLLECTIONS OF ESSAYS ON ADAM SMITH

Berry, Christopher J., Maria Pia Paganelli and Craig Smith (eds.), *The Oxford Handbook of Adam Smith*, Oxford University Press 2013

Haakonssen, Knud (ed.), *The Cambridge Companion to Adam Smith*, Cambridge University Press 2006

Hanley, Ryan Patrick (ed.), *Adam Smith: His Life, Thought, and Legacy*, Princeton University Press 2016

Hardwick, David F. and Leslie Marsh (eds.), *Propriety and Prosperity: New Studies on the Philosophy of Adam Smith*, Palgrave Macmillan 2014

Oslington, Paul (ed.), *Adam Smith as Theologian*, Routledge 2011

Wilson, Thomas and Andrew S. Skinner (eds.), *The Market and the State: Essays in Honour of Adam Smith*, Oxford University Press 1976

Wood, John C. (ed.) *Adam Smith: Critical Assessments*, 7 vols., Routledge 1983–94

Young, Jeffrey T. (ed.), *The Elgar Companion to Adam Smith*, Edward Elgar 2009

OTHER WORKS

Acemoglu, Daron and James A. Robinson, *Why Nations Fail*, Profile Books 2012

Akerlof, George A. and Rachel E. Kranton, *Identity Economics*, Princeton University Press 2010

Akerlof, George A. and Robert J. Shiller, *Animal Spirits*, Princeton University Press 2009

Akerlof, George A. and Robert J. Shiller, *Phishing for Phools: The Economics of Manipulation and Deception*, Princeton University Press 2015

Allen, Robert, *The British Industrial Revolution in Global Perspective*, Cambridge University Press 2009

Anderson, James, *An Enquiry into the Nature of the Corn Laws*, Mrs Mundell 1777

Ariely, Dan, *The (Honest) Truth about Dishonesty: How We Lie to Everyone— Especially Ourselves*, HarperCollins 2012

Arrow, Kenneth, *Social Choice and Individual Values*, John Wiley 1951

Arrow, Kenneth and Frank Hahn, *General Competitive Analysis*, Holden-Day 1971

Bagehot, Walter, *Economic Studies*, ed. R. H. Hutton, Longman, Green 1895

Banfield, Edward C., *The Moral Basis of a Backward Society*, Free Press 1958

Berkeley, George, *Siris: A Chain of Philosophical Reflexions and Inquiries Concerning the Virtues of Tar Water*, W. Innys, C. Hitch and C. Davis 1744

Berry, Christopher J., *The Idea of Commercial Society in the Scottish*

Enlightenment, Edinburgh University Press 2013

Besley, Timothy, *Principled Agents?: The Political Economy of Good Government*, Oxford University Press 2006

Bicchieri, Cristina, *The Grammar of Society: The Nature and Dynamics of Social Norms*, Cambridge University Press 2006

Binmore, Ken, *Natural Justice*, Oxford University Press 2005

Bisset, Robert, *Life of Edmund Burke* 2nd edn, 2 vols, George Cawthorn 1800

Blaug, Mark, *Economic Theory in Retrospect*, 5th edn, Cambridge University Press 1997

Boettke, Peter J., Stefanie Haeffele Balch and Virgil Henry Storr, *Mainline Economics: Six Nobel Lectures in the Tradition of Adam Smith*, Mercatus Center, George Mason University 2016

Boswell, James, *Boswell's Edinburgh Journals 1767–1786*, ed. Hugh Milne, Mercat Press 2001, rev. edn 2013

Boswell, James, *Correspondence of James Boswell and John Johnston of Grange*, ed. R. S. Walker, William Heinemann 1966

Boswell, James, *Dr Johnson's Table Talk*, J. Mawman 1807

Boswell, James, *The Life of Samuel Johnson*, Henry Baldwin, for Charles Dilly, London 1791 and 1793

Boswell, James, *London Journal 1762–3*, William Heinemann 1950

Boswell, James, *Boswell: The Ominous Years 1774–1776*, ed. Charles Ryskamp and Frederick A. Pottle, McGraw-Hill 1963

de Botton, Alain, *Status Anxiety*, Hamish Hamilton 2004

Bourke, Richard, *Empire and Revolution: The Political Life of Edmund Burke*, Princeton University Press 2015

Boushey, Heather, J. Bradford DeLong and Marshall Steinbaum (eds.), *After Piketty: The Agenda for Economics and Inequality*, Harvard University Press 2017

Braudel, Fernand, *Capitalism and Material Life 1400–1800*, Weidenfeld & Nicolson 1973

Brewer, John, *The Sinews of Power: War, Money and the English State 1688–1783*, Harvard University Press 1988

Broadie, Alexander (ed.), *The Cambridge Companion to the Scottish Enlightenment*, Cambridge University Press 2003

Brooks, David, *The Road to Character*, Allen Lane 2015

Brougham, Henry, *Lives of Men of Letters and Science, Who Flourished in the Time of George III*, Richard Griffin, London and Glasgow 1855

Brown, Gordon, 'Can Both the Left and Right Claim Adam Smith?', Enlightenment Lecture, University of Edinburgh, 25 April 2002

Brown, Gordon, Hugo Young Memorial Lecture, Chatham House, 13 December 2005

Buchanan, James and Gordon Tullock, *The Calculus of Consent*, University of Michigan Press 1962

Burns, Robert, *The Canongate Burns*, ed. Andrew Noble and Patrick Scott Hogg, Canongate Books 2001

Butler, Eamonn, *Adam Smith: A Primer*, Institute of Economic Affairs 2007

Butler, Eamonn, *The Condensed Wealth of Nations*, Adam Smith Institute 2011

Cairns, John W., *Enlightenment, Legal Education, and Critique*, Edinburgh University Press 2015

Campbell, Mungo, *Allan Ramsay: Portraits of the Enlightenment*, Prestel 2013

Chang, Ha-Joon, *Economics: The User's Guide*, Pelican Books 2014

Chang, Ha-Joon, *Kicking Away the Ladder: Development Strategy in Historical Perspective*, Anthem Press 2002

Chang, Ha-Joon, *23 Things They Don't Tell You about Capitalism*, Allen Lane 2010

Coase, Ronald H., *Essays on Economics and Economists*, University of Chicago Press 1994

Cohen, G. A., *Karl Marx's Theory of History*, Princeton University Press 1978

Collier, Paul, *The Bottom Billion*, Oxford University Press 2014

Congleton, Roger D. and Arye L. Hillman (eds.), *Companion to the Political Economy of Rent-Seeking*, Edward Elgar 2015

Cooper, George, *Fixing Economics*, Harriman House 2016

Cooper, George, *The Origins of Financial Crises*, 2nd edn, Harriman House 2010

Coyle, Diane, *GDP: A Brief but Affectionate History*, Princeton University Press 2014

Crawford, R. (ed.), *The Scottish Invention of English Literature*, Cambridge University Press 1998

Cropsey, Joseph, *Polity and Economy*, St Augustine's Press 2001

Deaton, Angus, *The Great Escape: Health, Wealth, and the Origins of Inequality*, Princeton University Press 2013

Defoe, Daniel, *A Tour Thro' the Whole Island of Great Britain*, G. Strahan 1724–6

DeMartino, George and Deirdre McCloskey (eds.), *The Oxford Handbook on Professional Economic Ethics*, Oxford University Press 2016

Devine, T. M. (ed.), *Recovering Scotland's Slavery Past: The Caribbean Connection*, Edinburgh University Press 2015

Devine, T. M., *Scotland's Empire: The Origins of the Global Diaspora*, Allen Lane 2003

Devine, T. M., *The Scottish Nation 1700–2000*, Allen Lane 1999

Devine, T. M., *To the Ends of the Earth: Scotland's Global Diaspora 1750–2010*, Allen Lane 2011

Emerson, Roger L., *An Enlightened Duke: The Life of Archibald Campbell, 3rd Duke of Argyll*, Humming Earth 2013

Ensminger, Jean and Joseph Henrich (eds.), *Experimenting with Social Norms: Fairness and Punishment in Cross-Cultural Perspective*, New York, Russell Sage Press 2014

Evensky, Jerry, *Adam Smith's Moral Philosophy*, Cambridge University Press 2005

Ewing, Jack, *Faster, Higher, Farther: The Inside Story of the Volkswagen Scandal*, Bantam Press 2017

Faujas Saint-Fond, Barthélemy, *Travels in England, Scotland and the Hebrides*, 2 vols., J. Ridgway, London 1799

Fay, C. R., *Adam Smith and the Scotland of his Day*, Cambridge University Press 1956

Ferguson, Adam, *An Essay on the History of Civil Society*, n.p. 1767

Ferguson, Adam, *Reflections Previous to the Establishment of a Militia*, R. & J. Dodsley 1756

Festinger, Leon, *A Theory of Cognitive Dissonance*, Stanford University Press 1957

Festinger, Leon, Henry W. Riecken and Stanley Schachter, *When Prophecy Fails*, University of Minnesota Press 1956

Fleischaker, Samuel, *On Adam Smith's Wealth of Nations*, Princeton University Press 2004

Folbre, Nancy, *Greed, Lust and Gender: A History of Economic Ideas*, Oxford University Press 2009

Force, Pierre, *Self-Interest before Adam Smith: A Genealogy of Economic Science*, Cambridge University Press 2003

Forman-Barzilai, Fonna, *Adam Smith and the Circles of Sympathy*, Cambridge University Press 2010

Foucault, Michel, *The Order of Things: An Archaeology of the Human Sciences*, repr. Routledge 2002

Fox, Justin, *The Myth of the Rational Market*, Harriman House 2009

Friedman, Milton, *Essays in Positive Economics*, University of Chicago Press 1953

Frydman, Roman and Michael D. Goldberg, *Imperfect Knowledge Economics*, Princeton University Press 2007

Galbraith, J. K., *A History of Economics: The Past as the Present*, Penguin 1989

Garber, Peter, *Famous First Bubbles: The Fundamentals of Early Manias*, MIT Press 2000

Gibbon, Edward, *Memoirs of my Life*, A. Strahan, T. Cadell Jun. and W. Davies, 1795–1815

Gintis, Herbert, Samuel Bowles, Robert Boyd and Ernst Fehr, *Moral Sentiments* and Material Interests: The Foundations of Cooperation in Economic Life, MIT Press 2005

Gjerstad, Steven D. and Vernon L. Smith, Rethinking Housing Bubbles: The Role of Household and Bank Balance Sheets in Modeling Economic Crises, Cambridge University Press 2014

Gordon, Robert J., The Rise and Fall of American Growth, Princeton University Press 2016

Graham, Benjamin, The Intelligent Investor, Harper & Bros. 1949

Greenberger, Martin (ed.), Computers, Communication, and the Public Interest, Johns Hopkins Press 1971

Griswold, Charles, Adam Smith and the Virtues of Enlightenment, Cambridge University Press 1999

Haakonssen, Knud (ed.), The Cambridge Companion to Adam Smith, Cambridge University Press 2006

Haakonssen, Knud, The Science of a Legislator: The Natural Jurisprudence of David Hume and Adam Smith, Cambridge University Press 1981

Hacker, Jacob S. and Paul Pierson, Winner-Take-All Politics: How Washington Made the Rich Richer—and Turned its Back on the Middle Class, Simon & Schuster 2010

Hanley, Ryan Patrick, Adam Smith and the Character of Virtue, Cambridge University Press 2009

Harris, James, Hume: An Intellectual Biography, Cambridge University Press 2015

Haskel, Jonathan and Stian Westlake, Capitalism without Capital: The Rise of the Intangible Economy, Princeton University Press 2017

Hayek, Friedrich, The Fatal Conceit, University of Chicago Press 1988

Henrich, Joseph, The Secret of our Success, Princeton University Press 2016

Hickok, Gregory, The Myth of Mirror Neurons, W. W. Norton 2014

Hirschman, Albert, The Passions and the Interests: Political Arguments for Capitalism before its Triumph, Princeton University Press 1977

Hirschman, Albert, Rival Views of Market Society and Other Recent Essays, Cambridge University Press 1992

Hont, Istvan, Jealousy of Trade: International Competition and the Nation-State in Historical Perspective, Harvard University Press 2005

Hont, Istvan, Politics in Commercial Society, Harvard University Press 2015

Hont, Istvan and Michael Ignatieff (eds.), Wealth and Virtue: The Shaping of Political Economy in the Scottish Enlightenment, Cambridge University Press 1986

Hoppit, Julian, Britain's Political Economies: Parliament and Economic Life 1660–1800, Cambridge University Press 2017

Horne, George, A Letter to Adam Smith LL.D. on the Life, Death, and Philosophy *of His Friend David Hume Esq. by One of the People Called Christians*, Clarendon Press 1777

Howell, Martha C., *Commerce before Capitalism in Europe 1300–1600*, Cambridge University Press 2009

Hume, David, *Essays Moral, Political and Literary*, ed. Eugene F. Miller, Liberty Fund [1752] 1985

Hume, David, *Letters of David Hume*, ed. J. Y. T. Greig, 2 vols., Oxford University Press 1932

Hume, David, *The Life of David Hume, Esq. Written by Himself*, W. Strahan and T. Cadell 1777, included in the edition of *Essays Moral, Political and Literary* above

Hume, David, *New Letters of David Hume*, ed. Raymond Klibansky, rev. edn, Oxford University Press 2011

Hume, David, *A Treatise of Human Nature*, ed. L. A. Selby-Bigge, rev. edn P. H. Nidditch, Oxford University Press 1978

Hutcheson, Francis, *An Inquiry into the Original of our Ideas of Beauty and Virtue*, J. Darby, London 1725

Hutcheson, Francis, *A System of Moral Philosophy*, 2 vols., A. Millar and T. Longman 1755

Hutchison, Terence W., *Before Adam Smith: The Emergence of Political Economy 1662–1776*, Basil Blackwell 1988

Hutton, Will, *The State We're In*, Jonathan Cape 1995

James, Oliver, *Selfish Capitalism*, Random House 2008

Jevons, W. S., *The Theory of Political Economy*, Macmillan 1888

Kaletsky, Anatole, *Capitalism 4.0: The Birth of a New Economy*, Bloomsbury 2010

Kay, John, *Other People's Money: Masters of the Universe or Servants of the People?*, Profile Books 2015

Kay, John, *The Truth about Markets: Why Some Nations are Rich but Most Remain Poor*, Allen Lane 2003

Kennedy, Gavin, *Adam Smith: A Moral Philosopher and his Political Economy*, Palgrave Macmillan 2008

Kerr, Robert, *Memoirs of the Life, Writing and Correspondence of William Smellie*, John Anderson 1811

Keynes, John Maynard, *Essays in Biography*, W. W. Norton 1963

Keynes, John Maynard, *The General Theory of Employment, Interest and Money*, Macmillan 1936

Kidd, Colin, *Union and Unionisms*, Cambridge University Press 2008

Kindleberger, Charles P., *Manias, Panics, and Crashes*, 4th edn, John Wiley 2000

King, Mervyn, *The End of Alchemy*, Abacus 2017

Klein, Naomi, *The Shock Doctrine*, Penguin 2008

Letwin, William, *The Origins of Scientific Economics*, Methuen 1963

Levitt, Steve and Stephen Dubner, *Freakonomics: A Rogue Economist Explores the Hidden Side of Everything*, HarperCollins 2005

Lewis, David, *Convention*, Harvard University Press 1969

List, Friedrich, *The National System of Political Economy*, J. B. Lippincott 1856

Lo, Andrew, *Adaptive Economics: Financial Evolution at the Speed of Thought*, Princeton University Press 2017

Locke, John, *Two Treatises of Government*, ed. Peter Laslett, Cambridge University Press [1689] 1967

Losurdo, Domenico, *Liberalism: A Counter-History*, Verso 2011

McCloskey, Deirdre N., *Bourgeois Dignity*, University of Chicago Press 2010

McCloskey, Deirdre N., *Bourgeois Equality: How Ideas, Not Capital or Institutions, Enriched the World*, University of Chicago Press 2016

MacGilvray, Eric, *The Invention of Market Freedom*, Cambridge University Press 2011

McLean, Iain, *Adam Smith, Radical and Egalitarian*, Edinburgh University Press 2006

Maddison, Angus, *Contours of the World Economy 1–2030 AD*, Oxford University Press 2007

Mallaby, Sebastian, *The Man Who Knew: The Life and Times of Alan Greenspan*, Bloomsbury 2016

Marçal, Katrin, *Who Cooked Adam Smith's Dinner?*, Pegasus Books 2016

Marglin, Stephen, *The Dismal Science: How Thinking Like an Economist Undermines Community*, Harvard University Press 2008

Marshall, Alex, *The Surprising Design of Market Economies*, University of Texas Press 2012

Martin, Felix, *Money*, Bodley Head 2013

Marx, Karl, *Capital: Critique of Political Economy*, Penguin [1867–83] 2004

Marx, Karl, *A Contribution to the Critique of Political Economy*, ed. Maurice Dobb, Lawrence & Wishart [1859] 1971

Mason, Paul, *Postcapitalism: A Guide to our Future*, Penguin Books 2015

Maugham, Frederic, *The Case of Jean Calas*, William Heinemann 1928

Mayer, Colin, *Firm Commitment: Why the Corporation is Failing Us and How to Restore Trust in It*, Oxford University Press 2013

Meek, Ronald L., *Social Science and the Ignoble Savage*, Cambridge University Press 1976

Meek, Ronald L., *Studies in the Labour Theory of Value*, Lawrence & Wishart 1956

Mercier, Hugo and Daniel Sperber, *The Enigma of Reason: A New Theory of Human Understanding*, Harvard University Press 2017

Milanovic, Branko, *Global Inequality: A New Approach for the Age of Globalisation*, Harvard University Press 2016

Milgate, Murray and Shannon C. Stimson, *After Adam Smith: A Century of Transformation in Politics and Political Economy*, Princeton University Press 2009

Miliband, Ralph, *Marxism and Politics*, Oxford University Press 1977

Mill, J. S., *Principles of Political Economy*, John W. Parker 1848

Minsky, Hyman P., *John Maynard Keynes*, McGraw-Hill [1975] 2008

Minsky, Hyman P., *Stabilizing an Unstable Economy*, Yale University Press 1986

Mirowski, Philip, *More Heat than Light*, Cambridge University Press 1989

Mitchell, B. R., *British Historical Statistics*, rev. edn, Cambridge University Press 2011

Mokyr, Joel, *The Enlightened Economy: Britain and the Industrial Revolution 1700–1850*, Yale University Press 2009

Monks, Robert A. G., *Corpocracy: How CEOs and the Business Roundtable Hijacked the World's Greatest Wealth Machine—and How to Get It Back*, John Wiley 2007

Monks, Robert A. G. and Nell Minow, *Power and Accountability*, HarperCollins 1991

Montes, Leonidas, *Adam Smith in Context: A Critical Reassessment of Some Central Components of his Thought*, Palgrave Macmillan 2004

Montes, Leonidas and Eric Schliesser (eds.), *New Voices on Adam Smith*, Routledge 2006

Montesquieu, Baron de (Charles-Louis de Secondat), *The Spirit of Laws*, 2 vols., J. Nourse & P. Vaillant 1750

Morris, Nicholas and David Vines, *Capital Failure: Rebuilding Trust in Financial Services*, Oxford University Press 2014

Mossner, Ernest Campbell, *The Life of David Hume*, 2nd edn, Oxford University Press 1980

Mullainathan, Sendhil and Eldar Shafir, *Scarcity: The True Cost of Not Having Enough*, Allen Lane 2013

Nelson, Julie, *Economics for Humans*, University of Chicago Press 2006

Nixon, Edna, *Voltaire and the Calas Case*, Victor Gollancz 1961

Norman, Jesse, *The Big Society*, University of Buckingham Press 2010

Norman, Jesse, *Compassionate Economics*, Policy Exchange 2008

Norman, Jesse, *Edmund Burke: Philosopher, Politician, Prophet*, William Collins 2013

Nussbaum, Martha, *Creating Capabilities: The Human Development Approach*, Harvard University Press 2011

Nussbaum, Martha, *The Fragility of Goodness*, Cambridge University Press 1986

Ó Gráda, Cormac, *Famine: A Short History*, Princeton University Press 2009

Oakeshott, Michael, *Rationalism in Politics*, Methuen 1962

O'Brien, Karen, *Women and Enlightenment in Eighteenth-Century Britain*, Oxford University Press 2009

Offer, Avner, *The Challenge of Affluence: Self-Control and Well-Being in the United States and Britain since 1950*, Oxford University Press 2006

Offer, Avner and Gabriel Söderberg, *The Nobel Factor*, Princeton University Press 2016

Otteson, James R., *Adam Smith's Marketplace of Life*, Cambridge University Press 2002

Peirce, Charles Sanders, *Reasoning and the Logic of Things*, ed. Kenneth Laine Ketner, Harvard University Press 1992

Phelps, Edmund, *Mass Flourishing: How Grassroots Innovation Created Jobs, Challenge, and Change*, Princeton University Press 2013

Phillipson, Nicholas, *David Hume: The Philosopher as Historian*, rev. edn, Penguin Books 2011

Piketty, Thomas, *Capital in the Twenty-First Century*, Allen Lane 2014

Pinker, Steven, *The Better Angels of our Nature: The Decline of Violence and its Causes*, Allen Lane 2011

Pinker, Steven, *Enlightenment Now*, Allen Lane 2018

Pirie, Madsen, *The Neoliberal Mind: The Ideology of the Future*, Adam Smith Institute 2017

Pocock, J. G. A., *Virtue, Commerce and History: Essays on Political Thought and History, Chiefly in the Eighteenth Century*, Cambridge University Press 1985

Polanyi, Karl, *The Great Transformation*, Farrar & Rinehart 1944

Pujol, Michèle A., *Feminism and Anti-Feminism in Early Economic Thought*, Edward Elgar 1992

Putnam, Hilary and Vivian Walsh (eds.), *The End of Value-Free Economics*, Routledge 2011

Raphael, D. D., *The Impartial Spectator: Adam Smith's Moral Philosophy*, Oxford University Press 2007

Rasmussen, Dennis, *The Infidel and the Professor: David Hume, Adam Smith, and the Friendship that Shaped Modern Thought*, Princeton University Press 2017

Rawls, John, *A Theory of Justice*, Harvard University Press 1974

Reinhart, Carmen and Kenneth Rogoff, *This Time is Different*, Princeton University Press 2011

Ricardo, David, *On the Principles of Political Economy, and Taxation*, John Murray 1817

Ridley, Matt, *The Rational Optimist*, Fourth Estate 2010

Robbins, Lionel, *An Essay on the Nature and Significance of Economic Science*, Macmillan 1932

Roberts, Russ, *How Adam Smith Can Change your Life*, Penguin 2014

Rodrik, Dani, *Economics Rules*, Oxford University Press 2015

Rodrik, Dani, *The Globalisation Paradox*, Oxford University Press 2011

Rosling, Hans, Ola Rosling and Anna Rosling Rönnlund, Factfulness: *Ten Reasons We're Wrong About the World—And Why Things Are Better Than You Think*, Sceptre 2018

Rothbard, Murray, *Economic Thought before Adam Smith: An Austrian Perspective*, Edward Elgar 1995

Rothschild, Emma, *Economic Sentiments: Adam Smith, Condorcet, and the Enlightenment*, Harvard University Press 2001

Samuelson, Paul, *Economics*, 19th edn, rev. W. D. Nordhaus, McGraw-Hill 2009

Sandel, Michael, *What Money Can't Buy: The Moral Limits of Markets*, Penguin 2012

Savage, Ruth (ed.), *Philosophy and Religion in Enlightenment Britain*, Oxford University Press 2012

Scott, W. R., *Adam Smith as Student and Professor*, Jackson 1937

Schelling, Thomas, *The Strategy of Conflict*, Harvard University Press 1980

Schumpeter, Joseph, *Capitalism, Socialism and Democracy*, rev. edn, Routledge 2015

Schumpeter, Joseph, *History of Economic Analysis*, Routledge [1954] 1987

Seabright, Paul, *The Comfort of Strangers: A Natural History of Economic Life*, Princeton University Press 2004

Sen, Amartya, *Collective Choice and Social Welfare*, 2nd edn, Penguin Books 2017

Sen, Amartya, *Development as Freedom*, Oxford University Press 2001

Sen, Amartya, *The Idea of Justice*, Allen Lane 2009

Sen, Amartya, *Poverty and Famines*, Oxford University Press 1981

Shiller, Robert, *Irrational Exuberance*, Princeton University Press 2000

Shleifer, Andrei, *Inefficient Markets*, Oxford University Press 2000

Shweder, Richard, *Why Do Men Barbecue? Recipes for Cultural Psychology*, Harvard University Press 2003

Skidelsky, Robert, *John Maynard Keynes 1883–1946: Economist, Philosopher, Statesman*, Macmillan 2003

Skinner, Andrew, *A System of Social Science: Papers Relating to Adam Smith*, Clarendon Press 1979

Skinner, Quentin, *The Foundations of Modern Political Thought*, 2 vols., Cambridge University Press 1978–97

Slacker, Paul, *The Invention of Improvement: Information and Material Progress in Seventeenth-Century England*, Oxford University Press 2015

Smellie, William, *Literary and Characteristical Lives of J. Gregory, M.D., Henry Home, Lord Kames, David Hume, Esq., and Adam Smith, LL.D.*, n.p. 1800

Smith, Craig, *Adam Smith's Political Philosophy*, Routledge 2013

Smith, Vernon, *Rationality in Economics: Constructivist and Ecological Forms*, Cambridge University Press 2008

Smout, T. C., *A History of the Scottish People 1560–1830*, William Collins 1999

Steuart, Sir James, *An Inquiry into the Principles of Political Economy*, ed. Andrew Skinner, Oliver & Boyd 1966

Stiglitz, Joseph E., *Globalisation and its Discontents Revisited*, Penguin Books 2017

Stiglitz, Joseph E., *The Price of Inequality*, Penguin Books 2012

Surowiecki, James, *The Wisdom of Crowds*, Doubleday Books 2004

Szechi, Daniel, *The Jacobites: Britain and Europe 1688–1788*, Manchester University Press 1994

Taleb, Nassim Nicholas, *The Black Swan*, Random House 2007

Tavris, Carol and Elliot Aronson, *Mistakes Were Made (But Not by Me)*, Mariner Books 2015

Thompson, Harold, *A Scottish Man of Feeling: Some Account of Henry Mackenzie . . . and of the Golden Age of Burns and Scott*, Oxford University Press 1931

Tirole, Jean, *Economics for the Common Good*, Princeton University Press 2017

Tytler, Alexander Fraser, Lord Woodhouselee, *Memoirs of the Life and Writings of the Honourable Henry Home of Kames*, T. Cadell & W. Davies 1814

Varoufakis, Yanis, *Talking to my Daughter about the Economy*, Bodley Head 2017

Veblen, Thorstein, *The Theory of the Leisure Class: An Economic Study in the Evolution of Institutions*, Macmillan 1899

Voltaire (François-Marie Arouet), *A Treatise on Religious Toleration*, T. Becket and P. A. de Hondt 1764

de Waal, Frans, *Our Inner Ape: The Best and Worst of Human Nature*, Granta Books 2006

Walpole, Horace, Earl of Orford, *Memoirs of the Age of King George III*, Richard Bentley 1845

Whatley, Christopher, *The Scots and the Union: Then and Now*, rev. edn, Edinburgh University Press 2014

Whyte, Ian D., *Scotland before the Industrial Revolution: An Economic and Social History c. 1050–c. 1750*, Routledge 2014

Winch, Donald, 'Adam Smith', *The Oxford Dictionary of National Biography*, Oxford University Press 2004

Winch, Donald, *Adam Smith's Politics: An Essay in Historiographic Revision*, Cambridge University Press 1978

Winch, Donald, *Riches and Poverty: An Intellectual History of Political Economy in Britain 1750–1834*, Cambridge University Press 1996

Wootton, David, *The Invention of Science*, Penguin Books 2015

Zingales, Luigi, *A Capitalism for the People: Recapturing the Lost Genius of American Prosperity*, Basic Books 2012

INDEX

state
  church and, 120–121
  commercial societies in, 327
  market pressures in, 305
state of nature, 77
Steuart, James, 154, 176
Stewart, Dugald, 3, 10, 21, 26,
    50–53, 137, 152–153
  on conjectural history, 77–78
  on government, 187
  Millar, J., and, 74
  on political economy, 162
  on Smith, M., 7–8, 218
  on *The Wealth of Nations,* 179
Stigler, George, 181
Strahan, William, 91, 129–131, 140,
    142, 302
Stuart, Charles Edward, 34–35
the Stuarts, 31–33
sympathy, 58–59, 62–65, 75, 105,
    220
system of natural liberty, 53, 177
  commerce in, 292
  free commerce and, 200
  freedoms in, 115–116
  inequality and, 272
  the invisible hand and, 253–254
  market imperfections and, 188
  regulation and, 254
systems, 45
systems of law, 75

tar water, 25
Tassie, 160
taxation, 71
  of American colonies, 101–102
  for commercial initiatives,
      116–117
  in England, 121–122
  four maxims of good, x, 122–123
  French system, 150–151

  by government, 189
  Townshend on, 102
  without representation, 103
technology, 280–284
"That Politics may be Reduced to a
    Science" (Hume), 28
Thatcher, Margaret, x–xi
theory of evolution, 168–170
The Theory of Moral Sentiments
    (Smith, A.), xi–xii, 27, 39, 44,
    53–54, 143, 168–169
  on behaviour, 201
  Burns and, 61
  on Calas, 289–290
  on compassion, 58
  corrections, to third edition of,
      87–88
  on economy of regard, 307–308
  French Revolution and, 150
  on government, 71, 271
  Hume on, 66–67
  on impartial spectator, 296
  on the invisible hand, 173
  on justice, 75–76
  moral philosophy in, 55, 146
  on norms, values, 230
  publication of, 65–66, 144–145
  on the rich, 185
  on selfishness, 183
  on slavery, 233, 235
  on sociability, 57
  on sympathy, 62–63
  on tranquility, 155
  on wealth, 172
  The Wealth of Nations and,
      160–161, 166–167, 178–180,
      237–238
  Wollstonecraft and, 220
  on women, 218
Thiel, Peter, 282
Thomas Aquinas, 163–164

Jesse Norman, MP, is widely regarded as one of the rising stars of the British House of Commons. A former Parliamentarian of the Year, he was educated at Oxford (BA) and holds a PhD in philosophy from University College London. His previous books include *Edmund Burke: The First Conservative.*